The Supreme Court

The Supreme Court

Third Edition

Lawrence Baum

Ohio State University

A Division of Congressional Quarterly Inc.
1414 22nd Street N.W., Washington, D.C. 20037

Library of Congress Cataloging-in-Publication Data

Baum, Lawrence.
    The Supreme Court/Lawrence Baum. — 3rd ed.
      p.   cm.
    Bibliography: p.
    Includes indexes.
    ISBN 0-87187-482-2   ISBN 0-87187-495-4 (pbk.)
    1. United States.   Supreme Court.   I. Title.
KF8742.B35 1989
347.73'26—dc19
[347.3.0735]   88-29374
                                                            CIP

To my parents
Ruth Klein Baum and Irving Baum

Contents

Preface   ix

1 **The Court**   1
A Perspective on the Court   2
The Court in the Judicial System   7
A First Look at the Court   12
The Court's History   18

2 **The Justices**   27
The Process of Selection   27
Who Is Selected   53
Leaving the Court   63
Conclusion   68

3 **The Cases**   71
A General View   71
Reaching the Court:
    Litigants, Attorneys, and Groups   74
Deciding What to Hear: The Court's Role   90
Caseload Growth and the Court's Burdens   104
Conclusion   109

4 **Decision Making**   113
Decisions and the Decisional Process   113
Influences on Decisions: Introduction   121
The State of the Law   122
The Court's Environment   127
Justices' Values   136

Group Interaction   149
Conclusion   158

5   Policy Outputs   165
Areas of Activity   165
Supreme Court Activism: Judicial Review   175
The Direction of Policy   182
Explaining the Court's Policies   192
Conclusions   197

6   The Court's Impact   201
Implementation of Decisions   201
Responses by Legislatures and Chief Executives   222
Impact on Society   237

Glossary   253
Supreme Court Nominations, 1789-1988   257
Selected Bibliography   261
Case Index   265
Index   271

Preface

In the preface of the first edition of this book, written in the early 1980s, I asserted that the Supreme Court stands at the center of American life. Now, at the end of that decade, the Court's importance is even more evident. The Court has been an issue in recent presidential elections, and national attention has focused on the appointments of new justices. This interest is justified because the Court continues to play a major role in resolving a wide range of policy questions and social issues.

In this third edition, like its predecessors, I attempt to provide an understanding of the Supreme Court as a political institution. The book is intended to serve students as a short but comprehensive guide to the Court. It also is meant as a general reference source for those who would like to learn more about the Court. I have sought to make this book useful to people with a wide range of backgrounds, from readers with little prior knowledge to experts on the Court. The book describes the Court's basic operation and offers explanations for the behavior of the Court and the people and institutions that affect it.

The basic approach of the third edition is similar to that of its predecessors. In building upon this structure, I have taken into account changes and developments that have influenced the work of the Court. Perhaps most important among these are President Reagan's appointments to the Court and how they have shifted its ideological balance and increased the potential for a strongly conservative Court in the future. This edition also makes use of new material on the Court from research by scholars and from other sources. Some of the new material included in this edition has come from the justices themselves, who in recent years have been unusually willing to speak openly about the Court.

The first chapter of the book serves as an introduction. It discusses the Supreme Court's role in general terms, examines the place of the

Court in the judicial system, takes a first look at the Court as an institution, and summarizes its history.

Each of the remaining five chapters deals with one important aspect of the Court. Chapter 2 examines the justices: their selection, their personal characteristics, and the circumstances under which they leave the Court. Chapter 3 discusses the processes by which cases reach the Court and are chosen for full decisions; the chapter also addresses the Court's caseload and efforts to deal with its growth.

Chapter 4 looks at the Court's decision-making process in the cases that it decides fully. After outlining the Court's decision-making procedures, I turn to the primary concern of the chapter: the factors that influence the Court's choices among alternative decisions and policies. Chapter 5 considers the kinds of issues on which the Court concentrates, the policies that it supports, and the extent of its activism in policy making. I examine these subjects as they stand today and as they have changed over time and suggest explanations for important patterns in Supreme Court policy.

The final chapter deals with the ways that other government policy makers respond to the Court's decisions and with the Court's impact on American society. This chapter is an appropriate conclusion to the book because the Court's significance ultimately depends on the effects of its decisions.

In previous editions I have thanked the many people who helped me. This edition continues to reflect their contributions. In addition, I have benefited from a great deal of new help in revising the book for this edition. Debra Gross, Anne N. Costain, Susan Lawrence, and Saul Brenner offered many useful suggestions for revision and improvement of this edition. Staci Rhine, John Kilwein, and Venita Martin provided valuable research assistance.

A number of people supplied information and ideas that were incorporated into the new edition: William Jenkins, John Kessel, Alfred Klein, Lynn Mather, Mark Miller, Richard Pacelle, Bradley Richardson, and Harold Spaeth. Toni House, the Supreme Court's public information officer, was very helpful in providing needed information. As in all my work, I appreciate the suggestions and encouragement of Gregory Caldeira and Elliot Slotnick, my fellow students of the courts in the Political Science Department at Ohio State University.

The people at CQ Press continue to provide extraordinary assistance in my efforts. I am especially grateful to Lys Ann Shore for her work as copy editor, to Kerry Kern for her tireless efforts as production editor, and to Joanne Daniels for her direction and encouragement.

All these people have my thanks for their help in making this book possible and in making it better.

1

The Court

In July 1987, President Ronald Reagan nominated federal judge Robert Bork to the U.S. Supreme Court. Nearly four months later, the Senate refused to confirm Bork's nomination. During that time, his candidacy for the Court became a national issue. An array of interest groups took positions for and against Bork's nomination, one spending more than $1 million to defeat him. President Reagan worked hard to win Senate votes for him. One former president supported Bork, while another opposed him. A public march against him was held in Indiana, and 75,000 people sent telegrams to Congress urging votes for or against him. The Senate hearings on Bork's confirmation received extensive coverage from the mass media, and by the time they ended a fairly obscure scholar and judge had become a familiar figure to a great many people.

The attention given to the Bork nomination was a reminder of the significance of the Supreme Court. Many people perceived that Bork would move the Court toward more conservative policies. They cared about this possibility because they believed that the Court's policies make a great deal of difference. They were correct in this belief. The Supreme Court helps to resolve many of the most important and controversial issues in the United States, and in doing so it shapes government policy in areas as diverse as civil rights and environmental protection.

The role that the Supreme Court plays makes it important to understand this institution. Who are the people who serve on the Court, and how do they get there? How is it determined which cases and issues the Court decides? In resolving the cases before it, on what bases does the Court choose between alternative decisions? In what policy areas is it active, and what kinds of policies does it make in those areas? Finally, what happens to the Court's decisions after they are handed down, and what effects do those decisions actually have?

1

This book is an effort to provide an understanding of the Supreme Court by answering these questions. Each question will be the subject of one of the chapters that follow. This chapter introduces the book by taking a general look at the Court, supplying the necessary background for the remainder of the book.

A Perspective on the Court

The Court in Law and Politics

The Supreme Court as a Political Body. People often speak of courts as if they are, or at least ought to be, "nonpolitical." In a literal sense, this is impossible: as part of government, courts are political institutions by definition. But many people believe that courts are nonpolitical in the sense that they are uninvolved in the political process and that their decisions are unaffected by nonlegal considerations.

Popular though this view of the courts may be, it is simply inaccurate. The Supreme Court is "political" in a variety of ways. Appointments to the Court frequently are the subject of considerable political contention. Interest groups often help to bring cases to the Court. Most of the justices were active participants in politics before their selection. The justices' political values and their perceptions of public and congressional opinion affect the Court's decisions. The decisions themselves often lead to controversies in government and the nation at large, and the Court and its rulings sometimes become important election issues.

Thus it is impossible to understand the Supreme Court except in the context of politics, and that will be the perspective of this book.

The Court as a Legal Institution. As a political body, the Supreme Court is similar to other government institutions, such as Congress and administrative agencies. Yet it would be a mistake to view the Court as identical to those other, nonjudicial policy makers. The Court's behavior and its position in the political system are affected in fundamental ways by the fact that it is a *court*.

First of all, the Supreme Court makes decisions within the framework of the law. The policy choices that the Court faces are framed as matters of legal interpretation. In this respect the Court's task differs from that of Congress and of some administrative agencies, and the legal context in which the justices work provides a constraint from which legislators are free.

Furthermore, the widespread belief that the Court should be nonpolitical leads to a certain degree of actual insulation from the political process. Supreme Court justices are given lifetime appointments that allow some freedom from concerns about public approval. Most justices remain fairly aloof from partisan politics, chiefly because open involvement in partisan activity is perceived as illegitimate. Justice Sandra Day O'Connor, for instance, turned down an invitation to appear at a "Salute to Republican Women" at the 1984 Republican national convention. Because most people view direct contact between lobbyists and justices as unacceptable, interest group activity in the Court is restricted primarily to formal channels of legal argument.

For these reasons, the Supreme Court should be viewed as a legal institution as well as a political one. What it does and how it operates are influenced by both the political process and the legal system. Such an ambiguous position makes the Court more complex in some ways than most political institutions, and it also helps to make the Court an interesting case study in political behavior.

The Court as a Policy Maker

This book will be concerned with the Supreme Court in general, but it will give particular emphasis to the Court's role in the making of public policy—the authoritative rules by which government institutions seek to influence the operation of government and to shape society as a whole. Legislation to provide subsidies for wheat farmers, a trial judge's sentence of a convicted criminal, and a Supreme Court decision laying down rules of procedure for an administrative agency are all examples of public policy. Thus the Court may be viewed as part of a policy-making system that includes lower courts as well as the legislative and executive branches of government. It will be useful at this point to look at some important aspects of the Court's policy-making role.

Policy Through Legal Interpretation. As noted above, the Supreme Court makes public policy through the interpretation of provisions of law. Issues of public policy come to the Court in the form of legal questions that the Court is to resolve. In this respect the Court's policy making differs fundamentally in form from that of Congress.

The Court does not face legal questions in the abstract. Rather, the Court addresses these questions in the process of settling specific controversies between parties ("litigants") that bring cases to it. In a sense, then, every decision by the Court has three levels: a judgment about the specific dispute brought to it, an interpretation of the legal issues involved in that dispute, and a position on the policy questions that are connected to the legal issues.

In a specific dispute, the Court determines how the parties to the case should be treated. In a tax case it may decide whether a business must pay taxes claimed by the Internal Revenue Service. In a criminal case it may choose to uphold a conviction, or it may overturn the conviction while allowing a retrial of the defendant. As this second example indicates, the Court often does not determine the final outcome of a case for the parties but instead directs a lower court in its further consideration of the case.

The Court's treatment of the parties is tied to its interpretation of the legal issues in the case. Some legal issues involve the interpretation of federal statutes, and statutory issues dominate many economic fields. The Court may rule in favor of a taxpayer on the basis of its reading of a section of the federal tax code. About half of the Court's decisions, including most of its decisions in civil liberties fields, rest on interpretations of the Constitution. In these cases the Court's task usually is to determine whether some government policy violates a provision of the Constitution. The Court may uphold the conviction of a criminal defendant on the ground that a disputed search for evidence in the case did not violate the Fourth Amendment.

Finally, the Court's legal interpretations also express policy positions, explicit or implicit. An interpretation of the Fourth Amendment may establish a position favorable to the search powers of law enforcement agencies. Often the Court's policy positions emerge most clearly from a series of decisions, such as a string of decisions in environmental law that support rigorous enforcement of environmental regulations. The positions that the Court establishes in a field such as tax law constitute part of the body of policy made by the various government institutions that work in that field.

The Court's Significance in Policy Making.   Through its interpretation of law the Supreme Court plays a critical role in the policy-making system of the federal government. The significance of that role is illustrated by some of the Court's major decisions during the 1970s and 1980s:

—In *Roe v. Wade* (1973), the Court drastically limited the power of states to prohibit abortions.[1] In a long series of later decisions, the Court struck down a variety of state laws regulating abortions but upheld legislation that limited government funding of abortions.[2]

—In a line of decisions since 1978, the Court has ruled on the legality of affirmative action plans that provide preferential treatment to women and racial minority groups. By upholding most of the plans before it, the Court has allowed and encouraged the use of affirmative action.[3]

—In a 1983 decision the Court held unconstitutional a provision that allowed Congress to veto certain decisions of the Immigration and Naturalization Service. In doing so the Court called into question more than one hundred legislative veto provisions through which Congress had sought to exert control over the president and the bureaucracy.[4]

—In *Bowsher v. Synar* (1986), the Court ruled that one provision of the Gramm-Rudman-Hollings deficit reduction law was unconstitutional. Its decision effectively made the law inoperative, postponing the move toward a balanced budget.

—Most important in its immediate effect was the Court's decision in *United States v. Nixon* (1974), perhaps the pivotal event in the process that led to the resignation of President Richard Nixon.

The Court's development of this role has been based on a favorable conjunction of circumstances. As the French observer Alexis de Tocqueville noted more than a century ago, "Scarcely any political question arises in the United States that is not resolved, sooner or later, into a judicial question."[5] Policy disputes tend to reach the courts largely because of the existence of a written Constitution, whose provisions offer a basis for challenges to the legality of government actions. Because so many policy questions come to the courts, the Supreme Court has the chance to rule on a large number of significant policy questions. Moreover, for much of its history the Court has welcomed that opportunity, first insisting on its supremacy as legal arbiter in the early nineteenth century and later making frequent use of its chances to speak on major issues. By doing so, of course, the Court has encouraged people to bring major policy issues to it.

Reaction to the Court's Role: Activism vs. Restraint. Inevitably, the Court's involvement in deciding major issues of public policy has led to controversy. Some of this controversy concerns the substance of the Court's decisions. Legal scholars debate the merits of the Court's rulings in relatively genteel terms. Supreme Court policies also are subject to less genteel discussion in the political arena, as exemplified by criticism of Court decisions on school prayer and abortion.

More fundamentally, people disagree about the Court's general role as a policy maker. That disagreement has taken many forms, but frequently it centers on the dichotomy between judicial activism and judicial restraint. The term *judicial activism* is used in many ways; one key element of the concept is a court's willingness to make significant changes in public policy, particularly in policies established by other institutions.[6] The most visible element of judicial activism is the issuance of decisions that overturn legislative and executive policies, but activism can take other forms. Judicial restraint is simply the avoidance of activism.

Some commentators, such as Robert Bork and former attorney general Edwin Meese, argue strongly for restraint.[7] In their view, the Court should work to limit its role in policy making and particularly to minimize its interference with the policies of the other branches. Advocates of judicial restraint attack activism on several grounds, of which three are especially important: activism is illegitimate because the Court is a relatively undemocratic institution; it is risky because the Court is vulnerable to attack when it takes controversial positions; it is unwise because courts lack the capacity to make effective policy choices.

Others, such as federal judge J. Skelly Wright, defend and support judicial activism. Some proponents of activism see it as a duty under the Constitution. Perhaps most important, proponents of activism see an activist Court as protecting fundamental values, such as liberty, that may be ignored elsewhere in government. Largely for this reason, the supporters of activism applaud the Supreme Court's assertion of a major policy-making role in civil liberties in the last thirty years—a development that many advocates of judicial restraint have criticized.

As we would expect, views about activism and restraint often reflect evaluations of the Court's decisions. Liberals who argued for judicial restraint in the 1920s and 1930s when the Court attacked government regulation of the economy later approved the Court's activism in defense of civil liberties in the 1960s. Today judicial activism continues to be used primarily to support liberal policies, so it is not surprising that conservatives generally advocate judicial restraint. But the debate over judicial activism is more than a dispute about the Court's policies. The Supreme Court's involvement in the making of important public policies raises fundamental questions about the appropriate role of a court, questions that transcend the substance of the Court's decisions at a given time.

Limitations on the Court as a Policy Maker.   The debate over activism and restraint underlines the importance of the Supreme Court's part in the policy-making process. But the Court's role in policy making is inherently limited by several factors. First, there is only so much that the Court can do with the rather small number of decisions that it makes each year. In the average year, the Court hands down decisions with full opinions in approximately 150 cases. In contrast, federal administrative agencies published about the same number of regulations in the first two weeks of 1988. In deciding such a small number of cases, the Court addresses only a select set of policy issues. Inevitably, there are whole fields of policy that it barely touches. Even in the fields in which the Court does act, it can deal only with a limited number of the issues that exist at a given time.

Second, even the most activist-minded justices support judicial restraint in some situations. This support stems in part from judges' training in a legal tradition that emphasizes the value of restraint, and in part from practical considerations. Judicial self-restraint is reflected in the Court's refusal to hear some important and controversial cases, such as the legal challenges brought against American participation in the war in Vietnam.[8] Another reflection of judicial restraint is a set of guidelines that the Court frequently uses to avoid deciding constitutional issues where it is possible to decide or dispose of a case on another basis. These guidelines are listed in a frequently cited opinion by Justice Louis Brandeis in *Ashwander v. Tennessee Valley Authority* (1936).

Finally, even a highly activist Court is limited in its impact by the actions of other policy makers. The Court seldom is the final government institution to deal with the policy issues that it addresses. Its rulings usually must be implemented by lower court judges and administrators, who often retain considerable discretion as to how they will put a Supreme Court decision into effect. Congress and the president influence the ways in which the Court's decisions are carried out, and they can overcome its interpretations of federal statutes simply by amending those statutes. The difference between what the Court rules on an issue and the public policy that ultimately results from government action on that issue may be considerable.

For these reasons, those who see the Supreme Court as the dominant force in American government almost surely are wrong. But if not dominant, the Court does play a very important part in the policy-making process. Certainly the extent of its role in that process is extraordinary for a court.

The Court in the Judicial System

In some respects the Supreme Court is unique among the courts of the United States. But it is also part of a system of courts, and it cannot be understood except in the context of that system. Accordingly, it is important to examine the structure of courts and the Supreme Court's place in that structure.

Structure of the System

Strictly speaking, it is inaccurate to refer to a single court system in the United States. In reality, the courts are divided between the federal system and a separate system in each state.

The federal system may be distinguished from the state systems in terms of jurisdiction, the power to hear and to decide a class of cases. Most of the jurisdiction of the federal courts can be placed in three categories. First are criminal and civil cases that arise under federal laws, including the Constitution. Second are all cases to which the U.S.

Figure 1-1   Most Common Forms of State Court Structures

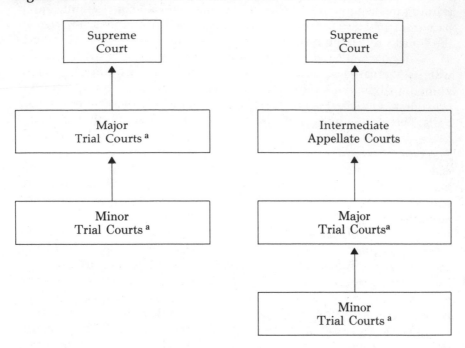

Note: Arrows indicate most common routes of appeals.

[a] In many states, major and/or minor trial courts are composed of two or more different sets of courts. For instance, minor trial courts in California include Municipal Courts and Justice Courts.

government is a party. Finally, in civil cases involving citizens of different states, if the amount in question is at least $10,000, either party may bring the case to federal court; otherwise, it will be heard in state court. Only a small minority of all cases fall into these categories. The trial courts of a single state as populous as California hear far more cases than do the federal trial courts. The average federal case, however, is more significant than the average state case.

State Court Structure.   The states vary considerably in the structures of their court systems. But a few general patterns can be described, and these are illustrated in Figure 1-1. Each state system includes trial courts, which generally hear cases initially as they enter the court system, and appellate courts, which generally review lower court decisions that are appealed to them. Most states have two sets of trial courts, one to handle major criminal and civil cases and the other to deal with minor cases. Major cases on the criminal side usually are those defined under the law as felonies, while major civil cases are those involving relatively large sums of money. Most often, appeals from decisions of minor trial courts are heard by the major trial courts. A few states have a single comprehensive set of trial courts.

Appellate courts are structured in two different ways, as illustrated in Figure 1-1. In about one-third of the states, including most of the less populous states, there is a single appellate court; this is usually called the state supreme court. All appeals from major trial courts go to this supreme court. The other two-thirds of the states have a set of intermediate appellate courts below the supreme court. These intermediate courts initially hear most appeals from major trial courts. The state supreme court may be required to hear certain appeals brought directly from the trial courts or from the intermediate courts, but for the most part it has discretionary jurisdiction over appeals from the decisions of the intermediate courts. The term *discretionary jurisdiction* means simply that a court has the right to hear some appeals and to refuse to hear others.

Federal Court Structure. The structure of federal courts is shown in Figure 1-2. The base of the federal court system is the federal district courts. There are ninety-four district courts in the United States, from one to four in each state along with a court in the District of Columbia and in some of the territories. The district courts hear all federal cases at the trial level, except for a few specialized classes of cases that go to the Tax Court, the Court of International Trade, and the Claims Court.

Above the district courts are the twelve courts of appeals. Each court of appeals has jurisdiction over appeals in one of the federal judicial circuits. The District of Columbia constitutes one circuit, while the other 11 each include three or more states. Appeals from the district courts in a circuit generally go to the court of appeals for that circuit, along with appeals from the Tax Court and from some administrative agencies. Patent cases and some claims against the federal government go from the district courts to the specialized Court of Appeals for the Federal Circuit, as do appeals from the Claims Court and Court of International Trade. The Court of Military Appeals hears cases from lower courts in the military system.

The Supreme Court stands at the top of the federal judicial system. The Court's jurisdiction requires a detailed examination, which follows in the next subsection.

The Court's Jurisdiction

The jurisdiction of the Supreme Court is summarized in Table 1-1. That authority can be divided into two parts. First, the Constitution gives the Supreme Court jurisdiction over certain specified classes of cases as a trial court, what is called original jurisdiction; those cases may

Figure 1-2 Basic Structure of Federal Court System

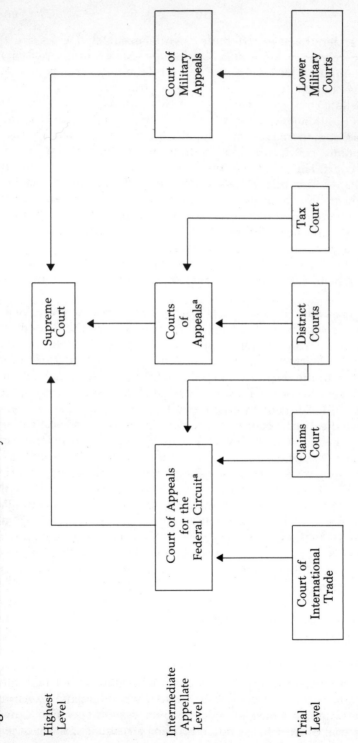

Note: Arrows indicate most common routes of appeals. Some specialized courts of minor importance are excluded.

[a] These courts also hear appeals from administrative agencies.

Table 1-1   Summary of Supreme Court Jurisdiction

I. Appellate jurisdiction [a]
   A. Mandatory cases (must be heard by the Court)
      1. Decisions of special three-judge federal district courts
   B. Discretionary cases (Court need not hear)
      1. All decisions of federal courts of appeals and specialized federal appellate courts
      2. All decisions of the highest state court with jurisdiction over a case, involving issues of federal law

II. Original jurisdiction
   A. Mandatory cases: none
   B. Discretionary cases
      1. Disputes between states [b]
      2. Cases brought by a state
      3. Disputes between a state and the federal government
      4. Cases involving foreign diplomatic personnel

[a] Some minor categories not listed.
[b] It is unclear whether these cases are mandatory or discretionary, but the Court treats them as discretionary.

be brought directly to the Court. The Court's original jurisdiction includes some cases to which a state is a party and cases involving ambassadors. Disputes between two states can be heard only by the Supreme Court. Other cases under the Court's original jurisdiction can be heard alternatively by a district court. Original cases account for few of the Court's full decisions—by one count, about 160 in its entire history.[9]

Second, under its appellate jurisdiction the Court may hear cases brought by parties dissatisfied with decisions of the federal courts of appeals and the specialized appellate courts in the federal system. Cases also may come directly from special three-judge district courts that are set up to hear a few classes of cases designated by Congress.

Cases can come to the Supreme Court after decisions by the state supreme courts if they involve claims under federal law or the Constitution. More precisely, a case can come to the Court from the highest state court with the power to hear it. The case of *Thompson v. City of Louisville* (1960) was brought to the Court directly from the police court of Louisville, Kentucky, because it involved a fine for loitering and disorderly conduct that was too small under state law to be appealed to any higher state court.

The rule by which state cases come to the Supreme Court may be confusing; as noted earlier, cases arising under federal law ordinarily are brought originally to federal court rather than state court. However, cases that are brought to court on the basis of state law, so that they are heard in state court, frequently contain issues of federal law as well. This distinction can be illustrated with reference to criminal cases. A person who is accused of violating a state criminal law will be tried in a state court. But during the state proceedings the defendant may argue that rights under the Constitution were violated in a police search or interrogation. The case eventually can be brought to the Supreme Court on that issue. If so, the Court will have the power to rule only on the federal issue, not on the issues of state law involved in the case. The Court cannot rule as to whether the defendant actually violated a state criminal law.

Nearly all cases brought to the Court are under its discretionary jurisdiction, so that it can choose whether or not to hear them. They come to the Court primarily in the form of petitions for a writ of certiorari, a legal device by which the Court brings up a case for decision. Until recently, several classes of cases from lower courts came to the Court as "appeals" under its mandatory jurisdiction; the Court was obligated to decide these cases. The Court developed mechanisms by which it gave some appeals only limited consideration, so that in practice their handling was similar to the handling of certiorari cases. In 1988, Congress narrowed the Court's mandatory jurisdiction to include only the small number of cases decided by three-judge federal district courts.

Of the cases brought to federal and state courts, the Supreme Court actually hears only a fraction of 1 percent. As this figure suggests, courts other than the Supreme Court have ample opportunity to make policy on their own. Moreover, their decisions help to determine the ultimate impact of the Court's policies. In focusing our attention on the Supreme Court, we must be careful to avoid what Jerome Frank called the "upper-court myth," the belief that little of consequence happens at the lower levels of the court system.[10]

A First Look at the Court

The Court's Physical Structure

The Supreme Court did not move into its own building until 1935. Before that time the Court sat in quarters borrowed from other institutions. Originally the Court met in the Royal Exchange Building in New York, then the Old City Hall in Philadelphia. The Court moved to Washington with the rest of the federal government at the beginning of the nineteenth century. For the next 130 years the Court sat at various places in the Capitol, as a "tenant" of Congress. In 1860 the Court obtained permanent quarters in the old Senate chamber in the Capitol.

The Court's accommodations in the Capitol increasingly were regarded as inadequate. The justices lacked office space and did most of their work at home. Largely at the behest of Chief Justice William Howard Taft, Congress appropriated money for a Supreme Court building in 1929. The building was completed in 1935, but the justices who served at that time found their quarters in the building too opulent for their tastes. "What are we supposed to do, ride in on nine elephants?" one justice asked.[11] Some chose to continue working at home rather than use their new chambers, which were occupied only as new justices came to the Court.

The Court's building *is* impressive. It occupies a full square block across from the Capitol and is five stories tall. The primary building material is marble, with liberal use of oak inside. The style is Corinthian, intended to give the Court building the same majesty as the neighboring congressional buildings. Not surprisingly, it has been referred to as a "marble palace."

The Court houses all the functions necessary for its operation as an institution. The most important rooms are on the first floor. The Court's formal sessions are held in the courtroom. The justices sit behind their bench at the front of the courtroom, with other participants and spectators in sections in the back and along the sides. Near the courtroom are the chambers that house offices for the associate justices and their staffs. Behind the courtroom is the conference room, where the justices meet to decide cases. The chief justice's chambers are attached to the conference room.

The Court's Personnel

The Justices. The Constitution requires that members of the Supreme Court be nominated by the president and confirmed by a majority of the Senate. It also establishes that they will hold office "during good behavior"—that is, for life unless they relinquish their posts voluntarily or are removed by impeachment proceedings. Beyond these basic rules, such issues as the number of justices, their qualifications, and their duties have been settled by law and tradition, rather than specified in the Constitution. The qualifications and selection of the justices will be covered in greater detail in Chapter 2.

We are accustomed to a Court of nine members, but the number of justices was changed several times during the Court's first century. The Judiciary Act of 1789 provided for six justices. Later statutes changed the number successively to five, six, seven, nine, ten, seven, and nine. The changes were made in part to accommodate the justices' duties in the lower federal courts, in part to serve partisan and policy goals of the president and Congress. The final change to nine members was made in 1869, and the Court has remained at that size; any further changes appear quite unlikely. In 1937 President Franklin Roosevelt's effort to gain ideological control of the Court by increasing the number of justices was defeated in part because the number nine had become well established.

In 1988 the associate justices received salaries of $110,000, the chief justice $115,000. (Congressional salaries were $89,500.) The primary duties of the justices, of course, involve participation in the collective decisions of the Court: determining which cases to hear, deciding cases, and writing and contributing to opinions.

Ordinarily, formal Court decisions are made by the full nine members. On occasion, however, fewer than nine justices sit on a case. A justice may sit out a specific case because of a conflict of interest, which might arise from stock holdings or earlier involvement in the case as a government lawyer. The individual justice alone decides whether it would be appropriate to participate in a case, and occasionally a justice is criticized for participating in a particular case.

The Court may operate with only eight members for an extended period of time because a justice is ill or a departing justice has not yet been replaced. Justice Lewis Powell was absent from the Court for two months in 1985 because of surgery. Powell retired two years later, and the Court was short one member for much of the 1987 term until Anthony Kennedy replaced him.

When only eight justices participate in a decision, the Court may divide 4-4; it did so eight times as a result of Powell's 1985 illness. A tie vote affirms the lower court decision. Ordinarily, individual votes are not announced and no opinions are written.

A quorum for decision on a case is six members. The Court seldom fails to achieve a quorum, but in 1987 it was unable to hear arguments in a case because it had only eight justices at the time, three of whom disqualified themselves from the case.[12] This failure, like a tie vote, resulted in affirmance of the lower court decisions.

Along with their participation in collective decisions, the justices have decision-making functions as individuals, primarily in their service as circuit justices. The country always has been divided into federal judicial circuits. Since 1891 each circuit has contained a court of appeals whose members decide appeals from district court decisions. Originally, appeals within a circuit generally were heard by ad hoc courts composed of a federal trial judge and two members of the Supreme Court assigned to that area as circuit justices. The circuit duties were arduous, particularly before the development of modern transportation systems. The justices' "circuit-riding" responsibilities were reduced in several stages, the first coming in 1793, until they were eliminated altogether by the creation of the courts of appeals in 1891.

The twelve judicial circuits continue to have circuit justices assigned to them, with three justices doing double duty. The current duties of the circuit justices are largely ceremonial. However, the circuit justices have primary responsibility to deal with applications for special action, such as a request to stay a lower court decision (preventing it from taking effect) until the Court decides whether to hear a case. Ordinarily, such an application must go first to the circuit justice, who usually rules on it as an individual but sometimes refers it to the Court as a whole. If the circuit justice rejects an application, it can then be made to a second justice; that justice usually refers it to the whole Court, which almost always rejects an application in this situation.[13]

This part of the Court's work has become more significant in recent years with an increasing number of requests to the Court to stay executions. Often these requests come very close to the scheduled time of execution, putting great pressure on the circuit justice or on the Court as a whole. Justice Harry Blackmun has referred to the "excruciating agony" of such cases.[14] Stays of execution have become a matter of contention within the Court, chiefly because of sharp disagreements about the death penalty itself. In recent years the Court has voted against stays in several cases by 5-4 votes and once on a 4-4 vote. Some of these decisions produced strong dissents by justices who favored stays.[15]

The position of chief justice carries with it a number of special roles.[16] Within the Court, the chief justice presides over public sessions and conferences and has primary responsibility for administration of the Court. The chief justice also holds administrative responsibilities in the federal judicial system as a whole, such as chairing its Judicial Conference. Warren Burger was a particularly active chief justice, devoting considerable energy to his administrative duties. Like some predecessors, Burger also sought to exert leadership in the legal system as a whole; he acted as advocate for such goals as prison reform and improvement in lawyers' skills.

The press of work and the desire to maintain the appearance of impartiality limit the outside activities of justices. But justices do engage in other pursuits, which have included making a cameo appearance in a Gilbert and Sullivan opera (William Rehnquist), playing on a bridge team facing British opponents (John Paul Stevens), and ruling at a hearing on whether William Shakespeare actually wrote the plays credited to him (William Brennan, Harry Blackmun, and Stevens).

Some outside activities involve the Court's work more directly. In forums such as speeches and interviews, several justices in recent years have been willing to air their views on public issues, to discuss details of the Court's internal processes, and even to complain about Court practices. Some justices have become involved in the political process more directly, primarily through informal consultation with presidents. Such consultation troubles some observers of the Court, because it may compromise a justice's impartiality. Abe Fortas's continuing service as a close adviser to President Lyndon Johnson after he joined the Court in

1965 provided ammunition for those senators who successfully opposed his confirmation as chief justice three years later.

Law Clerks and Other Support Staff.   The justices are supported by a staff that included about 320 people in 1988.[17] More than half serve custodial and police functions under the marshal of the Court. About thirty people work for the clerk of the Court, who is responsible for clerical processing of all the cases that come to the Court. The reporter of decisions supervises preparation of the official record of the Court's decisions, the *United States Reports.* The librarian is in charge of the set of libraries in the Supreme Court building.

Each justice is served directly by secretaries and law clerks. (There also are a counsel and a staff counsel for the Court as a whole who aid the Court and individual justices on several kinds of matters, including applications for special action.) The law clerks are the most important part of the support staff. In 1988 seven of the justices employed four clerks each, while Justices William Rehnquist and John Paul Stevens chose to use three each. The clerks traditionally are recent law school graduates who have compiled exceptional records, primarily in prestigious schools. Nearly all Supreme Court clerks in recent years already had served as clerks for judges in lower federal courts. Usually clerks serve a justice for one year, though a few stay for two or more years. After leaving the Court, clerks frequently go on to distinguished careers. Among the eighteen law clerks who worked in the 1957 term, by 1983 one was deputy secretary of state, a second was president of the American Civil Liberties Union, and a third was president of the Pacific Stock Exchange; three others were judges on state supreme courts and a federal court of appeals.[18] Three of the justices in 1988 (Rehnquist, Stevens, and White) once were law clerks in the Court.

Clerks serve their justices in several ways. Most clerks spend the largest part of their time on the petitions for hearing by the Court, digesting information in the petitions and lower court records and summarizing this information for the justices. Because of the large number of cases brought to the Court, this function is indispensable. The clerks also help with tasks such as the research used as a basis for deciding cases that the Court has accepted for full consideration and for the drafting of opinions. Many justices give their clerks considerable responsibility for the actual writing of opinion drafts.

It is difficult to assess the influence of the clerks on the Court's decisions. Because so much work is delegated to clerks, it is inevitable that they have some impact on what the justices do. At the same time, most justices seem to work hard to retain control over their decisions. It may be, as Chief Justice Rehnquist suggested after his own service as a clerk,[19] that law clerks have greater influence over decisions about which cases to hear than over decisions on the merits of the cases that the Court does hear. The availability of clerks as drafters probably encourages justices to write separate opinions expressing their own views in cases and increases the length and complexity of opinions.

The Court's Schedule

The Schedule by Year. The Court holds one "term" each year, which lasts from the first Monday in October until the beginning of the succeeding term a year later. The term is designated by the year in which it begins. With some exceptions, the Court's collective work is restricted to the period from late September to late June or early July. This work begins when the justices meet to dispose of the large number of petitions for hearing that have accumulated during the summer and ends when the Court has issued all its decisions in cases it heard during the term.

Most of the term is divided into "sittings" of approximately two weeks and "recesses" of almost two weeks, sometimes longer. During the sittings the Court meets in open session and holds internal conferences. Some conferences are held during the recesses as well. The Court departs from this schedule in mid-May, holding one or more sessions each week for the next several weeks.

Early in the term the Court hears oral argument in cases but issues few decisions on argued cases, because the process of decision for most cases takes from several weeks to several months. Later the Court begins to hand down significant numbers of decisions. Oral argument for the term generally is completed by late April or early May. From this point on the Court's sessions will be devoted chiefly to the announcements of its decisions. When the Court has reached and announced decisions in all the cases that it heard during the term, the long summer recess begins. Cases that the Court accepted for hearings but that were not argued during the term are carried over until the next term.

During the summer the justices spend some time away from Washington but continue their work on the petitions for hearing that arrive at the Court. During that time the Court and individual circuit justices respond to applications for special action, and on rare occasions the Court holds a special summer hearing on an urgent case such as *United States v. Nixon* (1974). When the justices meet at the end of summer to dispose of the accumulated petitions, the cycle begins again.

The Schedule by Week. The schedule of activities during the week, like the annual schedule, is fairly regular. During the sittings, the Court holds sessions on Mondays, Tuesdays, and Wednesdays. In recent terms the most common pattern has been to hold sessions Monday through Wednesday of two weeks and Monday of the third week. As I noted, toward the end of the term one or more sessions are held each week to announce decisions in the form of orders and opinions.

The sessions generally are held from 10:00 a.m. until about 3:00 p.m. with a one-hour break at noon. Oral arguments are held in each session except the last Monday of the sitting. They may be preceded by several types of business. On Mondays the Court announces the filing of its order list, which reports the Court's decisions on petitions for hearing and other action in its conference of the preceding Friday. Opinions in cases that the Court has resolved may be announced or read. New members of the Supreme Court bar, attorneys who may handle cases before the Court, are admitted early in the sessions.

The oral arguments consume most of the time of the sessions. Most often one hour is allocated for argument in a case, divided equally between the two sides. Thus the Court generally hears four cases in a session.

During sittings the Court holds two conferences each week. The Wednesday afternoon conference is used to discuss the cases that were argued on Monday. A longer conference on Friday includes discussion of the cases argued on Tuesday and Wednesday, as well as all the other matters that must be taken up by the Court. Most numerous of these matters are the petitions for hearing.

The Court also holds a conference on the last Friday of each recess to deal with the continuing flow of business to the Court. The remainder of the justices' time during recess periods is devoted to their individual work: preparatory work on petitions for hearing and cases scheduled for argument, the writing of opinions, and reaction to other justices' opinions. These activities continue during the sittings, but less time can be devoted to them then.

The Court's History

This book is concerned primarily with the Supreme Court at present and in the recent past. However, to understand the current Court it is necessary on occasion to look to its history. To provide some context for the excursions into history later in the book, it will be useful at this point to examine some relevant highlights of Supreme Court history.

The Court from 1790 to 1865

The Constitutional Context. The Constitution explicitly created the Supreme Court, giving Congress discretion as to the creation of lower federal courts. But the Constitution said much less about the Court than it did about Congress and the president. Article III laid out the Court's basic jurisdiction and gave Congress power to regulate the appellate part of that jurisdiction. The Constitution also indicated the mode of selection and the tenure of Supreme Court justices. Otherwise it was silent as to the Court's position in government and role in the making of policy.

The Judiciary Act of 1789, which set up the federal court system, used the Court's jurisdiction under the Constitution as a basis for granting it broad powers. The Court explicitly was given power to hear certain cases brought from lower federal courts as well as from state courts. It also was given power to direct action by federal judges and any other federal officials. Still, what the Court would do with its powers was uncertain, in part because the scope of those powers was somewhat ambiguous. Perhaps the most important of the uncertainties was the issue of judicial review: did the Court have the power to declare statutes (acts of Congress and other legislatures) or other government action void on grounds of inconsistency with the Constitution?

A Slow Start.   During its first decade, between 1790 and 1799, the Court decided only about fifty cases. A few of these decisions were significant. The Court's ruling in *Chisholm v. Georgia* (1793) embroiled it in controversy; the decision, which allowed a citizen of one state to sue another state in federal court, was attacked and quickly overturned with passage of the Eleventh Amendment. In some other cases justices seemed to claim the power of judicial review, though they did not exercise that power clearly. But the Court was not yet a major participant in national policy making.

The Court's relative unimportance was reflected in matters of personnel. Several people rejected offers of nominations to the Court. Chief Justice John Jay and Justice John Rutledge left the Court for more attractive opportunities in state government.

John Marshall and Judicial Review.   The rise in the Court's fortunes following this early period was directed by John Marshall, chief justice from 1801 to 1835. Marshall, a last-minute appointment by President John Adams, came to dominate the Court to a degree that no other justice has matched. He used his dominance to advance the policies that he favored as well as the position of the Court itself.

The key assertion of power by the Court under Marshall probably was its famous decision in *Marbury v. Madison* (1803), in which the Court struck down a federal statute for the first time. Marshall's opinion for the Court argued that where a federal law is inconsistent with the Constitution, the Court must uphold the supremacy of the Constitution by declaring the law unconstitutional and refusing to enforce it. A few years later Marshall also claimed the right of judicial review over state acts, and during his tenure the Court overturned more than a dozen state statutes on constitutional grounds.

The Court's aggressiveness brought denunciations and threats, including an effort by President Jefferson to secure the removal of at least one justice through impeachment. But Marshall's finesse helped to protect the Court from a successful attack. Gradually the powers that he claimed for the Court and the Court's central role in the policy-making process came to be accepted by the other branches of government and by the citizenry in general.

This acceptance was tested by the Court's decision in *Scott v. Sandford* (1857). Until that decision the Court had overturned only one federal statute, the minor law involved in *Marbury v. Madison*. In the *Dred Scott* case, however, Chief Justice Roger Taney held for the Court that Congress had exceeded its constitutional powers in adopting the Missouri Compromise prohibiting slavery in some territories. That decision was intended to resolve the legal controversy over slavery. Instead, the level of controversy increased, and the Court was vilified in the North. Yet, although the Court's prestige suffered mightily, the Court itself and its basic powers survived without serious challenge.[20]

The Court and Federalism.   During this period the Court was concerned with more than its own position. It addressed major issues of public policy as well. The primary area of its concern was federalism, the legal relationship between the national and state governments.

Under Marshall, the Court gave strong support to national powers. Marshall was especially interested in restricting state policy where that policy interfered with activities of the national government, especially its power to regulate commerce. His position was exemplified by *Gibbons v. Ogden* (1824), which overturned a state monopoly over steamboat transportation that impinged upon national control over interstate commerce, and by *McCulloch v. Maryland* (1819), which limited state power to tax a nationally chartered bank.

Marshall was succeeded by Chief Justice Roger Taney, who served from 1836 to 1864. During this period the Court's position was more complex and less uniformly favorable to the national government. Taney and his colleagues did not reverse the direction of the Court under Marshall, however. As a result the constitutional power of the federal government remained strong; the Court had subtly altered the lines between national and state governments in support of the former.

The Court from 1865 to 1937

Issues of Economic Regulation.   In the first two decades after the Civil War, the Court was faced with several issues arising out of that conflict. The Court did not address the constitutionality of the Reconstruction policy of military control over the South, in part because Congress acted to limit the Court's jurisdiction in that area. However, the Court did rule against the use of military courts to try civilians in *Ex parte Milligan* (1866). In 1870 a narrow majority ruled that the Civil War policy of issuing paper money without backing in coin was unconstitutional in part. One year later, after two new appointments, the Court reversed its position. This abrupt shift later was cited by Chief Justice Charles Evans Hughes as one of the Court's "self-inflicted wounds." [21]

Gradually, however, the Court turned its attention primarily to issues of government authority to regulate private economic behavior. By the late nineteenth century, all levels of government had begun to adopt laws regulating business activities. Among those laws were the federal antitrust laws, state regulations of railroad practices, and federal and state laws concerning employment conditions. Inevitably, much of this legislation was challenged in the courts on constitutional grounds, and the Court's work in this area increased.

Early in this period, the Supreme Court's position on government authority to regulate business was quite mixed. But the Court increasingly became unfriendly to regulatory policies. That position was reflected in the development of constitutional doctrines that limited government powers to control business activities. Those doctrines were used with increasing frequency to attack regulatory legislation; in the 1920s, the Supreme Court held unconstitutional more than 130 regulatory laws.[22] Federal statutes were overturned because the Court viewed them as unsupported by the Constitution's grants of powers to Congress; state and local laws were overturned primarily as violations of economic rights protected by the Fourteenth Amendment.

The New Deal Conflict. This line of policy was criticized heavily by supporters of regulatory legislation. By the 1920s liberals freely attacked the Court for what they perceived as its friendliness toward business interests. However, the Court did not face a serious threat until the 1930s, when its majority brought it into direct conflict with President Franklin Roosevelt and the New Deal.

Roosevelt's program to combat the Great Depression included sweeping measures to control the economy. The Agricultural Adjustment Act was an effort to limit farm production in order to stabilize commodity prices. The National Industrial Recovery Act was established to bring about agreements on labor and trade practices within whole industries.

In a series of decisions in 1935 and 1936 the Court struck down these two acts and other federal recovery legislation, generally by 6-3 and 5-4 margins.[23] As a result, the New Deal program was weakened seriously. Inevitably, the Court was criticized with a new fervor. Roosevelt led the criticism, and after his overwhelming reelection in 1936 he proposed to deal with the situation through legislation under which an additional justice could be added to the Court for every sitting justice over seventy years old. The result would have been to increase the Court's size temporarily to fifteen, allowing Roosevelt to "pack" the Court with justices favorable to his programs.

While this plan was being debated in Cong:ess, the Court took away most of the impetus behind it. In a series of decisions in 1937, the Court upheld New Deal legislation and similar state legislation by narrow margins, taking positions contrary to its collective views in recent cases.[24] This shift came because Chief Justice Hughes and Justice Owen Roberts changed their votes to establish majority support for the Roosevelt-sponsored legislation and thereby turned the Court around. They almost surely did so in response to the conflict between the Court and the president and the resulting threat to the Court's autonomy. As a result of this shift, which became known as "the switch in time that saved nine," the Court-packing plan died.

During the congressional debate, one of the conservative justices retired. Several other justices left the Court in the next few years, so that Roosevelt was able to obtain the ideological control of the Court that he had sought through the Court-packing legislation. The new Court created by his appointments accepted unequivocally the economic regulation that its predecessor had viewed unfavorably.

The Court from 1937 to the Present

A Shift to Civil Liberties Concerns.　Since the Court's retreat in the late 1930s, it has continued to accept major government economic policies. The Court hears many cases involving economic regulation, but this field has become less important as part of its work and as a source of major decisions.

Instead, the Court's emphasis in the current era is on civil liberties. More precisely, the Court has focused primarily upon the interpretation of constitutional guarantees of protection for freedom of expression and freedom of religion, for the procedural rights of criminal defendants and other persons, and for equal treatment of racial minorities and other disadvantaged groups by the government. These issues had concerned the Court since the late nineteenth century, but not until the current era did they become the primary focus of the Court's work.

The Court's general position on civil liberties issues has varied a good deal during this period. At some times it has provided strong support for expansive protections of civil liberties, while at other times it has taken a mixed position. The Court's position has been especially sensitive to changes in its membership. The appointment of one or two new justices may affect the handling of civil liberties issues a great deal. The one constant factor has been the willingness of most justices to give serious consideration to claims of violations of civil liberties.

Activism in the Warren Court. The Court was most uniformly supportive of civil liberties and most activist in its policy making during the period in which Earl Warren was chief justice (1953-1969), particularly during the last half of that period. As a result, the policies of the Court during that period often are identified with Warren. However, other liberal justices played roles of at least equal importance. Especially important were Hugo Black and William Douglas, Roosevelt appointees who served through Warren's entire tenure, and William Brennan, an Eisenhower appointee.

Probably the best known decision of this period was *Brown v. Board of Education* (1954), which ordered a desegregation of southern school systems and began the long process of desegregation that continues today. The Court also supported the rights of black Americans in several other areas of policy. During the 1960s, the Court expanded the rights of criminal defendants in state trials, most notably in landmark decisions on the right to counsel (*Gideon v. Wainwright*, 1963), police search and seizure practices (*Mapp v. Ohio*, 1961), and questioning of suspects (*Miranda v. Arizona*, 1966). The Court supported freedom of expression by expanding First Amendment rights in several fields, particularly obscenity and libel. In a series of cases beginning with *Baker v. Carr* (1962), the Court required that legislatures be apportioned according to population.

These policies led to heavy criticism of the Court. In the late 1950s members of Congress attacked the Court for a series of liberal decisions, particularly those concerning the rights of allegedly subversive persons, and proposed legislative action against the Court. These proposals failed, in part because the Court engaged in a more limited version of its retreat in the New Deal period. The liberal policies of the 1960s drew further criticism in Congress and elsewhere. Some legal scholars joined in the criticism, charging the Court's majority with taking untenable positions and engaging in unjustified activism. The Court also had a good many defenders, and the level of controversy over its work reached a level unprecedented since the 1930s.

Partial Retrenchment in the 1970s and 1980s. Earl Warren retired in 1969 and was replaced as chief justice by Warren Burger, President Nixon's first appointment to the Court. Nixon made three more appointments in 1970 and 1971, producing a Court whose aggregate viewpoint was more conservative. The Court's membership changed much more slowly after that, but each new justice over the next seventeen years was selected by a conservative Republican president—one by Gerald Ford and three by Ronald Reagan. In 1986 Reagan named Nixon appointee William Rehnquist, the most conservative member of the Court, to replace Warren Burger as chief justice.

As of 1988, these appointments had not changed the Court's policies as much as some observers had expected. (One collection of commentaries on the Burger Court was subtitled *The Counter-Revolution That Wasn't.*[25]) Rather, the Court developed a mixed position, taking strongly conservative positions on some issues but maintaining liberal positions on others.

The Court took its sharpest turn in a conservative direction in the area of criminal justice. It became less sympathetic to defendants, interpreting procedural rights narrowly in a series of mostly undramatic decisions. For instance, in *United States v. Leon* (1984) it created an important exception to the rule barring illegally seized evidence from court. In freedom of expression the Court's decision in *Miller v. California* (1973) gave government more power to regulate obscene materials, and the Court reduced protection of the mass media against libel suits in decisions such as *Wolston v. Reader's Digest Association* (1979).

Even in these fields there were important exceptions to the dominant pattern, and in other fields the Court was more favorable to civil liberties. It was in the 1970s that the Court gave its first significant support to legal equality for women, striking down a variety of laws that treated women and men differently. The Court showed a willingness to support other disadvantaged groups as well; this was symbolized by its decision in *Plyler v. Doe* (1982), holding that the children of people who entered the country illegally have a right to a public education. In *Roe v. Wade* (1973), the Court virtually eliminated the power of states to prohibit abortions, and over the next decade it reinforced that decision by restricting the power of states to regulate abortions.

The most dramatic decision during this period was the Court's ruling in *United States v. Nixon* (1974), which required that President Nixon yield recordings of his conversations to a federal court. The expectation of compliance with the decision was so great that Nixon had little choice but to comply, even though the result was to expose evidence fatal to his defense against impeachment. Nixon resigned two weeks later.

The decision in *United States v. Nixon* was unanimous, but the Court of the 1970s and 1980s was deeply divided in most major cases. The division reflected a close balance between liberals and conservatives, with a middle group of moderates who usually determined the Court's position. It was not surprising that the nomination of Robert Bork in 1987 became controversial, because even a single change in personnel could result in more consistently conservative policies. As the development of the post-Warren Court continues, the Court inevitably remains a subject of national interest and concern.

Notes

1. Full legal citations to cases mentioned in this book are provided in the Index of Cases.
2. *Thornburgh v. American College of Obstetricians and Gynecologists* (1986); *Harris v. McRae* (1980).
3. See, for instance, *Sheet Metal Workers' International Association v. Equal Employment Opportunity Commission* (1986) and *Johnson v. Transportation Agency* (1987).
4. *Immigration and Naturalization Service v. Chadha* (1983).
5. Alexis de Tocqueville, *Democracy in America*, trans. Henry Reeve, rev. Francis Bowen (New York: Alfred A. Knopf, 1945), 1:280.
6. Bradley C. Canon, "A Framework for the Analysis of Judicial Activism," in *Supreme Court Activism and Restraint*, ed. Stephen C. Halpern and Charles M. Lamb (Lexington, Mass.: Lexington Books, 1982), 385-419.
7. The views on activism and restraint discussed here are presented in *The Supreme Court in American Politics: Judicial Activism vs. Judicial Restraint*, ed. David F. Forte (Lexington, Mass.: D.C. Heath, 1972); and in *Supreme Court Activism and Restraint*, ed. Halpern and Lamb. For some views of the commentators mentioned here, see Robert H. Bork, "Neutral Principles and Some First Amendment Problems," *Indiana Law Journal* 47 (Fall 1971): 1-35; Edwin Meese, III, "Construing the Constitution." *U. C. Davis Law Review* 19 (Fall 1985): 22-30; and J. Skelly Wright, "The Judicial Right and the Rhetoric of Restraint: A Defense of Judicial Activism in an Age of Conservative Judges," *Hastings Constitutional Law Quarterly* 14 (Spring 1987): 487-523.
8. *Mora v. McNamara* (1967); *Massachusetts v. Laird* (1970); *Sarnoff v. Shultz* (1972).
9. Henry J. Abraham, *The Judicial Process*, 5th ed. (New York: Oxford University Press, 1986), 178-179, updated by the author.
10. Jerome Frank, *Courts on Trial* (Princeton: Princeton University Press, 1950), 222.
11. Richard L. Williams, "Supreme Court of the United States: The Staff That Keeps It Operating," *Smithsonian*, January 1977, 42.
12. Marcia Chambers, "Supreme Splits," *National Law Journal*, November 30, 1987, 37.
13. This discussion draws from the material in Robert L. Stern, Eugene Gressman, and Stephen M. Shapiro, *Supreme Court Practice*, 6th ed. (Washington, D.C.: Bureau of National Affairs, 1986), 674-705.
14. "Death Cases Straining Justices," *New York Times*, May 13, 1986, A18.
15. See *Green v. Zant* (1985), *Wainwright v. Booker* (1985), and *Rook v. Rice* (1986).
16. Peter G. Fish, "The Office of Chief Justice of the United States: Into the Federal Judiciary's Bicentennial Decade," in *The Office of Chief Justice*, ed. White Burkett Miller Center of Public Affairs, University of Virginia (Charlottesville: University of Virginia, 1984), 1-153.
17. Information on the number of personnel, as of February 1, 1988, is taken from an information sheet compiled by the Public Information Office of the Court.
18. James F. Clarity and Warren Weaver, Jr., "High Court Graduates," *New York Times*, October 7, 1983, B9.
19. William H. Rehnquist, "Who Writes Decisions of the Supreme Court?" *U.S. News and World Report*, December 13, 1957, 74-75.
20. Robert G. McCloskey, *The American Supreme Court* (Chicago: University of

Chicago Press, 1960), 98-100.

21. Charles Evans Hughes, *The Supreme Court of the United States* (Garden City, N.Y.: Garden City Publishing Co., 1936), 50. The cases were *Hepburn v. Griswold* (1870) and the *Legal Tender Cases* (1871).

22. This figure was calculated from data in Congressional Research Service, *The Constitution of the United States of America: Analysis and Interpretation* (Washington, D.C.: Government Printing Office, 1987).

23. The cases included *Carter v. Carter Coal Co.* (1936), *United States v. Butler* (1936), and *Schechter Poultry Corp. v. United States* (1935).

24. The cases included *National Labor Relations Board v. Jones & Laughlin Steel Corp.* (1937), *Steward Machine Co. v. Davis* (1937), and *West Coast Hotel Co. v. Parrish* (1937).

25. Vincent Blasi, ed., *The Burger Court: The Counter-Revolution That Wasn't* (New Haven: Yale University Press, 1982).

2

The Justices

The attention given to Robert Bork's nomination to the Supreme Court in 1987 underlines the importance of the Court's membership. What any policy-making body does is determined in part by the attitudes and perspectives of the people who serve in it. This is particularly true of the Supreme Court, whose members are relatively free from the electoral controls that legislators face and from the organizational constraints that limit the choices of administrators. Indeed, the single most important factor shaping the Court's policies at any given time may be the identity of its members.

This chapter is concerned with the members of the Supreme Court: their selection, backgrounds, and tenure on the Court. First, I will examine the process by which justices are selected. Second, I will discuss the characteristics of those who become justices and the implications of those characteristics for the Court's policies. Finally, and more briefly, I will discuss how and why justices leave the Court.

Through mid-1988 there have been 144 nominations to the Supreme Court, and 104 people have sat on the Court. Four people were nominated and confirmed twice, eight declined appointments or died before beginning service on the Court, and twenty-eight did not secure Senate confirmation.[1] In discussing the recruitment process I will focus on the fifty-eight nominations that were made and the forty-seven justices who were selected during this century (see Table 2-1).

The Process of Selection

The selection of a Supreme Court justice begins with the creation of a vacancy, when a member of the Court dies or steps down from the Court. Inevitably, vacancies occur at an irregular rate. There were no vacancies to fill in Franklin Roosevelt's first term, but five in his second term. Four

Table 2-1 Twentieth-Century Nominations to the Supreme Court

Name	Nominated by	Replaced	Years served
Oliver Wendell Holmes	T. Roosevelt	Gray	1902-32
William Day	T. Roosevelt	Shiras	1903-22
William Moody	T. Roosevelt	Brown	1906-10
Horace Lurton	Taft	Peckham	1910-14
Edward White (CJ)[a]	Taft	Fuller	1910-21
Charles Evans Hughes	Taft	Brewer	1910-16
Willis Van Devanter	Taft	White	1911-37
Joseph Lamar	Taft	Moody	1911-16
Mahlon Pitney	Taft	Harlan	1912-22
James McReynolds	Wilson	Lurton	1914-41
Louis Brandeis	Wilson	Lamar	1916-39
John Clarke	Wilson	Hughes	1916-22
William Howard Taft (CJ)	Harding	White	1921-30
George Sutherland	Harding	Clarke	1922-38
Pierce Butler	Harding	Day	1923-39
Edward Sanford	Harding	Pitney	1923-30
Harlan Fiske Stone	Coolidge	McKenna	1925-46
Charles Evans Hughes (CJ)	Hoover	Taft	1930-41
John Parker	Hoover	(Sanford)	Defeated for confirmation, 1930
Owen Roberts	Hoover	Sanford	1930-45
Benjamin Cardozo	Hoover	Holmes	1932-38
Hugo Black	F. Roosevelt	Van Devanter	1937-71
Stanley Reed	F. Roosevelt	Sutherland	1938-57
Felix Frankfurter	F. Roosevelt	Cardozo	1939-62
William Douglas	F. Roosevelt	Brandeis	1939-75
Frank Murphy	F. Roosevelt	Butler	1940-49
James Byrnes	F. Roosevelt	McReynolds	1941-42
Harlan Fiske Stone (CJ)[a]	F. Roosevelt	Hughes	1941-46

Name	President	Seat	Notes
Robert Jackson	F. Roosevelt	Stone	1941-54
Wiley Rutledge	F. Roosevelt	Byrnes	1943-49
Harold Burton	Truman	Roberts	1945-58
Fred Vinson (CJ)	Truman	Stone	1946-53
Tom Clark	Truman	Murphy	1949-67
Sherman Minton	Truman	Rutledge	1949-56
Earl Warren (CJ)	Eisenhower	Vinson	1953-69
John Harlan	Eisenhower	Jackson	1955-71
William Brennan	Eisenhower	Minton	1956-
Charles Whittaker	Eisenhower	Reed	1957-62
Potter Stewart	Eisenhower	Burton	1958-81
Byron White	Kennedy	Whittaker	1962-
Arthur Goldberg	Kennedy	Frankfurter	1962-65
Abe Fortas	Johnson	Goldberg	1965-69
Thurgood Marshall	Johnson	Clark	1967-
Abe Fortas (CJ)[a]	Johnson	(Warren)	Nomination withdrawn, 1968
Homer Thornberry	Johnson	(Fortas)	Nomination became moot, 1968[b]
Warren Burger (CJ)	Nixon	Warren	1969-86
Clement Haynsworth	Nixon	(Fortas)	Defeated for confirmation, 1969
G. Harold Carswell	Nixon	(Fortas)	Defeated for confirmation, 1970
Harry Blackmun	Nixon	Fortas	1970-
Lewis Powell	Nixon	Black	1971-87
William Rehnquist	Nixon	Harlan	1971-
John Paul Stevens	Ford	Douglas	1975-
Sandra Day O'Connor	Reagan	Stewart	1981-
William Rehnquist (CJ)[a]	Reagan	Burger	1986-
Antonin Scalia	Reagan	Rehnquist	1986-
Robert Bork	Reagan	(Powell)	Defeated for confirmation, 1987
Douglas Ginsburg	Reagan	(Powell)	Withdrew before formal nomination, 1987
Anthony Kennedy	Reagan	Powell	1988-

[a] Nominated as chief justice while serving as associate justice.
[b] When Fortas's nomination for chief justice was withdrawn, no vacancy for his seat as associate justice existed.

justices left the Court in Richard Nixon's first three years in office. The absence of any vacancies in the four years from 1977 through 1980 made Jimmy Carter the first president in more than a century—and the only president who served a full term—not to select any justices.

The formal selection process for justices is rather simple. When a vacancy occurs, the president makes a nomination, and the nomination must be confirmed by a majority of those voting in the Senate. When the chief justice's position is vacant, the president may nominate a sitting justice to that position and also nominate a new associate justice, or simply nominate a person as chief justice from outside the Court. Most of the time presidents have taken the latter course, chiefly to have a wider field from which to select this important leader.

Ordinarily the president's nominee is not actually "appointed" and cannot join the Court until confirmed by the Senate. In a few circumstances the president may make a "recess appointment" to the Court that becomes effective immediately, without Senate approval. The most important of these circumstances is when a vacancy occurs in the last month of a Senate session or when the Senate is not in session. The Senate retains the power to vote on the appointee's confirmation when it returns, but the confirmation process inevitably is affected by the fact that the person in question is already acting as a justice. Four of President Eisenhower's five nominations were recess appointments, and in 1960 the Senate expressed its disapproval of the practice. There have been no recess appointments since that time, in part because congressional recesses have become much shorter.

The actual process of selection, of course, is far more complicated than the simple formal procedure would suggest. The president and Senate make their decisions in an environment of individuals and groups highly interested in these decisions, and the process by which they reach their decisions is quite complex. In examining this process it will be useful first to discuss the roles of unofficial participants in the selection of justices and then to discuss how the president and Senate reach their decisions.

Unofficial Participants

Because of the importance of appointments to the Supreme Court, a variety of individuals and groups seek to influence the president and Senate. Apart from members of the president's administration, whose activities will be discussed later in this section, the most important of these participants fall into three categories: the American Bar Association and the legal community in general; nonlegal interest groups; and members of the Supreme Court. The roles of each of these participants, along with the activities of those who seek nominations for themselves, will be discussed in turn.

The ABA and Legal Community. The American Bar Association (ABA) is a national voluntary organization of attorneys organized in 1878. Because of its large membership and national scope, the ABA has come to be accepted as the major voice of the legal profession in the United States.

Much of the ABA's activity concerns politics and government policy, and among the most important of its policy interests is the selection of judges. At the state level the ABA and other bar associations have worked for the adoption of so-called merit selection of judges, by which the explicit role of partisan politics in judicial recruitment would be reduced. These efforts have been a major factor in the growing adoption of merit selection by the states.

At the federal level the ABA generally has accepted the existing formal method for the selection of judges, but it has sought to influence the selections that are made. Its attempts to influence judicial selection were unsystematic and occasional until the creation of its Committee on the Federal Judiciary in 1946. This committee is composed of fifteen members selected by the ABA president on a regional basis. It has sought to obtain a regular role in the selection process, particularly the opportunity to approve or disapprove of potential nominees before the president's final choice is made.

Presidents and senators have been relatively cooperative with the ABA in appointments below the Supreme Court level. The committee regularly is allowed to make recommendations to the president's administration concerning the qualifications of serious candidates for lower court judgeships. This participation is accepted in part because it serves presidential purposes in avoiding unqualified nominees, particularly where senators are supporting candidates who appear to be unqualified. However, presidents have been less willing to give the committee a significant role in Supreme Court nominations. In 1969, for instance, the Nixon administration gave the committee a veto power over nominations to all federal courts except the Supreme Court. This difference stems from the fact that presidents care far more about Supreme Court nominations than about lower court judgeships and wish to minimize constraints over their nominations to the Court.

The ABA committee's participation in Supreme Court nominations has varied according to the attitudes of the existing presidential administration. The committee would prefer to help screen prospective nominees before the president makes a choice. The Eisenhower and Nixon administrations allowed the committee to undertake such screening for some of their nominations. Gerald Ford did so for his only nomination, giving the committee fifteen names to consider. But presidents generally have preferred to exclude the ABA from the nomination process, because its inclusion would limit the president's freedom. Leaks of mixed and negative ratings for two prospective nominees in 1971 effectively prevented their selection; the Nixon administration immediately retracted its acceptance of the ABA committee's prescreening. Other administrations, such as the Reagan administration, have refused to allow committee prescreening for any of the vacancies that they have filled.

When it receives no advance notice of prospective nominees, the ABA committee is limited to making formal ratings of nominees after their selection. The committee undertakes an investigation, after which its members rate a nominee as "well qualified," "not opposed" (minimally qualified), or "not qualified." Acting after a nomination is made, the committee is understandably reluctant to call nominees unqualified. Indeed, a committee majority has never done so—even in the case of G. Harrold Carswell, a nominee of seemingly dubious qualifications who was defeated for confirmation by the Senate in 1970.

The ABA's position as the most prestigious organization of lawyers lends considerable weight to its ratings of nominees. The ABA committee usually votes unanimously that a nominee is well qualified, and such a vote makes Senate confirmation of a nomination easier. The unanimous approval of Anthony Kennedy in 1987, for instance, undoubtedly strengthened senators' positive views of Kennedy.

In contrast, the committee's split vote on Robert Bork, nominated for the same vacancy earlier that year, added to Bork's difficulties. Ten members of the committee rated Bork as well qualified, but four others rated him not qualified, and one voted "not opposed." Senate opponents of Bork used the negative votes as ammunition, and this probably helped to prevent Bork's confirmation.

The ABA's power in the selection process is a matter of controversy, and people who disagree with its ratings sometimes attack the ABA in strong terms. After it prevented his two prospective nominations in 1971, President Nixon dismissed the ABA with an expletive.[2] The committee members who voted against Robert Bork received strong criticism from some supporters of the nominee, who argued that these members were substituting political considerations for objective judgments about Bork's qualifications. Whatever the merits of this criticism, it underlines the significance of the role that the ABA committee has attained.

Other legal groups and individual lawyers also participate in the selection process. For instance, law professors and other prominent attorneys often give evaluations of nominees the Senate is considering. A great many lawyers publicly supported or opposed Robert Bork, and several testified before the Senate Judiciary Committee.

In some instances, such attorneys have considerable impact. In 1932, for instance, President Herbert Hoover nominated Benjamin Cardozo in response to the lobbying activities of a number of legal scholars. Another notable example of non-ABA legal influence was the criticism of Nixon's nominees Clement Haynsworth and Carswell by prominent attorneys. This criticism helped to counterbalance the ABA's official judgment that the nominees were qualified. For instance, legal scholar Louis Pollak apparently had some impact when he stated that Carswell "presents more slender credentials than any nominee for the Supreme Court put forth in this century." [3]

Other Interest Groups. The decisions of the Supreme Court affect the interests of most organized interest groups in the United States. While the Court's work in the general area of civil liberties is best publicized, the Court is also active in economic fields such as antitrust and labor law, and certainly most major economic interests have a real stake in the Court's policies. Thus interest groups would be pleased to influence the selection process, and often groups seek to exert such influence.

Relatively little open lobbying takes place over presidential nominations, the key decisions in the process. To the extent that groups seek to influence nominations, private efforts are likely to be the most effective. Because such efforts *are* private, however, it is difficult to determine their extent and impact.

A few conclusions are possible. Certainly we can assume that groups associated with the president's party and political fortunes will have some impact on the nomination decision even without active lobbying. A Democratic president, for instance, probably would not select a candidate whose views are opposed to those of organized labor. In addition, groups that enjoy close relations with the administration may affect decisions by communicating their general concerns or their feelings about particular candidates to the president.

Once a nomination is announced, groups may work for or against confirmation in the Senate. Group opposition to a nominee is more common than support, because it constitutes an effort to overcome the presumption in favor of confirmation. In this century, liberal groups frequently have sought to defeat nominees whom they perceived as too conservative on relevant issues. In 1930, labor groups and the National Association for the Advancement of Colored People (NAACP) opposed the confirmation of federal judge John Parker, a Hoover nominee, because of his conservative decisions on labor relations and racial issues. Parker's eventual defeat by a two-vote margin in the Senate was made possible by their activity. Forty years later, the same groups opposed President Nixon's nominations of Haynsworth and Carswell on similar grounds, and again they were successful by small margins in the Senate. Liberal groups have opposed other conservative nominees with less success. Several groups worked against the elevation of William Rehnquist to chief justice in 1986, helping to build significant opposition, but ultimately Rehnquist was confirmed with about a two-thirds majority.

Conservative groups also have opposed some nominees. A variety of individuals and groups attacked the nomination of Louis Brandeis in 1916, because they regarded Brandeis as a dangerous radical. They succeeded in delaying, but not preventing, Brandeis's confirmation. In the 1950s and 1960s anti-civil rights groups attacked some nominees with whose views they disagreed, most notably Thurgood Marshall in 1967, without great success.

The nomination of Robert Bork in 1987 produced an unprecedented level of group activity. Liberal groups saw Bork as a highly conservative judge whose confirmation to replace the moderate Lewis Powell would move the Court strongly to the right. Accordingly, they devoted great efforts to his defeat. Among the groups working against Bork were the NAACP, the American Civil Liberties Union, the National Organization for Women, the AFL-CIO, the Sierra Club, and Common Cause. The anti-Bork groups held press conferences, sent mailings to members, organized rallies, took out newspaper advertisements, and lobbied senators directly. These efforts were coordinated by the Leadership Conference on Civil Rights, a coalition of 185 groups concerned with civil rights and civil liberties; the Leadership Conference had also led the successful opposition to G. Harrold Carswell in 1970.

Groups favorable to Bork's nomination took action as well. Among them were the American Conservative Union, the National Right to Work Committee, the National Conservative Political Action Committee, and the Fraternal Order of Police. Right-to-life groups and other conservative organizations initiated campaigns of letters and telephone calls from their members to senators. The pro-Bork groups were at a disadvantage, however, because conservative support for the nominee undercut the arguments of some supporters that Bork was actually a moderate rather than a conservative. In part for this reason, these groups did not mobilize as quickly or as fully as the opposition groups. The higher level of activity against Bork was one factor in his defeat for confirmation. In this instance as in others, however, the outcome reflected not only group efforts but also conditions beyond the groups' control, such as the party composition of the Senate.

Sitting Justices.   Sitting members of the Supreme Court frequently have played active roles in the selection process. The extent of their activity may be surprising, because we might expect justices to remain aloof from politics outside the Court. But members of the Court frequently have participated in external politics when the stakes seemed sufficiently high, and there are few matters as important to justices as the selection of new colleagues. Whether they wish to obtain ideologically compatible colleagues, to maintain the Court's collective competence, or to bring friends onto the Court, they frequently will have an interest in intervening in the selection process.

Indeed, research by two political scientists identified sixty-four separate efforts by justices to influence Supreme Court nominations between 1902 and 1969.[4] Most of these efforts were in support of potential nominees. Often the lobbying was relatively mild, involving no more than a letter of recommendation for an individual, and in several instances it came at the request of the administration. In a few cases, however, justices have engaged in rather intensive lobbying. When Justice Oliver Wendell Holmes retired in 1932, Justice Harlan Stone undertook a strong campaign in favor of New York judge Benjamin Cardozo, while six of his colleagues worked against Cardozo by supporting another candidate. Cardozo eventually was nominated, although Justice Stone's efforts probably were less significant than other sources of support for Cardozo.

The most active Supreme Court lobbyist in the twentieth century was Chief Justice William Howard Taft, who intervened continually during his tenure in the 1920s. Taft, a former president, felt no hesitancy about tendering his advice to his successors. Indeed, Taft personally directed a successful campaign for the nomination and confirmation of Pierce Butler in 1922. Chief Justice Warren Burger was another active participant in the selection process. He lobbied in the Senate for Haynsworth and Carswell and, a year after his retirement, testified on behalf of Bork. He also played a role in nominations, suggesting the name of his long-time friend Harry Blackmun to the Nixon administration and recommending Sandra Day O'Connor to the Reagan administration. While chief justices have been particularly active in the selection process, associate justices also have been involved. William Rehnquist gave a strong endorsement of his law school classmate O'Connor to the White House, and John Paul Stevens publicly endorsed Bork after his nomination.

It is difficult to gauge the effects of judicial intervention. Active justices such as Taft have obtained the desired outcomes more often than not, but their activity may not have been the crucial factor in producing these outcomes. Taft did appear to have considerable influence over President Warren Harding. In a few instances, such as Burger's suggestion of Blackmun, the intervening justice played a key role by putting the eventual nominee's name into consideration. Where several members of the Court stand together on a recommendation, as occasionally has happened, their views may carry particular weight. But most justices lack the leverage to secure decisive influence over selections, and concerted campaigns may even backfire if the president resents interference. Felix Frankfurter's pressure on Franklin Roosevelt to select federal judge Learned Hand in 1943 was one reason that Roosevelt chose Wiley Rutledge instead of Hand. "This time," Roosevelt reportedly said, "Felix overplayed his hand."[5]

Prospective Nominees.   People who wish to become members of the lower federal courts often engage in very active campaigns for these positions, seeking to secure support from the officials who select judges and from those with influence over these officials. Indeed, such campaigns are almost a necessity. In most circumstances, Joel Grossman has written, "the candidate who does not make at least a minimum effort in his own behalf is likely to remain a private citizen."[6]

The Supreme Court appears to be somewhat different. People often are chosen as justices without campaigning actively for the job. Because presidents see Court appointments as so important, they look for candidates who best serve presidential purposes rather than restricting their choices to people who seek the job openly. Further, the Court's standing makes some potential justices hesitant to conduct campaigns on their own behalf.

Some people do work to obtain appointments, however, and some of them are successful. Of the successful campaigns, the best documented and almost surely the most elaborate was conducted by William Howard Taft. Taft was a somewhat reluctant president who really wanted to be chief justice of the Supreme Court. Even as president he worked toward his eventual selection by appointing a relatively aged chief justice, Edward White, to help guarantee a vacancy in that position in the foreseeable future. White returned the compliment by refusing to retire or die, despite his extreme disability, until a Republican replaced President Wilson. When White died early in President Harding's term, Taft was appointed to replace him; the appointment came after an intensive campaign by Taft that had begun even before Harding's election. One commentator has appropriately spoken of Taft as "virtually appointing himself" Chief Justice, as one commentator has said.[7]

According to Justice William Douglas, Sherman (Shay) Minton obtained his nomination in 1949 through a far simpler campaign. President Truman had agreed to nominate another candidate for a vacancy on the Court when Minton, a federal judge and close personal friend, walked into the White House to see Truman. Douglas reported that the following conversation ensued:

"What can I do for you, Shay?"

"Harry, I want you to put me on the Supreme Court to fill that new vacancy."

"Shay, I'll do just that."[8]

Other justices who reportedly worked to obtain their nominations were Douglas himself, Truman appointee Tom Clark, and Warren Burger. In the account of President Nixon's aide John Ehrlichman, Burger "wanted a seat on the Supreme Court so passionately that he would have agreed to almost anything to get it." Ehrlichman claimed that Burger even promised to retire before the end of Nixon's tenure as president so that Nixon could appoint a younger chief justice to serve for a long period.[9] A lower court judge could try to win promotion to the Supreme Court by writing opinions that concurred with the president's views, and a few observers suggested that Antonin Scalia might have done so before President Reagan nominated him.[10]

While some people actively seek appointments to the Court, others are reluctant to accept them. Several people have declined nominations or taken themselves out of the running when they appeared likely to be nominated. John W. Davis, a highly successful lawyer and later a presidential nominee, declined a possible nomination in 1922. One reason was financial; Davis explained to a friend that "I have taken the vows of chastity and obedience but not of poverty."[11] Sen. Howard Baker declined a nomination by President Nixon in 1971; reaffirming his lack of interest in a nomination in 1987, he said, "I've seen funeral homes that are livelier than that court."[12] Abe Fortas in 1965 and Lewis Powell in 1971 turned down nominations and then changed their minds only because of presidential persuasion.

Such cases, however, are exceptions. Whether or not they worked for a position on the Supreme Court, most of those who are offered a nomination have little difficulty in accepting it. Speaking of William Brennan's appointment in 1956, President Eisenhower's press secretary reported, "I never saw a man say 'yes' so fast when the President asked him to take the job."[13]

The President's Decision

Every president must make thousands of appointments to positions in the executive and judicial branches. For most of these posts, the real process of selection is handled by subordinate officials. The president's time is considered too important to be spent in filling posts that are not viewed as critical.

In particular, the president is not a major participant in the selection of judges for the lower federal courts. The task of identifying candidates and negotiating with other participants in the selection process falls chiefly to officials in the Department of Justice, although the Carter administration instituted a system of commissions of private citizens to identify possible nominees. The president ordinarily does little more than ratify these choices.

The president plays a much more active role personally in the selection of Supreme Court justices. Presidents recognize the importance of the Court and of its membership. As a result, most give nominations to the Supreme Court a degree of personal attention that is paralleled only by that given to Cabinet appointments. This attention is exemplified by the personal interviews that President Reagan conducted with some prospective nominees.

In identifying candidates for nomination to the Supreme Court and making a final selection, the president usually receives help from high officials on the White House staff and in the Justice Department. The attorney general often plays the most important advisory role in the selection process.

In 1987, the Reagan administration's effort to choose a successor to Lewis Powell produced conflicts between the highly conservative Justice Department under the leadership of Attorney General Edwin Meese and the more moderate White House staff under Chief of Staff Howard Baker. Robert Bork was primarily the choice of the Justice officials, while Baker was somewhat reluctant because of concerns about Senate confirmation. After Bork was defeated in the Senate, Meese fought for the nomination of Douglas Ginsburg while Baker supported Anthony Kennedy, who was seemingly more moderate; Meese won in a hard-fought battle. When Ginsburg withdrew from consideration because of damaging disclosures, Baker was able to secure Kennedy's nomination.

In making their selections the president and administration officials hear from a variety of individuals and groups. The information that these sources provide can help in choosing a nominee, but external pressures also can limit the president's options. For most presidents, the ideal situation might be the one that Reagan enjoyed in 1986. Chief Justice Burger gave the administration advance notice of his impending retirement, so the president could announce his nominations of William Rehnquist to succeed Burger and Antonin Scalia to take Rehnquist's seat at the same time that he announced Burger's retirement. This prevented any lobbying on the nominations.

Presidents make selections based on a broad range of considerations. These considerations can be placed in four general categories: the "objective" criteria of competence and ethics; policy preferences; reward to political and personal associates; and the pursuit of future political support. Each of these categories merits consideration in some detail.

Competence and Ethics.   In the selection of judges to the lower federal courts, "objective" qualifications traditionally have played a relatively limited role. Because of the perceived lesser importance of the lower courts, the Justice Department and relevant senators often elevate other considerations over a candidate's merits. As a result, the quality of lower court nominees varies from very high to fairly low.

Quality plays a more important role in the selection of nominees for the Supreme Court, because presidents have strong incentives to select persons of high competence and ethical behavior. A candidate who falls short on either of these standards is likely to embarrass the president and may even be defeated in the Senate. A highly skilled justice has relatively great influence on the Court; if such a justice shares the president's policy goals, the president's own effect on the Court is thereby increased. Finally, most presidents have sufficient respect for the Supreme Court that they wish to uphold high standards in selection.

In general, the choices made by presidents have reflected a concern for competence. In this century, as Robert Scigliano points out, the great majority of nominees had achieved eminence in political or legal careers.[14] Oliver Wendell Holmes and Benjamin Cardozo, for instance, were distinguished state appellate judges. This does not mean that all nominees are highly skilled in the law, but only in a few cases has the competence of a nominee to serve on the Court been questionable.

The ethical behavior of the great majority of nominees has been unexceptionable, at least so far as that behavior was known. There have been a few exceptions in this century. Louis Brandeis was accused of improper practices as a private attorney when he was nominated by President Wilson. More recently, Abe Fortas (when nominated for chief justice) and Clement Haynsworth were attacked for alleged financial improprieties, and Fortas also was criticized for his continuing consultation with President Johnson after he had joined the Court. The charges against Fortas and Haynsworth aided in producing their defeats in the Senate. After Douglas Ginsburg was announced as a nominee, disclosures were made about a possible financial conflict of interest when he was in the Justice Department and about his past use of marijuana. The latter disclosure was especially damaging, and under pressure Ginsburg withdrew from consideration.

Competence and ethics can be considered screening criteria for potential nominees. These criteria may eliminate some people from consideration, but enough candidates survive the screening process to give presidents a wide range of choices for a nomination. In one instance, President Hoover's nomination of Benjamin Cardozo, these criteria played a more central role; Cardozo was so well respected for his work as a state judge that Hoover received strong pressure to elevate him to the Supreme Court. Ordinarily, however, a concern for objective qualifications leaves the president with a great deal of freedom.

Policy Preferences. By policy preferences, I mean a person's attitudes toward policy issues. Until recently, these preferences generally were of limited importance in the selection of lower federal judges. Now, with the policy-making role of the federal courts increasingly apparent, presidents are giving more attention to the attitudes of prospective nominees for lower court judgeships. The Carter administration sought to appoint liberals, while conservatism on issues such as abortion was an important criterion for the Reagan administration.

For the Supreme Court, policy preferences are the president's single most important consideration. Presidents recognize the importance of their power to reshape the Court through their appointments; according to one aide, Ronald Reagan considered the Court "his most important legacy." [15] On leaving the presidency, William Howard Taft reported that he had told his six appointees, "If any of you die, I'll disown you." [16] Thus all presidents seek to put on the Court people whose views on important policy questions are similar to their own.

The seriousness of this effort has varied among presidents. For some presidents a person's ideological position was the overwhelming criterion for selection, because they had special reason to be concerned with the direction of Supreme Court policy. Thwarted by the Court's attacks on his economic policies, Franklin Roosevelt was careful to select justices who supported his views on the economic powers of the federal government. It was only after he had gained a clear majority for his position on the Court that Roosevelt's interest in nominees' attitudes declined somewhat. President Nixon felt that the Court's liberalism on criminal procedure questions in the 1960s had helped to weaken law enforcement, so he was meticulous in finding conservatives to put on the Court. Presidents less concerned with the Court's direction, such as Harry Truman, have put less emphasis on policy preferences as a basis for their choices.

It is not always easy to ascertain the policy preferences of a potential nominee and to determine how the preferences would be reflected in votes and opinions on the Supreme Court. The task generally is easiest in the case of sitting federal judges; as Reagan's attorney general Edwin Meese said, "You know the judicial philosophy of those judges because they've had experience and they've written opinions you can look at." [17] Reagan's nominees were all judges. After his disappointment with the liberalism of his appointee Earl Warren, who had never been a lower court judge, President Eisenhower restricted his future nominations to sitting judges to avoid another such disappointment. But William Brennan, one of the judges promoted by Eisenhower, also surprised the president with his liberal positions on the Court. The administration, however, had given limited scrutiny to Brennan's judicial record. Especially in recent years, administrations usually examine a judge's record with some care and act on what they discover; the Nixon administration, for instance, shied away from one near-nominee because of his position on rules for police questioning of suspects. Notably, sitting judges as a group have been less likely to disappoint their nominators with their Supreme Court decisions than have other justices.[18]

The views of a candidate who is not a judge may be gauged in several ways. A president may have a good sense of a nominee's views from personal association, such as the friendship between Lyndon Johnson and Abe Fortas. Partisan affiliation provides one indicator of preferences; in the present era, Democrats are likely to be liberal, Republicans conservative. This tendency helps to explain presidents' preference for selecting nominees from their own party. A nominee's public expressions on relevant issues also may offer some clues to the president.

Sometimes presidents or their representatives question prospective nominees directly about their views, even when the candidate is a sitting judge. Harry Blackmun reports that before his nomination by President Nixon, "I was rather cross-examined by two members of the Department of Justice," and it is likely that one prominent subject was his policy preferences.[19] (One of the cross-examiners was William Rehnquist, who joined Blackmun on the Court a year later.) During the Reagan administration several prospective nominees were asked about their views. Sandra Day O'Connor, for instance, was questioned by two sets of administration officials and then by President Reagan himself, with whom she discussed abortion and other issues.

Observers of the Court give considerable attention to the instances in which justices have dismayed the presidents who selected them with their policies on the Court. The liberal Wilson was shocked by the extreme conservatism of James McReynolds, just as conservative Coolidge later was upset with Harlan Stone's liberalism. As noted earlier, Eisenhower was unhappy with the liberalism of both Warren and Brennan; asked if he had made any mistakes as president, Eisenhower replied, "Yes, two, and they are both sitting on the Supreme Court."[20]

Such instances are not rare; Robert Scigliano has estimated that at least one quarter of the justices have deviated from the expectations of their appointers.[21] But most justices do turn out to be ideologically compatible with the presidents who appoint them. Moreover, presidents who were especially careful to select compatible justices have suffered relatively few disappointments. Both Franklin Roosevelt and Richard Nixon, for instance, did rather well in getting what they wanted from the justices they selected, although Harry Blackmun's increased liberalism over time has marred the Nixon record of success somewhat. Presidents who have emphasized other criteria or who chose with less care often have done less well.

No justice, of course, will please the appointing president with every decision. This is inevitable for an appointee to any position. It is particularly common for judges because the facts of particular cases and the state of the law may move them to reach decisions contrary to their general predispositions. Whatever his pleasure with most of his appointees' votes on the Court, President Nixon certainly was not happy with their votes against his position in *United States v. Nixon* (1974), in which a unanimous Court required him to yield recordings of his conversations as president. When he saw the decision, Nixon reportedly "exploded, cursing the man he had named chief justice, reserving a few choice expletives for Blackmun and Powell, his other appointees." [22] As this reaction illustrates, even the most careful selections do not provide a president with "control" over the Supreme Court.

Certainly the power of appointment does provide presidents with an opportunity to shape the Court's general direction. The impact of this power on the Court's policies will be examined in Chapter 5.

Political and Personal Reward. Nominations to the Supreme Court are among the most important prizes that presidents can bestow. It should not be surprising that they frequently offer these prizes to people who have been political associates or personal friends. Not only do such people seem deserving of positions on the Court, but a president can have the most confidence in the ability and ideological "correctness" of associates and friends.

Indeed, about 60 percent of the nominees to the Court personally knew the nominating president.[23] Of the most recent presidents, Franklin Roosevelt, Truman, Kennedy, and Johnson all selected primarily acquaintances. For Truman, reward for political associates seemed to be the predominant criterion for selection. But among the justices chosen by Nixon, Ford, and Reagan, only William Rehnquist—an official in the Nixon Justice Department—might qualify as a close associate. And Nixon, three months before nominating Rehnquist, recalled his name as "Renchburg." [24] This trend among recent presidents may reflect an increased emphasis on policy preferences as the primary criterion for nominations; Reagan, for instance, was quite willing to select judges who seemed reliably conservative even if he was unacquainted with them personally.

Occasionally appointments to the Court are direct rewards. Presidents may feel the need to compensate someone for past service with an appointment of this magnitude. Eisenhower selected Earl Warren to serve as chief justice in part because of a debt owed for Warren's crucial support of Eisenhower's cause in the 1952 Republican convention. As governor of California and leader of that state's delegation, Warren had provided needed votes on a preliminary issue concerning contested state delegates, and Eisenhower's success in that contest helped to secure his nomination. Franklin Roosevelt nominated James Byrnes in 1941 partly to compensate for Byrnes's being denied the Democratic vice-presidential nomination in 1940 after his loyal service to Roosevelt.

A rather different kind of "reward" is the use of a Supreme Court appointment to remove a troublesome individual to a presumably safer place. It has been suggested that Wilson's appointment of James McReynolds and Coolidge's appointment of Harlan Stone came about in part because these individuals had created difficulties as attorney general. If these allegations are true, then Wilson and Coolidge "deserved" the disappointments that they received from these men as justices. Earl Warren's appointment to the Court served the purposes of Vice President Nixon and other rival California Republicans in removing him from the political scene, and this fact apparently played a role in his selection.

About 90 percent of all nominees to the Court have been members of the president's party. This statistic, similar to those for the lower federal courts, reflects several factors: the relationship between party and ideology, the tendency for presidents' associates to come from the same party, and the desire to reserve the patronage of seats on the Supreme Court for the party faithful. Nominees who were not of the president's party have been appointed because they appealed to the president on other grounds. Harold Burton, for instance, had served with Truman in the Senate, and they were close friends. Eisenhower chose William Brennan in part to appeal to Democratic and Catholic voters in the 1956 election. Lewis Powell, nominated by Nixon, was an eminent lawyer who fulfilled the president's goal of putting a southerner on the Court.

Pursuit of Political Support. Like other appointments, such as those to the Cabinet, seats on the Supreme Court provide means for a president to build political support. By selecting justices with particular characteristics, presidents often have sought to gain the gratitude of voters who share those characteristics. Similarly, presidents seek to avoid choices that will alienate people.

For most of our history, efforts to obtain political support with appointments to the Court focused heavily on geography. Presidents sought to provide each region of the country with representation on the Court in order to please a maximum number of voters. This interest was strengthened by the practical value of geographical diversity. Until 1891 the justices "rode circuit," helping to staff the lower federal courts in designated regions of the country, and it made most sense to select justices from the circuits that they would represent.

Geography has continued to be a consideration in some nominations. For instance, Franklin Roosevelt nominated Wiley Rutledge in 1943 partly because of Rutledge's Iowa residence. Occasionally geography becomes very important, as it was when Nixon struggled mightily to put a southerner on the Court to strengthen his electoral support in that region. But in general, geography has become a less important criterion. As circuit-riding responsibilities declined and then were abolished, one important rationale for concern with geography disappeared. Presidents also seem to have perceived a decline in sectional consciousness, so that geography has become less important to them as a means of building support. As a result of both factors, the Court has become less balanced geographically.

During the twentieth century an interest in providing representation to religious and ethnic minority groups has affected some nominations, though generally as a relatively minor consideration. Examples include the selection of two Jewish nominees, Arthur Goldberg by Kennedy and Douglas Ginsburg by Reagan, and Reagan's choice of Antonin Scalia as the first justice of Italian ancestry.

Representation by race and sex has become important in the current era. Thurgood Marshall's selection in 1967 brought the first black member to the Court, and in the future presidents will feel some pressure to maintain black representation on the Court. The pressure for the appointment of a woman to the Court in 1981 would have been difficult for President Reagan to resist, and even while Sandra Day O'Connor remains on the Court presidents may see some advantage to appointing additional women.

Of course, the president can also try to build political support by selecting nominees who appeal to important political interest groups. President Reagan received considerable criticism from conservative leaders and groups that were disappointed with some of his policies, and his lower court nominations were intended in part to appeal to those groups. The same consideration may have affected his choices of Robert Bork and Douglas Ginsburg, both of whom were popular with conservative groups.

To some degree, nominations can help presidents gain support from political leaders and activists. It seems less likely that presidents obtain significant electoral advantages from nominations. Important though they are, Supreme Court nominations seldom are conspicuous to most voters, and in themselves it is unlikely that they have great impact on election results. But the practice of using judicial and other appointments to appeal to voters is so well established that it continues even in the absence of any clear effect.

Summary. As the discussion of these four kinds of considerations should suggest, nominations to the Supreme Court rest on a variety of criteria, and most appointments serve multiple goals. Perhaps the only safe generalizations are that all four categories of considerations are important and that their relative importance varies considerably.

The perceived importance of the Court has at least two effects on the criteria for selection of justices. First, it makes presidents weigh all the criteria more carefully than their representatives generally do for lower court nominations. Second, it gives emphasis to the factors of competence and policy preferences as opposed to the "political" considerations of reward and support building. If Supreme Court justices are better jurists and better reflections of their nominators' views than are lower court judges, it is largely because presidents have an interest in producing both of those results.

Senate Confirmation

Once the president has nominated someone for a vacancy on the Supreme Court, the nomination goes to the Senate for confirmation. Ordinarily the nomination is referred to the Judiciary Committee, which holds hearings and then votes its recommendation for Senate action. After committee action the nomination is referred to the floor, where it is debated and a confirmation vote taken. The length of this process depends on the degree of controversy concerning the nomination. If there is no opposition to a nominee, hearings may be pro forma and take only a single day, the nomination will be reported to the full Senate rather quickly, and the nominee will be confirmed quickly with little debate. However, the hearings on Thurgood Marshall, Clement Haynsworth, Abe Fortas, and Robert Bork all lasted five days or more—Bork himself testified for five days—and the Judiciary Committee reported Louis Brandeis's nomination 122 days after it was made.[25] Most important, some nominations have been debated vigorously on the floor, and four have been defeated since 1968.

The Senate's Role. The role of the Senate in the selection of Supreme Court justices can best be understood in contrast with its role at the district court level. For district judges the practice of "senatorial courtesy" has given a quasi-veto power to senators of the president's party from the state for which an appointment is made; if they disapprove of a nomination, their colleagues will defeat it. Because of this power, the administration ordinarily consults with the appropriate senators before making a nomination. These senators often play a very active role at the nomination stage, suggesting and sometimes insisting upon particular candidates. Then, if the administration and these senators agree upon a nominee, the Senate as a whole usually confirms the nominee with little scrutiny. Since the late 1970s senatorial courtesy has become less automatic; most notably, some nominees approved by senators from their state have faced serious opposition from other senators. Still, at the district court level, the Senate's role is concentrated primarily in a few of its members.

The situation is quite different for the Supreme Court. In this century, senators from a nominee's home state hold no special power. Thus, the Senate's role in the selection process is more widely dispersed among its members. At the nomination stage, senators may be consulted, but on the basis of their standing in the Senate and with the administration rather than on the basis of their state. The Reagan administration, for instance, discussed potential nominees with leaders of the two parties in the Senate before nominating Robert Bork. After Bork's defeat, strong objections from conservative senators whose political support was important to the administration influenced the choice of Douglas Ginsburg over Anthony Kennedy. When Ginsburg withdrew, Senate conservatives were consulted before Kennedy was nominated.

Because no single senator can veto a nominee, the administration has greater freedom to select nominees on its own, leaving the Senate to react to people who already have been chosen. This reactive role puts the Senate at a disadvantage in the confirmation process, because the presumption is always in favor of confirming a presidential nominee. But the Senate gives Supreme Court nominations a collective scrutiny that district court nominations seldom receive, and the occasional defeats of nominees are reminders that confirmation is not automatic. In turn, this gives the president good reason to take the Senate's likely reaction into account in making a nomination. A president may choose a nominee who is certain to face serious opposition in the Senate, such as Bork, but the desire to gain an easy confirmation often influences the president's choice: the selection of Anthony Kennedy is an example. Certainly the Senate's role in the process is a significant one.

The Senate's Record.   Through mid-1988 the Senate had failed to confirm twenty-six of the president's nominations to the Supreme Court, either through an adverse vote or through a refusal to act. These twenty-six cases constituted about 20 percent of the nominations that the Senate considered. This proportion of defeats is higher than for any other position to which the president makes appointments. For instance, only eight cabinet nominees have been defeated.

Presidents have been more successful with Supreme Court nominations in the twentieth century than in the nineteenth. Since 1900, only five of the fifty-six nominations considered by the Senate have failed: Hoover's nomination of John Parker in 1930, Johnson's elevation of Abe Fortas to chief justice in 1968 (withdrawn after Fortas's supporters failed to end an anticonfirmation filibuster), Nixon's nominations of Clement Haynsworth in 1969 and G. Harrold Carswell in 1970 for the same vacancy, and Reagan's nomination of Robert Bork in 1987. Moreover, only two successful nominees were confirmed by less than a two-thirds margin in the Senate.

This record of success is impressive, but it may be a bit misleading. During two periods in this century a high proportion of nominees have faced serious opposition. The first was between 1910 and 1930, when several nominees were attacked by senators on ideological grounds. The second began in the late 1940s and continues today. Of the twenty-four nominees considered by the Senate from 1949 through mid-1988, four were defeated, six others received more than ten negative votes, and still others were opposed seriously. The Senate votes in this period are shown in Table 2-2. Meanwhile, Senate care in scrutinizing nominations, as indicated by such measures as the length of time spent in hearings, has increased markedly. Although nominations usually have been successful even during these periods, clearly the Senate has not adopted a policy of automatic confirmation for nominees.

The relative success of nominations to the Court in this century and the serious opposition that frequently arises both can be understood in terms of the sources of opposition to nominees. I will examine those sources in general terms and then illustrate their impact by looking at recent presidential nominees.

The Sources of Opposition. Nominees to the Supreme Court have attracted opposition on a variety of grounds, and confirmation defeats have resulted from very different mixes of negative factors. Still, it is possible to identify four sources of opposition to nominees that have been particularly important. Of these, two are related to the president who makes the appointment, two to the nominee.

For the president, the likelihood of defeat increases a good deal with the strength of the opposition party in the Senate. Indeed, whether or not the president's party has a Senate majority seems to make a tremendous difference in the confirmation decision. When the president's party has a majority, 91 percent of the nominees have been confirmed; when the president faces an opposition majority, only 48 percent have been confirmed.[26]

The timing of a nomination in the president's term also has an effect on the chances for confirmation. Historically, only about two thirds of the nominations made in the last year of the term have been confirmed. Timing is important in part because a president's power sometimes declines toward the end of the term. More important, partisanship may increase in presidential election years, and the opposition may seek to delay an appointment until its own candidate can come into office. When the Senate was controlled by the opposition party, nominations made in the presidential election year or during the "lame duck" period between the election and the inauguration of a new president were defeated eleven out of fifteen times.

One important characteristic of nominees is their objective quali-

Table 2-2   Senate Votes on Supreme Court Nominations, 1949-1988

Nominee	Year	Vote
Tom Clark	1949	73-8
Sherman Minton	1949	48-16
Earl Warren	1954	NRV[a]
John Harlan	1955	71-11
William Brennan	1957	NRV
Charles Whittaker	1957	NRV
Potter Stewart	1959	70-17
Byron White	1962	NRV
Arthur Goldberg	1962	NRV
Abe Fortas	1965	NRV
Thurgood Marshall	1967	69-11
Abe Fortas[b]	1968	withdrawn[c]
Homer Thornberry	no action	
Warren Burger	1969	74-3
Clement Haynsworth	1969	45-55
G. Harrold Carswell	1970	45-51
Harry Blackmun	1970	94-0
Lewis Powell	1971	89-1
William Rehnquist	1971	68-26
John Paul Stevens	1975	98-0
Sandra Day O'Connor	1981	99-0
William Rehnquist[b]	1986	65-33
Antonin Scalia	1986	98-0
Robert Bork	1987	42-58
Douglas Ginsburg	no action	
Anthony Kennedy	1988	97-0

Source: Congressional Quarterly, *The Supreme Court: Justice and the Law* (Washington, D.C.: Congressional Quarterly Inc., 1983), 179, updated by the author.

[a] No recorded vote.
[b] Elevation to chief justice.
[c] Nomination withdrawn after Senate vote failed to end filibuster against nomination; vote was 45-43 to end filibuster, and two-thirds majority was required.

fications, as assessed by senators. Nominees who appear to lack the competence to do their job effectively or the ethical standards demanded of justices tend to attract great opposition. Scrutiny of qualifications seems to have increased in this century.

Another important characteristic of nominees in the Senate has been their policy preferences. Where a nominee's views are anathema to a significant number of senators, the nomination is likely to face difficulty. Interest groups play an important role in calling ideology to the attention of senators. When organized labor opposes a nominee on grounds of unfriendliness to the labor movement, for instance, liberal senators will be moved to examine the candidate from an ideological perspective.

In the twentieth century, nominees' policy preferences have been the primary source of Senate opposition to nominations. Where nominees in this century have received ten or more negative votes, the most important reason for opposition nearly always has been disagreement about policy. During the 1950s and 1960s, for instance, the eleven votes cast against John Harlan and Thurgood Marshall and the seventeen in opposition to Potter Stewart were based primarily on conservative southern disagreement with the views of the nominees on racial issues. Similarly, several conservative nominees have received negative votes from liberal senators.

The relative success of twentieth-century presidents in obtaining confirmation for their nominees stems in part from the infrequency of unfavorable circumstances. Only sixteen of the fifty-eight nominations in this century were made when the Senate was controlled by the opposition party, and few have been made in election years except under conditions favorable to the president's nominee. Presidential success also seems to stem from an increased willingness of the Senate to defer to the president's choice if that person's competence and adherence to ethical standards are clear. Although party and policy disagreement frequently produce opposition to a nomination, that opposition is unlikely to be successful unless it can be buttressed with weaknesses in the nominee's competence or ethics. The existence of such weaknesses provides a rationale for opposition and helps to attract ideological moderates to the opposition cause. Their absence makes opponents appear to be unfair and partisan, and it increases the difficulty of building a coalition against the candidate.

These generalizations may be illustrated through a discussion of the Senate's treatment of nominations since 1968. The Senate's actions in this period fall into three categories: confirmations involving little difficulty, confirmations that came with greater difficulty, and defeats of nominees.

The Easy Confirmations. Of the thirteen nominees who were considered by the Senate, seven achieved relatively easy confirmations: Warren Burger, Harry Blackmun, Lewis Powell, John Paul Stevens, Sandra Day O'Connor, Antonin Scalia, and Anthony Kennedy. Burger received three negative votes; none of the others received more than one.

This does not mean that these nominees enjoyed near-unanimous enthusiasm. Certainly liberal Democrats would have preferred people less conservative than Burger and Scalia. Antiabortion groups opposed O'Connor because they feared that she was insufficiently conservative on that issue. But these nominees escaped strong challenges because their objective qualifications seemed clear and because serious concern about their ideological positions did not become widespread.

Circumstances favored some of these nominees. Blackmun probably would have won confirmation easily in any case, but that result was ensured by the Senate's collective desire to avoid a third consecutive battle over a Nixon nomination. Scalia, about as conservative as Robert Bork, might have attracted serious opposition. But he was aided by several conditions, including the Senate's focus on the simultaneous nomination of William Rehnquist to become chief justice and the fact that Scalia in effect would replace another conservative (Burger). As a result, his nomination went through the Senate with ease.

The Difficult Confirmations.   The two nominations of Rehnquist, as associate justice in 1971 and as chief justice in 1986, both faced strong opposition. This opposition was based on the distaste of Senate liberals for Rehnquist's pronounced conservatism on civil rights and civil liberties issues.

When Rehnquist was first nominated in 1971, the Leadership Conference on Civil Rights led the opposition. Rehnquist's opponents argued that his conservatism on civil liberties was so extreme as to be unacceptable for a Supreme Court justice. But the case against him was weakened by the general perception that he was a highly competent person who would serve effectively on the Court. The opposition thus had to rest almost entirely on ideological grounds, and even for some liberals those grounds were insufficient to justify a negative vote. As a result, Rehnquist was confirmed by a 68-26 vote.

Rehnquist's record as an associate justice was as conservative as his opponents had feared, and his prospective elevation to chief justice in 1986 also aroused strong opposition from liberal interest groups and senators. These opponents sought to gain support by raising questions about Rehnquist's ethical standards. They charged that Rehnquist had sought to intimidate black and Hispanic voters in Arizona in the 1960s, that he had participated in a 1972 decision despite his earlier involvement in the government policy that was challenged, and that he had bought two pieces of property with deeds that barred sales to racial or religious minority groups.

These charges were given considerable attention, but they proved insufficient to expand the opposition much beyond its liberal core. After a long debate on the Senate floor, Rehnquist was confirmed by a 65-33 vote, a margin ten votes closer than in 1971; with a few exceptions, northern Democrats voted against Rehnquist and other senators voted for him.

The Defeats. Of the four confirmation defeats since 1968, three came in a two-year period between 1968 and 1970. The first was that of Abe Fortas, a sitting justice nominated for chief justice by President Johnson in 1968. Fortas's strong liberalism on the liberal Warren Court aroused early opposition from conservative senators, and some Republicans wanted to prevent Fortas's confirmation to reserve the vacancy for a new president—expected to be Republican—in 1969. These partisan and ideological considerations were strengthened by two activities of the nominee that raised doubts about his ethical fitness: his continued consultation with the president about policy matters while a member of the Court, and an arrangement by which he gave nine lectures at American University, in Washington, D.C., for a fee of $15,000 raised from businesses. After the Judiciary Committee approved the nomination by a divided vote, it ran into a filibuster on the Senate floor. A vote to end the filibuster fell fourteen votes short of the two-thirds majority then required; the opposition came almost entirely from Republicans and southern Democrats. At Fortas's request, his nomination was then withdrawn.

In 1969, Fortas resigned from the Court. President Nixon selected Clement Haynsworth, chief judge of a federal court of appeals, to replace him. Haynsworth was opposed by labor groups and the NAACP, both of which disliked his judicial record. Liberal senators, concerned by this record, were motivated by their anger over Fortas's defeat as well. Charges of unethical conduct also arose against Haynsworth: it was learned that he had sat in two cases involving subsidiaries of companies in which he owned stock, and that in another case he had bought the stock of a corporation between the time of his court's decision in its favor and the announcement of the decision. These charges attracted additional opposition from Senate moderates. Haynsworth ultimately was defeated by a 45-55 vote, with a large minority of Republicans voting against confirmation.

Following Haynsworth's defeat, President Nixon nominated another court of appeals judge, G. Harrold Carswell. After the fight over Haynsworth, most senators were inclined to support the next nominee. But Carswell drew quick opposition from civil rights groups for what they perceived as his hostility to their interests, and their cause gradually gained strength from a series of revelations about Carswell that suggested an active opposition to black civil rights. Carswell also was criticized for an alleged lack of judicial competence. Legal scholars attested to his limited abilities, and data showed that an unusually high proportion of his decisions had been reversed on appeal. Carswell's supporters were not able to counter this attack successfully. The nomination was defeated by a 45-51 vote, with the lineup similar to the vote on Haynsworth.

Robert Bork's 1987 defeat differed from the three preceding it in that no serious charges were made against his competence or his ethical standards. His nomination drew strong liberal opposition from the start, both because he seemed to be a highly conservative judge on civil liberties issues and because his replacement of the moderate Lewis Powell on a closely divided Court might have considerable impact on the Court's policies. President Reagan's political power had been weakened by time and by difficulties in his second term, and the Democrats had regained control of the Senate in the 1986 elections; under these circumstances, some Democrats thought that they could prevent Reagan from filling Powell's position with a strong conservative.

Liberal interest groups launched a campaign of unprecedented scope against Bork in the Senate and the country, helping to arouse doubts about the nominee. Bork's closely watched testimony before the Senate Judiciary Committee, in which he was questioned in detail about his positions on issues such as the right to privacy, intensified these doubts. Gradually, liberal and moderate senators announced their opposition to Bork because of the prospect that he would help to reverse important Court doctrines favorable to civil liberties. The Judiciary Committee recommended against confirmation by a 5-9 vote, and two weeks later the full Senate defeated Bork by a 42-58 vote. All but eight senators voted along party lines, with the overwhelming and unexpected opposition of southern Democrats making the difference.

Conclusions. The four defeats of Court nominees since 1968 underline the close scrutiny that the Senate gives to nominees. But it should be recalled that the defeats were possible only because of circumstances particularly adverse to the nominees, including credible challenges to the objective qualifications of three of them. Even during this unusual period, nine other nominations were confirmed, seven of them with little difficulty.

The Bork episode was extraordinary for the level of interest group activity, the closeness with which the nominee was questioned about his views, and the willingness of so many senators to vote against a nominee on ideological grounds alone. Undoubtedly, this episode will have an impact on future confirmation decisions. But in itself, Bork's defeat does not indicate a fundamental change in the confirmation process. The easy confirmation of Anthony Kennedy a few months later is a reminder that, even in the current era, most nominees are successful in the Senate.

Who Is Selected

From the process of selecting Supreme Court justices, we turn to the characteristics of those who have been selected. These characteristics should be examined to determine what kinds of people reach such exalted positions in the American political system and how they reach the point of being considered for selection. This examination is useful for a second reason as well. The characteristics of the justices potentially have a major impact on their policy choices, so observers of the Court who wish to understand those choices need to take into account the backgrounds of justices.

First, I will examine the major paths by which people reach the Court. These paths are significant in themselves. In addition, they help in understanding why justices tend to share certain characteristics. Those characteristics themselves will be the subject of the second part of the section.

As in the preceding section, I will focus on the justices selected in the twentieth century. Because paths to the Court have changed somewhat even in this century, I will give particular attention to the period beginning with the presidency of Franklin Roosevelt, which includes the twenty-nine justices selected from Hugo Black in 1937 through Anthony Kennedy in 1988. Some important characteristics of those justices are listed in Table 2-3.

Career Paths

The Legal Profession. The Constitution does not restrict membership on the Supreme Court to attorneys. In practice, however, this restriction has been absolute. Most people involved in the selection process have assumed that a person must have legal training to serve effectively on the Court, although Justice Black thought otherwise.[27] Certainly the large number of attorneys in the Senate and the strength of the organized bar help to ensure that this rule never will be violated.

This means that a person who does not undertake legal training early in life is disqualified from consideration for the Supreme Court; the willingness and capacity to obtain a legal education, then, is the first and least flexible requirement for recruitment to the Court. For the first century of the Court's history, most justices had undergone apprenticeship under a practicing attorney, as was the predominant pattern at that time. In several cases the practicing attorney was a leading member of the bar.[28] More recently, law school education has predominated, with James Byrnes (chosen in 1941) the last justice to study law through apprenticeship. A high proportion of justices have gone to the more prestigious schools. Of the nine justices sitting in 1988, for instance, seven had been educated in the Harvard, Yale, or Stanford law schools.

Table 2-3 Selected Characteristics of Justices Appointed Since 1937

Justice	Age[a]	State of residence[b]	Law school	Position at appointment[c]	Years judge	Elective office[d]	Administrative position[e]
Black	51	Ala.	Alabama	Senator	1	Senate	—
Reed	53	Ky.	Columbia	Solicitor General	0	State leg.	Solicitor General
Frankfurter	56	Mass.	Harvard	Law professor	0	—	Subcabinet
Douglas	40	Wash.	Columbia	Chairman, Sec. & Exchange Comm.	0	—	Sec. & Exchange Comm.
Murphy	49	Mich.	Michigan	Attorney General	7	Governor	Attorney General
Byrnes	62	S.C.	None	Senator	0	Senate	—
Jackson	49	N.Y.	Albany	Attorney General	0	—	Attorney General
Rutledge	48	Iowa	Colorado	U.S. Ct. App.	4	—	—
Burton	57	Ohio	Harvard	Senator	0	Senate	—
Vinson	56	Ky.	Centre (Ky.)	Sec. of Treasury	5	House of Rep.	Sec. of Treasury
Clark	49	Texas	Texas	Attorney General	0	—	Attorney General
Minton	58	Ind.	Indiana	U.S. Ct. App.	8	Senate	Asst. to president
Warren	62	Calif.	Calif.	Governor	0	Governor	—
Harlan	55	N.Y.	New York	U.S. Ct. App.	1	—	Asst. U.S. Attorney
Brennan	50	N.J.	Harvard	State Sup. Ct.	7	—	—

Whittaker	56	Mo.	Kansas City	U.S. Ct. App.	3	—	—
Stewart	43	Ohio	Yale	U.S. Ct. App.	4	City council	—
White	44	Colo.	Yale	Dep. Atty. General	0	—	Dep. Atty. General
Goldberg	54	Ill.	Northwestern	Sec. of Labor	0	—	Sec. of Labor
Fortas	55	D.C.	Yale	Private practice	0	—	Subcabinet
Marshall	59	N.Y.	Howard	Solicitor General	4	—	Solicitor General
Burger	61	Minn.	St. Paul	U.S. Ct. App.	13	—	Asst. Atty. General
Blackmun	61	Minn.	Harvard	U.S. Ct. App.	11	—	—
Powell	64	Va.	Wash. & Lee	Private practice	0	—	State Bd. of Education
Rehnquist	47	Ariz.	Stanford	Asst. Atty. General	0	—	Asst. Atty. General
Stevens	55	Ill.	Northwestern	U.S. Ct. App.	5	—	—
O'Connor	51	Ariz.	Stanford	State Ct. App.	6	State leg.	State Asst. Atty. General
Scalia	50	D.C.	Harvard	U.S. Ct. App.	4	—	Asst. Atty. General
Kennedy	51	Calif.	Harvard	U.S. Ct. App.	11	—	Asst. Atty. General

Sources: Leon Friedman and Fred L. Israel, *The Justices of the United States Supreme Court 1789-1969: Their Lives and Major Opinions* (New York: R. R. Bowker Co., 1969; 1978 supplement); Harold W. Chase and Craig R. Ducat, *Constitutional Interpretation,* 2d ed. (St. Paul: West Publishing Co., 1979), 1361-1376; Congressional Quarterly, *The Supreme Court and Its Work* (Washington, D.C.: Congressional Quarterly Inc., 1983), 169-187, updated by the author.

[a] Age at time of appointment.
[b] Primary state of residence prior to selection.
[c] In this and following columns, positions are federal except where noted otherwise.
[d] Highest office.
[e] Highest appointive administrative position. Minor positions omitted.

High Positions.   If legal education is a necessary first step in the path to the Court, almost as necessary as a last step is the holding of a high position in government or the legal profession. The importance of such a position stems largely from the credibility that it gives a person for consideration by the selectors. Obscure private practitioners or state trial court judges might be superbly qualified for the Court, but their qualifications would be questioned because of their lowly positions. A high government or legal position also helps to make a person visible to the president and others involved in the nomination process and helps to bring about the acquaintanceship with presidents that has been a factor in a great many nominations.

The twenty-nine appointees since 1937 have held four kinds of positions at the time that they were selected. Ten held federal administrative positions. Seven of the ten served in the Justice Department, either as attorney general or in a lower administrative position. The attorney general's central role in the selection process certainly has much to do with this large number. The other three served as chairman of the Securities and Exchange Commission (Douglas), Secretary of the Treasury (Vinson), and Secretary of Labor (Goldberg).

Twelve of the justices in the most recent period have been appellate judges, ten on the federal courts of appeals and two (Brennan and O'Connor) on state courts. The predominance of federal judges is a recent phenomenon, in large part because the intermediate appellate courts in the federal system were not created until 1891. Three of the ten federal judges (Rutledge, Burger, and Scalia) came from the District of Columbia circuit, which is particularly visible to the president and other officials in Washington.

Four justices came from high elective office, three as senators (Black, Byrnes, and Burton) and the fourth as the governor of California (Warren). It may be more than coincidence that the three members of Congress were from the Senate and that the governor was from a major state. These positions provide more visibility and prestige than do the House of Representatives and governorships of small states.

The remaining three justices appointed to the Court since 1937 held positions outside government, in private practice or university teaching. Each had acquired unusual success and prestige in his field. Felix Frankfurter was a renowned legal scholar who had worked a good deal in the federal government, both formally and informally. Abe Fortas was a highly successful Washington lawyer who had held positions in the executive branch, argued an important Supreme Court case, and served as a presidential adviser. Lewis Powell was a leader of the legal profession whose important positions included the presidency of the American Bar Association. Even among successful attorneys, their records were extraordinary.

The Path Between. The discussion thus far has described the first and last rungs of the ladder by which people ascend to the Supreme Court. Also important is the path between these stages. By what process do people move from membership in the bar to the high positions from which justices are selected? There are several recognizable career paths that the justices have taken.

One common path is through partisan elective office. Throughout the Supreme Court's history, many of its members have had careers in politics, advancing in office until they reach positions in which they can be considered for the Court. Eight of the last twenty-nine justices fit into this category. Some, such as Earl Warren, spent virtually all of their careers in political office. Warren practiced law for only three years, then held a series of appointive and elective offices. He was elected state attorney general at the age of forty-seven, then was elected governor three times, becoming a party leader and serious candidate for the Republican nomination for president (he was the vice-presidential nominee in 1948). For others, the final move from private practice into politics as a career came somewhat later. Hugo Black held some minor offices in Alabama early in his career, but he did not leave private practice permanently until he was forty years old, when he was elected to the Senate; his next step was to the Court.

A majority of the recent justices have followed a second path. This path begins with a private practice, followed at some point by elevation to a high administrative or judicial position from which the selection to the Court was made, or to a series of positions in administration and the judiciary and then to the Court.

The careers of the justices who fit into this category have differed in the length of time that the person spends in the "intermediate" positions. For some justices, this is a relatively long period that constitutes an important part of their pre-Court work. For instance, after a private practice of about twenty years, Warren Burger served for three years in the Department of Justice, then thirteen years on the Court of Appeals for the District of Columbia before his elevation to the Court. For other justices, the intermediate position is only a very short way station. President Kennedy's appointees, Byron White and Arthur Goldberg, served in his administration for less than two years before they were selected as justices. In instances such as these, the intermediate position provides a stamp of legitimacy for the person in question and gives the president more information about that person's views, but it does not constitute a significant part of the pre-Court experience.

A smaller third group of justices has come to the Court directly from the private sector, skipping intermediate positions. The three recent justices in this category—Frankfurter, Fortas, and Powell—all have been discussed. In each case the justice had achieved eminence through the practice or teaching of law, and each had gained attention through governmental service during his professional career.

As this discussion makes clear, there are multiple paths from membership in the bar to the positions from which Supreme Court appointments are made. Certainly the careers of the persons selected as justices differ a great deal. At any given time, the nine members of the Court are likely to have brought with them a broad range of career experiences. What they will share is their membership in the legal profession and their success at reaching the higher levels within that profession or within government.

Implications of the Career Paths

On the basis of this analysis of paths to the Supreme Court, it is possible to explore some significant issues concerning the kinds of people who become justices. These issues include age at time of appointment; the role of "social background" characteristics such as class, race, and sex; the significance of prior judicial service; partisan political activity as a requisite for selection; and the role of chance in recruitment to the Court.

Age. Young people are not appointed to the Supreme Court. Most of the justices selected in this century were in their fifties when they joined the Court, and of the remainder most were over sixty. William Douglas was the youngest appointee at forty, and only two other appointees—Potter Stewart and Byron White—were under forty-five.

This pattern is surprising in at least one sense. We might expect presidents to select relatively young people in order to increase the length of time during which "their" justices would serve. In this way, presidents could increase their indirect influence over the Court's future policies. Given this advantage of young appointees, why do presidents generally choose persons over fifty and frequently choose persons over sixty?

One major reason for the predominance of older justices is the time required to achieve the high positions from which most justices are selected and to attain the eminence that makes one a "candidate" for selection. The groups from which justices are chosen, such as appellate judges and high administrators, are populated chiefly by people of at least middle age. Another reason is that at least some participants in the selection process would regard truly young persons as lacking the experience to serve effectively on the Court. The American Bar Association prefers more than a decade of experience as an attorney even for prospective lower court judges. Thus it is easiest for presidents to select older persons as justices, even though in doing so they are limiting their own influence over the Court.

Class, Race, and Sex. The Supreme Court's membership has been quite unrepresentative of the general population in social class backgrounds, with most justices coming from upper-status families. John Schmidhauser has concluded that "only a handful of the members of the Supreme Court were of essentially humble origin." [29] Schmidhauser's definition of humble origin may be overly restrictive, but he is certainly correct in pointing out that rather few children of the working class and poor have reached the Court.

The period since 1937 has differed somewhat from the general pattern, in that the number of justices from relatively low-status backgrounds has been relatively large. Although the group of recent justices is still of higher average status than the population as a whole, the gap is narrower than in any previous period. Democratic appointees since the 1930s have been especially likely to come from humble backgrounds.[30]

The tendency for justices to come from higher-status backgrounds can be understood in terms of the career paths that justices take. First and most important, a justice must obtain a legal education. To do so is easiest for people with high status, because of the costs of law training and the education that precedes it. When apprenticeships provided the major source of legal education, high social status was important in obtaining an apprenticeship with a leading practitioner. Second, people of high-status backgrounds have a variety of advantages in their post-educational careers. Those who can afford to attend elite law schools, for instance, have the easiest time finding positions in successful law firms.

The partial deviation from this pattern since 1937 may be explained in part by the increasing availability of legal education. Warren Burger, with few financial resources, could attend law school at night while selling insurance during the day. It may also be that the growth of the legal profession, the judiciary, and the federal government has opened access to high positions in these sectors for people of lower-status backgrounds who might have been shut out of the limited opportunities that existed earlier. If these explanations have some validity, then we should expect that the proportion of justices from lower-status backgrounds will remain relatively high and perhaps increase in the future.

With the exceptions of Thurgood Marshall and Sandra Day O'Connor, the Supreme Court has been composed entirely of white males. This pattern is not difficult to understand. Until very recently, women and blacks had extreme difficulty pursuing legal educations due to legal and other restrictions. As a result, the pool of potential justices from these groups who passed the first barrier to selection was quite small. Moreover, prejudice against women and members of racial minority groups has limited their ability to advance in the legal profession and in politics, so that very few people from these groups could reach the high positions from which justices are selected. It is notable that Thurgood Marshall became a renowned attorney not through the usual process of advancement in a major law firm—which would have been nearly inconceivable—but through his work for the NAACP. Similarly, Sandra Day O'Connor graduated near the top of her class at Stanford Law School but found the law firms of Los Angeles and San Francisco unwilling to hire her as an attorney.

The representation of women and racial minority groups on the Court probably will increase significantly in the future. One reason, already noted, is the growing willingness of presidents to consider women and blacks in selecting justices from those holding high positions. More important, increased educational and career opportunities for both groups will augment their representation in those positions. Still, the various advantages of white males are likely to keep them numerically dominant on the Court for some time.

If the Court has been composed primarily of white men from upper-status backgrounds, what impact has this composition had on its policies? The impact of these characteristics is difficult to ascertain, but some tentative judgments are possible. In the case of race and sex, the legal claims of racial minority groups and of women might have been taken seriously at an earlier time had these groups enjoyed even limited representation on the Court. During the 1960s Congress took its first steps to support equality for women, largely through the efforts of its female members; during the same decade, the all-male Supreme Court gave no support to those litigants who brought sex discrimination complaints to the Court despite its general support for civil liberties.

For social class the picture is more complicated. Certainly a person of high socioeconomic status tends to develop certain attitudes that differ from the predominant attitudes in lower-status groups. But this is only a tendency. Moreover, some of those born relatively poor became fairly wealthy in adulthood; Warren Burger is one example. The sympathies of those who have "climbed" from low-status backgrounds may differ little from those who started out with social and economic advantages. Notably, the justices from humble backgrounds have included solid conservatives such as Warren Burger as well as liberals such as Earl Warren. If the Supreme Court's decisions have reflected "essentially the conscience of the American upper middle class," it is only in part because most justices originated in that class.[31]

Prior Judicial Service.   A majority of all the justices have served as judges on state courts or in lower federal courts. The importance of such service has been debated. For some observers of the Court, experience as a lower court judge is a prerequisite to superior work on the Supreme Court. Indeed, in recent years members of Congress have made several efforts to create a formal requirement of such experience. These efforts have stemmed largely from conservatives' belief that judicial activism is encouraged by an absence of lower court service. On the other side, a number of commentators—including Justice Felix Frankfurter—have argued that lower court experience is not a necessity for a justice. A few have even suggested that nonexperienced justices have a better record on the Court. Certainly it is not difficult to find justices without prior experience who have distinguished themselves on the Court, from John Marshall to Earl Warren.

Of the sixteen justices since 1937 who had lower court experience, the longest experience was thirteen years (Burger), and nine justices had been lower court judges for five years or less. Undoubtedly even a short period on a lower court provides experiences that shape a justice's perspective, but a stint of three or five years—or even of thirteen years—is not likely to have as much impact on a person's thinking and approach to judicial policy issues as the much longer period of education and professional development that preceded it.

For this reason, it is not surprising that justices with lower court experience have not behaved very differently as a group from justices without that experience. Service on lower courts may offer one benefit, that of easing the difficulties of new justices. But even this benefit is limited by the differences between the Supreme Court and other courts, which make the Court's work a challenge for experienced judges as well as other people.

Partisan Political Activity.   Most justices have had significant involvements in partisan politics prior to their selection, as holders of partisan offices and participants in political campaigns. This pattern differs from that in many other countries, and it is a source of dissatisfaction for many observers of the courts.

The use of nominations as political rewards causes presidents deliberately to select politicians for some vacancies. But the importance of partisan activity also can be understood as a result of the established paths to the Court. First, high partisan office has come to constitute one recognized source of potential nominees, both because of the achievement that it signifies and because of the visibility of those who hold such offices. Second, appointment to the high judicial and administrative posts that constitute the major source of Supreme Court justices in the current period is itself heavily based on partisan politics.

Whether the preponderance of politicians on the Court is desirable constitutes a more difficult question. Certainly people uninvolved in partisan activities have a substantial disadvantage in reaching the Court; some highly qualified but less visible people have little chance of appointment. Yet there always will be far more qualified people available than vacancies on the Court, and this would be the case even if justices were recruited only from professional politicians. Moreover, it can be argued that involvement in partisan politics is useful preparation for the Court, particularly insofar as it provides a broad understanding of the policy issues that the Court's decisions touch. In any case the current pattern is unlikely to change radically.

The Role of Chance.   Perhaps the clearest conclusion to be reached from an examination of the path to the Supreme Court is that people do not become justices through an inevitable process. At any given time the number of people considered eligible for appointment to the Court because of their high positions in government or the bar will be very large. Even those people who attain high positions are a small proportion of those who might have reached them. Nor are these two kinds of advancement based on a rational selection of the most able or a "survival of the fittest." Rather, much of the advancement from membership in the bar to the Court is a result of luck as much as anything else. Chance factors such as geography and a president's need to appeal to a major interest group may be decisive in determining whether a person becomes a justice. For this reason an ambitious person hardly could guarantee eventual selection to the Court by choosing a particular career path.

The impact of luck is clear when we consider that presidents ordinarily select members of their own party, and that when they do cross party lines they seldom cross ideological lines at the same time. All the appointments to the Court between 1969 and 1988 were made by Republican presidents. As a result, potential justices who were liberal Democrats and who were of prime age for appointment in this period have had to watch their chances slip away.

Indeed, most justices probably would not have reached the Court under any other president. The case of Byron White is typical of many. White was a highly successful attorney in Denver who became involved in John Kennedy's campaign for the presidency because of their personal friendship. When Kennedy was elected, White received first a position in the Department of Justice and then a Supreme Court appointment. Had Kennedy not become president, it is almost certain that White never would have reached the Court.

The role of luck in the selection of justices does not mean that the Court's direction, as determined by its membership, is entirely random. Although Warren Burger's selection as chief justice was hardly inevitable, President Nixon was certain to select a political conservative for the position. However, this discussion does suggest that membership on the Supreme Court is attained through good fortune as well as a person's own qualities. "You have to be lucky," said Sandra Day O'Connor;[32] that statement reflects realism as well as modesty.

Leaving the Court

Thus far, this chapter has examined the process by which people get to the Supreme Court. Also of importance is the process by which justices' careers end, and that process will be examined briefly in this final section.

Voluntary Resignation and Retirement

When the Supreme Court's importance as a policy maker was established, one effect was to increase the willingness of justices to remain on the Court. In the Court's first decade, its members frequently resigned to seek more attractive opportunities. For instance, John Jay, the first chief justice, left the Court to become governor of New York. Since the early years, however, the great majority of Supreme Court justices have stayed on the Court either until their death or until they were overtaken by age or ill health.

Some notable exceptions to this rule have occurred, including several in this century. Charles Evans Hughes resigned in 1916 on receiving the Republican nomination for president; he lost a close race, and fourteen years later he returned to the Court as chief justice. John Clarke resigned in 1922 largely because of dissatisfaction with the Court and his life as a justice. James Byrnes left the Court in 1942 to become director of the Office of Economic Stabilization, a crucial post during World War II. Arthur Goldberg resigned in 1965 to become U.S. ambassador to the United Nations. Warren Burger retired in 1986 at the age of seventy-eight to devote full time to his service as chairman of the Commission on the Bicentennial of the Constitution, although his age also may have played a role in his decision. But these cases *are* exceptions. Most justices have found the Court sufficiently attractive to remain on it until the end of their professional lives.

The desire to remain on the Court can cause problems when justices suffer from serious infirmities that limit their effectiveness. In an effort to prevent such problems, since 1869 Congress has encouraged aging justices to leave the bench by providing that their salaries will continue if they do so. Today justices who are at least seventy years old and who have served for at least ten years may resign and continue to receive the salaries that they earned prior to resignation. Justices who meet those criteria, or who are sixty-five years old with fifteen years of service, may retire and still obtain any salary increases granted those still on the Court. (A person who resigns relinquishes the position of justice, whereas one who retires retains that position formally. In either case, the person gives up a seat on the Court and ceases to participate in the Court's decisions.)

These financial benefits seem to have had the desired effect, in combination with an apparent growth in the responsibility that justices feel for the Court's work. In the twentieth century, unlike the nineteenth, a majority of justices have left the Court before their deaths. Indeed, as Table 2-4 shows, none of the ten justices who left the Court between 1965 and 1987 died in office, although Black and Harlan died soon afterward. The table also shows that old age and health problems have been the primary reasons for resignations and retirements in recent years.

Potter Stewart and Lewis Powell exemplify the justices who wish to leave the Court before their performance begins to decline. Stewart retired in 1981 at the age of sixty-six, while he remained healthy and vigorous. In explaining his retirement, he said, "I've always been a firm believer in the principle that it's better to go too soon than to stay too long." [33] Powell was seventy-nine years old when he retired in 1987; he cited his age and the possibility of a recurrence of past illnesses that had created problems for the Court. In terms similar to those used by Stewart, Powell quoted his son as saying, "It's a whole lot better to go out when some people may be sorry than it is to wait until, when you decide to go . . . people say, 'Thank God, we got rid of that old gent.' " [34]

But a few twentieth-century justices have remained on the Court when their faculties were impaired, leaving their colleagues with the delicate task of trying to convince them to retire. The most recent instance involved William Douglas. Justice Douglas delayed his retirement in 1975 until it was absolutely clear that he could not recover from his physical problems, and his delay disrupted the Court's work during that year. Douglas did not want to yield his liberal voice on the Court when his replacement would be chosen by the conservative Gerald Ford—who, moreover, had sought to impeach Douglas a few years earlier.

The Court of the 1980s was notable for the refusal of several members to retire despite advanced age. As noted already, Burger and Powell were nearly eighty when they left the Court. At the beginning of 1988, Brennan, Marshall, and Blackmun remained on the Court, although they ranged in age from seventy-nine to eighty-one. These three justices and John Paul Stevens (who was sixty-eight years old in 1988) were the four most liberal members of the Court, and some conservatives wished fervently that they would depart. Evangelist and presidential candidate Pat Robertson said in 1987 that most of the country's social concerns "would be solved if Justice Marshall, Justice Brennan and Justice Stevens were to be either retired or to be promoted to that great courtroom in the sky." [35] But the same ideological concerns strengthened the desire of the older liberal justices to remain on the Court while a conservative president was in office. Although they were not free of health problems, these problems were not as serious or as disruptive as

Table 2-4 Reasons for Leaving the Court, Since 1965

Year	Justice	Age	Primary reasons for leaving	Length of time from leaving until death
1965	Goldberg	56	Appointment as ambassador to U.N.	—
1967	Clark	67	Son's appointment as attorney general	10 years
1969	Fortas	58	Pressures based on possible ethical violations	13 years
1969 [a]	Warren	78	Age	5 years
1971	Black	85	Age and ill health	1 month
1971	Harlan	72	Age and ill health	3 months
1975	Douglas	77	Age and ill health	4 years
1981	Stewart	66	Age	4 years
1986	Burger	78	Responsibilities for Commission on the Bicentennial of the Constitution, possibly age	—
1987	Powell	79	Age and health concerns	—

Sources: Congressional Quarterly, *The Supreme Court: Justice and the Law* (Washington, D.C.: Congressional Quarterly Inc., 1983), 165-183, 244-245; other biographical sources.

[a] Warren originally announced intent to leave Court in 1968.

the incapacities of some past justices. Mindful that serious problems might strike in the future, Blackmun at a 1985 judicial conference asked, "When I show more than the usual signs of senility, for goodness sakes, let me know." [36]

External Pressure

Beyond the provision of retirement benefits, Congress and the president may try to induce specific justices to leave the Court. Presidents have a special incentive to do so, because they can fill vacancies with new justices of their choice, and they may be impatient for vacancies to arise. Thurgood Marshall suspected such impatience when he was hospitalized for pneumonia and President Nixon called to inquire about the state of his health. Marshall gave permission to pass his prognosis on to Nixon, but "only on one condition: that you put at the bottom of it, quote, NOT YET." [37]

One action that the president can take is to offer inducements for justices to take other positions. President Roosevelt was able to appeal to James Byrnes to resign from the Court to accept a central position in the war effort in World War II. A quarter-century later Arthur Goldberg resigned to become U.S. ambassador to the United Nations under heavy pressure from President Johnson. In 1987 the Reagan administration sounded out Byron White about becoming director of the FBI, but White rejected the idea.

Alternatively, the president can try to encourage a justice to leave the Court through indirect pressure. Theodore Roosevelt sought to induce the resignations of Chief Justice Melville Fuller and Justice John Marshall Harlan, in part through leaks to newspapers. Roosevelt's efforts only stiffened the two justices' resolve to stay on the Court; they reportedly made a pact not to resign "until they have to take us out feet foremost." [38] Lyndon Johnson effectively brought about Justice Tom Clark's retirement by appointing Clark's son Ramsey as attorney general. Because the federal government is a party to a high proportion of Supreme Court cases, Justice Clark had little choice but to leave his post.

Very different is impeachment or its threatened use. Under the Constitution justices, like other federal officials, can be removed through impeachment proceedings for "treason, bribery, or other high crimes and misdemeanors." [39] President Jefferson actually sought to gain control of the largely Federalist (and thus anti-Jefferson) judiciary through the liberal use of impeachment, and Congress did impeach and convict a federal district judge in 1803. Meanwhile, Justice Samuel Chase made himself vulnerable to impeachment through his participation in President John Adams's campaign for reelection in 1800 and some injudicious and partisan remarks to a Maryland grand jury in 1803. He eventually was impeached, with the action justified chiefly by his handling of political trials, but the Senate acquitted him in 1805. His acquittal effectively ended Jefferson's plans to bring impeachment against other members of the Court.

This episode discredited impeachment as a means to remove justices. Later, the near-success of the effort to remove President Andrew Johnson from office through impeachment helped to establish a belief that impeachment was a potentially dangerous procedure that should be reserved for extraordinary situations. In this century impeachment proceedings have been brought against a few federal judges, but each instance involved alleged corruption. In more ambiguous situations, such as judicial senility, impeachment has proved to be a useless procedure.

It is true that justices, like presidents, occasionally are subject to demands for impeachment from their opponents. The ultraconservative John Birch Society engaged in a prolonged campaign to impeach Chief Justice Warren, but there was never any real possibility that Congress would respond to its urgings. Somewhat more serious were several efforts to remove Justice Douglas, with his strong liberalism as the underlying motivation. The most significant of these efforts came in 1969 and 1970, based publicly on his financial connections with a foundation and on his outside writings. The public leader of this effort was House minority leader Gerald Ford, who apparently was set in motion by President Nixon.[40] The impeachment resolution against Douglas was disapproved by a special committee and died.

Justice Fortas is the one exception in this century to the general rule that justices need not fear impeachment; had he not resigned from the Court in 1969, he might well have been removed through impeachment proceedings. Fortas had been criticized for his financial dealings when he was nominated unsuccessfully for chief justice in 1968. A year later it was disclosed that he had a lifetime contract as a consultant to the Wolfson Foundation and had received money from that foundation at a time when its head was being prosecuted by the federal government. The Nixon administration orchestrated a campaign of pressure on Fortas through the mass media and through the Court itself, and after Fortas's explanation of his conduct proved unsatisfying, he resigned fairly quickly. The resignation came too early to determine how successful an impeachment effort would have been, but almost certainly it would have been serious.

A repetition of the Fortas episode may be unlikely, if only because the justices have become more aware of the dangers of questionable financial conduct. Notably, Justice Douglas severed his own foundation connection shortly after Fortas's resignation, and Justice Brennan cut back on his investments and other extra-Court activities. Although the effort to impeach President Nixon in 1974 seemed to revive impeachment as a serious option for Congress, it is still likely to remain a last resort and one used only in extreme circumstances.

Thus the timing of a justice's leaving the Court is chiefly a matter of that person's own inclinations, health, and longevity. Other people seeking to influence the Court's composition may have their say when a vacancy occurs, but they have relatively little control over the vacancies.

Conclusion

One theme that emerges from this chapter is that the recruitment process for Supreme Court justices is affected considerably by the Court's accepted importance. The importance of the Supreme Court in the political system gives presidents an interest in controlling these appointments and causes them to stress competence and policy preferences as well as "political" considerations in selecting justices. For the same reason, the Senate gives nominations to the Court a degree of scrutiny that is unusual for presidential appointments. The prestige attached to the Court helps to limit the selection of its members to those who have achieved high positions in the law or in politics. Finally, the attractiveness of the Court has reduced the willingness of justices to leave it before they are overtaken by old age or death.

Beyond this generalization, it should also be clear that the recruitment of justices is a complex process, whether seen from the perspective of the president or from the perspective of those who aspire to the Court. The Supreme Court is not a body to which people "rise" in an orderly and rational fashion. Rather, people reach the point of being considered for the Court and actually obtain appointments through a process that involves a great many participants, in which a great many considerations are weighed, and in which chance plays a considerable role.

The significance of the recruitment process lies largely in the impact of the Court's membership on its decisions. That impact will be discussed in succeeding chapters, in the examination of the factors that shape the Court's policy choices and determine its general direction.

Notes

1. The four who were nominated and confirmed twice include three individuals elevated from associate justice to chief justice (Edward White, Harlan Stone, and William Rehnquist), as well as one (Charles Evans Hughes) who resigned from the Court and was later appointed chief justice. Douglas Ginsburg is counted as a nominee throughout this chapter even though he withdrew from consideration in 1987 before he was officially nominated.
2. James Goodman, "The Politics of Picking Federal Judges," *Juris Doctor*, June

1977, 26; cited in Henry J. Abraham, *Justices and Presidents: A Political History of Appointments to the Supreme Court*, 2d ed. (New York: Oxford University Press, 1985), 21.

3. U.S. Congress, Senate, *Congressional Record*, 91st Cong., 2d sess., 1970, 116, pt. 3:2860.
4. Henry J. Abraham and Bruce Allen Murphy, "The Influence of Sitting and Retired Justices on Presidential Supreme Court Nominations," *Hastings Constitutional Law Quarterly* 3 (Winter 1976): 37-63.
5. William O. Douglas, *Go East, Young Man: The Early Years* (New York: Random House, 1974), 332.
6. Joel B. Grossman, *Lawyers and Judges: The ABA and the Politics of Judicial Selection* (New York: John Wiley & Sons, 1965), 42.
7. Abraham, *Justices and Presidents*, 184.
8. William O. Douglas, *The Court Years 1939-1975: The Autobiography of William O. Douglas* (New York: Random House, 1980), 247.
9. John Ehrlichman, *Witness to Power: The Nixon Years* (New York: Simon and Schuster, 1982), 114-115. The quotation is on p. 114.
10. Evan Thomas, "Reagan's Mr. Right," *Time Magazine*, June 30, 1986, 26; William Safire, "Free Speech v. Scalia," *New York Times*, April 29, 1985, A17.
11. William H. Harbaugh, *Lawyer's Lawyer: The Life of John W. Davis* (New York: Oxford University Press, 1973), 192.
12. "No Wonder They're So Stiff," *California Lawyer*, December 1987, 12.
13. Abraham, *Justices and Presidents*, 263.
14. Robert Scigliano, *The Supreme Court and the Presidency* (New York: Free Press, 1971), 107-108.
15. Elizabeth Olson, "Judging the Effect of a Reagan Court," *San Francisco Examiner*, December 2, 1984, E1.
16. Henry F. Pringle, *The Life and Times of William Howard Taft* (New York: Farrar & Rinehart, 1939), 854.
17. Fred Barnes, "Reagan's Full Court Press," *The New Republic*, June 10, 1985, 18.
18. Data supporting this conclusion are presented in David W. Rohde and Harold J. Spaeth, *Supreme Court Decision Making* (San Francisco: W. H. Freeman & Company, 1976), 107-109.
19. John A. Jenkins, "A Candid Talk with Justice Blackmun," *New York Times Magazine*, February 20, 1983, 24.
20. Abraham, *Justices and Presidents*, 263.
21. Scigliano, *Supreme Court and the Presidency*, 147-148.
22. J. Anthony Lukas, *Nightmare: The Underside of the Nixon Years* (New York: Viking Press, 1976), 569.
23. Scigliano, *Supreme Court and the Presidency*, 95.
24. Abraham, *Justices and Presidents*, 314.
25. Data on the length of the process are collected in Joel B. Grossman and Stephen L. Wasby, "The Senate and Supreme Court Nominations: Some Reflections," *Duke Law Journal* (1972): 563-566.
26. These figures and those in the following paragraph are based primarily on data in Scigliano, *Supreme Court and the Presidency*, 97-99.
27. "Justice Black and the Bill of Rights," *Southwestern University Law Review* 9 (1977): 939-940.
28. For this observation and much of the information on which the analysis in this section is based, I am indebted to John R. Schmidhauser, *Judges and Justices: The Federal Appellate Judiciary* (Boston: Little, Brown & Co., 1979), 41-100.
29. Ibid., 49.

30. Sheldon Goldman and Thomas P. Jahnige, *The Federal Courts as a Political System*, 3d ed. (New York: Harper & Row, 1985), 52.
31. Schmidhauser, *Judges and Justices*, 99.
32. Laurence Bodine, "Sandra Day O'Connor," *American Bar Association Journal* 69 (October 1983): 1394.
33. Fred Barbash, "Student Query Moved Stewart to Quit," *Washington Post*, June 20, 1981, A9.
34. Ruth Marcus, "The Other Pivotal Figure in the Powell Family," *Washington Post*, June 28, 1987, A10.
35. "Overheard," *Newsweek*, May 18, 1987, 21.
36. "High Court Not 'Great,' Not 'Worst,'" *Washington Post*, July 28, 1985, A5.
37. From an interview conducted by Carl Rowan, quoted in "The Justice and the President," *Washington Post*, September 11, 1987, A23.
38. John E. Semonche, *Charting the Future: The Supreme Court Responds to a Changing Society, 1890-1920* (Westport, Conn.: Greenwood Press, 1978), 202.
39. U.S. *Constitution*, Art. 2, sec. 4.
40. Ehrlichman, *Witness to Power*, 122.

3

The Cases

In recent years the Supreme Court has decided an average of about 150 cases with full opinions each term. In these cases the Court not only rules on the legal rights of specific parties but also lays down general principles that apply to the nation as a whole. It is primarily these cases that the Court uses to make law and policy.

These 150 cases, of course, involve only a minute proportion of the situations that might have resulted in full Supreme Court decisions. This fact gives great importance to the Court's agenda-setting process, the series of choices that determine which cases it decides. This chapter will examine that complex process by discussing the roles of the various participants who help to set the Supreme Court's agenda. The first section will take a brief, general view of the agenda-setting process. The following two sections will look at how cases are brought to the Court and how the Court chooses which of these cases it will hear. A final section will discuss the growth in the Court's caseload and its significance for the Court's capacity to function.

A General View

Steps in the Process

The Supreme Court's agenda-setting process ordinarily involves several steps. First, a case is initiated in a state or federal trial court. This first step is significant, since only a small minority of the legal disputes that might be taken to court actually result in civil suits or criminal prosecutions.

In the second step, that case must proceed through the court system to a court from which a dissatisfied party can bring a case to the Supreme Court. This means, of course, that the parties have not settled the case somewhere along the way; approximately 90 percent of all civil and criminal cases are settled prior to a trial court decision. It also means that at least one of the parties must appeal from the court's decision at each step.

Third, the party who is dissatisfied with the decision of a court below the Supreme Court—usually a federal court of appeals or a state supreme court—petitions the U.S. Supreme Court to hear the case. Petitions are brought in only a minority of cases. One study found that 30 percent of the losing parties in the federal courts of appeals took their cases to the Supreme Court.[1] The petition rate from state supreme courts is lower; a high proportion of cases in state supreme courts are ineligible for hearing by the Supreme Court because they involve no issues of federal law.

Finally, the Supreme Court agrees to accept the case for decision on the merits and then renders a decision with full opinion. By its own rule the Court does not accept a case for decision on its merits unless four justices agree that the case should receive that treatment; this is the "rule of four." Even when the Court does accept a case, it may render only a summary decision rather than a full ruling on the legal issues. The Court is highly selective in its choices; for every case it accepts and decides fully, more than twenty are rejected or decided summarily.

Two classes of cases take routes to the Court that differ somewhat from the one that I have described. Some cases originate in federal administrative agencies and go next to the courts of appeals, only one step below the Supreme Court. A few cases arise under the Court's original jurisdiction and come directly to the Court. Like other cases, however, these cases reach the Court's ultimate agenda through action by one or more parties and by the Court itself.

The Participants

In the agenda-setting process for the Supreme Court, three sets of participants play crucial roles. The first is Congress, which influences the agenda in several ways. Most broadly, Congress has general power over the Court's appellate jurisdiction. Through this power Congress can determine what classes of cases may come to the Court and from what courts they may be brought.

Congressional legislation can affect the agenda in other ways. For instance, new statutes often lead to federal court litigation that creates potential business for the Supreme Court. In recent years, the Court has decided significant numbers of cases under such statutes as the environmental protection laws of the 1960s and 1970s and the Civil Rights Act of 1964.[2] When Congress creates a large number of new federal judgeships, as it did in 1984, it may reduce the delay in lower federal courts and thus encourage litigants to use those courts, and in turn a larger number of cases may reach the Supreme Court. Although the impact of a specific congressional action on the Court's agenda frequently is too subtle to measure, the overall impact of Congress on that agenda is tremendous.

The impact of litigants and potential litigants is much more direct. Like most courts, the Supreme Court cannot hear a case on its own initiative. Thus the Court is dependent upon people and institutions that bring cases to court originally and then bring cases up to the Supreme Court. Moreover, the Court must address the facts of the particular cases that come to it. It cannot reach out for a case with a "better" set of facts if no such case has been brought to it. Litigants also help to determine the Court's range of options with the issues that they raise.

Finally, the Court itself plays a most important role in the process. The Court has total control over its agenda in a negative sense by retaining an absolute power to forgo full decision in any given case. No matter how many cases are brought to the Court concerning a particular issue, no matter how urgent that issue seems, nobody can require the Court to give a case full consideration. When the Court does agree to hear a case, it can determine which issues in the case it will address, and in this respect too the Court is master of its own agenda. One striking example is *Mapp v. Ohio* (1961), in which the Court turned what had been brought to it and argued before it as an obscenity case into a landmark decision on police searches and seizures.

The Court also can encourage and discourage cases in particular areas through the cues that its decisions provide for potential litigants. For example, the Court's two 1987 decisions sustaining the rights of property owners against regulations of land use undoubtedly will spur other property owners to challenge such regulations.[3] Sometimes the cue is quite direct. In a 1985 decision two justices strongly hinted that the Court would uphold some laws providing for a moment of silence in public schools, thus encouraging states to bring to the Court cases in which lower courts had struck down such laws.[4]

Assessing the Court's Position

In a general way, the Supreme Court's position in the setting of its agenda may be considered a hybrid of the positions of most courts and that of Congress. In its dependence on the legislative branch for most of its jurisdiction and on litigants to bring cases the Court is similar to other courts but very different from Congress. Unlike the Supreme Court, Congress can address whatever policy questions it chooses. It is subject to few constraints from other institutions in this respect, and it can act on an issue whether or not it has received any requests for such action. In this sense Congress has a significant degree of freedom that the Court lacks.

In its capacity to choose from the cases brought to it, however, the

Supreme Court is more typical of a legislature than of a court. All courts have some ability to screen the litigation brought to them, but few have as complete a freedom to reject cases as does the Supreme Court. Moreover, the very large number of requests for hearings allows the Court to be highly selective.

The Court's control over its agenda is greater than this hybrid position might suggest. First, the practical impact of the Court's enforced passivity is more limited than it appears to be. As I have noted, the Court can encourage and discourage litigation of a particular type through its pattern of decisions. Moreover, because so many cases are brought to the Court, justices probably will find in these cases nearly all the questions that they would like to decide.

The Court also draws freedom from its relative isolation in the political system. While Congress technically is totally free to decide which issues it will address seriously, in practice its choices are dictated in part by pressures upon it to act. Today, for instance, Congress has little choice but to grapple with the foreign trade deficit. Further, Congress is burdened by recurring issues such as the budget which must be addressed regularly. The Court is nearly free of those constraints. An occasional case will be regarded as so important that the Court feels some pressure to decide it, but for the most part the Court has practical as well as technical freedom to turn aside whatever litigation it chooses.

Thus the Supreme Court has almost as much control over its agenda as does Congress, despite the seemingly fundamental differences between their positions. Certainly the Court possesses great freedom to determine the issues it will address.

Reaching the Court: Litigants, Attorneys, and Groups

In the 1987 term about 4,500 cases were filed in the Supreme Court.[5] These cases came from a great many different courts, primarily federal courts of appeals and state supreme courts. Their subject matter was diverse; the largest number arose from criminal prosecutions, but the others included a wide variety of policy issues in civil cases. What all of these cases had in common, of course, was that a party who was dissatisfied with a lower court decision sought action by the Supreme Court.

In this section I will consider how and why these cases came to the Supreme Court by examining the roles of three sets of participants: the litigants who are parties to the cases; the attorneys who represent them; and the interest groups that frequently play either central or peripheral roles in the litigation process. After discussing these sets of participants, I will give separate attention to the litigation activities of the federal government, the single most frequent participant in Supreme Court cases and one whose role is rather distinctive.

Litigants

Every case that comes to the Supreme Court has at least two formal parties, one on each side, and frequently more than two. For a case to reach the Court, of course, one or more of the parties must have taken action to initiate the litigation and to move it upward through the court system. Parties who have played this role in Supreme Court cases may be referred to generally as litigants.

As we would expect, litigants in the Supreme Court are a rather diverse lot. Many are individuals. Most individual litigants are criminal defendants, but individuals also appear in disputes concerning such civil matters as civil rights issues or personal injuries. Others are private institutions, such as businesses, labor unions, colleges, and foundations. Still others are state and government agencies, most commonly the agencies responsible for prosecution of criminal cases. Finally, agencies of the federal government become litigants in the Court. As this range of litigants suggests, it is difficult to generalize about the participants in Supreme Court cases.

The Motivations of Litigants. Perhaps the most important question concerning litigants is why they have become involved in court cases and carried them to the Supreme Court. The significance of this question is underlined by the fact that most people seek to avoid litigation or to terminate it as early as possible, chiefly because of its expense and the conflict and risk that it engenders. The motives of litigants can be thought of as taking two general forms, resulting in two "ideal types" of Supreme Court litigation. In reality some litigation falls between the two types, because it is based on mixed motives, but the distinction is still a useful one.

The first type may be called "ordinary" litigation because of its relative frequency. Ordinarily, people bring cases to court or appeal adverse judgments because of a direct personal or organizational interest that they seek to advance. Plaintiffs take personal injury suits to court because they perceive that they will obtain a monetary advantage from litigation. Prosecutors file criminal cases to fulfill the goals of the prosecuting agencies for which they work. Similarly, litigants usually appeal court decisions because they believe that their potential gain from a successful appeal and the likelihood of success are sufficient to justify additional trouble and expense.

The second type may be called "political" litigation. Here the goal of litigants is not self-interest but the advancement of policies that they favor. Most often, political litigation involves an effort to obtain a judicial decision that supports the litigant's policy goals. For instance, a person concerned with environmental protection might bring a suit to obtain a stringent interpretation of a statute that regulates air pollution. Someone who seeks to promote equality for disabled people may challenge the constitutionality of a state law that allegedly discriminates against the disabled.

The proportion of litigation that can be classified as political increases with each step upward in the judicial system, and political litigation is most common in the Supreme Court. This pattern is not accidental. Ordinary litigation tends to be terminated at a relatively early stage because participants find it more profitable to settle their dispute or even to accept a defeat than to fight on. In contrast, political litigants often can obtain significant victories only by getting a case to the highest levels of the system; a favorable verdict at the local level may do little to advance their policy goals. Moreover, political litigation often attracts support from interest groups that help to shoulder financial and other burdens of carrying a case through the judicial system.

Still, the great majority of cases brought to the Supreme Court would be classified as ordinary litigation. A large share are criminal cases in which the primary goal of the convicted defendant who seeks a hearing is to get out or stay out of prison. Other cases involve business corporations that have a sufficient economic stake in the outcome to justify a petition to the Court. Still other cases involve a variety of individual grievances, big or small, in which the aggrieved party cannot resist going to the Supreme Court for one final effort at redress.

Political litigation is more common in the set of cases that the Court agrees to hear, because these cases are more likely to involve the broad issues in which the justices are interested. Yet ordinary litigation is by no means absent from this set of cases. Even in the biggest cases, the ones that attract attention from large numbers of interest groups, the litigants themselves often are motivated primarily by personal self-interest.

Some Examples.   A few examples of Supreme Court litigants will suggest the range of goals that motivate them. Cecelia Young is a good representative of the litigant with a personal grievance. Young lived on the edge of Atlantic Beach, North Carolina. She kept two goats and a pony on her property. In 1979 Atlantic Beach passed an ordinance barring residents from keeping on their property a number of animals, including horses and goats. When town officials tried to evict Young's animals, she argued in court that her animals fell under a "house pets" exception in the ordinance. After the state supreme court ruled against her, Young took her case to the Supreme Court on constitutional grounds. While she may have been trying to make a point, her primary interest was in keeping her animals. Her case attracted the attention of neither interest groups nor the Supreme Court itself; her petition for a hearing was turned down in June 1983.[6]

An even clearer instance of ordinary litigation was the dispute between the Pennzoil and Texaco oil companies. After Texaco acquired Getty Oil in 1984, Pennzoil sued Texaco for allegedly inducing Getty to breach a contract to sell its stock to Pennzoil. Pennzoil won a Texas jury verdict for $10.5 billion, the biggest damage award ever. Faced with possible financial ruin, Texaco sought a federal court injunction against enforcement of the monetary award. Ultimately, the case reached the Supreme Court on issues concerning the power of federal courts to intervene in state cases, and the Court ruled in favor of Pennzoil in 1987. Neither company cared about the issues before the Court as such; rather, both were concerned with their very considerable financial stakes in the case.[7]

A case of ordinary litigation that also involved political elements is that of Ishmael Jaffree, a lawyer in Mobile, Alabama, who objected to prayers and other religious observances at the public schools that his children attended. When teachers continued these practices over his objection, Jaffree filed a lawsuit in federal district court. The Alabama governor and legislature responded to the lawsuit by enacting a statute providing for a state-composed prayer that could be recited in class, and the suit was amended to attack that statute and a related one that was already on the books. A federal district judge upheld the statutes and the Mobile schools' practices, but his decision was overturned by a court of appeals. By the time the Supreme Court accepted the case to consider the constitutionality of the statutes, it had become highly visible. Several interest groups submitted legal briefs to supplement those of the parties, and the federal government participated in oral argument on behalf of the state. But Jaffree and his attorney, another Mobile lawyer with a new practice, remained in control of their own case throughout the proceedings. The Supreme Court ruled in Jaffree's favor in 1985.[8]

One example of "pure" political litigation is another religion case, which arose from a city-sponsored nativity scene in Pawtucket, Rhode Island. The case was brought in 1980 by four individuals, some of whom were members of the Rhode Island affiliate of the American Civil Liberties Union (ACLU), and by the affiliate itself. The individual plaintiffs had nothing to gain personally from the litigation; indeed, people who challenge government involvement with religion sometimes suffer abuse. Rather, the lawsuit was an expression of the goals of the ACLU in supporting the separation of church and state. After winning in the lower federal courts, the opponents of the nativity scene lost in the Supreme Court in 1984.[9] The loss, like the case itself, affected the plaintiffs' policy goals far more than their personal interests.

Lawyers

In the great majority of cases that come to the Supreme Court, the parties seeking a hearing from the Court are represented by attorneys. Almost without exception, oral arguments before the Court are made by attorneys. Thus an examination of Supreme Court litigation must take into account the roles of lawyers.

The participation of attorneys in cases that reach the Court varies in timing. In many cases a litigant is represented by the same lawyer from the initiation of the case through the Supreme Court decision. In others, the lawyer who handled a case in the lower courts will be succeeded by a new attorney at the Supreme Court level. Criminal defendants often are represented by a series of attorneys as their cases progress. Some indigent defendants and prisoners draft their petitions for a hearing in the Court without legal representation; if the Court accepts such a case, it will appoint an attorney to represent the successful petitioner.

Members of the Court and other observers have complained about the competence of many attorneys who appear before the Court. Justice William Douglas, a harsh critic, concluded: "Few truly good advocates have appeared before the Court. In my time 40 percent were incompetent." [10] In 1972 a study group on the Court's caseload reported that "the average level of oral advocacy in the Court is judged to be disappointingly low." [11]

To the extent that problems of competence exist, they stem to some degree from inexperience. In the nineteenth century a high proportion of Supreme Court cases were handled by a few attorneys who argued regularly before the Court. The picture is quite different today; probably a majority of attorneys who argue cases before the Court do so only once. Lawyers, of course, are unlikely to do their best work in an unfamiliar setting.

Some lawyers do bring considerable experience with them when they argue cases before the Court. Attorneys for the federal government in the solicitor general's office gain expertise from their regular involvement in Supreme Court litigation. In the private sector, several attorneys handle cases in the Court with some frequency. Often, these are lawyers who first became familiar with the Court through service for the federal government. Erwin Griswold, solicitor general under Presidents Lyndon Johnson and Richard Nixon, had argued 127 Supreme Court cases by the end of the 1986 term. Solicitor General Rex Lee, who served in the Reagan administration until 1985, argued six cases in the 1986 term—an unusually large number for a lawyer outside the solicitor general's office. Others who have made several appearances in the Court include Laurence Gold of the AFL-CIO and Washington lawyer E. Barrett Prettyman. [12]

In the legal system as a whole, a relationship exists between the wealth of an individual or institution and the quality of the legal services available to that party. Certainly wealth has some impact on representation before the Supreme Court. Large corporations with big stakes in a case, for example, can afford to hire the best legal talent available. In the Pennzoil-Texaco case, both sides were represented by attorneys with very high reputations; as one commentator observed, "It was, without doubt, the most expensive single hour of oral argument the Supreme Court will hear all year." [13]

But the overall relationship between wealth and quality of legal services in the Court is complex. Many of the attorneys who appear before the Court with some frequency and who are most skilled in arguing before the Court represent some of the poorest and most powerless groups in society. Attorneys such as Thurgood Marshall and Jack Greenberg of the NAACP Legal Defense Fund and Hayden Covington of the Jehovah's Witnesses have been frequent and effective advocates for their groups in the Court. Lawyers for state and local governments who must contend with more experienced advocates for civil rights and civil liberties groups often are outmatched. This imbalance helped to spur the development of organized programs in the 1980s to provide better preparation for these government lawyers when they come to the Court.

Even a poor person without support from an interest group is likely to get very good legal services in a case that the Court accepts, because the Court appoints some of the best attorneys in the country to represent indigent litigants; a lawyer who is offered such an appointment seldom declines. For instance, Abe Fortas, then a renowned Washington lawyer, was appointed to represent Clarence Earl Gideon in the famous case of *Gideon v. Wainwright* (1963), which concerned the right to counsel for indigent criminal defendants.

Once in a great while a Supreme Court litigant who is not an attorney wishes to argue the case personally. Twice during the 1970s the Court allowed litigants to do so. But in 1982 it refused that right to a litigant who was challenging a California loitering statute as unconstitutional; the relative importance of this case may explain the refusal.[14]

Interest Groups

Supreme Court decisions are an important part of public policy making; as a result, political interest groups seek to influence what the Court does. The ways in which interest groups operate differ from one institution to another, and their role in the Court is quite different from their role in Congress. The Court is insulated from interest group influence in the sense that these groups have little to offer the justices in comparison with the services that interest groups can perform for legislators and administrators. Nonetheless, in the Court, as in the other branches, interest groups are major participants in the policy-making process.

The Forms of Group Activity.   The activity of interest groups in the Supreme Court is limited by a well-accepted norm. It is considered highly improper to lobby judges directly, as a group would lobby legislators. In general, because of this norm, Supreme Court justices seek to avoid contact with litigants and others interested in the outcomes of particular cases.

But interest groups can attempt to influence action by the Court in other ways. As noted in Chapter 2, they can participate informally in the nomination and confirmation of justices. A group that helps to determine the Court's membership may affect its policies in a fundamental way.

Groups also can participate directly in the litigation process. First, a group can help to get cases to the Court. It may initiate a "test case" designed to obtain a ruling from the Court on a policy issue that is important to the group, locating people who can serve as plaintiffs in the case and directing the litigation from the start. Alternatively, a group can become involved in cases that others already have initiated, helping to bear financial costs and supplying legal services and advice.

Second, a group can attempt to influence the Court's decisions whether to accept cases and how to decide those that are accepted through participation in oral argument or the submission of legal briefs. If a group is effectively in control of a case, its attorneys will submit the brief in support of (or in opposition to) the Supreme Court's acceptance of the case. If the case is accepted for full decision, the group's attorneys will submit further briefs and participate in oral argument.

When a group does not control the case, it still may submit arguments to the Court through what are called *amicus curiae* ("friend of the court") briefs. With the consent of the parties to a case or by permission of the Court, any person or organization may submit an *amicus* brief to supplement the arguments of the parties. (Legal representatives of the various levels of government do not need to obtain permission.) When the Court's permission is needed, it is granted far more often than it is refused.[15] *Amicus* briefs can be submitted on the issue of whether a case should be heard or, after a case is accepted for hearing, directly on the merits of the case. An *amicus* can also participate in oral argument if the Court allows it; in practice, it is rare for an *amicus* other than the federal government to argue a case.

Preparation and submission of an *amicus* brief can involve considerable expense, but it is still the easiest and most common form of group involvement in cases. In the 1983 term, at least one *amicus* brief was

Table 3-1 Selected Groups and Organizations Submitting *Amicus* Briefs in Cases Decided by the Supreme Court, 1987 Term

Businesses

Shell Oil Company
Universal Tool & Stamping Company

Trade associations

Air Transport Association
California Association of Realtors

Labor unions

American Federation of Government Employees
United Mine Workers of America

Professional associations

American Association of University Professors
National Association of Secondary School Principals

Legal groups

American Bar Association
Mid-Atlantic Legal Foundation

Governments

United States
State of Vermont
City of Morgan Hill, California

Other interest groups

Competitive Enterprise Institute
People for the American Way
Sierra Club

submitted in more than 80 percent of the cases in which the Court heard oral arguments. A high proportion of *amicus* briefs come from interest groups. The wide array of groups and organizations that submit *amicus* briefs is suggested by Table 3-1, which offers a sampling of the sources of such briefs in cases decided during the 1987 Supreme Court term.

Finally, a group can lobby the Court outside the litigation process. Occasionally a group will hold demonstrations concerning a decision. Both sides in the abortion controversy have staged marches on anniversaries of *Roe v. Wade* (1973), in part as an effort to put pressure on the Court. On a quite different level, groups sometimes attempt to get articles favorable to their positions published in law journals and other prestigious outlets. In its efforts to overturn restrictive covenants that limited blacks' access to housing, the NAACP stimulated several publications to publish articles designed to obtain support from the public and the Court.

Taken together, these avenues of potential influence may provide groups with significant roles in Supreme Court policy making. At this point I will focus primarily on the part groups play in getting cases to the Court. Their influence over the Court's decisions will be considered later in this chapter and in Chapter 4.

Group Involvement in the Supreme Court.   Because the Supreme Court deals with a broad range of policy issues, a great many interest groups of various types seek to bring cases to the Court. While most of these groups do so only occasionally, some are fairly regular participants in Supreme Court litigation. These "regulars" are those groups for which litigation seems most likely to pay significant dividends, because the policy issues that concern these groups fall within the Court's own major concerns and because the Court appears to be sympathetic to these groups' claims.

In the early twentieth century the Supreme Court was receptive to conservative arguments on economic issues. Groups representing the business community participated in several Court cases during this period, and they won some noteworthy victories.[16] Between 1908 and 1915 the American Anti-Boycott Association won three decisions limiting labor union practices. The Executive Committee of Southern Cotton Manufacturers sponsored a successful attack on federal regulation of child labor in *Hammer v. Dagenhart* (1918). But in 1937 the Court began to adopt a more liberal stance on economic issues, and this policy change helped to reduce conservative litigation activity for a time.

Liberal groups also participated in litigation early in the century. Most notably, the National Consumers' League involved itself in Court cases to defend legislation favorable to workers, and it achieved some successes. The NAACP and ACLU were founded during this period and began to litigate on behalf of civil liberties, in part because the other branches of government were inhospitable to their concerns. The Court's growing liberalism after 1937 encouraged these groups to expand their litigation efforts. Also active after 1937 were other groups with civil liberties interests such as the Jehovah's Witnesses, who sought to protect the proselytizing activities of their members.

In the last two decades new kinds of groups have played a significant part in the litigation process. The NAACP has been joined by groups that represent more recent civil rights interests, such as the National Organization for Women and the Mexican-American Legal Defense and Education Fund. Groups supporting consumers and environmental protection have also become involved in litigation. The Sierra Club, for instance, has sponsored environmental cases that reached the Supreme Court.

One important structure that has emerged in recent years is the public interest law firm, a concept pioneered by Ralph Nader in the 1960s. These firms devote themselves to cases that they see as serving the public interest in general. They are not tied directly to a particular interest group, and the activities of any particular firm may range broadly. The first public interest firms were ideologically liberal, and these groups have brought litigation with liberal goals such as protection of civil liberties and the environment. One liberal firm active at the Supreme Court level is the Public Citizen Litigation Group, whose director, Alan Morrison, argued and won the cases in which the Court struck down the legislative veto and the Gramm-Rudman-Hollings deficit reduction law.

In the 1970s and 1980s conservative groups have become increasingly frequent participants in Supreme Court litigation.[17] They have been motivated in part by the success of liberal groups in the courts, which they seek to counter. Several conservative public interest law firms have been created, primarily on a regional basis, and these firms participate in a wide range of cases. Among the other conservative groups involved in Court cases are the National Right to Work Legal Defense Fund and Americans for Effective Law Enforcement. Some of these groups emphasize the submission of *amicus* briefs, in part because their positions usually put them in support of government agencies that are the actual litigants. But other groups directly sponsor litigation in some cases.

The ideological change in the Court in the last two decades undoubtedly has encouraged litigation activity by conservative groups. The same change has made the Court less attractive to liberal groups, and some have become less active in Court litigation as a result. Should the Court become even more conservative in the 1990s, both these trends in interest group activity may accelerate.

The involvement of groups in the Supreme Court clearly has increased over time. Research by Karen O'Connor and Lee Epstein, for instance, shows that the proportion of cases with *amicus* briefs has grown substantially over the last half century.[18] One reason may be increased awareness of the Court's importance as a public policy maker. Another, probably, is the examples that some groups set for others. Several groups have patterned legal defense funds after the one established by the NAACP, and liberal public interest firms have served as a model for conservative counterparts. Whatever the causes, the Court gradually has become more of a focus for interest group activity.

Group Approaches and Strategies. Of the various groups involved in Supreme Court litigation, some are far more active than others. The groups that participate most often in litigation merit further scrutiny.

These groups differ a good deal in such characteristics as the scope of their activities and the ways that they make litigation decisions. One key similarity among them is the desire to develop effective long-term strategies for litigation. Ideally, a group interested in the favorable development of legal policy in a particular field would bring a series of cases to the Supreme Court through which the Court gradually would move doctrine in the direction the group favors. To achieve this result, groups look for cases that will serve their interests at a particular time. "Good" cases have such characteristics as favorable factual situations and attractive plaintiffs. For instance, in a case attacking government involvement in religion, a devout churchgoer serves as a better plaintiff than an outspoken atheist. Because of the rule of precedent and the caution that frequently characterizes courts, a group ordinarily seeks a case in which the Supreme Court must move only a short distance from its existing position to rule in the group's favor rather than a case in which a favorable decision requires that existing doctrine be uprooted.

This kind of strategy is easier to describe than to achieve. First of all, groups are constrained by limited resources. Litigation is expensive, and many groups—even some that represent business interests—have had difficulty in financing their court activities. This is especially true of groups with very broad interests, such as the ACLU and the NAACP Legal Defense Fund, which could not possibly finance major campaigns in each area of concern to them. Certainly, what such groups are able to do depends heavily on their success in raising money through memberships, foundation grants, and other sources.

Even if finances are no problem, the task of carrying out an ideal litigation program is complicated by other practical considerations. The case that would meet a group's needs perfectly often does not exist, and a group then must accept a less attractive vehicle for its legal arguments. Further, no group has total control over the initiation of litigation in its area of interest. A group cannot prevent individuals from bringing cases, and in criminal justice the initiative lies with prosecutors rather than with the groups that seek to expand or to narrow defendants' rights. The groups that work against capital punishment have no choice but to enter cases in which prosecutors have sought and obtained death sentences. Often multiple groups are active on the same side of an issue; this is the case, for instance, with women's rights litigation, in which the ACLU and several women's groups are active. This situation may create problems of coordination, especially when groups have different goals.

Of course, the courts themselves are not always cooperative. A group may select a case as the appropriate vehicle to establish a principle from which it can work in future cases. But if the Supreme Court refuses to hear that case or explicitly rejects the principle in question, the strategy must be reconsidered.

This discussion suggests that groups must be satisfied with something less than well-coordinated long-term litigation campaigns. "Despite talk of 'strategy,' " Stephen Wasby has concluded, "it is problematic whether interest groups do more than respond idiosyncratically to cases one at a time." [19] As one lawyer told Wasby, "The nature of the business prevents it from being a grand design." [20] From this perspective it is all the more impressive that at least a few groups have enjoyed considerable success over a long period in getting cases to the Supreme Court. It will be useful to take a further look at the two litigating groups that have been the most important over the past few decades.

The NAACP Legal Defense Fund. The NAACP was organized in 1909.[21] Early in its history it began to devote extensive efforts to litigation, largely because the executive and legislative branches were unfriendly to the interests of black citizens. In 1939 the NAACP established the Legal Defense and Educational Fund, usually called the Legal Defense Fund or simply the Fund, as a separate organization for legal activity. The Fund gradually became more independent of the NAACP, and the two organizations now are entirely separate.

The Fund does not have a mass membership, and much of its activity is centralized in a national office in New York City. Its litigation activities operate primarily through its staff lawyers and a network of cooperating attorneys throughout the country. Possible cases come from a variety of sources, and the Fund's staff attempts to choose among them on the basis of priorities and strategic considerations.

The Fund is best known for its work in school desegregation, especially for its management of the attacks on southern school segregation that led to the Supreme Court's decision in *Brown v. Board of Education* (1954). But the Fund has been involved in a variety of other areas as well. Voting rights is a long-standing and continuing priority. After Congress adopted the Civil Rights Act of 1964, the Fund initiated a concerted litigation campaign to obtain effective enforcement of its provision on employment. It also undertook a long-term campaign against capital punishment.

In part because it is not a membership group, the Fund has some advantages in carrying out general strategies. But its orchestration of the *Brown* case probably has been exaggerated. "If the military metaphor referring to a litigation campaign is helpful," according to one scholar, "the campaign was conducted on a terrain that repeatedly required changes in maneuvers." [22] In some other instances the organization has been unable to develop and implement effective strategies. One problem is that the Fund cannot always choose the cases that it handles; another is that in most areas of its work other organizations also are engaged in litigation.

Nonetheless, the achievements of the NAACP Legal Defense Fund are impressive. It has brought a substantial number of cases to the Supreme Court concerning legal equality and other issues that affect the status of black citizens. One ironic tribute to the Fund's effectiveness is the efforts that southern opponents of civil rights expended in the 1950s and 1960s to cripple its litigation activities. A more straightforward tribute is the establishment of similar litigation operations by a variety of other organizations that seek to influence judicial policy.

The American Civil Liberties Union. The ACLU was established after World War I as an organization to protect civil liberties, and it has always emphasized litigation as a means to that end.[23] Its range of interests is even broader than that of the NAACP; it has given particular emphasis to freedom of expression, but by no means does it specialize in that field. During the Supreme Court's 1986 term, the ACLU participated in cases on such matters as police searches of automobiles, state taxes on newspapers, free speech rights in airports, and affirmative action in local government employment.

The ACLU participates in a great many Supreme Court cases as *amicus,* but its central activity is sponsoring cases. To a great extent, this sponsorship role is triggered by the action of people outside the organization. People bring complaints of civil liberties violations to local ACLU affiliates, which then determine whether to take legal action. Litigation is undertaken primarily by volunteer attorneys attached to affiliates. The national office has a fairly small staff and budget. Its litigation activity comes largely at the Supreme Court level, where it reserves the right to take charge of ACLU cases.

The obvious disadvantage of this system is its fragmentation, which aggravates the difficulty of coordinating litigation and selecting appropriate cases to take to the Supreme Court. The ACLU is not well structured to carry out an ideal litigation strategy. But the ACLU's decentralization makes it accessible to people with civil liberties complaints and thus maximizes the number of potential cases from which the organization can choose. (Not incidentally, ACLU affiliates also can help to solve individual problems without engaging in litigation.)

Certainly the ACLU has been quite active as a Supreme Court litigator. It has aided litigants in such important cases as *Engel v. Vitale* (1962), in which the Court ruled against recitation of prayers in public schools, and *Buckley v. Valeo* (1976), in which the Court struck down part of the Federal Election Campaign Act. Its resources and the skills of its attorneys often make it possible for a significant case to get to the Court and strengthen cases as candidates for hearings by the Court.

During the last two decades the ACLU has operated several special projects that undertake concerted campaigns in specific areas. Among the projects set up are those dealing with capital punishment, children's rights, prisons, and national security. These projects have made a mark; through its Women's Rights Project, for instance, the ACLU has been the primary sponsor of sex discrimination cases decided by the Supreme Court since 1971. Because of the coordination that these projects provide, they offer a useful complement to the traditional mode of ACLU litigation activity.

Conclusions: The Significance of Groups. It is clear that interest groups are heavily involved in Supreme Court litigation, but how important are they in getting cases to the Court? In this respect, cases may be placed in three general categories.

The largest category includes the cases that come to the Court without any participation by interest groups. For the most part, these cases constitute what I have called "ordinary" litigation. The issues in these cases are too narrow to interest any group. These cases get to the Court because the parties and attorneys have sufficient motivation on their own to seek a Supreme Court hearing and sufficient resources to finance the litigation costs. As suggested earlier, these conditions often exist in litigation involving businesses and in criminal cases.

A second category consists of cases in which group help is unnecessary to get to the Court, but one or more groups are involved in some way. An interest group may aid one of the parties with legal services or financing to ensure that the case does reach the Supreme Court and to gain some control over its form. More often, a group supplements the legal arguments of a party with an *amicus* brief. The group's participation may enhance the chances of getting a hearing from the Supreme Court, particularly by providing effective legal arguments in favor of hearing the case.

Finally there are the cases that would not reach the Court without the initiative or aid of interest groups. In areas such as civil liberties there often are important legal questions that no individual litigant has sufficient incentive or capability to take to the Supreme Court. Ordinarily it would be impossible for one parent or even several parents to arrange and finance a school desegregation suit on their own. To take another example, a man named Stephen Wiesenfeld believed that he had been subjected to sex discrimination when he was denied Social Security benefits under statutory rules after his wife's death, but a successful suit against the federal government would have cost more than any benefits that he could have gained. When the ACLU offered to handle his case, he asked only one question: "How much will it cost me?" Because the group would pay all the costs, he agreed to pursue the case, which resulted in a significant Supreme Court decision in 1975.[24]

The general importance of interest groups in the agenda-setting process is greater than the proportions of cases in the second and third categories would indicate. Groups are especially likely to participate in and to sponsor the most significant cases, those that have the potential to produce major legal rulings. According to one study, more than half of the important constitutional cases decided between 1870 and 1969 were sponsored by interest groups.[25] Further, groups have their greatest effect in the civil liberties area, which is most central to the Court's work in the current era. Thus interest groups are of considerable significance in setting the agenda.

The Federal Government as Litigant

Most cases in the Supreme Court have governments as parties, and governments and their officials play important roles as litigants in the Court. State and local governments frequently are called upon to defend their policies in the Court, and it has become common for states to submit *amicus* briefs supporting their interests.[26] Congress comes to the Court as a litigant in cases involving issues such as the legislative veto, and in recent years members of Congress sometimes have submitted *amicus* briefs to the Court offering their interpretations of statutes such as the Voting Rights Act.

The Justice Department, as primary legal representative of the federal government, plays a special role in the Supreme Court, largely because the United States is a party in a high proportion of all federal cases. The Justice Department is the prosecutor in criminal cases and appears in a wide range of civil litigation. As a result, the department is involved in many cases that might come from lower federal courts to the Supreme Court.

At the trial level, litigation decisions for the Justice Department are divided among the U.S. Attorneys who serve in each of the federal judicial districts and lawyers for other federal departments. Decisions to appeal, however, are controlled primarily by the Office of the Solicitor General in the Justice Department, which had twenty-three attorneys in 1987. At the Supreme Court level, this control is almost total; only a few federal agencies can take cases to the Court without the solicitor general's approval. Moreover, the solicitor general's office does most of the legal work in Supreme Court cases in which the federal government participates, including petitions for hearings and oral arguments.

The solicitor general's office stands out for its self-restraint as a legal advocate. One aspect of this restraint is a rationing of requests for hearings from the Supreme Court. In the 1984 term, for instance, the office filed 36 petitions for certiorari, while in 637 cases it decided not to petition. In contrast, the government's opponents filed 1,421 petitions, undoubtedly a much higher proportion of the cases in which such petitions were possible.[27] The office's restraint is the product of a deliberate policy; as former solicitor general Erwin Griswold said, "In effect, the Solicitor General does most of the screening which is done in other cases by the Supreme Court. . . ." [28]

Another aspect of the office's restraint is a willingness to take a more neutral role than other litigants. This relative neutrality is symbolized by the practice of "confessing error"—agreeing with the position of the government's opponent. In a 1987 case, for instance, the office agreed with its opponent that a court of appeals decision affirming a criminal conviction should be overturned. [29] The office's neutrality also has been reflected in a degree of independence from the president and even from the attorney general. Administration officials outside the office have intervened in some cases; President Jimmy Carter and a number of officials, for instance, helped to determine the government's position in the *Bakke* case on affirmative action in school admissions. [30] But to a surprising degree the solicitor general has been left alone. Notably, lawyers often remain in the office when a new president takes office. Griswold was solicitor general in both the Johnson and Nixon administrations, and Philip Elman was the civil rights specialist in the office from 1944 to 1961.

The self-restraint of the solicitor general's office is both cause and effect of a unique relationship with the Supreme Court, which might be called a quasi-partnership. For example, the Court provides an office for the solicitor general's staff to use at the Court. The Court frequently requests the solicitor general to participate in a case as *amicus* by submitting a brief or offering oral argument. Unlike the situation with other litigants and lawyers, justices interact with lawyers in the solicitor general's office, both formally and informally, with some frequency.

This relationship is based in part on the credibility of the solicitor general. The justices know that the government ordinarily will petition for certiorari only in the cases that are most deserving of hearings. They also expect that the solicitor general's arguments can be relied upon more than those of most other parties; Justice William Douglas once expressed his appreciation that he could rely even on the footnotes in a brief from the solicitor general. [31] This is one reason that the Court is inclined to treat the federal government more favorably than other parties.

Some observers perceived a change in the relationship between the Court and the solicitor general during the Reagan administration. The administration came into office with the goal of moving the Court in a conservative direction on a variety of issues. Reflecting this goal, Justice Department officials outside the solicitor general's office had more direct influence on litigation decisions than in most past administrations. The solicitor general's office pressed the administration's policy positions on the Court to an unusual degree, especially in the second term. It took a sweeping position against affirmative action, for instance, and asked the Court to overrule its 1973 decision legalizing abortion.

As a result, some observers believed, the Court's collective attitude toward the solicitor general became less favorable. In 1987 one justice was quoted anonymously as saying, "I look at things from the SG's office a lot more closely than I felt I had to in the days of anyone else." [32] Some Court opinions criticized the government's arguments or refuted them at length.[33] The Court also seemed less willing than in the past to let the solicitor general participate as *amicus* in oral argument.[34]

The change in the office's position, though significant, was not fundamental. Rex Lee, who served as solicitor general from 1981 to 1985, was heavily criticized by conservatives for maintaining considerable independence from the administration. Charles Fried, his successor, seemed to follow administration positions more faithfully. But he too felt free to take an independent line, and by 1988 disappointed conservatives were attacking him as well. The solicitor general's office still maintained its special position in the Court, one that gives it a significant advantage over other litigants.

Deciding What to Hear: The Court's Role

Overview

When a litigant brings a case to the Supreme Court, the Court decides whether to hear the case. If it refuses to hear the case, as it did 94 percent of the time in the 1986 term,[35] it leaves the lower court decision standing. If it accepts the case, the Court will decide whether to affirm the lower court or overturn its decision to some degree. But the Court's choices are broader and more complicated than this simple dichotomy suggests.

First, the Court does not screen petitions for hearing in isolation from each other; often, cases are linked. The justices may accept a case to clarify or expand on an earlier decision in the same policy area. They may accept several cases raising the same issue to address that issue more fully than a single case would allow. They may even reject a case because they are looking for a more suitable case on the same issue.

A second complication was noted earlier: when the Court accepts a case, it retains choices as to which issues in the case it will address. The Court can limit its grant of certiorari to one issue raised by the petitioner, or it can ask the parties to address an issue that neither had raised. After it hears a case, the Court can choose whether to address the broadest legal questions in the case or to decide it on narrower grounds. These choices are sometimes a matter of contention. In a 1985 decision, Chief Justice Burger chastised the Court's majority for what he considered evasion of the constitutional issue in the case, and Justice Stevens has attacked the Court for bringing new issues into some cases.[36]

Finally, if the Court accepts a case, it can handle the case in different ways. It may provide "full treatment," including oral argument before the Court and a decision on the merits with a full opinion explaining the decision. Alternatively, it may give the case summary treatment. Most often, this means that the case is decided without oral argument and that the Court issues only a brief, uninformative opinion that is labeled *per curiam* ("by the Court") rather than being signed by a justice. About one third of the cases that the Court accepts receive summary treatment.

The choice of summary treatment for a case is often routine. For instance, after the Court lays down a new rule of law, it may accept other cases simply to return them to the lower courts to reconsider in light of the new rule. But sometimes this choice is less routine, and over the past several years the Court has been divided over some uses of summary decisions. Liberal justices have complained that the Court is overusing this mode of decision as a means to overturn liberal rulings by lower courts. Sometimes, these justices argue that a case deserves full treatment because of its importance or complexity; at other times, they argue that a case is too trivial to be decided at all. But their fundamental concern is the use of summary decisions to reach conservative results. In a 1986 decision, Justice Brennan cited a "trend to grant summary dispositions only in favor of the prosecutor" in criminal cases. Noting that prosecutors had won twenty-six of the last thirty summary decisions in which they were parties, he wrote that "only a one-sided exercise of discretion can explain these results." [37]

Procedures

The Court's procedures for the screening of petitions are somewhat complex. I will look first at the treatment of two special types of cases and then discuss screening procedures more generally.

The Handling of Mandatory Cases. Until recently, several types of cases came to the Court as appeals. While appeals accounted for fewer than 10 percent of the cases brought to the Court, there were enough to constitute a significant burden if all actually were decided. Because of this potential burden, and because the justices considered many of them to be unimportant, the Court used summary decisions to evade the statutory requirement that appeals must be heard. Parties who brought appeals had to file a statement of the grounds on which they contended that their cases merited hearing. Their opponents then could request that the Court dismiss the appeal or summarily affirm the lower court decision. The Court was not reluctant to grant such requests; in a sample of terms in the 1970s and 1980s, about 80 percent of the appeals were dismissed or summarily affirmed. [38] But the Court gave full consideration to a higher proportion of appeals than of discretionary cases.

In 1988, after several years of urging by members of the Court, Congress eliminated all mandatory appeals except in the few cases in special categories that are decided by three-judge federal district courts. These cases are unlikely to impose a heavy burden on the Court. But its rules continue to allow for summary decisions in appeals, and the justices may use this device to avoid cases that they see as unworthy of their time.

Paupers' Cases.   About half of the requests for hearing that arrive at the Supreme Court are "paid" cases, in which the Court's filing fee of $200 is paid and all required copies of materials are provided. The other half are filed *in forma pauperis,* by indigent persons for whom the fee and requirement of multiple copies are waived. Perhaps 80 percent of the "paupers' cases" are criminal, brought primarily by prisoners in federal and state institutions. (A person responding to a petition also may be given pauper's status.)

Criminal defendants who have had appointed counsel in the lower federal courts automatically are entitled to file paupers' cases. Other litigants must support with an affidavit their motion for leave to file as paupers. The Court has never developed precise rules as to when a litigant can claim pauper's status, and traditionally it focused on the petition for hearing rather than passing on the question of pauper status. In the 1980s the Court has taken a different approach, frequently denying motions for pauper's status that it views as unjustified. Justices Brennan and Marshall regularly dissent from these denials, and they are often joined by Justices Blackmun and Stevens. The dissenters argue that it would be more efficient simply to deny a writ of certiorari when a petition is clearly unmeritorious. But in one case three of the dissenters indicated that they might follow the majority's approach in extreme cases, such as one in which a person with approximately $1 million in net assets sought pauper's status.[39]

The paupers' cases have been handled by the Court in a somewhat different way from the paid cases. Until 1970 they were placed on a separate docket, and even now they are listed separately on the Court's docket. Until the 1970s these cases were reviewed by the chief justice's law clerks, and other justices received materials only on cases deemed to merit serious consideration. Under Chief Justice Burger the procedure for handling paupers' cases became similar to that for paid cases.

Most of the petitions from indigent persons are rejected as having little merit. In the 1986 term, about 1 percent were accepted for decisions on the merits, in contrast with 12 percent for the paid cases.[40] Even so, the paupers' cases are an important source for the Court's decisions on issues of criminal procedure, because few convicted defendants can afford to meet the Court's requirements for paid cases.

Prescreening: The Discuss List. The ultimate decision to hear a case is made at the Court's conference. But not all requests for hearing are discussed at conference. Under a procedure that reached its present form in the 1970s, the chief justice places cases on what is called the "discuss list," to be voted on in conference, if they are thought to merit full consideration. All other cases are denied hearings automatically unless another justice asks that they be added to the discuss list.

At least 70 percent of petitions fail to get on the discuss list, so this prescreening procedure is a significant one.[41] Of the cases that do reach the list, the majority are placed on the list by the chief justice. Other justices vary considerably in the numbers of cases that they add to the list.[42]

The discuss list procedure is intended to limit the Court's workload. The Court now receives more than 4,000 cases each term, and elimination of discussion for most of these cases saves the justices considerable time. But the justices also feel that most petitions do not require collective consideration, because they have essentially no chance of receiving the necessary four votes. A great many petitions are poor candidates for acceptance because they raise narrow issues, often focusing on the facts of the specific case. In 1983 Chief Justice Burger estimated that something like two-thirds of the petitions for hearing are "utterly frivolous." [43] Although other justices might disagree with this figure, some petitions clearly are frivolous by any standard. A good example is the three cases that one litigant brought to set aside the 1980 presidential election, followed by another attacking the 1984 election.[44]

Action in Conference. The cases on the discuss list are considered and voted upon in conference.[45] The chief justice or the justice who added a case to the discuss list will open discussion of the case. In order of seniority, from senior to junior, the justices speak and generally announce their votes. If the discussion does not make justices' positions clear, a formal vote will be taken in the same order. One kind of vote that some justices cast is a "join 3," meaning that they will provide the necessary fourth vote if three colleagues have voted to hear the case; one justice characterized this as "a timid vote to grant." [46] Despite this practice and the prescreening of weak cases, a majority of petitions considered in conference are denied.

Most cases receive very brief discussion in conference, and ordinarily justices simply state the positions that they have reached individually before the conference. In this sense, the conference usually serves only as a place for individual votes to be added together. This is true even though justices often disagree: In the 1947-1958 terms little more than half the conference decisions were unanimous, and in the 1981 term 29 percent of the accepted cases received the bare minimum of four votes.[47]

But some cases are given more extensive consideration, and this consideration can go beyond the initial discussion. In conference any justice can ask that a case be "relisted" for a later conference. This might be done to obtain additional information, such as the full record of the case from the lower courts. A justice also might ask for relisting to circulate an opinion dissenting from the Court's tentative denial of a hearing and thus try to change the Court's decision. As Justice Stevens once noted, such an opinion "sometimes persuades other Justices to change their votes and a petition is granted that would otherwise have been denied." [48] On rare occasions, a case will be considered over a long period; reportedly, a 1985 case involving state regulation of abortion was debated for several months before the Court granted a hearing. [49]

When it accepts a case, the Court also decides whether to allow oral argument or to decide the case summarily on the basis of the available written materials. Four votes are required for oral argument. When the Court hears oral argument it generally decides the case with a full opinion, so the case receives what I have called full treatment; when oral argument is bypassed, the decision usually is announced with a very brief *per curiam* opinion. A case given less than full treatment may be granted a hearing and decided on the merits at the same conference, so that the two stages of decision in effect become one.

No opinion is written for the Court to explain its acceptance or rejection of a case, and ordinarily no individual votes are announced. But justices increasingly record their dissents from denials of petitions for hearing. In the 1986 term, 499 dissenting votes were announced in 267 cases. Many dissenting votes are accompanied by opinions, which often originated as efforts to convince colleagues to hear a case. In recent years most dissenting votes (about three-quarters in the 1986 term) have announced objections by Brennan and Marshall to the denial of hearings in capital punishment cases, with restatements of their belief that the Court should overturn the death penalty in all cases. On rare occasions, a justice will publish an opinion concurring with a denial or grant of certiorari or dissenting from a grant.

The Clerks' Role.   Probably the most important function of justices' law clerks is to help in scrutinizing requests for hearings. Clerks carry out this function primarily by writing memoranda, which typically summarize the relevant facts and the parties' contentions and recommend whether the case should be accepted. Since 1972, several justices have pooled their resources by designating a single clerk to prepare a memo for their mutual use in each case. That memo is then supplemented by clerks serving each justice. The justices who do not participate in the pool—as of 1988, Brennan, Marshall, and Stevens—rely entirely on their own clerks.

The clerks receive surprisingly little guidance in learning how to write memos. Chief Justice Rehnquist has reported that he was basically left on his own when he became a clerk.[50] Gradually clerks develop a feel for the job, which includes a sense of what their justice wants in a memo.

The press of work makes the usual clerk's memo rather dull and routine, but there are occasional exceptions. One such exception, produced by one of Justice Harold Burton's clerks in the 1954 term, merits quotation to illustrate the weakness of some requests for hearing:

> Petitioner is a big Cadillac dealer who got caught buying the local Alderman; he has been fighting conviction for four years; his case has no merit and his brief is replete with overstatements, innuendo, speculation, and almost untruth. It would be a crime to touch this case.[51]

As noted in Chapter 1, the influence of the clerks has been debated. The potential for clerks' influence in the screening of petitions varies among the justices. Justice Stevens relies heavily on his clerks; he reported in 1982 that his clerks examine all the petitions "and select a small minority that they believe I should read myself. As a result, I do not even look at the papers in over 80 percent of the cases that are filed." [52] In contrast, Justice Brennan has his clerks work on petitions for hearing only during the summer and occasionally on cases for which he wants more information. With these exceptions he handles the petitions himself, often reaching judgments on them quickly.[53]

Brennan seems to be unique in this respect; the other justices give larger roles to their clerks, roles that involve significant decision-making power. For the most part, however, clerks can be expected to exercise this power in a way consistent with the needs and goals of their justices. Moreover, justices are aware of the potential loss of control that their delegation of responsibility to their clerks entails, and this awareness undoubtedly increases their independence from their clerks' recommendations.

The Criteria for Decision

The Supreme Court's decisions on requests for hearings clearly are significant. These decisions determine which litigants are given a chance to challenge unfavorable decisions. They also determine which policy issues the Court addresses. In this section I will examine the criteria on which these decisions are based, focusing on the Court's selection of cases to be given full treatment in its decisions on their merits.

The Court offers only limited guidance concerning its decisions whether to hear specific cases. Frequently the Court's opinion on a case offers an explanation of its acceptance of that case, but the rationale tends to be brief and unilluminating. The Court seldom explains denials of petitions for hearing.

The Court does provide some general guidance on its treatment of petitions. Its Rule 17 proclaims some of the conditions under which the Court will hear a case. The rule emphasizes the Court's role in enhancing the certainty and consistency of the law: The criteria it lists for accepting a case include the existence of important legal issues that the Court has not yet decided, conflict among courts of appeals on a legal question, conflict between a lower court and the Supreme Court's prior decisions, and departure "from the accepted and usual course of judicial proceedings" in the courts below.

These criteria make sense, but they suggest a conception of the Court's function and of its members' interests that is unrealistically narrow. Accordingly, it is necessary to take a broader view of the criteria for decision. Evidence from the Court's pattern of screening decisions and from other sources suggests the significance of several criteria, which I will discuss in succession.

The Technical Criteria.   To merit acceptance by the Supreme Court a case must meet certain technical requirements. First of all, the petition for hearing must comply with the Court's rules. A petition may be denied, for instance, because the petitioner has not supplied the required number of copies of the papers in the case. These requirements are relaxed for the paupers' petitions, but even these petitions may be denied if their deviation from the rules is extreme.

More important, the Court imposes the same kinds of general technical requirements for the hearing of cases that other courts apply. The most fundamental requirements are jurisdiction and standing. The Court's jurisdiction was discussed in Chapter 1. If the Court receives a case that clearly falls outside its jurisdiction, it cannot accept the case for hearing. For instance, the Court could not hear a state case in which the petitioner raised no issues of federal law. Further, the Court rejects petitions from litigants who try to attach federal issues to cases that clearly involve only state law.

The rule of standing holds that a court may not hear a case unless the party that brings the case is properly before it. Standing is a complex concept with several aspects. It primarily concerns the requirement that a party in a case have a real and direct stake in its outcome. This requirement precludes hypothetical cases, cases brought on behalf of another person, "friendly suits" between persons who are not really adversaries, and cases that have become "moot" (purely academic) because the parties no longer can be affected by the outcome.

One effect of the standing requirement is to complicate the task of challenging governmental practices on constitutional grounds. Individuals or groups unhappy with a particular practice cannot bring suit in their own names unless they have a direct personal stake; if they do not, a party with that stake must be found to serve as the official challenger. The NAACP Legal Defense Fund cannot challenge school segregation in its own name. Rather, in each district it must support cases brought in the names of students in the district.

Even after the Court accepts a case, it may determine that jurisdiction or standing is lacking and dismiss the case, no matter how important the issues involved. In two 1987 cases the Court held that a dispute over the president's power to kill legislation through a pocket veto had become moot and that the Court lacked jurisdiction to decide a challenge to a New Jersey law creating a "minute of silence" period in the state's public schools.[54]

Because of their complexity and ambiguity, the rules of jurisdiction and standing require occasional interpretation, and as the highest federal court the Supreme Court is the most important interpreter. In recent years the Court has dealt with such issues as the standing of environmental groups to challenge projects that may damage the environment. In deciding these issues, the Court helps to determine access to all federal courts including itself.

The technical requirements are not always easy to interpret, and justices sometimes differ in their interpretations. In a 1988 decision, for instance, the justices disagreed as to whether the case was moot.[55] Often, such disagreements reflect the views of justices about the underlying merits of cases. The justices most likely to grant standing to environmental groups generally are those who are most favorable to the policy positions of those groups. As this example indicates, the rules of jurisdiction and standing are not only requirements imposed upon the Court but also means by which the Court itself can regulate access to its judgments in accord with its members' goals.

The technical criteria serve as preliminary screening devices by which some cases are eliminated. But most cases meet these criteria, and the Court must use others to choose among them.

Conflict Between Courts.   One of the criteria suggested by Rule 17 is the existence of conflicting legal interpretations between courts, such as a conflict between federal courts of appeals or between a state or federal appellate court and the Supreme Court. The existence of a conflict should provide the justices with an incentive to hear a case, both to enhance the consistency of the law and—where the conflict is with the Court's own decision—to vindicate its authority as the highest court. Indeed, we might expect the Court to accept any case involving intercourt conflict.

Conflict does strongly incline the Court to hear a case. A substantial minority of the cases that the Court accepts involve conflicts among courts, and frequently the existence of a conflict seems to be the primary reason that a case is heard. Most law clerks interviewed by H. W. Perry said that the first thing they looked for in a petition was a genuine conflict.[56] Research by Gregory Caldeira and John Wright found that intercourt conflict was one of the strongest factors inclining the Court to accept a case.[57]

But the Court does not automatically accept cases in which there is a possible conflict between courts, in part because justices differ in the priority they give to resolving conflicts.[58] Each term Justice White writes a number of dissenting opinions where the Court denies certiorari but he feels that the case should be heard because a conflict exists; he wrote eighteen such opinions in the 1986 term. The presence of a conflict is often ambiguous, so commentators disagree on the number of conflicts the Court refuses to resolve. It is clear, however, that an apparent conflict does not guarantee a hearing by the Court.

Whether a conflict case is accepted depends in part on the extent of the conflict. Another key criterion is the practical effect of the conflict. Some conflicts are so serious that the Court may have little choice but to resolve them, while others are more tolerable. But occasionally the Court allows conflicts to continue even if they seem fairly serious. In 1986 it refused to hear a challenge to states' use of roadblocks to detect drunk driving, even though many states used them and state courts had disagreed as to whether they violated the constitutional protection against unreasonable searches and seizures.[59]

Importance.   The importance of the issues in a case is a second criterion suggested by Rule 17, and it seems to be very useful in explaining the Court's screening decisions. It is reasonable for the justices to emphasize importance as a criterion; the best way for the Court to maximize its impact is to decide the cases that affect the most people and include the most significant policy issues.

The criterion of importance eliminates from consideration a high proportion of the cases that come to the Court. Since 1980 the Court's rules have required that petitions for hearing list the "questions presented" by the case on the very first page, and a perusal of petitions makes it clear why the Court does so: in a great many cases the questions presented almost certainly are too narrow to merit the Court's attention. Yet even cases that seem to be of minor importance will be heard from time to time, particularly if four justices perceive a grave injustice in a lower court decision. In 1987 Justice Stevens criticized his colleagues for accepting a case in which the facts were "surely unique" and "do not give rise to any issue of general or recurring significance." [60]

A case may seem important to members of the Court for various reasons. A few individual cases are important in themselves, aside from the broader legal issues that they contain; a good example is the 1974 case concerning President Nixon's duty to surrender tape recordings of his conversations to a federal court. Other cases, such as serious challenges to the constitutionality of major statutes, raise legal issues of obvious significance. *Amicus* briefs may suggest that a case is important. Caldeira and Wright found that a petition for certiorari was more likely to be accepted if *amicus* briefs were submitted; even a brief *opposing* the granting of certiorari increased the chances that a case would be heard.[61] At a more general level, one or more justices may feel that certain policy areas merit attention because of their importance. This feeling helps to account for the Court's long-standing interest in federalism cases and the prominence of civil liberties cases on its agenda in the current era.

Although a case that appears to be important has a relatively good chance to be accepted by the Court, it is common for the Court to reject such cases. Justices may vote against hearing them for a variety of reasons, including their agreement with the lower court decision in a case and a desire to delay before tackling a difficult issue. The latter reason may explain the Court's 1986 refusal to hear either of two cases raising the issue of when court-ordered busing in a school district could be terminated, an issue with enormous impact and one on which the two lower court decisions seemed to conflict.[62] Seldom, if ever, is a case so important that the justices feel compelled to hear it.

Policy Preferences. Rule 17 does not mention justices' personal values as a basis for case-screening decisions. But inevitably justices respond to petitions for hearing in part on the basis of their policy preferences. Because acceptance and rejection of cases is such an important part of the Court's policy making, members of the Court hardly could resist use of the agenda-setting process as a way to advance their policy goals.

The most straightforward effect of justices' concern with their policy goals is that they are more likely to vote to accept a case when they disagree with the position of the lower court. Chief Justice Rehnquist has said that "the most common reason members of our Court vote to grant certiorari is that they doubt the correctness of the decision of the lower court." [63] Justices and clerks have attested that cases sometimes are accepted simply because the decision under review was "egregious." [64] These statements suggest that the Court will overturn most of the lower court decisions that it reviews, and this is indeed true; in certiorari cases with full opinions in the 1986 term, the affirmance rate was only 32 percent.[65] While evaluation of the lower court's action is hardly the Court's only consideration, it is an important one.

Of course, justices' evaluations of lower court decisions are based largely on their ideological positions. A liberal justice will be most skeptical of conservative decisions. In the 1947-1956 terms, for instance, the Court's liberals were more likely than conservatives to vote to hear criminal cases when the defendant had lost in the lower courts.[66] When justices record their dissents from certiorari denials, liberals usually want to review conservative decisions, while conservatives want to review liberal decisions.

As a result, the Court's ideological center of gravity influences the kinds of cases that it accepts. Because of the conservative shift in the Court's membership in the 1970s and 1980s, the Court has become more willing to accept cases in which the lower court reached a liberal result. Caldeira and Wright found that by the 1982 term the Court was significantly more likely to accept a case with a liberal result, even if other case characteristics were taken into account.[67]

This shift is particularly clear in criminal cases, where the Court's collective point of view has changed sharply. As Table 3-2 shows, the Warren Court accepted primarily cases brought by defendants, while the Burger and Rehnquist Courts have been relatively willing to accept cases brought by prosecutors. The Court's recent support for prosecutors is even stronger than the figures suggest, since the great majority of all petitions in criminal cases come from defendants. The Court's liberals have complained bitterly about their colleagues' interest in hearing cases brought by prosecutors. In one dissent, Justice Stevens said that the Court's eagerness to hear cases in which the lower courts had suppressed evidence from a police search "encouraged state legal officers to file petitions for certiorari in even the most frivolous search and seizure cases."[68]

A more complex effect of justices' policy preferences is that they may take into account an estimate of what the Court would decide if a particular case were accepted. It is common for justices to vote against hearing a case because they fear that the Court would reach a result they dislike if the case were accepted. H. W. Perry found that justices and clerks routinely referred to this practice as "defensive denials." As one justice told Perry, "I might think the Nebraska Supreme Court made a horrible decision, but I wouldn't want to take the case, for if we take the case and affirm it, then it would become a precedent."[69] On the other side, justices who think that the Court would decide a case in accord with their preferences may vote to hear it for that reason. But this strategy is more difficult, because the Court's general inclination is to reject cases rather than accept them.[70]

Defensive denials are especially appealing to the members of the Court's ideological minority at a given time, since they have the most reason to fear the Court's prospective decisions. In the Burger and

Table 3-2   Criminal Cases Decided by the Supreme Court After Oral Argument, by Petitioning Party, in Selected Terms

	Percentage filed by	
Terms	Defendant	Prosecutor
1965-1966	79.5	20.5
1970-1971	69.1	30.9
1975-1976	49.3	50.7
1980-1981	41.7	58.3
1985-1986	43.8	56.2

Notes: The percentages are the total for cases decided in the two terms listed. The term *prosecutor* includes all parties in opposition to defendants in the categories of cases included. Cases are included if they arose from criminal prosecutions, including postconviction challenges to trial and pretrial procedures. Cases concerning parole and prison conditions are excluded.

Rehnquist Courts, liberals seem more inclined than conservatives to take into account the Court's likely decision when they vote whether to hear a case. As long ago as 1975, a reporter indicated that "the liberal Justices have an 'unwritten agreement' to try to keep many cases out of the hands of the Court so long as the conservatives have the five-vote majority needed to carry a decision." [71] Whether or not that report is accurate, some version of this strategy almost surely existed, and it probably has become even stronger as the Court's membership has become more conservative.

Identity of the Petitioner.   Some litigants and interest groups are more successful than others in getting their cases heard by the Supreme Court. To some extent, this variation may simply reflect the policy positions that they take and the perceived importance of the issues in which they are involved. The success of the NAACP Legal Defense Fund has resulted in part from the sympathy of most recent justices for the civil rights positions that it espouses. Another reason for the success of certain litigants and groups is their skills in developing litigation and presenting cases. The attitudes of the justices toward a litigant may also make a difference. In interviews with justices, O'Connor and Epstein found that at least some are favorably disposed to hear cases brought by interest groups in whose work they have confidence.[72] Other litigants are viewed less favorably. Justice Marshall, who is ordinarily sympathetic to criminal defendants, has said, "If it's a dope case, I won't even read the petition. I ain't giving no break to no drug dealer." [73]

The one party whose identity has the greatest impact on the Court's responses to petitions for hearing is the federal government. Earlier in this chapter I discussed the government's behavior as a litigant; here I will look at its success in obtaining hearings. That success is striking. Over the 1959-1984 terms, the Court accepted 69 percent of the federal government's petitions for certiorari and 82 percent of petitions brought by other parties and supported by the government with an *amicus* brief. In contrast, petitions not brought or supported by the federal government had a 5 percent success rate.[74]

The government's success should not be exaggerated. In policy areas of little interest to the Court a relatively low proportion of government petitions is accepted. Further, the government—like other litigants—does best when its arguments are ideologically acceptable to at least four justices. But the solicitor general's overall record is quite impressive.

The federal government's success can be ascribed to the fact that it is what Marc Galanter calls a "repeat player," a litigant engaged in many related cases over time.[75] The federal government has far more cases that it could take to the Supreme Court than does any other party. This situation provides at least three advantages to the government.

First, by bringing only a small minority of a large pool of cases to the Court, the solicitor general can select those whose characteristics make them most likely to be accepted. Almost any litigant who could be so selective would enjoy a fairly high rate of success in the Supreme Court.

Second, the solicitor general's selectivity earns some gratitude from the Court and builds credibility as well. If the federal government brought petitions at the high rates of other litigants, the Court's caseload problems would be aggravated considerably. Thus the solicitor general plays an important role in easing pressures on the Court. The justices reciprocate by viewing the government's petitions in a favorable light. Further, the justices know that the government takes to the Court only the cases that its lawyers deem most worthy, so they too are inclined to view those cases as worthy.

Finally, the attorneys in the solicitor general's office handle a great many Supreme Court cases, so they can develop an unusual degree of expertise. Few other lawyers learn as much about how to appeal to the Court's interests. As a result, the government can do more than most other litigants to make cases appear worthy of acceptance.

At least through the 1984 term, the Reagan administration maintained the high success rate of its predecessors; in 1983 and 1984, 80 percent of its certiorari petitions were accepted.[76] Its aggressive litigation program may have weakened its credibility with the Court, but for the most part the sources of the federal government's success, particularly the solicitor general's selectivity in submitting petitions for hearing, continued to work in its favor.

Avoiding Problematic Cases. Whatever their value in other respects, some cases will be rejected by the Court because of characteristics
that make their acceptance inconvenient. These characteristics are of two
types.

First, the facts of some cases may be inappropriate, particularly in
relation to the decision the justices expect to reach. The facts may be too
muddled to allow a clear decision, or they may require justices to reach a
decision on grounds different from the ones they would like to use. In
other cases, the circumstances of a dispute or the identity of the litigants
may cast an unfavorable light on the Court's likely decision.

Sometimes the justices select the "best" case on an issue after
rejecting a large number of related cases because of their facts. In 1961
members of the Court had resolved that they would establish the right
of indigents to a free attorney in felony cases. Then, with their clerks,
the justices searched for a case whose facts were appropriate for the
establishment of that principle. A large number of cases were rejected
before Clarence Gideon's petition was accepted. His case was ideal for
the Court's purposes, in part because it involved the relatively minor
felony of breaking and entering a poolroom with intent to commit a
misdemeanor. A reversal of Gideon's conviction would arouse less
public wrath than would the reversal of a conviction for a violent
offense.

Second, justices may seek to avoid issues altogether because of their
controversial character, which can make them difficult to decide and—
more important—can make the Court vulnerable to attack for the
decisions that it does reach. One good example is the Court's refusal to
rule on the constitutionality of American participation in the war in
Vietnam. Few issues brought before the Court have been as important,
but the Court refused to hear the cases that raised this question between
1967 and 1972. In recent years the Court has ducked such controversial
issues as the comparable worth theory of sex discrimination in employment and the conditions under which school busing orders can be
terminated.

This does not mean, of course, that the Court uniformly refuses to
decide the most controversial issues; quite frequently, it does rule on
such issues. Sometimes the Court accepts a case after rejecting others
raising the same difficult question over a period of time, thereby
allowing the issue to "percolate" and gaining the benefit of several
lower court decisions. In recent terms the Court has dealt with such
matters as partisan gerrymandering of state legislatures, criminal prohibitions of homosexual behavior, and affirmative action programs in
employment. In light of the difficulties that decisions on such issues can
create for the Court, it is noteworthy that the justices address as many
controversial issues as they do.

Conclusion. As this discussion suggests, the Court's decisions whether or not to hear cases are based upon a complex set of considerations. This complexity should not be surprising, given the variety of goals that justices are interested in advancing.

It should be clear that votes whether to hear cases are subjective decisions, which depend upon the values and perspectives of the justices. Individual justices differ in the priority they give to resolving conflicts between lower courts. They assess the importance of cases in various ways. And they differ fundamentally in their policy preferences.

It follows that the selection of cases to decide fully, like everything else that the Court does, is affected by the membership of the Court at a given time. Many cases are unlikely to be accepted no matter who is on the Court. But the composition of the few dozen that the Supreme Court actually does accept will be largely a function of who the justices are in a given term.

Caseload Growth and the Court's Burdens

The Growth in Caseload

The Process of Growth. Litigants brought 4,493 cases to the Supreme Court during the 1987 term. That figure reflects a massive increase in the number of filings during the 1950s and 1960s, followed by a more moderate increase in the 1970s and a significant but more limited increase in the 1980s. The growth in the Court's caseload is depicted in Figure 3-1, which shows that the Court's caseload in the 1980s was double that of the 1958-1962 period and more than three times that of the 1948-1952 period.

The growth in the Court's business has come disproportionately in certain areas.[77] Perhaps most important, the number of criminal cases has risen tremendously. Fifty years ago, the great majority of the Court's cases were civil. Since then, criminal cases have increased in number to the point that they constitute about half of a much larger docket.

Criminal cases usually involve issues of constitutional due process, and in that respect they comprise part of a general growth in civil liberties cases brought to the Court. Half a century ago, cases concerned with constitutional freedoms, other than those arising from regulation of business, were fairly rare. Now constitutional cases dominate the Court's docket, and the largest portion of these cases raise civil liberties issues.

Explaining the Growth. The spectacular growth in the Court's caseload, with the attendant changes in the composition of that caseload, has stemmed from several sources. One of these sources is societal change. First of all, the population of the United States has increased

Figure 3-1 Cases Filed in Supreme Court, by Five-Year Averages, 1948-1987 Terms

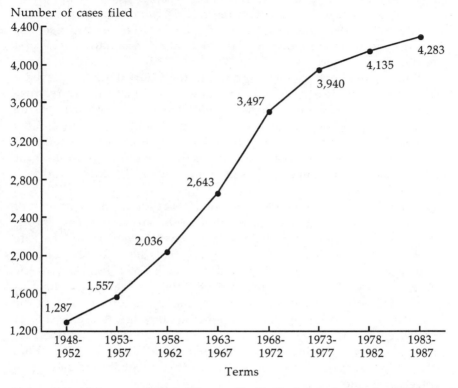

Number of cases filed

Sources: Gerhard Casper and Richard Posner, *The Workload of the Supreme Court* (Chicago: American Bar Foundation, 1976), 3; "Statistical Recap of Supreme Court's Workload," *United States Law Week*, vols. 44-57.

about 60 percent since 1950, and that growth in population might have produced a similar increase in litigation even if nothing else had changed. Not just the Supreme Court but most other government institutions as well have been subject to an increasing volume of demands for action. During the same period, according to the best estimates, crime has increased far more rapidly than population. This increase inevitably has affected the Supreme Court's criminal caseload. Finally, there has been a general growth in "rights consciousness," in which Americans have shown an increased willingness to take action— including litigation—to protect what they see as their rights. The single most important example of increased rights consciousness is the black civil rights movement, which has been directly responsible for an impressive number of Supreme Court cases.

A second source of the growth is congressional action, particularly the adoption of legislation that creates new sources of litigation. The civil rights legislation of the 1960s and 1970s provided an important basis for legal action. So did economic legislation such as the Social Security Act of 1935, the environmental laws of the last two decades, and the considerable expansion of the federal criminal laws in the past few decades.

Finally, and perhaps most important, the Court itself has played a major role. Most clearly, its willingness to waive its ordinary requirements for the filing of cases has made possible the growth of the paupers' petitions so that they now constitute about half of the Court's caseload. The Court's establishment of the right to counsel for indigent criminal defendants and its elimination of the cost of the first appeal for indigent defendants have increased tremendously the opportunity to challenge convictions.

The Court's general policy direction also has spurred the growth of certain kinds of litigation. Since the 1940s the Court has shown considerable sympathy for challenges to government action that are based on alleged violations of civil liberties. This sympathy has encouraged those with civil liberties-related grievances to bring cases to the Court. The Court's support for civil liberties probably has had its greatest impact in two issue areas: criminal procedure, in which the Court has encouraged appeals by defendants through its tightening of due process requirements; and equality, in which the Court's support for equality for racial minorities and other disadvantaged groups has spurred challenges to government action that allegedly violates equal protection of the laws.

In light of all these forces, why has the rate of growth in the Court's caseload slowed so dramatically in recent years? Part of the answer probably is that some of these forces—the growth in rights consciousness and in crime, the Court's opening of access to the indigent and to criminal defendants—had exerted almost their full impact by the mid-1970s. The same is true of the Court's receptivity to civil liberties claims; indeed, its reduced sympathy for such claims in the 1970s and 1980s probably has discouraged some potential litigants from coming to the Court. Thus the caseload may remain relatively stable unless new sources of growth arise.

Responding to Caseload Growth

A Historical View. The growth in the Court's caseload in the last few decades is not unprecedented. During most periods in the Court's history there has been substantial growth in the number of cases brought to the Court.

At least since the late nineteenth century, increases in the Court's business have led to complaints by the justices that they were overburdened and unable to handle their work effectively. As a result, members of the Court and sympathetic observers have sought to provide it with greater control over its docket through an expansion in its discretion whether to hear cases.

Congress has responded favorably in several instances. Two of these instances were particularly important. The first was the Court of Appeals Act of 1891, which created a new set of intermediate appellate courts and gave the Court discretionary jurisdiction over a large proportion of cases for the first time. The second was the Judiciary Act of 1925. This act provided that most cases would come to the Court as requests for writs of certiorari, which the Court could reject, rather than as mandatory appeals. The result was to expand considerably the Court's ability to choose the cases it would hear. The Supreme Court's jurisdiction has changed relatively little since that time.

The impact of the 1925 statute was tremendous. Its most obvious effect was to limit justices' workloads by allowing them to concentrate on a limited portion of the cases brought to them. More subtly, the Court obtained greater freedom to shape its own scope of activity, to determine the kinds of issues it would address and its role as a policy maker. The justices have used that freedom to concentrate on what they see as the most significant and worthy issues raised by the cases that come to the Court. As a result, according to one commentator, the Court evolved from "a supreme corrector of errors" to "the effective arbiter of the federal form of government."[78]

Current Concerns. The 1925 law gave the Court freedom to determine which cases it would hear fully, but it could not prevent continued growth in the number of cases and legal issues brought to the Court. With that growth, justices and observers of the Court increasingly have argued that the Court is overburdened. The Court's burdens in turn are seen as creating problems for the Court itself and for the federal law.

For the Court itself, the perceived problem is that the Court's capacity to do its job effectively is compromised. The Court is faced with more petitions for hearing to screen and more cases that seem to merit full consideration. As a result, the justices can give less careful consideration to their work, particularly to each case that they hear fully. Two legal scholars, for instance, argue that the Court's burdens have led to a "sleaziness of the opinions on the merits."[79] Some commentators also argue that increasing workloads and a resulting growth in the responsibilities of law clerks have weakened the Court by reducing justices' control over the Court's output.

For the federal law, the perceived problem is one of uniformity and consistency. As the numbers of federal cases and judges have increased, so has the potential for conflicting interpretations of the law. But there is a limit to the number of cases that the Supreme Court can accept. Therefore, according to Justice White and others, the Court fails to resolve a good many conflicts in the law and thus leaves the law too unsettled.

Shortly after he came to the Court, Chief Justice Burger began to call attention to these problems, and in 1971 he created a Study Group on the Caseload of the Supreme Court to propose solutions. While some colleagues supported Burger's efforts, during the 1970s liberals on the Court such as Douglas and Brennan argued that Burger exaggerated the problems. Apparently the liberals feared that measures to reduce the Court's workload also would reduce its role as a protector of civil liberties.

By the early 1980s there was more of a consensus among the justices that the Court faced serious problems. In 1982 and 1983 a majority of the justices talked about workload issues in speeches. They differed in their diagnoses and prescriptions, but they agreed on the need to consider action to deal with the workload. Ironically, this increased agreement came while the volume of petitions for hearing was leveling off.

Attacking the Problems. The Court's perceived workload problems could be addressed in a variety of ways,[80] some of which can be undertaken by the Court itself. In 1970 the Court shortened the time for oral argument, and since 1972 most of the justices have pooled their clerks to help in screening petitions for hearing. In the early 1980s the Court began to deny pauper's status to some petitioners and to levy money damages for what it saw as frivolous petitions, though with opposition from the four most liberal justices.

Other internal actions have been proposed. Some justices and observers argue that the Court should be more selective in accepting cases for hearings, and that the justices should write fewer and shorter opinions. As yet, the Court has not altered its practices significantly in either respect.

The Court also has looked to Congress for relief. Taking a step that the justices had requested for several years, Congress in 1988 adopted legislation that eliminated nearly all the remaining categories of appeals, cases that the Court is obliged to hear. Chief Justice Burger argued for a reduction in the jurisdiction of the federal courts, which indirectly would limit demands on the Court.

A New Court? The most sweeping proposals are for creation of one or more new courts above the federal courts of appeals and below the Supreme Court. A number of such plans have been put forward over the past two decades. The one that has received the most attention recently was advocated by Burger in a 1983 speech.[81] The then-chief justice suggested that Congress create a temporary court as a panel of the specialized Court of Appeals for the Federal Circuit. The panel would draw members on a rotating basis from the federal courts of appeals. Its job would be to decide cases involving conflicts among courts of appeals and perhaps some category of statutory interpretation cases, thus relieving the Supreme Court of the burden of deciding such cases. After a set period, no more than five years, Congress could make the new court permanent or take some alternative action.

Burger's proposal received serious attention. Four other justices endorsed it, including William Rehnquist, who as chief justice has continued to support the new court. Congressional committees have considered the proposal, and in 1986 the Senate Judiciary Committee approved it—though with a modification that caused Burger to oppose the amended bill.

But support for the proposed court, specific provisions aside, is far from unanimous. Several commentators have argued against the court, suggesting that it is unnecessary and that it would not reduce the Supreme Court's burdens. After Justices Scalia and Kennedy joined the Court, there was no longer a majority in favor of a new court. Further, the American Bar Association voted against it. In light of this opposition and the magnitude of the structural change involved, creation of the proposed court seems highly unlikely. As one writer said in 1988, it is "an idea whose time has gone." [82]

Conclusion

A central theme of this chapter has been the Supreme Court's capacity to set its own agenda. Congress and litigants play important parts in shaping the Court's agenda, but what the Court hears is largely under its own control. From a very broad range of legal and policy questions brought to the Court the justices can choose those few that they will address fully.

The justices have made effective use of their agenda-setting powers. Cases are selected and rejected on the basis of individual and collective goals, such as the avoidance of troublesome issues and the establishment of policies that the justices favor. Thus the process of selecting cases for full decision helps to determine the Court's role as a policy maker.

After the Court selects the cases to be decided fully, of course, it must actually decide those cases. Ultimately, its role depends on the decisions that it does reach. The next chapter will examine the process by which the Court makes its decisions.

Notes

1. J. Woodford Howard, Jr., *Courts of Appeals in the Federal Judicial System: A Study of the Second, Fifth, and District of Columbia Circuits* (Princeton: Princeton University Press, 1981), 63-64.
2. Arthur D. Hellman, "Case Selection in the Burger Court: A Preliminary Inquiry," *Notre Dame Law Review* 90 (1985): 992-996.
3. *First Lutheran Church v. Los Angeles County* (1987); *Nollan v. California Coastal Commission* (1987).
4. *Wallace v. Jaffree* (1985).
5. "Statistical Recap of Supreme Court's Workload During Last Three Terms," *United States Law Week* 57 (July 26, 1988): 3074.
6. *Young v. Town of Atlantic Beach* (1983). The case is described in Jim Mann, "Season of Lost Causes," *The American Lawyer* (November 1983): 112-113.
7. The case was *Pennzoil Co. v. Texaco, Inc.* (1987). Its background is discussed in Thomas Petzinger, Jr., *Oil and Honor: The Texaco-Pennzoil Wars* (New York: G. P. Putnam's Sons, 1987).
8. The case, *Wallace v. Jaffree* (1985), is discussed in Patrick Malone, "Prayers for Relief," *American Bar Association Journal* 71 (April 1985): 60-64.
9. *Lynch v. Donnelly* (1984).
10. William O. Douglas, *The Court Years 1939-1975: The Autobiography of William O. Douglas* (New York: Random House, 1980), 183.
11. Federal Judicial Center, *Report of the Study Group on the Caseload of the Supreme Court* (Washington, D.C., 1972), 42.
12. John Greenya, "Supreme Lawyers," *The Washington Lawyer* 1 (May/June 1987): 34-47.
13. David Lauter, "The Best Argument That Money Can Buy?" *National Law Journal*, January 26, 1987, 1.
14. The case was *Kolender v. Lawson* (1983).
15. Karen O'Connor and Lee Epstein, "Court Rules and Workload: A Case Study of Rules Governing Amicus Curiae Participation," *Justice System Journal* 8 (1983): 40-41.
16. Lee Epstein, *Conservatives in Court* (Knoxville: University of Tennessee Press, 1985), chap. 2.
17. This discussion draws from Karen O'Connor and Lee Epstein, "The Rise of Conservative Interest Group Litigation," *Journal of Politics* 45 (May 1983): 479-489; and Epstein, *Conservatives in Court.*
18. Karen O'Connor and Lee Epstein, "Amicus Curiae Participation in U.S. Supreme Court Litigation: An Appraisal of Hakman's 'Folklore,' " *Law & Society Review* 16 (1981-1982): 316.
19. Stephen L. Wasby, "Interest Groups in Court: Race Relations Litigation," in *Interest Group Politics*, ed. Allan Cigler and Burdett Loomis (Washington, D.C.: CQ Press, 1983), 256.
20. Stephen L. Wasby, "How Planned is 'Planned Litigation'?" *American Bar Foundation Research Journal*, Winter 1984, 87.
21. This discussion of the Legal Defense Fund draws from Stephen Wasby's work on the organization, including "Interest Groups in Court."
22. Mark V. Tushnet, *The NAACP's Legal Strategy Against Segregated Education, 1925-1950* (Chapel Hill: University of North Carolina Press, 1987): 145-146.
23. Much of the information presented on the ACLU's activities is drawn from *Civil Liberties*, the organization's newsletter.
24. Ruth B. Cowan, "Women's Rights Through Litigation: An Examination of

the American Civil Liberties Union Women's Rights Project, 1971-1976," *Columbia Human Rights Law Review* 8 (Spring-Summer 1976): 385. The case was *Weinberger v. Wiesenfeld* (1975).

25. Karen O'Connor and Lee Epstein, "The Role of Interest Groups in Supreme Court Policy Formation," in *Public Policy Formation*, ed. Robert Eyestone (Greenwich, Conn.: JAI Press, 1984), 71-77.

26. Thomas R. Morris, "States Before the U.S. Supreme Court: State Attorneys General as *Amicus Curiae*," *Judicature* 70 (February-March 1987): 298-305.

27. *Annual Report of the Attorney General of the United States, 1985* (Washington, D.C.: Government Printing Office, 1986), 5, 7. The figure of 637 cases apparently is based on a somewhat different time period from the others.

28. Erwin N. Griswold, "Rationing Justice—The Supreme Court's Caseload and What the Court Does Not Do," *Cornell Law Review* 60 (March 1975): 344.

29. "Admits Error," *National Law Journal*, May 25, 1987, 16. The case was *Petty v. United States* (1987).

30. Lincoln Caplan, *The Tenth Justice: The Solicitor General and the Rule of Law* (New York: Alfred A. Knopf, 1987), 39-48.

31. Caplan, *The Tenth Justice*, 51.

32. Caplan, *The Tenth Justice*, 266.

33. An example is *Immigration and Naturalization Service v. Cardoza-Fonseca*, 94 L.Ed.2d 434, 455 (1987).

34. Findings by Richard Revesz on this issue are reported in "Solicitor General Box Score," *Legal Times*, August 18, 1986, 3.

35. "The Supreme Court, 1986 Term," *Harvard Law Review* 101 (November 1987): 366.

36. See, respectively, *Baldwin v. Alabama*, 472 U.S. 372, 390 (1985); and *New Jersey v. T.L.O.*, 468 U.S. 1214, 1215-1216 (1984).

37. *Colorado v. Connelly*, 474 U.S. 1050, 1051 (1986).

38. Robert L. Stern, Eugene Gressman, and Stephen M. Shapiro, *Supreme Court Practice*, 6th ed. (Washington, D.C.: Bureau of National Affairs, 1986), 239.

39. *Brown v. Herald Co., Inc.*, 464 U.S. 928, 931 (1983).

40. "Supreme Court, 1986 Term," 366.

41. See Jeffrey B. Morris, "Can the Supreme Court Be Led: A Reevaluation of the Role of Chief Justices" (paper presented at the annual conference of the American Political Science Association, Washington, D.C., August 1986), 41: and Byron R. White, "The Work of the Supreme Court: A Nuts and Bolts Description," *New York State Bar Journal*, October 1982, 349.

42. H. W. Perry, Jr., "Deciding to Decide: Agenda Setting in the United States Supreme Court" (Ph.D. dissertation, University of Michigan, 1987), 113-114.

43. "Chief Justice Burger's Challenge to Congress," *U.S. News and World Report*, February 14, 1983, 40.

44. Hellman, "Case Selection in the Burger Court," 964.

45. This discussion of the conference owes much to Perry, "Deciding to Decide."

46. Perry, "Deciding to Decide," 185.

47. Doris Marie Provine, *Case Selection in the United States Supreme Court* (Chicago: University of Chicago Press, 1980), 32; John Paul Stevens, "The Life Span of a Judge-Made Rule," *New York University Law Review* 58 (April 1983): 17; William J. Brennan, Jr., "The National Court of Appeals: Another Dissent," *University of Chicago Law Review* 40 (Spring 1973): 481-482.

48. *Singleton v. Commissioner of Internal Revenue*, 439 U.S. 940, 945-946 (1978).

49. Linda Greenhouse, "Court Will Hear Appeal on Pennsylvania Abortion Control Act," *New York Times*, April 16, 1985, A23.

50. William H. Rehnquist, *The Supreme Court: How It Was, How It Is* (New York: William Morrow, 1987), 26-38.
51. Provine, *Case Selection in the Supreme Court*, 22.
52. John Paul Stevens, "Some Thoughts on Judicial Restraint," *Judicature* 66 (November 1982): 179.
53. Perry, "Deciding to Decide," 89-92.
54. *Burke v. Barnes* (1987); *Karcher v. May* (1987).
55. *Honig v. Doe* (1988).
56. Perry, "Deciding to Decide," 283.
57. Gregory A. Caldeira and John R. Wright, "Organized Interests and Agenda-Setting in the Supreme Court," *American Political Science Review* 82 (December 1988).
58. Perry, "Deciding to Decide," 283-285.
59. *Lowe v. Virginia* (1986).
60. *Connecticut v. Barrett*, 93 L.Ed.2d 920, 933 (1987).
61. Caldeira and Wright, "Organized Interests and Agenda-Setting."
62. *Riddick v. School Board* (1986); *Board of Education v. Dowell* (1986).
63. William H. Rehnquist, "Oral Advocacy: A Disappearing Art," *Mercer Law Review* 35 (1984): 1027.
64. Perry, "Deciding to Decide," 135-139.
65. "Supreme Court, 1986 Term," 366.
66. S. Sidney Ulmer, "Supreme Court Justices as Strict and Not-so-Strict Constructionists: Some Implications," *Law & Society Review* 8 (Fall 1973): 13-32.
67. Caldeira and Wright, "Organized Interests and Agenda-Setting."
68. *California v. Carney*, 471 U.S. 386, 396 (1985).
69. Perry, "Deciding to Decide," 226-236. The quotation is from p. 228.
70. Perry, "Deciding to Decide," 236-243.
71. Nina Totenberg, "Behind the Marble, Beneath the Robes," *New York Times Magazine*, March 16, 1975, 60.
72. Karen O'Connor and Lee Epstein, personal communication.
73. "Justice Revealed," *Life Magazine*, Fall 1987, 109.
74. Rebecca M. Salokar, "The Solicitor General Before the Supreme Court, 1959-1982: A Descriptive Analysis" (paper presented at the annual conference of the Law and Society Association, Washington, D.C., June 1987), 30-31; *Annual Report of the Attorney General, 1985*, 7.
75. Marc Galanter, "Why the 'Haves' Come Out Ahead: Speculations on the Limits of Legal Change," *Law & Society Review* 9 (Fall 1974): 97-125.
76. *Annual Report of the Attorney General, 1985*, 7.
77. This discussion draws from material in Gerhard Casper and Richard A. Posner, "A Study of the Supreme Court's Caseload," *Journal of Legal Studies* 3 (1974): 339-362.
78. Eugene Gressman, "Much Ado About Certiorari," *Georgetown Law Journal* 52 (1964): 756, 762.
79. Philip B. Kurland and Dennis J. Hutchinson, "The Business of the Supreme Court, O.T. 1982," *University of Chicago Law Review* 50 (Spring 1983): 648.
80. The discussion of proposals draws from Note, "Of High Designs: A Compendium of Proposals to Reduce the Workload of the Supreme Court," *Harvard Law Review* 97 (November 1983): 307-325.
81. Warren E. Burger, "Annual Report on the State of the Judiciary," *American Bar Association Journal* 69 (April 1983): 442-447.
82. Al Kamen, "National Appeals Court Appears to Be Lost Cause," *Washington Post*, May 13, 1988, A21.

4

Decision Making

Each term the Supreme Court selects, out of thousands of petitions for hearing, fewer than two hundred cases to be given full decisions on the merits. The Court does its most critical work in deciding these cases, explicitly making policies that can affect the nation as a whole. This chapter examines how and why the Court makes its decisions on the merits.

The first section of the chapter will consider the character of the Court's decisions and the procedural steps through which the Court reaches its decisions. The remaining sections will focus on the primary concern of the chapter, the factors that shape the Court's decisions on the merits, to provide a sense of the reasons for the Court's choices among alternative policies.

Decisions and the Decisional Process

The Court's Dual Decision

A full decision by the Supreme Court has several levels. We may examine those levels in terms of two components: the Court's treatment of the parties to the case and its establishment of a position on the legal and policy issues raised by the case.

First, cases come to the Court as disputes between contending parties with specific interests in the case. The parties that bring cases to the Court may have broad policy concerns, but at the most basic level they are asking the Court simply to upset a ruling against them in a lower court. A person convicted of a crime wants the Court to overturn the conviction. A litigant who was denied a monetary award by a lower court wants the Court to grant the award.

The Court's task is to decide whether and in what ways to change the lower court's allocation of benefits and burdens between the parties.

It may affirm the lower court, leaving undisturbed that court's treatment of the parties. Alternatively, it may modify or reverse the lower court decision, changing the judgment in some way. The terms *modify* and *reverse* are imprecise. Reversal generally refers to a fairly complete overturning of the lower court's decision, while modification is a more limited, partial overturning. The Court also may "vacate" (make void) the lower court decision; the effect is similar to that of reversal.

In some cases, the parties are so important that what happens to them specifically is crucial. In *United States v. Nixon* (1974), for instance, the Court's determination that President Nixon must yield certain tape recordings to the courts helped to ensure his resignation from office. More often, the Court's treatment of the parties has little impact on the nation as a whole. Nonetheless, the Court's decisions in such cases may be very important because of their second component, the statement of general principles of law on which the Court bases its treatment of the parties.

The statement of general principles comes in the Court's opinion. In every case that the Court decides fully, the decision is accompanied by an opinion that explains the decision. Generally at least five justices subscribe to this opinion, so that it constitutes an authoritative statement for the Court.

The opinion serves several functions. First, it is an effort to justify the Court's decision. When the Court overturns a criminal conviction, it can explain the principles that led it to that decision and thus seek to convince its audiences that its decision was correct. Second, if the Supreme Court modifies or reverses a lower court decision, the case usually will be sent back, "remanded," to the lower court to be reconsidered; the Court's opinion provides directions for that reconsideration. If a court of appeals has refused to issue an injunction in a freedom of speech case and the Supreme Court overturns its refusal, the Court's opinion can express the principles of interpretation for the First Amendment that the court of appeals should follow in rehearing the case.

Finally, and most important, the opinion lays down general principles of law that are applicable to other cases, principles that theoretically are binding on lower court judges whenever they are relevant. Together, the principles that the Court establishes in an issue area constitute its policies in that area.

The importance of the opinion as a source of law and policy is illustrated by the Court's opinion in *Immigration and Naturalization Service v. Chadha* (1983). In this case the House of Representatives acted under a "legislative veto" provision to overrule an administrative ruling and require that Jagdish Rai Chadha leave the United States. The Supreme Court ultimately ruled that Chadha must be allowed to remain in the country. In its opinion the Court's majority based that ruling on the unconstitutionality of the legislative veto provision that Congress used, and its reasoning indicated that a variety of other legislative veto provisions in federal law also were unconstitutional. Without this opinion, the Court's decision would have been of great importance to Chadha personally but of little significance to the nation as a whole. With the opinion, the *Chadha* decision had a tremendous potential impact on the legal and policy relationships between Congress and the executive branch on issues as important as the commitment of troops to combat.

Just as the Court can choose which party to favor in its decision, so it can choose the basis on which its decision rests. A particular treatment of the parties may be justified on a variety of different grounds, and which ground the Court adopts will help to determine the long-term impact of its decision. If the Court overturns the death penalty for a particular defendant, it might rest that decision on a whole range of possible grounds—from the existence of a specific error in that defendant's trial to the unconstitutionality of the death penalty under all circumstances. Obviously, a decision based on the second ground will have a good deal more impact than one based on the first ground.

The Decision-Making Process

Presentation of Cases to the Court. The written briefs that the Court receives when it considers whether to accept a case may address the merits of the case as well as the desirability of hearing it. Once a case is accepted for full consideration, attorneys for the parties submit new briefs that focus solely on the merits. In addition, in most cases that reach this stage, individuals and groups other than the parties submit *amicus curiae* briefs stating their own arguments on the merits.

The primary material in these briefs generally concerns the legal issues in the case. The parties muster evidence to support their interpretations of relevant constitutional provisions and statutes. Some briefs offer policy arguments as well, seeking to convince the justices that support for their position constitutes not only good law but also good public policy. In a sense, the Court made this practice legitimate in a 1908 decision, *Muller v. Oregon*. In upholding a state law, the Court praised a lengthy analysis of sociological data presented by attorney Louis Brandeis—who later became a justice—in support of the policy that underlay the law. A brief that addresses sociological issues sometimes is called a "Brandeis brief."

Material in briefs is supplemented by attorneys' presentations in oral argument before the Court. Oral argument is strictly limited in time. At present, each side generally is provided half an hour for argument to the Court. Attorneys for the parties to the case nearly always participate in the argument. Occasionally they are joined by the lawyer for an *amicus*, most often the federal government.

Oral argument provides an opportunity for attorneys to supplement the material in their briefs. More important, perhaps, it provides the justices with a chance to probe issues that concern them. Presentations by lawyers are interrupted frequently by questions and comments from members of the Court, frequently more than one hundred times in an hour of argument on a case. As a result, the course of the argument usually is determined more by the justices than by the attorneys, who often find the discussion going in unexpected—and undesired—directions. The justices differ in the frequency with which they pose questions; in one set of eight cases in 1987, Scalia asked 126 questions while Brennan asked none.[1]

The justices' questions and comments sometimes stray from legal issues, and justices often indulge in the opportunity to amuse their colleagues and the courtroom audience—usually at the expense of the lawyer before them. One attorney in a 1986 case complained of his opponent's style of argument but said, "I doubt very much that it will fool this Court." Chief Justice Rehnquist replied, "Don't overestimate us."[2]

Justices use their questions in part to influence their colleagues' perceptions of a case. As Rehnquist points out, this is the only time before conference discussion of a case "when all of the judges are expected to sit on the bench and concentrate on one particular case."[3] But the opportunity to influence colleagues may be reduced by their lack of complete concentration on the proceedings. When Rehnquist and Blackmun sat together at oral argument, for instance, Rehnquist's clerks sometimes handed him trivia questions, which Rehnquist in turn passed on Blackmun.[4]

Tentative Decisions.   After oral argument on a case is held, the Court discusses it in one of its conferences later in the same week. The conference is held in a closed session from which all people other than the justices are barred. The chief justice presides at the conference. The chief opens discussion on each case. The other justices follow, from the most senior member (in service on the Court, not in age) to the most junior.

The form of the discussion has varied with the style of the chief justice and other members of the Court, but in the current era it is fairly structured.[5] The chief justice begins by summarizing the case, then offers personal views of the case. The associate justices, starting with the most senior and ending with the most junior, then present their own views and votes. Because their colleagues already have voiced similar positions, the more junior justices generally speak quite briefly. Typically, little or no additional discussion follows this presentation of positions. When consideration of a case has ended, the chief justice indicates the breakdown of votes, subject to disagreement by other justices.

We might expect a more freewheeling discussion of cases, with justices arguing at length and votes changing as a result of the give and take. The usual absence of such discussion results in part from the Court's workload: Time pressures abbreviate the consideration given to cases in conference. Just as important, however, is that the justices usually bring to conference fixed views of the cases. They have already read the materials in a case, have listened to oral argument, and often have discussed the case with their law clerks. Furthermore, they approach cases on the basis of their own, frequently strong, attitudes about policy. As a result, according to Chief Justice Rehnquist, "it is very much the exception" for justices' minds to be changed in conference, and extended discussion ordinarily would have little impact on their positions.[6]

After each two-week sitting, the writing of the Court's opinion in each case is assigned to a justice. If the chief justice voted with the majority, the chief assigns the opinion; in other cases, the most senior justice in the majority makes the assignment. Because so many conference votes are unanimous or nearly so, the chief justice is usually among the majority. If there is no majority, either because some justices wish to reserve judgment or because the Court is split in complex ways, the chief justice assigns the opinion. The assignment power is important, because the justice who writes the opinion can determine the grounds on which the Court's decision rests as well as the ultimate size of the majority. The use of this power will be discussed later in this chapter in connection with the role of the chief justice.

Reaching Final Decisions. Following the conference the justice who was assigned the opinion begins work, drafting an initial version of the opinion. This justice will be guided by the views expressed in conference concerning the appropriate rationale for the Court's decision. Other justices also may work on the case, reconsidering their positions and—particularly if they voted with the minority—writing alternative opinions. During this process views of the case may change even before the assigned opinion is produced in draft form.

Once the opinion is completed and circulated, it often becomes a focus of negotiation. Ordinarily the assigned justice wishes to obtain the support of as many colleagues as possible for the opinion. The writer will seek to convince justices who were originally in the minority to change positions, and it also may be necessary to discourage allies in conference from leaving the fold. At the very least, the assigned justice will wish to maintain the original majority for the outcome supported by the opinion and a majority in support of the rationale expressed in the opinion, so that the opinion becomes the official statement for the Court. The justice may fail in this task, so that another justice's opinion reaching the same outcome or a different one becomes the opinion of the Court.

The negotiation that occurs during this period focuses on the wording of the opinion. The assigned justice and rival opinion writers may be willing to change arguments or the ways in which they are expressed in order to satisfy other justices and thus to enlist their support. When the Court is deeply divided, this process may be quite complex and difficult, and the result often is an opinion that lacks clarity and coherence because of the need to appeal to other justices.

Occasionally no opinion gains the support of a majority. This has happened fairly often in the 1970s and 1980s. Table 4-1, which describes several characteristics of the Court's decisions in the 1986 term, shows that there were six decisions without majority opinions in 1986 and another eight decisions in which a majority could be mustered for only part of the Court's opinion. Over the years some major decisions have lacked majority opinions; one example is *Regents v. Bakke* (1978), in which the Court ruled on the constitutionality of affirmative action programs for medical school admissions.

When a majority opinion is lacking, there is no authoritative statement of the Court's position on the legal issues in the case. Confusion is reduced if the opinion on the winning side that the largest number of justices sign—the "plurality opinion"—delineates the points for which majority support exists. Sometimes the Court provides a short *per curiam* opinion that serves the same function. Lower court judges and other observers also can attempt to discern a "least common denominator" from the positions of the justices on the majority side, but this task may be quite difficult. In *Furman v. Georgia* (1972), the five justices in the majority expressed quite different reasons for concluding that the existing death penalty laws were unconstitutional. As a result, legislators and others had difficulty determining just what kinds of death penalty laws, if any, were acceptable in the Court's collective view.

Concurring and Dissenting Opinions. An opinion may gain a majority but lack unanimous support. Disagreement with the majority opinion can take two forms. First, a justice may cast a dissenting vote, which expresses disagreement with the result reached by the Court as it affects the parties to a case. If a criminal conviction is reversed, for instance, dissent indicates a belief that it should have been affirmed. Second, a justice may concur with the Court's decision, agreeing with the result in the specific case, but differing with the rationale expressed

Table 4-1 Selected Characteristics of Supreme Court Decisions, 1986 Term

Characteristic	Number	Percentage
Vote for Court's decision[a]		
Unanimous	41	26
Nonunanimous	115	74
Support for Court's opinion		
Unanimous for whole opinion	29	19
Unanimous for part of opinion	5	3
Majority but not unanimous	108	69
Majority for only part of opinion	8	5
No majority for opinion	6	4
Cases with		
Dissenting opinions[b]	115	74
Concurring opinions[c]	59	38
Total number of		
Dissenting opinions	156	
Concurring opinions	82	

Note: The 156 cases included are those with decisions on the merits that were listed in the front section of *Supreme Court Reports, Lawyer's Edition*.

[a] Partial dissents are not counted as votes for the decision.
[b] Opinions labeled as "concurring and dissenting" are treated as dissenting opinions.
[c] Some concurring opinions are written by justices in full agreement with the Court's opinion.

in the Court's opinion. Both kinds of disagreement are common; in the 1986 term, as Table 4-1 shows, only 19 percent of the Court's majority opinions enjoyed full support from every justice.

Generally, a justice who disagrees with the majority opinion will write or sign on to a dissenting or concurring opinion. Since it does not need to express an authoritative statement of the law, such an opinion can range widely in the issues and concerns that it raises. And justices who write concurring and dissenting opinions have considerable freedom to express themselves as they see fit. In a 1986 case concerning whaling rules, Justice Marshall concluded his dissenting opinion by quoting *Moby Dick;* such a flourish is less likely to appear in a majority opinion.[7] Certainly concurring and dissenting opinions reveal much more about the views of their authors than do the Court's majority opinions.

Dissenting opinions are written for several reasons. Most generally, they allow justices who disagree with the result in a case to express unhappiness with that result and to justify their disagreement. At a more practical level, the opinion may be intended to subvert the Court's decision by pointing out how lower courts can interpret it narrowly or by encouraging Congress to overturn the Court's reading of a statute.

Finally, the dissenting opinion may be a kind of appeal to the future, when, as Chief Justice Hughes said, "a later decision may possibly correct the error" that the dissenter believes the Court has made.[8] Indeed, in several cases a dissenting view on an issue later became the Court's majority position. One famous example is Justice Black's dissent in *Betts v. Brady* (1942), in which he argued that indigent criminal defendants had the right to a free attorney in any serious case. The Court reversed itself twenty-one years later in *Gideon v. Wainwright,* and Black had the rare satisfaction of writing the Court's opinion that turned his long-standing position into the law of the land.

When more than one justice dissents, all the dissenters may join in a single opinion. Alternatively, they may write multiple opinions; occasionally, as in a 1984 immigration case, there are four dissenting opinions.[9] In such instances dissenters may express agreement with each other's opinions.

Concurring opinions differ considerably in their positions relative to the majority opinion. Some express full disagreement with the majority's rationale for the decision. In a 1987 decision, for instance, the Court ruled against a labor union that challenged an Interstate Commerce Commission decision. Justice Scalia's majority opinion held that the federal courts lacked jurisdiction to review the Commission's decisions under certain conditions. Justice Stevens's concurring opinion disagreed vehemently with that holding but concluded that the Commission had acted properly in this case. Thus the differences between the two opinions were far more significant than their similarities.[10]

In contrast, a concurring opinion often will disagree with the majority only to a limited degree. Sometimes it does not disagree at all: a justice will sign on to a majority opinion but write a separate concurrence to express personal views. The most common reason for doing so is to "interpret" the majority opinion in a particular way, to influence how lower courts and other institutions apply it. In a 1987 case involving rights to distribute literature in airports, Justice White wrote, "I join the Court's opinion but suggest that it should not be taken as indicating that a majority of the Court considers the Los Angeles International Airport to be a traditional public forum." [11] A justice may even write a concurring opinion to take issue with a dissenting opinion, as Chief Justice Burger did in *Darden v. Wainwright* (1986).

Frequently, an opinion will be labeled as "concurring and dissenting." Such an opinion agrees with the Court's treatment of the parties in part, but disagrees with some aspect of that treatment.

Announcing the Decision. The process of decision making in a case ends when all the opinions are written and all justices have determined which opinions they will join. At this time the decision will be announced in open court.

The justices sometimes read the entirety of their opinions in court, but more often they summarize them. Occasionally justices engage in outbursts of anger in reporting their opinions. One example occurred in 1984, when Justice Stevens read his dissent from a decision limiting prisoners' rights and accused the majority of violating "any civilized standard of decency." [12]

The Court suffers from relatively few "leaks" of decisions prior to their formal announcement. In 1985 a group called the Fund for a Conservative Majority predicted the date and direction of the Court's decision in a case to which it was a party; when both turned out to be correct, the group's lawyer said that he had simply guessed correctly. [13] In 1979 an ABC television reporter predicted some impending decisions, possibly through information provided by a Court printer. In 1986 the same reporter announced that the Court would strike down part of the Gramm-Rudman-Hollings budget deficit reduction law the next day. The report was accurate in most respects, but the decision was not handed down until three weeks later; the Court may have delayed it in reaction to the report. [14]

The length of time required for a case to go through all the stages from filing to decision can vary a good deal, depending chiefly on the backlog of cases scheduled for oral argument and the time that the justices take to settle on a decision and set of opinions. In June 1987 the Court decided cases filed as early as August 1985 and as late as September 1986. Of the cases argued in October 1986, three decisions were announced in early November but one only in late June 1987.

After the Court decides a case—or declines to hear it—the losing party may petition for a rehearing. Occasionally such a petition is granted, sometimes when the Court decides a case by a tie vote and a ninth justice then becomes available. But such action is rare; in the 1976-1982 terms, only six of 735 petitions for rehearing were granted. [15]

Influences on Decisions: Introduction

The rest of this chapter will be concerned with explanation of the choices made by the Supreme Court and by its individual members in reaching decisions. As I have indicated, these choices have two components: the treatment of the parties to the case and the Court's position on the general legal and policy issues in the case. For individual justices, we need to explain their votes on the outcome of the specific case and the content of the opinions to which they subscribe.

Explanation of policy choices anywhere in government is difficult. Policy makers are influenced by a broad range of considerations that interact in a complex way. We hardly can say that a particular policy chosen by a legislature or an administrative agency resulted from a specific set of influences and specify the importance of each influence with precision. We can, however, point to the general kinds of factors that do shape policy choices in significant ways.

The factors that affect decisions of the Supreme Court can be placed in four general categories: (1) the state of the body of law that is applicable to a case; (2) the external environment of the Court, including other policy makers, interest groups, and public opinion; (3) the personal values of the justices concerning the desirability of alternative decisions and policies; and (4) interaction among members of the Court.

Each of the following four sections of the chapter will examine one of these categories: its significance as an influence on the Court's decisions and the ways in which it operates. Together, these sections should provide a sense of the bases for the decisions that the Court reaches.

The State of the Law

It should be clear by now that the Supreme Court makes its policy choices in a legal context. Like all other courts and most administrative agencies, the Court selects among alternative policies in the form of interpreting provisions of law. Accordingly, an examination of influences on the Court's decisions must begin with a look at the ways that the Court interprets the law and a discussion of the law's significance in determining what the Court does.

Means of Interpretation

The law that the Supreme Court interprets comes primarily from the United States Constitution and from federal statutes. In deciding cases, members of the Court must exercise their judgment as to the meaning of one or more provisions of the Constitution, of statutes, or both. They can utilize several time-honored judicial techniques to make their interpretations.

"Plain Meaning."   The most basic of these techniques is analysis of the literal meaning of the words in question. In some instances the plain meaning of a provision of law will be sufficiently clear to resolve a case. For instance, the Twenty-second Amendment to the Constitution states, "No person shall be elected to the office of the President more than twice." The Supreme Court would reject almost automatically a claim that a twice-elected person could run for a third term.

But the Court seldom faces such easy cases, because the justices see little purpose in reviewing a lower court judgment that has reached an obvious result. Most of the Court's decisions involve ambiguous provisions such as the Fourteenth Amendment's protection of "due process of law," for which there is no plain meaning.

Moreover, justices may not agree on the plain meaning of a provision. The First Amendment states that "Congress shall make no law . . . abridging the freedom of speech." Justice Black argued that the meaning of this language was clear: Congress could not restrict speech in any way. But some commentators argue that in the period when the First Amendment was written, "freedom of speech" meant only a limited protection for speech from government control, and this is the interpretation that most members of the Court have adopted.[16]

Legislative Intent. Where the plain meaning of a legal provision is unclear, justices can seek to ascertain the intentions of those who wrote the provision into the law. Indeed, if there is a conflict between the literal meaning of a provision and the intent that seems clearly to underlie it, the Court may follow the latter. Evidence concerning legislative intent can be found in congressional committee reports and floor debates or—for provisions of the original Constitution—in records of the Constitutional Convention.

Unfortunately, the intent of the Convention or of Congress often is itself quite unclear. Statements of purpose for a provision may be contradictory; members of Congress frequently offer conflicting interpretations of a statute under consideration. Sometimes, such statements are absent altogether. Justice Stevens suggested in one case that, where Congress passed a highly detailed budget act in a considerable hurry, there effectively was *no* legislative intent behind a provision of the act that the Court was interpreting.[17]

A broad constitutional provision such as the Fourteenth Amendment applies to many different situations, some of which will not have occurred to the people who wrote the provision, so a search for their intent may be futile. Wiretapping became technologically possible more than a century after the Fourth Amendment's requirements for searches and seizures were written; thus, the writers of that amendment could have had no intent concerning the legal status of wiretapping. In such a situation, the justices may rely upon "purposive" interpretation, in which they seek to apply the general goal that underlies a provision to the specific issue in question, but this may be a difficult process.

The use of intent has been the subject of considerable controversy in constitutional interpretation. Some people argue that the Court should adhere to the intent of the framers of each provision as closely as possible, while others believe it is appropriate to interpret the Constitution in terms of the current meaning of its language and underlying values.

This controversy achieved unusual visibility in 1985, when Attorney General Edwin Meese called for a "Jurisprudence of Original Intention" and criticized the Court for what he saw as departing from the intent of the framers in its expansions of constitutional rights. Partly in response, Justices Brennan and Stevens spoke in defense of the Court, pointing to the ambiguity of the framers' intent and arguing that the meaning of the Constitution changes over time. In Brennan's view, "the ultimate question must be, what do the words of the text mean in our time." [18] Thus, not only is legislative intent often difficult to ascertain, but in addition people differ on the weight that it should be given in interpreting the Constitution.

Precedent.   Another means of interpretation is analysis of the Supreme Court's own past decisions, its precedents. A basic doctrine of the law is *stare decisis* ("let the decision stand"). Under this doctrine a court is bound to follow the interpretations of constitutional provisions and statutes that have been established by higher courts; as a general rule, a court is expected to follow its own past interpretations as well. Aside from legal doctrine, precedents have a practical value. The following of precedent allows a judge to rely on past practice rather than to take new and perhaps dangerous directions in legal interpretation; more generally, it eases the task of decision making.

Technically, a court is bound to follow not everything stated in a relevant precedent but only the rule of law that was necessary for decision in that case, what is called the "holding." Other statements, called *obiter dicta* or simply *dicta* (pl.; singular, *dictum*), have no legal force. In *Jones v. Barnes* (1983), the Supreme Court held that a defendant's constitutional right to counsel was not violated when the assigned counsel did not raise all the issues urged by the client in appealing a conviction. Chief Justice Burger's opinion for the Court laid down rules on the obligations of appointed counsel in appeals; because the decision was based on these rules, they may be considered the holding of the decision. The opinion also stated, "There is, of course, no constitutional right to an appeal";[19] because that judgment was unnecessary to decide the case, it may be considered *dictum.* In this case the distinction between holding and *dictum* is fairly clear, but often it is difficult to discern the distinction. This difficulty gives a court some freedom to choose what it will regard as binding in a precedent.

In any case, the rule of precedent hardly eliminates all ambiguity in legal interpretation. Most cases before the Supreme Court involve issues that are at least marginally different from those decided in past cases, so precedent seldom determines a decision in a strict way. Indeed, the precedents that are relevant to a case often point in more than one direction. More fundamentally, because a court is not absolutely bound to adhere to its own precedents, the Court is always free to reconsider a past decision. This freedom in turn requires the justices to make choices.

The Significance of the Law in Shaping Decisions

To what extent are the Supreme Court's decisions determined by the state of the applicable law? Some justices and legal scholars have argued that the law is the key factor in determining what the Court does. This argument probably was best expressed by Justice Owen Roberts in a 1936 decision for which he knew the Court would be criticized heavily. Seeking to turn back such criticism, Roberts wrote as follows:

> It is sometimes said that the court assumes a power to overrule or control the action of the people's representatives. This is a misconception.... When an act of Congress is appropriately challenged in the courts as not conforming to the constitutional mandate the judicial branch of the Government has only one duty—to lay the article of the Constitution which is invoked beside the statute which is challenged and to decide whether the latter squares with the former. All the court does, or can do, is to announce its considered judgment upon the question. The only power it has, if such it may be called, is the power of judgment.[20]

The discussion thus far should make clear the weakness of Roberts's argument. Even if members of the Supreme Court wanted only to follow the law, the state of the law seldom is sufficiently certain to allow such a passive approach. In this respect the Court differs from appellate courts that must decide all the cases brought to them. Judges on these courts often say that most of their cases can be decided only one way under the law. But the Supreme Court ordinarily chooses to hear only cases that involve ambiguous applications of the Constitution and statutes. As a result, the justices have no choice but to exercise discretion.

Moreover, few justices would be content to take a passive approach even if it were possible. Justices often have strongly held preferences about the policy issues that come before them, and they wish to see their preferences reflected in the Court's decisions. Accordingly, they not only accept the freedom provided by the law's ambiguity but also use that freedom to advance the policies they prefer.

This attitude is reflected in the justices' willingness to abandon a precedent when this is the only means to change a policy that the Court's majority strongly disfavors. The Court has been particularly willing to overrule precedents in the last thirty years. By one count, the Court overturned prior decisions in eighty-eight decisions between 1961 and 1986, in contrast with a total of ninety-six overturnings during the

Court's entire history through 1960.[21] The fragility of precedent is suggested by the issue as to whether the federal minimum wage law could be applied to state and local government employees; in 1968 the Court said that the law could be applied, in 1976 it overturned that decision and held that the law could not be applied, and in 1985 it overturned *that* decision and returned to its 1968 position—which one justice in dissent predicted the Court would abandon again.[22] In their opinions, several justices have indicated that they view the Court's precedents as mild constraints rather than strong limits on its action.

The justices' desire to use their freedom in interpreting the law is reflected in other practices as well. Sometimes the Court reaches a decision that seems contrary to the best interpretation of the law. Article I, section 10, of the Constitution prohibits the states from adopting laws "impairing the obligation of contracts." But in *Home Building & Loan Assn. v. Blaisdell* (1934), the Supreme Court upheld a Minnesota law that postponed payments on home and farm mortgages as a means to prevent wholesale foreclosures during the Great Depression. Chief Justice Hughes's opinion in that case employed circuitous and rather unsatisfying legal reasoning to justify a decision that the majority wanted to reach because of the circumstances of the case.

The Court also has adopted major legal doctrines that seem to have little basis in any recognized mode of legal interpretation. One classic example is the establishment of a new constitutional right to privacy in *Griswold v. Connecticut* (1965). In that case seven of the nine justices agreed that a right to privacy existed, but they could not agree on the provisions that provided an implicit basis for this liberty; this disagreement suggests that they reached their conclusion first and then searched for a supporting rationale. Their decision can be explained more satisfactorily by their belief that a right to privacy was desirable than by anything in the law.

The best evidence that the law does not fully govern the Court's decisions is the frequency of disagreement among the justices. The Court is unanimous on the outcome and on the legal rules that govern it in only a minority of cases. This pattern is inevitable in light of the uncertainty of the legal issues that the Court addresses and the differing personal perspectives from which the justices view cases.

It would be a mistake, however, to dismiss the law altogether as a factor in Supreme Court decisions, because those decisions are made in a legal context. Justices are trained in a tradition that emphasizes the law as a basis for judicial decisions. They are judged by a legal audience largely in terms of their adherence to what are regarded as good legal principles. Perhaps most important, they work in the language of the law, and this language channels judges' thinking and constrains their choices.[23]

Because justices approach decisions in a legal context, some possible policies that cannot easily be justified legally are eliminated from consideration. The Court's effective range of alternatives often is narrowed by the state of the law at a given time. Even among the policies that could be justified legally, justices may perceive that the law lies so heavily on the other side that they cannot support a policy that they prefer personally. Harry Blackmun and Potter Stewart both voted to uphold capital punishment laws. But Blackmun expressed his "distaste, antipathy, and, indeed, abhorrence, for the death penalty," and Stewart said, "If I were a legislator, I wouldn't ever vote for it." [24] In 1982 Chief Justice Burger wrote in an opinion that a policy to deny education to illegal aliens was "senseless," "folly," and "wrong," but nonetheless he dissented from a decision overturning that policy.[25] And a concurring opinion by William Brennan in a 1988 case shows how a justice's perception of the law can override other considerations:

> Were I judging on a clean slate, I would still be inclined to adopt the view that the entrapment defense should focus exclusively on the government's conduct. But I am not writing on a clean slate; the Court has spoken definitively on this point. Therefore I bow to stare decisis, and today join the judgment and reasoning of the Court.[26]

The state of the law, then, operates as one element in the decision process. Although it seldom forces the Court to adopt a particular policy, it often exerts an impact by narrowing and channeling the Court's choices. In this sense decision making on the Supreme Court differs somewhat from decision making by legislators and chief executives. As C. Herman Pritchett has said, "Judges make choices, but they are not the 'free' choices of congressmen." [27] The considerable freedom that the justices do possess requires that factors other than the law be considered in explaining the Court's decisions.

The Court's Environment

Public policy makers are subject to influence from at least four elements of their environments: the mass public; relevant elite groups in the population; those who bring demands to them, especially interest groups; and other governmental institutions. Certainly congressional behavior reflects influence from each of these sources. Indeed, some commentators argue that decisions by members of Congress can be explained chiefly by their desire to appeal to their constituents to ensure reelection. Similarly, the policies of some administrative agencies, such as the independent regulatory commissions of the federal government, have been ascribed primarily to their relationships with the private groups that are most concerned with their decisions.

Courts are not immune to influence from their environments, but most courts do possess a degree of freedom that distinguishes them from most other policy makers. The Supreme Court's freedom is particularly great, and it helps to make the Court a rather different kind of institution from, say, Congress. As Justice Harold Burton replied when he was asked about his move from Congress to the Court, "Have you ever gone direct from a circus to a monastery?" [28]

The Court's insulation has several sources, some of which are common to other courts.[29] The most important source of the Court's freedom from influence is the lifetime term, which reduces tremendously justices' dependence upon public opinion and upon other policy makers. Formal and practical constraints on interest group activity in the judiciary augment the Court's freedom. Finally, the Court's status as the highest judicial body eliminates the review by judicial superiors that limits the autonomy of lower courts.

Nonetheless, each element of the environment that I have listed exerts a meaningful influence on the Court. Collectively, they have a significant impact on the Court's decisions. Their impact merits examination.

Mass Public Opinion

Legislators may wish to act in accordance with public opinion for two general reasons. Most important, they wish to maintain public support in order to secure reelection or political advancement. In addition, they may feel some responsibility to represent their constituents' views in order to serve their district effectively. Both of these motives have limited relevance to the Supreme Court. Justices do not depend on public opinion to keep their positions, and few are interested in other positions. Moreover, the Court is not intended to be a representative body. The relative unimportance of public opinion for the Court is reflected in its adoption of some highly unpopular policies. The Court's decisions prohibiting organized prayers in public schools and promoting busing of students for racial desegregation have been supported by a relatively small minority of the public and opposed strongly by large segments of that public. Its support for the rights of criminal defendants, particularly during the 1960s, has been equally unpopular.

Yet the justices certainly are aware of public opinion. The mass media provide information on public attitudes. Members of the Court receive letters supporting or opposing their positions. At public appearances they come into contact with people who express views on their decisions; indeed, protesters disrupted a speech by William Rehnquist at the Indiana University law school in 1986. In recent years, antiabortion groups and gay rights advocates have held demonstrations at the Court.

There are several reasons why public opinion might influence the Court's decisions. At least some justices have a personal concern about the popularity of their actions. This may arise simply from the desire to be liked, but in rare instances it may stem from an interest in future elective office. William Douglas apparently had some ambition for the presidency, and some of his colleagues believed this ambition affected his decisions.[30] Sandra Day O'Connor has received attention as a potential candidate for president or vice president, and there is some speculation that this possibility might influence her course as a justice.

Perhaps more important, justices know that a willingness to carry out the Court's decisions depends in part on agreement with those decisions and on acceptance of the Court's general authority. This concern may affect some decisions involving controversial issues. A particularly clear example is the Court's implementation decision in *Brown v. Board of Education* (1955). The Court chose to establish an indefinite timetable for school desegregation in the South rather than demanding immediate action. This choice was based in part on a calculation that flexibility on the part of the Court would make southern whites more likely to accept the obligation to desegregate. A concern with public opinion also may affect how decisions are presented. One example may be Chief Justice Burger's opinion for the Court in *United States v. Will*, a 1980 decision that had the effect of increasing the justices' salaries. Apparently recognizing the potential for criticism, Burger stressed why the Court needed to decide a case that had a direct monetary impact on its members.

Finally, public opinion can affect the justices' own perceptions of issues. For example, public concern about illegal drugs may affect the view that justices take of drug cases. Chief Justice Rehnquist has suggested that the unpopularity of President Truman and of the Korean War influenced the Court's 1952 ruling against Truman's seizure of steel mills,[31] and widespread public disagreement with American participation in the Vietnam conflict may subtly have encouraged the Court to overturn penalties against opponents of the war in several cases.

Asked what impact public opinion has on the Court, Justice Brennan answered emphatically, "None!"[32] Nonetheless, for the reasons I have noted, it seems certain that the views of the public exert some influence. As Rehnquist concludes:

> Judges, so long as they are relatively normal human beings, can no more escape being influenced by public opinion in the long run than can people working at other jobs. And if a judge on coming to the bench were to decide to hermetically seal himself off from all manifestations of public opinion, he would accomplish very little; he would not be influenced by current public opinion, but instead would be influenced by the state of public opinion at the time he came to the bench.[33]

Elite Opinion: The Mass Media and the Legal Community

Along with general public opinion, the opinion of narrower groups may have some effect on the Supreme Court. Two groups whose opinions potentially are relevant to all justices are the mass media and the legal community. Ordinarily, neither is likely to exert more than a subtle influence on the Court, but even that subtle influence may be significant under some conditions.

The mass media are the Court's primary source of information on public opinion and on the views of other policy makers. The media also are significant in themselves because they serve as visible reviewers of the Court's work. Justices have shown some sensitivity to criticism in the press, and Potter Stewart once wrote a letter to the *Wall Street Journal* to refute the *Journal*'s criticism of a decision.[34]

Media criticism may have had considerable impact on a 1980 decision. In *Gannett v. De Pasquale* (1979), the Court held that judges could bar the public—including the press—from pretrial proceedings, and it implied that the First Amendment does not provide the public with a right of access to trials. The decision was attacked a good deal in the press, which was very concerned with its own access to court proceedings, and four justices took the unusual step of making public statements about the decision and its meaning. Only a year later, in *Richmond Newspapers v. Virginia* (1980), the Court "retreated" by holding that the First Amendment does guarantee the public a right of access to most trials. "Without *Gannett,* and the critical reaction it aroused," wrote the journalist Anthony Lewis, "I doubt that the Supreme Court would soon have found in the First Amendment a public right to know about public institutions."[35]

The media may have a broader impact on the Court's decisions. Two commentators have speculated that the relatively favorable treatment of the Warren Court's liberal activism by the Washington and northeastern media might have reinforced those policies.[36] And one legal scholar suggested that media emphasis on the Court's conservative civil liberties decisions in the 1983 term affected the Court's decisions the following term: "The very fact of the media saying there is a trend sets up a magnetic pull in the opposite direction."[37]

The legal community is important as a professional reference group. Justices draw many of their acquaintances from this community, and most of them continue to interact a good deal with lawyers and lower court judges after they join the Court. The legal community also serves as the primary source of expert evaluation of the Court, particularly in the law reviews published by law schools and edited by their students. As I suggested earlier, the legal community helps to make legal considerations important to the Court's decisions. Where a particular view of legal issues is dominant in the bar or in a segment of the bar relevant to a justice, that view may affect the one that the justice adopts.

The law reviews can have another kind of impact as well. As cited in briefs and read by justices and clerks, law review articles constitute an important source of the information about legal questions that enters into decisions. Justices frequently cite law review articles in support of their positions, and on occasion articles may help to determine the positions themselves.

Of course, a justice may take cues and information from a wide range of individuals and groups. Undoubtedly, some justices are influenced by their own friends and acquaintances—whether or not they are attorneys. Justice Harry Blackmun once served as counsel for the Mayo Clinic, and he has drawn a good deal from medical scholarship for some of his opinions. Justice Tom Clark once telephoned J. Edgar Hoover to ask for information relevant to a case.[38]

Litigants and Interest Groups

In Chapter 3, I discussed the roles of litigants and groups in the Supreme Court, with emphasis on how they bring cases to the Court. Here I will focus on their direct impact on decisions on the merits. Because of the requirement that communications to the Court go through formal channels, the potential for such impact comes primarily through advocacy in written briefs and oral arguments.

It is reasonable to expect that advocacy influences some Court decisions, because it can shape justices' perceptions of cases. Justice Brennan has said that often his "whole notion of what a case is about crystallizes at oral argument," and Justice Harlan said that oral argument "may in many cases make the difference between winning and losing." [39] The federal government is highly successful in winning cases on the merits, as shown by its 70 percent victory rate in the 1959-1982 terms.[40] While this success has several bases, one surely is the expertise of the experienced advocates in the solicitor general's office. *Amicus* briefs may suggest options and arguments to the Court, and the fact that justices occasionally cite them in opinions suggests their possible influence.[41]

But the impact of advocacy should not be exaggerated. The Court is not entirely dependent upon litigants and *amici* for information and arguments, and justices may approach cases with very strong predispositions. According to one writer, "the best guess among careful students of the Supreme Court is that 15 percent of the cases are substantially affected by oral argument." [42] In many other cases, the best or worst advocacy may have no effect on the outcome, because the justices' attitudes combine with the facts of the case to ensure victory for one side.

The importance of a case to the justices helps to determine the potential effects of lawyers' advocacy. John Frank, a former law clerk, suggested that in many cases justices are not open to persuasion because of their strong feelings. "On the other hand, in a very large number of cases the Justices are pursuing no special enthusiasms and invoking no sentiments. In those cases the function of counsel may be controlling." [43]

Frank's first generalization is supported by accounts of two landmark decisions. In the famous *Gideon* case on counsel for indigent criminal defendants, future justice Abe Fortas employed his own considerable skills and the services of a large law firm on behalf of Gideon, while his opponent was a young and inexperienced attorney who developed his case virtually alone and part time. Yet the disparity between the two sides probably had no effect on the Court's decision, because most justices already had decided to adopt the policy supported by Fortas even before they accepted Gideon's case. As legal scholar Bernard Schwartz wrote, "The Fortas eloquence was only the battering of an open door." [44] Similarly, in *Brown v. Board of Education*, according to one government attorney involved in the case, "nothing that the lawyers said made a difference." Thurgood Marshall, who argued the case for school desegregation, "could have stood up there and recited 'Mary had a little lamb,' and the result would have been exactly the same." [45] These examples suggest that in the Court, as in Congress, interested parties generally have the least impact on issues that concern policy makers the most.

Congress, the President, and Other Policy Makers

Several sets of policy-making institutions are important to the Court. Lower courts and some administrative agencies are responsible for implementation of the Court's decisions. The president plays some role in enforcement of decisions, helps to shape public attitudes toward the Court, and may have close personal relations with some justices. Congress holds crucial powers over the Court as an institution as well as power to change Court-made policies.

Understandably, members of the Court make some effort to achieve good relations with each of these institutions. For instance, individual justices sometimes seek to develop friendly contacts with lower court judges. The Court's expressions of deference to administrative expertise in its opinions also may reflect a desire for support from other policy makers. Most important, an interest in maintaining the support of other policy makers may influence the substance of the Court's decisions.

Congress and the president probably are the policy makers that affect the Court's decisions most. The potential influence that Congress gains through its powers over the Court deserves relatively lengthy discussion here. I will discuss the influence of the president more briefly; some of the most significant forms of presidential influence already have been considered, and another is linked to congressional powers.

Congressional Powers. The array of congressional powers over matters important to the Court is impressive. First, Congress largely controls the structure and powers of the Court. It can narrow the Court's appellate jurisdiction—its power to hear cases—as it did in 1868 to prevent the Court from ruling on the constitutionality of Reconstruction-era legislation. (The extent to which Congress can narrow the Court's jurisdiction is not fully settled.) It can set the justices' salaries, although those salaries cannot be reduced; at times Congress has expressed its displeasure with the Court by holding salaries constant during times of inflation. Congress also sets the number of justices and has changed that number several times, although the current number of nine has become so well established that it would be difficult to alter.

Further, congressional legislation on substantive matters can be important to the Court. The establishment of new legal rights can increase the Court's caseload. Statutes may strengthen or overturn the policies that the Court makes in particular areas of law, and congressional overturning of a Court policy may be intended as a rebuke to the Court. These substantive powers, in combination with congressional control over the Court as an institution, make Congress very relevant to the Court.

The Court's Behavior. Members of the Supreme Court hardly can be unconcerned with the relevant actions of Congress. Occasionally justices directly lobby Congress for or against legislation. Chief Justice Taft worked hard to obtain the Judiciary Act of 1925, the statute that gave the Court its broad discretionary jurisdiction. Some members of the Court intervened to help defeat Franklin Roosevelt's "Court-packing plan" in 1937. Chief Justice Burger was an active advocate on legislation that concerned him, particularly laws affecting federal court structure and jurisdiction.

More important, the Court's policies may be affected by a desire to deter Congress from enacting legislation that attacks the Court in some way. During several periods in the Court's history justices seemed to be motivated by the goal of avoiding decisions that would arouse—or aggravate—the displeasure of Congress. At the beginning of the nineteenth century John Marshall's Court faced congressional attacks because of its activist policies, and Marshall was careful to limit the occasions on which the Court reached decisions that would further anger its opponents. After the Civil War the Court retreated from conflict with the Radical Republicans in Congress, primarily through its acceptance of a statute that removed its jurisdiction over the Reconstruction laws while it considered a case involving those laws. Probably the most striking instance of the Court's efforts to avoid congressional attack was its shift from opposition to support of New Deal legislation in 1937 while Congress was considering President Roosevelt's Court-packing plan; this episode was discussed at greater length in Chapter 1.

A more recent episode with some drama occurred in the late 1950s. From 1954 to 1957 the Court adopted civil libertarian policies in several areas and thereby aroused a good deal of displeasure in Congress and the country at large. Members of Congress introduced bills to attack the Court's policies and to limit its jurisdiction, and a few of the bills received serious consideration. Meanwhile, in 1958 and 1959 the Court handed down some decisions in which it retreated from policies that had displeased Congress, including a virtual reversal of its position on congressional investigation of subversive activities. This shift seems to have constituted what one commentator called "a tactical withdrawal," [46] and it helped to quiet congressional attacks on the Court.

No dramatic events like these have taken place since the 1950s, and it is difficult to point to recent decisions that clearly were influenced by congressional pressure. Yet the pressure itself has existed. The Court has been attacked in Congress for its position on a variety of civil liberties issues, including school desegregation, legislative reapportionment, abortion, and school prayer. On each of these issues efforts have been made to overturn the Court's decisions, to limit its jurisdiction, or both.

The Court has adhered to some of its disfavored policies, and its continued support for school busing in the face of strong congressional opposition is striking. In other areas it has altered its positions. While most of the alterations seem best explained by other factors, a desire to reduce conflict with Congress may have played a part in some.

Church-state cases in the 1980s are interesting in this respect.[47] The Court has reiterated its opposition to organized school prayer, an unpopular position in Congress. But other decisions have been favorable to religious activities. In 1983 the Court upheld the use of legislative chaplains; as Justice Brennan's dissent said, the opposite decision "would likely have stimulated a furious reaction." [48] And in *Lynch v. Donnelly* (1984), the Court allowed a government-sponsored nativity scene. Presumably by coincidence, that decision was announced on the day that the Senate began debate on a constitutional amendment to allow school prayer exercises; a decision in the opposite direction probably would have increased interest in attacking the Court on church-state issues through support of the amendment.

Conclusions.   The impact of Congress on the Court should not be exaggerated. The instances in which congressional attacks have affected

Supreme Court policies are significant, but they hardly dominate the Court's history. Only occasionally has the Court faced a serious possibility of adverse action by Congress, and even at these times conflict between Congress and the Court has involved only a limited set of issues. Nor does the Court always retreat under pressure. In recent years the Court has maintained very liberal policies on several civil liberties issues despite considerable criticism from Congress.

But we also should be careful not to assume that Congress is irrelevant to the Court most of the time. Undoubtedly most justices are constantly aware of Congress as well as other elements of their environment. All else being equal, justices would prefer to take actions that please their audiences, and concern with congressional reaction may exert influence on their decisions from time to time that is too subtle for outsiders to recognize.

The President. Presidents have multifaceted relationships with the Supreme Court, and these relationships provide several sources of potential influence. Two of these, which already have been discussed, are quite important. First, the appointment power gives presidents considerable ability to determine the direction of the Court. Second, the president helps to shape government litigation policy—and thus affects the Court's decisions—through appointment of the solicitor general and occasional intervention in specific cases.

Another source of influence is the personal relationships between justices and presidents. Some members of the Court were close associates of presidents who later selected them. Moreover, justices may interact with presidents while serving on the bench. Some, such as Abe Fortas, have been frequent visitors to the White House for advisory or social purposes. Such relationships hardly compel justices to support the president's position in litigation, but they may exert a subtle impact on a justice's responses to cases with which the president is concerned.

Finally, the president helps to determine the Court's effectiveness by shaping responses of other institutions to the Court's decisions as well as the public's view of the Court. The president can support anti-Court action in Congress, as Franklin Roosevelt and Ronald Reagan did, or defend the Court against such action. Presidents can aid the Court in obtaining implementation of its policies, or they can refuse to help. They can lend their own prestige to the Court or undercut public support by criticizing it.

Because the president can help or hurt the Court in these ways, justices have reason to keep the peace with the president just as they do with Congress. This does not necessarily mean, however, that presidents can get what they want from the Court by pressuring it. During the Reagan administration, both President Reagan and Justice Department officials criticized the Court and some of its justices, but it does not appear that the Court retreated at all in the face of these attacks. This example illustrates a more general point: the considerable power of the president and Congress over the Supreme Court ordinarily falls far short of control over the Court's policies.

Justices' Values

The Role of Policy Preferences

Preferences and Decisions. In 1971, Supreme Court nominee William Rehnquist told the Senate Judiciary Committee, "My fundamental commitment, if I am confirmed, will be to totally disregard my own personal belief." [49] In making this statement, Rehnquist was asserting the view that justices' policy preferences can be irrelevant to their decisions.

This view seems untenable. The discussion of the law earlier in this chapter showed that the state of the law does not dictate justices' positions. Choices among legally acceptable policies must be based on other factors. If justices had only weak preferences about the issues that they face, perhaps those preferences would not be an important factor in their decisions. But justices come to the Court with stong views about many of the policy questions they will be called upon to decide, and they develop strong views on other issues as they confront cases raising those issues. As a result, their policy preferences serve as a powerful force shaping how they view cases and choose among alternative policies. Like other policy makers, members of the Supreme Court make decisions largely in terms of their personal attitudes about policy.

Indeed, policy preferences may play a larger role in the Court than in legislatures and administrative agencies. While justices' policy choices are constrained by the state of the law, this constraint may be outweighed by the Court's relative freedom from environmental pressures. In any case, it can be argued that justices' policy preferences are the most important of the factors that affect Supreme Court decisions.

Several kinds of evidence suggest the significance of preferences in decisions. The writings and public statements of some justices express the same views about policy that their votes and opinions indicate; Thurgood Marshall's support for affirmative action in the Court's decisions, for instance, is mirrored by his defense of affirmative action off the bench.[50] Similarly, some biographies of individual justices trace the ways in which their attitudes toward policy issues are reflected in their behavior on the Court. Another kind of evidence is the consistency that most justices show in the positions that they take on particular sets of issues, not only from case to case but also from year to year. Justice Brennan's regular support for civil liberties from the mid-1950s through the late 1980s is difficult to explain except in terms of a strong personal commitment to those liberties.

Whatever their importance in explaining decisions generally, policy preferences almost certainly provide the best explanation for differences among the justices in decisional behavior. This is true because no other factor varies so much from one justice to another. Most efforts by scholars to examine the effects of preferences on decisions have focused on differences among justices, using the assumption that differences in their voting behavior generally reflect differences in personal views about policy issues.[51] This procedure is reasonable so long as we avoid assuming that *all* Supreme Court behavior is based solely on policy preferences. Later in this section I will use comparisons among justices to probe the role of their policy preferences in the Court's decisions.

The Sources of Preferences.   The views of Supreme Court justices on policy issues, of course, derive from the same general sources as political attitudes generally. Family socialization is a key element in the development of attitudes. Other institutions such as schools and the mass media also are important. Certainly, career experiences can help to shape justices' attitudes.

Some scholars have sought to explain justices' preferences, and thus their behavior, in terms of specific "background" characteristics.[52] Certainly these characteristics do help to shape the attitudes that justices bring to cases. Male and female justices are likely to have differing perspectives on issues affecting women, a difference underlined when Justice O'Connor in 1986 cast the only public dissent against the Court's refusal to hear a sex discrimination case.[53] Justice Powell said that his experience as a college trustee influenced his opinion that determined the Court's position on affirmative action in college admissions.[54] But the relationship between specific characteristics and attitudes is complex, and a judge's attitudes cannot be explained completely in terms of those characteristics. Certainly justices whose backgrounds were rather similar in many respects have behaved quite differently as members of the Supreme Court.

The Ideological Dimension

The pattern of a justice's preferences on the various issues addressed by the Supreme Court is not random. Rather, the attitudes that each justice holds tend to be interrelated in a fairly logical way. As Benjamin Cardozo wrote before he reached the Court,

> There is in each of us a stream of tendency, whether you choose to call it philosophy or not, which gives coherence and direction to thought and action. Judges cannot escape that current any more than other mortals.[55]

In this respect, of course, judges are similar to others with active interests in political issues.

Liberalism and Conservatism.   The coherence that exists in the attitudes of Supreme Court justices and other people can be understood in terms of liberalism and conservatism. In the United States one set of preferences on a wide range of issues is labeled liberal, while the opposing preferences are called conservative. Most of the issues that come to the Supreme Court involve conflicts between liberal and conservative positions. As described by David Rohde and Harold Spaeth, those issues can be placed in three general categories.[56]

The first category is called "freedom," and it includes issues involving conflicts between individual freedoms and government action. These freedoms are of two types: procedural rights, such as the rights of criminal defendants, and substantive rights, such as freedom of expression and of religion. The liberal position gives heavy weight to these rights, while the conservative position gives relatively heavy weight to values that compete with these rights, such as the capacity to fight crime effectively.

The second category is labeled "equality." It includes issues involving the right to equal treatment by government and private institutions under the Fourteenth Amendment and other provisions of law, including civil rights statutes. The liberal position is more sympathetic toward challenges to inequality than is the conservative position.

Rohde and Spaeth call the third category "New Dealism," though it might also be called economic regulation. This category contains issues resulting from government regulation of the economy, an activity associated with President Franklin Roosevelt's New Deal program. The liberal and conservative positions are more difficult to define in this area, though liberals are basically more sympathetic to the positions of economic "underdogs" and to regulatory policies intended to serve those groups. Thus, liberals are more likely than conservatives to support government regulation of business and to favor labor unions against businesses.

Ideology and Decisions.   Throughout government, liberalism and conservatism provide organizing principles for people's views and actions on policy issues. Any individual policy maker tends to stand at about the same position on the continuum from liberalism to conservatism on most issues. Thus, a senator who takes a strong conservative position on public welfare is likely to adopt a conservative position on national defense as well.

The same is true of Supreme Court justices. In their votes and opinions, most justices establish fairly consistent positions on the ideological spectrum, positions that span the broad range of issues the Court decides. This is especially true of the justices who stand close to either end of the spectrum. There is no difficulty in characterizing Justices Brennan and Marshall as liberals or Chief Justice Rehnquist as a conservative.

This does not mean that a justice will be equally liberal or conservative on all issues. Some justices deviate considerably from that pattern; Justice White, for instance, has been more liberal on equality cases than on freedom cases. While some justices are considered moderates because they take middle-of-the-road positions on most issues, others appear to be moderates because they combine liberal positions on some issues with conservative positions on others. Ideological consistency across issues is a strong tendency but not an absolute rule.

The level of ideological consistency is higher within the three categories of cases identified by Rohde and Spaeth. This is illustrated by the voting patterns in fifty-eight nonunanimous decisions on freedom cases that the Court reached in the 1986 term. These patterns are depicted in Figure 4-1, in what is called a scalogram. In a scalogram, justices and cases are both put in order primarily according to the number of liberal votes (with some rearrangements to improve "scalability"), so that the observer can determine how consistently the overall ideological rankings of justices are reflected in individual cases.

Figure 4-1 shows, first of all, that the justices varied considerable in their support for liberal outcomes, from Marshall at the liberal end of the spectrum to Rehnquist at the conservative end. For the most part, the divisions in individual cases followed the same lines as the overall rankings of justices. For instance, when the Court divided 5-4 in a conservative direction, in thirteen of seventeen cases it was the four justices with the most liberal overall records who dissented. There were many exceptions to perfect ideological consistency, but most were moderate rather than extreme. To take one example, when Stevens did not join Brennan and Marshall as the third liberal vote in a 6-3 or 5-3 conservative decision, in six of seven cases it was Blackmun—fourth in overall liberalism—who cast that third vote. Aside from Blackmun, Scalia cast the largest number of "inconsistent" votes, a pattern that might result from a complex set of attitudes toward freedom issues or from his newness on the Court.

The pattern shown in the figure is similar to that found in other issue categories and other years, though in recent years economic regulation seems to show less consistent voting than the other categories.[57] (If we defined issue areas more narrowly, voting consistency would appear much greater; for example, criminal procedure cases, which constitute nearly two-thirds of the cases in Table 4-1, show a very high level of consistency.)

Figure 4-1 Scalogram of Justices' Votes in Cases Involving "Freedom" Issues, 1986 Term

Justices

Cases[a]	Marshall	Brennan	Stevens	Blackmun	Powell	Scalia	White	O'Connor	Rehnquist	*Liberal votes*
94 - 190	+	+	+	+	+	+	+	+	+	8
95 - 209	+	+	+	+	+	−	+	+	−	7
96 - 510	+	+	+	+	+	−	+	+	−	7
94 - 347	+	+	+	+	−	+	+	−	−	6
96 - 398	+	+	+	+	−	+	−	−	−	6
93 - 649	+	+	+	+	+	+	−	+	−	6
93 - 539	+	+	−	−	+	+	+	+	−	5
97 - 56	+	+	+	+	+	−	−	−	−	6
96 - 303	+	+	+	+	+	−	−	−	−	6
95 - 622	+	+	+	+	+	−	−	−	−	5
95 - 772	+	+	+	+	+	−	−	−	−	5
96 - 440	+	+	+	+	+	−	−	−	−	5
97 - 37	+	+	+	+	+	−	+	−	−	5
97 - 315	+	+	+	+	+	−	−	−	−	5
93 - 514	+	+	−	+	+	−	−	−	−	5
94 - 267	+	+	−	+	+	+	−	−	−	4
97 - 638	+	+	−	+	+	+	−	−	−	4
95 - 740	+	+	+	+	+	−	−	−	−	5
95 - 162	+	+	+	+	+	−	−	−	−	5
94 - 714	+	+	+	+	−	−	−	−	−	4
95 - 127	+	+	+	+	−	−	−	−	−	4
95 - 458	+	+	+	+	−	−	−	−	−	4
95 - 262	+	+	+	+	−	−	−	−	−	4
97 - 709	+	+	+	+	−	−	−	−	−	4
97 - 1	+	+	+	+	−	−	−	−	−	4
97 - 90	+	+	+	+	−	−	−	−	−	4
93 - 934	+	+	+	+	−	−	−	−	−	4
94 - 405	+	+	+	+	−	−	−	−	−	4
95 - 439	+	+	+	+	−	−	−	−	−	4
96 - 282	+	+	+	+	−	−	−	−	−	4

Citation[a]	57	56	40	37	15	9	7	7	0	
96-64	+	+	+	−	−	−	−	−	−	4
96-654	+	+	+	+	−	−	−	−	−	4
93-334	+	+	+	+	−	−	−	−	−	4
94-40	+	+	+	−	−	+	−	−	−	4
94-364	+	+	+	−	−	+	+	−	−	4
93-473	+	+	+	−	−	−	−	−	−	3
95-176	+	+	+	−	−	−	−	−	−	3
95-354	+	+	+	−	−	−	−	−	−	3
95-539	+	+	+	−	−	−	−	−	−	3
95-697	+	+	+	−	−	−	−	−	−	3
96-631	+	+	+	−	−	−	−	−	−	3
97-336	+	+	+	−	−	−	−	−	−	3
97-523	+	+	+	−	−	−	−	−	−	3
95-415	+	+	+	+	−	0	−	−	−	3
97-485	+	+	−	+	−	−	−	−	−	3
97-144	+	+	−	+	−	−	−	−	−	3
97-618	+	+	−	+	−	−	−	−	−	3
97-364	+	+	−	+	−	−	−	−	−	3
94-72	+	+	−	−	−	−	−	−	−	3
96-601	+	+	−	−	−	−	+	−	−	3
93-954	+	+	−	−	−	−	−	−	−	2
94-326	+	+	−	−	−	−	−	−	−	2
93-739	+	+	−	−	−	−	−	−	−	2
93-499	+	+	−	−	−	−	−	−	−	2
97-427	+	+	+	−	−	−	−	−	−	2
93-920	+	−	−	−	−	−	−	−	−	2
93-305	+	−	−	−	−	−	−	−	−	1
97-473	−	+	+	−	−	−	−	−	−	1
Total liberal votes	57	56	40	37	15	9	7	7	0	

Note: Cases were included if the Court decided issues of procedural due process or substantive civil liberties, except equality issues, by nonunanimous vote. Liberal votes are designated +; conservative votes, −; nonparticipating judges are designated 0. The stepped vertical rule divides justices into two groups according to conventional rules of scalogram analysis; − signs to left of the line and + signs to the right may be interpreted as votes inconsistent with the ideological ordering of the justices.

[a] Numbers represent volumes and pages of case citations in *Supreme Court Reports, Lawyers' Edition.*

Figure 4-2   Median Percentages of Cases in Which Pairs of Justices Supported the Same Opinion, 1985-1986 Terms

	Br	St	Bl	Po	Wh	O'C	Bu	Re	Sc
					Justices[a]				
Marshall	95	68	81	53	47	49	41	39	41
Brennan		68	79	56	51	51	46	42	42
Stevens			68	56	57	55	48	49	51
Blackmun				64	58	59	50	50	52
Powell					76	85	85	87	73
White						76	78	81	78
O'Connor							82	85	74
Burger								92	—
Rehnquist									86
Scalia									

Sources: "The Supreme Court, 1985 Term," *Harvard Law Review* 100 (November 1986): 305; "The Supreme Court, 1986 Term," *Harvard Law Review* 101 (November 1987): 363.

Note: Numbers are medians, for the two terms, of the percentages of cases in each term in which a pair of justices agreed on an opinion. Both unanimous and nonunanimous cases are included. Burger served only in the 1985 term, Scalia only in the 1986 term.

[a] Br = Brennan, St = Stevens, Bl = Blackmun, Po = Powell, Wh = White, O'C = O'Connor, Bu = Burger, Re = Rehnquist, Sc = Scalia.

This pattern suggests that within a broad category of cases justices divide primarily on the basis of a single ideological dimension. Not only are justices' policy preferences largely responsible for differences in their decisional behavior, but to a considerable degree those preferences are expressed in a moderately simple ideological form.

Patterns of Agreement.   Another perspective on the Court's ideological divisions can be obtained by examining the patterns of agreement among justices. Figure 4-2 shows the mean proportions of cases in which each pair of justices supported the same opinion during the 1985 and 1986 terms. (It should be noted that Burger served only in the 1985 term, Scalia only in 1986.) This figure, unlike Figure 4-1, includes cases in all issue categories. As the figure shows, some pairs of justices agreed with each other a good deal more than other pairs, though the differences are not as sharp as we might have expected.

Not surprisingly, levels of agreement are highest for the justices whose ideological positions in Court decisions are closest. Figure 4-2 shows that Marshall and Brennan supported the same opinion in nineteen of every twenty cases, an extraordinarily high proportion, and the rate of agreement for Burger and Rehnquist was nearly as high. By the same token, the lowest rates of agreement were between justices who were ideologically distant from each other; Marshall and Brennan supported the same opinion as Rehnquist only about two fifths of the time. The figure indicates that Powell was in the ideological center of the Court but that he agreed with his conservative colleagues more often than with the more liberal justices. Of the eighty-one cases decided by 5-4 votes in these two terms, forty-four found Powell joining the four most liberal members or the four most conservative members, and in thirty-one of those cases he joined the conservatives.[58]

We should be careful not to make too much of these patterns. First, as some of the votes in Figure 4-1 suggest, the justices do not always line up in expected ways. Indeed, in cases that lack clear-cut ideological conflicts, rather unusual alliances may appear. Second, we should not assume that patterns of agreement reflect self-conscious alliances or blocs of justices. To some degree justices who hold similar policy preferences work together to achieve favorable outcomes; indeed, Warren and Brennan met on Thursdays to discuss cases before the Court's Friday conferences.[59] And certainly members of the Court are aware of general patterns of agreement among themselves. But it is their shared preferences, not the existence of concerted action, that best explain the tendency for certain justices to support the same opinion.

Preferences and Policy Change

The process of policy change on the Supreme Court is difficult to analyze, because the issues before the Court constantly are changing. In tax law, for example, if the proportion of decisions favorable to taxpayers declines, the decline might reflect a change in the Court's policies on tax law or simply a change in the kinds of tax cases that reach the Court, and it is not always easy to distinguish between the two possibilities. Still, at times it is clear that the Court's collective approach to a policy area or a set of policy areas (such as civil liberties) has changed.

Such changes can occur for a variety of reasons. But the discussion of policy preferences in this section suggests that a primary source of policy change on the Court must be changes in the preferences of the justices as a group. Such changes can come in two ways: from changes in the views of people already serving on the Court and from change in the Court's membership. In practice, both kinds of change are significant.

Changes in Views. Justices come to the Supreme Court with fundamental values that are well formed. Yet as justices they are exposed to new influences and confront issues in new forms. The result is a general stability in the preferences that justices express in their votes and opinions but many minor changes in their views—and, occasionally, a fundamental change.

Certainly most justices retain the same basic ideological position throughout their careers. A justice who begins as a liberal, such as William Brennan, generally remains a liberal; the same is true of a conservative such as William Rehnquist. When a justice's position shifts relative to other members of the Court, it is usually because new appointments have changed the Court's ideological center of gravity while the justice retains the same general views. This was the case with Potter Stewart, who moved toward the liberal side of the Court as new justices more conservative than Stewart joined the Court.

Even a justice who retains the same general preferences is likely to shift positions on specific issues. In 1973, for instance, Brennan announced a fundamental change in his position on the application of the First Amendment to obscenity.[60] Some justices experience a more systematic, but fairly limited, shift in their general views. Some observers have perceived a conservative shift in Byron White, and others—including her colleague Harry Blackmun—have seen Sandra Day O'Connor as moving at least slightly to the left.[61]

Blackmun himself is an example of the relatively rare cases in which a justice's basic views seem to undergo a fundamental shift. Blackmun came to the Court in 1970 as a Nixon appointee, and early in his career he aligned himself chiefly with the other conservative justices. He and Chief Justice Burger, boyhood friends from Minnesota, were dubbed the "Minnesota Twins." In the 1973 term Blackmun agreed with Burger on opinions in 84 percent of the decisions, with Brennan in only 49 percent.[62] But gradually Blackmun moved toward the center of the Court, and from the 1980 term on he usually had higher agreement rates with Brennan than with Burger—in 1985, Burger's last term, 30 percent higher. In an interview published in 1983, Blackmun indicated that one personal goal was to prevent the Court "from plunging rapidly to the right." He also referred obliquely to his changed views: ". . . I think, clearly, this is an educational process—and I would hope that one matures as the years go by." [63]

More common than individual ideological shifts are changes in the views of the justices as a group on a particular issue. I have already suggested that public opinion can affect how justices perceive an issue at a particular time. In some instances, external events such as wars and social movements can influence the justices in a deeper way, affecting their basic attitudes about an issue. Such an impact might be characterized as a special kind of environmental influence on the Court.

One example is the development of the black civil rights movement in the 1950s and 1960s. That movement enlisted the sympathies of many Americans, apparently including most members of the Supreme Court. The Court's support for the positions of the civil rights movement across a broad range of cases is striking; especially noteworthy was its extraordinary willingness to overturn convictions of civil rights demonstrators who had been arrested for their activities.

A similar and even more striking example concerns the legal status of women. The Warren Court gave unprecedented support to equality under the law, but it did not attack legal provisions that treated women and men differently. Its successor, a more conservative Court on most issues, nonetheless handed down a series of decisions promoting legal equality for the sexes. This seemingly anomalous change resulted in part from an upsurge in cases challenging sex discrimination, but a more fundamental cause seemed to be the impact of the women's liberation movement on justices' views about women's social roles. Most of the Court's moderates and conservatives took positions supportive of sexual equality in the 1970s that even some liberals might not have adopted in the 1960s. This example underlines the potential for significant changes in justices' collective attitudes toward policy issues.

Membership Change. Although shifts in the positions of sitting justices can produce major policy changes on the Court, more often such changes result from new appointments to the Court. Membership change is probably the most important source of policy change on the Court. Indeed, the importance of appointments should be evident from the discussion thus far: If Supreme Court policies are primarily a product of the justices' preferences, and if those preferences tend to be stable, then change will come most easily through the replacement of one justice with a successor who has a different set of policy preferences.

The Court's civil liberties policies since the 1950s demonstrate the significance of membership change. The early Warren Court was closely divided between liberals and conservatives, and from 1958 until 1961 there was a relatively stable division between a four-member liberal bloc and a moderate to conservative bloc of five. By the standards of the 1920s and 1930s the Court's decisions were quite liberal, but Table 4-2 shows that parties with civil liberties claims won only a little more than half their cases.

In 1962 President Kennedy made two appointments to the Court. The moderate Byron White replaced conservative Charles Whittaker, and the liberal Arthur Goldberg replaced Felix Frankfurter. On a closely divided Court, these appointments were sufficient to change the general direction of policy. Their effects were reinforced by the selection of

Table 4-2 Percentages of Supreme Court Decisions Favorable to Parties with Civil Liberties Claims, 1958-1987 Terms

Terms	Percentage
1958-1961	57.8
1962-1968	74.1
1969-1975[a]	48.8
1975-1980[a]	39.1
1981-1985	37.2
1986-1987	46.0

[a] 1969-1975 includes the part of the 1975 term with Douglas on the Court; 1975-1980 includes the part of that term with Stevens on the court.

Thurgood Marshall in 1967 to replace Tom Clark. (In 1965, Goldberg was replaced by another liberal, Abe Fortas.) The period from 1962 to 1969 probably was the most liberal in the Court's history. The Court established strikingly liberal positions in a variety of policy areas, and the proportion of pro-civil liberties decisions increased substantially.

Between 1969 and 1971, President Nixon was able to fill four vacancies on the Court, and he used these opportunities to move the Court in a conservative direction. Liberals Warren and Fortas, along with Harlan and Black, were replaced by four justices who ranged from moderately conservative (Powell and Blackmun) to strongly conservative (Burger and Rehnquist) in their views. Later the very liberal Douglas was succeeded by the moderate-to-liberal Stevens (in 1975) and the moderate Stewart was succeeded by the conservative O'Connor (in 1981). These changes made the Court still more conservative, though they were balanced somewhat by Blackmun's move in a liberal direction. More time will be necessary to ascertain the impact of the last two appointments, those of Antonin Scalia (replacing Burger in 1986) and Anthony Kennedy (replacing Powell in 1988).

As noted in Chapter 1, the impact of these membership changes on the Court's civil liberties policies has been somewhat ambiguous. On the one hand, the Court has adhered to some policies of the Warren Court and has even taken new liberal directions on issues such as women's rights. Yet, on the whole, the Burger and Rehnquist Courts have been considerably less supportive of civil liberties than the Court of the 1960s. As Table 4-2 shows, the successive appointments from 1969 through 1981 reduced the proportion of decisions favorable to civil liberties. (The table may exaggerate the Court's conservative movement because the issues faced by the Warren and Burger Courts were not fully compara-ble.)[64] The surprising increase in pro-civil liberties decisions in the first two terms of the Rehnquist Court probably is a temporary phenomenon that will be reversed as that Court continues.

The limits on the Supreme Court's policy shift in the 1970s and 1980s caution against exaggerating the impact of membership change. But the change in policies that did occur is noteworthy. Certainly it provides evidence that the appointment process is the most important mechanism by which the Court's policies may be altered, at least in the short run.

Role Values

Thus far the discussion of justices' values has been limited to their policy preferences. But these are not the only kinds of values that may affect the Court's decisions. The choices that justices make also may be influenced by their role values, their views about what constitutes appropriate behavior for the Supreme Court and its members. In any body, whether it is a court or a legislature, members' conceptions of how they should carry out their jobs will structure what they do and affect their policy decisions.

In the Supreme Court, perhaps the most fundamental role value is that decisions are to be founded on the law and justified in legal terms. No member of the Court has disagreed with this value, though justices may vary in the extent to which they think that legal considerations should determine their judgments.

Other sets of role values also can affect decisions. Views about the legitimacy of dissenting opinions may help to determine the frequency of unanimous decisions. Attitudes concerning the desirability of judicial activism may influence decisions whether to overturn acts of Congress. Justices who believe that the Court should take public opinion into account may be especially unwilling to adopt unpopular positions on policy issues. These values are likely to vary considerably among members of the Court.

Attitudes toward activism and the law as a constraint both were expressed in the quite different ways that Oliver Wendell Holmes and Hugo Black summarized their roles on the Court. Once, when bidden by a friend to "do justice," Holmes replied, "That is not my job. My job is to play the game according to the rules." [65] In contrast, when Black was asked what he conceived his basic task to be, "His eyes blazed, his right hand shot into the air, and without hesitation he fervently said, 'To do justice!' " [66] While both statements oversimplify the views of the justices who made them, they reflect real and significant differences in role conceptions.

It is difficult to reach firm conclusions about the impact of role values on justices' behavior, and observers of the Court differ in their judgments. In one sense, role values clearly are important, because they structure the ways in which justices perceive their jobs. Certainly members of the Court speak frequently about these values; some opinions, for instance, emphasize the desirability of judicial restraint.

Yet justices could be expected to adopt, consciously or unconsciously, role values that are consistent with their policy goals. If this is the case, then justices' values concerning matters such as judicial activism might simply reflect their preferences rather than exerting an independent impact on their behavior. The most fundamental value, adherence to the law as a basis for decision, would seem on its face to be a powerful constraint on the justices; we have seen, however, that the ambiguity of the law in Supreme Court cases usually leaves justices with considerable freedom to choose among alternative decisions.

On the whole, I think the evidence indicates that role values have only a limited impact. The positions that justices adopt in decisions generally appear to be consistent with their personal policy preferences. Thus it is their conceptions of good public policy that seem most responsible for their policy choices, and role values seem to play a considerably more limited part in the decision process.

This conclusion is supported by the history of the debate over judicial activism and restraint in this century. During the 1920s and early 1930s, activist Supreme Court policies generally involved attacks on government regulation of the economy. Conservative justices took the most activist positions, while liberals on the Court and elsewhere argued for judicial restraint. Since the 1940s, however, activism has meant primarily support for civil liberties against legislative and executive action. In this context it is liberals who have given the most support to Supreme Court activism, while conservatives have argued for judicial restraint. This history suggests that positions on activism and restraint have served chiefly as justifications of policy choices rather than determining those choices themselves.

One possible exception is Felix Frankfurter. As a liberal law professor in the 1920s and 1930s, Frankfurter argued strongly for judicial restraint. After joining the Court in 1939, he supported restraint not only on issues of economic regulation but also on civil liberties questions, where most liberals supported activism. This pattern suggests that Frankfurter's decisions were motivated primarily by his conception of the Court's role of government, which overrode his liberal policy preferences. Frankfurter himself interpreted his behavior in this way, and some commentators agree. Others argue that Frankfurter really had become a conservative on civil liberties issues and masked his conservatism with rhetoric about judicial restraint.[67]

The debate about Frankfurter's motives is difficult to resolve. But it should not obscure the fact that Frankfurter is, at most, an exceptional case. If his behavior was determined primarily by his role values, he stands out among justices whose role values seemed to have only a limited independent effect on their decisions. For the justices as a group, policy preferences are the most important values that influence their decisions.

Group Interaction

A Quasi-Collegial Body

For the most part, Supreme Court justices do their work as individuals, with the help of their law clerks and in isolation from each other. Justice Powell observed that "for the most part, perhaps as much as 90 percent of our total time, we function as nine small, independent law firms." [68] A Court secretary expressed a similar thought: "There are nine separate kingdoms here." [69]

But there is also a critical group element to the Court's decision making. Part of the decisional process occurs in the group settings of oral argument and the Court's conferences. Further, justices have incentives to interact and work together on decisions outside of conference. The shared goal of seeking majority approval for an opinion in each case often requires interaction. The desire to obtain as much consensus as possible gives justices further reason to work together to reach agreement on outcomes and opinions. On a different level, justices who feel strongly about cases will attempt to persuade colleagues to accept their viewpoints, and there may be a good deal of competition between opposing sides to win votes in a close case. Perhaps it is best to call the Court a quasi-collegial body, one in which group interaction plays a limited but significant role in the decision-making process.

Interaction among justices has a considerable effect on some decisions. Most frequently, the Court's opinion is shaped through negotiation between the assigned justice and other members of the Court. Indeed, the final opinion sometimes is fundamentally different from its first draft, even when the official author is the same. This apparently was the case in *United States v. Nixon* (1974), in which Chief Justice Burger's original opinion was found unsatisfactory by several colleagues. Reportedly they worked together to produce a more acceptable final opinion, which nonetheless was issued in Burger's name.[70]

Group interaction also accounts for much of what J. Woodford Howard called "the fluidity of judicial choice," [71] the shifting of individual votes and collective decisions after tentative decisions in conference. A justice may change a position independently after further study of a case, but frequently it is input from colleagues that spurs reconsideration of an initial position. Certainly group interaction was crucial in the single most famous instance of fluidity, the process by which a Court that had been closely divided eventually produced a unanimous decision in *Brown v. Board of Education.*[72] Histories of the Court offer other accounts of cases in which persuasion within the Court shifted votes and sometimes majorities.

But the effects of group interaction should not be exaggerated. Once a justice has developed a position on a case or on an issue that runs through several cases, over time, a colleague may have considerable difficulty in dislodging the justice from that position. As noted earlier, for example, conference discussion of a case often has little impact on justices' views. As Chief Justice Rehnquist wrote, when justices who have prepared themselves "assemble around the conference table on Friday morning to decide an important case presenting constitutional questions that they have all debated and written about before, the outcome may be a foregone conclusion." [73]

A more systematic picture of the impact of group processes can be obtained through Saul Brenner's work on decisional fluidity. In the 1956-1967 period, 10 percent of the justices' votes shifted from one side to the other between the conference and the Court's announcement of its decision, and at least one shift occurred in about half of the cases. Most of the vote changes increased the size of the original majority, as the Court worked toward consensus. But in eighty-five cases during those years (about 9 percent of the total) an initial minority became a majority through vote shifts or shifts between participation and nonparticipation in a vote.[74] Brenner has examined another indication of fluidity, the frequency with which the justice originally assigned the Court's opinion does not end up writing for the Court; during the 1946-1952 terms, this kind of shift occurred in 6 percent of the Court's decisions.[75]

These findings do not give a perfect indication of group impact on decisions. Not all vote or opinion shifts stem from group influences, and group influences may be reflected in initial conference votes as well as shifts later in the process. But the findings nonetheless are noteworthy. On the one hand, they suggest that group processes do make a difference. Perhaps more important, the stability of most votes cast in conference suggests that there are limits to the impact of colleagues on the positions that justices take. Individual policy preferences appear to be considerably more important than group processes in shaping the Court's decisions.

The group life of the Court can have an effect on its decisions that is broader and more subtle than shifts of position in individual cases. A Court may have patterns of influence that give special weight to the positions of some justices in determining the Court's policies. The Court's ability to reach consensus may depend on the extent of conflict among its members. In the rest of this section I will examine those two issues and through them look in more detail at the characteristics of the Court as a group.

Patterns of Influence

Sources of Influence. Except for the chief justice, all members of the Supreme Court are essentially equal in their formal powers. Each has one vote. In a sense, then, the justices begin with equal opportunities for influence over their colleagues.

As in other groups, however, members of the Supreme Court differ in what they make of these opportunities. In part, these differences result from variation in the desire for influence. Justice Douglas wrote that "most judges content themselves with making up their own minds," but Stone, Black, and Frankfurter "were evangelists," "active proselytizers." [76] Douglas himself was an extreme case of a justice who is uninterested in exerting influence; one colleague reported, presumably with some overstatement, that "Bill Douglas is positively embarrassed if anyone on the court agrees with him." [77]

In addition, justices differ in qualities that help to determine interpersonal influence on the Court. One crucial quality is skill in legal reasoning and argumentation. Ultimately, policy positions must be justified within the Court and to its audiences as good law and, to a lesser extent, as good policy. For this reason a justice who can make very strong arguments for personal positions will have disproportionate influence. A good example might be John Harlan, a conservative on the distinctly liberal Warren Court. Despite his minority position, Harlan seemed to have considerable influence with his colleagues because of his extraordinary skills as a legal analyst. On the Burger Court Lewis Powell may have held special influence because of his widely acknowledged strengths as a legal scholar. On the other side, justices with clearly limited skills are likely to wield relatively little influence in the decisional process.

A second relevant quality is a justice's personality. Supreme Court justices, like other people, vary in their likability and their skills in personal relations, and these characteristics inevitably will affect their influence. Justice James McReynolds, who alienated his colleagues with his unpleasantness, was not likely to have much impact on their decisions. Certainly he did not improve his chances of changing his colleagues' positions with his practice of noting on drafts of opinions, "This statement makes me sick." [78] In contrast, a person who gets along well with colleagues—as William Rehnquist, for instance, appears to do—is likely to gain in influence as a result.

In this respect, Felix Frankfurter and William Brennan provide an interesting contrast. Frankfurter came to the Court in 1939 expecting to play a major leadership role, and he made great efforts to influence his colleagues. He gave special energy to courting new colleagues. But these efforts suffered from his arrogance and his tendency to lecture to his colleagues. His messages to other justices during the decision-making process included an abundance of statements like the following: "And so please, Mr. Jackson, do find time to read, if you have not already read, the chapter on Presumption in J. B. Thayer's Preliminary Treatise." "I would like to ask you to read or reread in cold blood the following cases." [79] He also reacted sarcastically to opinions with which he disagreed. Frankfurter unintentionally alienated several colleagues with his behavior, and his influence within the Court was fairly limited. Indeed, one study of four Court terms concluded that Frankfurter exerted less leadership in decisions than any of his colleagues. [80]

Brennan's efforts to exert influence have been considerably more successful. As a member of the Warren Court, working closely with Warren, he helped to forge a liberal majority for expansions of civil liberties; in the Burger and Rehnquist Courts, he has done much to shape the Court's decisions so as to limit the Court's movement to the right. One former law clerk for another justice described Brennan as "the best coalition builder ever to sit on the Supreme Court." [81] Brennan has the advantage of a personal style far warmer than Frankfurter's. Just as important are his focus on the task of developing support for his positions and his willingness to compromise as much as necessary to move the Court in his direction. Whatever the precise measure of Brennan's influence, he demonstrates that a committed and effective justice can do a good deal to affect the Court's decisions.

Equality of Influence. It is important not to exaggerate the influence—or lack of influence—of individual justices. First of all, under today's conditions it is doubtful that a single justice could dominate the Court or even approach a position of dominance. For the most part, members of the Court are strong-minded people who care deeply about many of the issues on which they rule.

Further, the fact that each justice holds a single vote provides an important equalizing force. No matter how limited a justice's skills or how weak a justice's personality, that member still has the power to vote to affirm or reverse, to support one opinion or another. Particularly on a closely divided Court, every justice has the capacity to secure changes in opinions to meet objections. When Justice Stewart joined an ideologically split Court in 1958, he reportedly was "wooed" by the competing factions "in much the manner of an uncommitted delegate at a political convention." [82] Stewart's colleagues could have known little about his professional and personal qualities at that time, but his mere presence on the Court as a potentially pivotal member gave him real influence.

The Chief Justice

As a leader of the Court, the chief justice occupies an ambiguous position. The limitations of the position as a source of leadership stand out, but the chief also holds some significant formal powers.

One limitation lies in the increasing burden of administrative duties that have fallen on the chief. Jeffrey Morris, a close observer of the Court, concludes that the chief "may well stand at a relative disadvantage" in the rewriting and bargaining over opinions "because of the unique demands upon his time." [83] Perhaps a more fundamental limitation is the difficulty of leading twentieth-century justices, whose resistance to control already has been described. In the early nineteenth century, Chief Justice John Marshall exerted tremendous influence over the Court, an influence reflected in his writing of the Court's opinion in a majority of cases. But today's members of the Court would be impossible to lead so strongly. Indeed, they accord little special deference to the chief justice. As William Rehnquist has written, the chief

> presides over a conference not of eight subordinates, whom he may direct or instruct, but of eight associates who, like him, have tenure during good behavior, and who are as independent as hogs on ice. He may at most persuade or cajole them.[84]

Yet the formal powers that the chief possesses provide a special potential for influence over the Court's decisions, and these powers require examination.

The Chief Justice's Powers. Perhaps the most important power attached to the position of the chief justice is that of presiding over the Court in oral argument and in conference. In presiding over conference, the chief can direct discussion and frame alternatives, thus helping to shape the outcome of the discussion. It is especially important that the chief is the first to speak on a case in conference.

Two other powers are quite important. The first is the chief's part in creating the discuss list, the set of petitions for hearing to which the Court will give full consideration. The chief, aided by clerks, makes up the initial version of the discuss list. This task gives the chief the largest role in determining which cases are set aside without group judgment. The second is the power of opinion assignment, which merits discussion in some detail.

Opinion Assignment. By custom, the chief justice assigns the Court's opinion whenever the chief is in the majority on the initial vote in conference. (In other cases, the senior justice in the majority makes the assignment.) As a result, the chief ordinarily assigns the great majority of opinions.

The significance of the assignment power should be underlined. First of all, the selection of the opinion writer may determine whether the initial majority stands up and what its ultimate size will be, since different justices may produce opinions with different effects on their colleagues. More directly, the policy proclaimed by the Court may depend in large part on who writes the opinion—if the selected writer can maintain the support of at least four colleagues for the opinion. In addition, the assignment power allows the chief to reward and punish colleagues and thus provides an extra degree of leverage over them.

To some extent, patterns in opinion assignment are dictated by the need to ensure that the Court's work gets done.[85] The chief justice usually will try to assign approximately equal numbers of opinions to the justices to spread out the workload, but speedier writers may receive more than their share.[86]

But the chief has considerable room to use opinion assignments to advance personal policy goals. Most important, the chief can choose to write the Court's opinion or give it to an ideological ally to obtain an opinion that accords with the chief's views. Indeed, the chief justice tends to follow this strategy in the more important cases, with justices who are ideologically distant from the chief receiving most of their opinion assignments in cases that the chief views as less critical. The chief also may use desirable assignments to try to gain influence with a colleague, while Justice Blackmun has said that a justice who is "in the doghouse" may be assigned one of the "crud" opinions "that nobody wants to write."[87]

Other factors come into play in assignment decisions. One reason why the chief justice is especially likely to write the opinion in very important cases is that the chief's name on the opinion may lend it greater weight. The chief may assign a disproportionate number of cases in a technical area of law to a member who has expertise in that area. Because so many factors contribute to opinion assignment decisions, the pattern of assignments is complex.

Variation in Leadership. What particular chief justices make of their formal powers and how strong a leadership role they play have varied a good deal during this century. Charles Evans Hughes, for instance, was a relatively powerful leader of the Court, particularly in its conference deliberations; his successor, Harlan Stone, played a far more limited leadership role. Such differences result from several conditions, including the chief's interest in exerting leadership, the chief's skill as a leader, and the general willingness of the associate justices to be led.

The last two chief justices preceding William Rehnquist, Earl Warren and Warren Burger, are of particular interest. Their tenure is too recent and the evidence too ambiguous to provide a clear picture of their roles. Still, it is possible to sketch out their positions generally.

Earl Warren could not compete with some colleagues as a scholar. He presided over a Court with several skillful and strong-minded members, such as Douglas and Frankfurter, and the Court was closely divided between liberals and conservatives during most of his tenure. These conditions would have made it very difficult for Warren to establish himself as dominant in the Court's decision making, and he did not do so. Indeed, some observers see Brennan as the real leader of the Warren Court, while Justice Stewart thought that Black had occupied that role.[88]

But Warren did have some major assets. Most important, he possessed a high level of leadership skills, which stemmed largely from his personality and his experience as a political leader. Those skills were demonstrated at the beginning of his career on the Court. He came to the Court in 1953 during the deliberation over the school desegregation cases, which had divided the Court sharply. Chiefly through what Justice Douglas called "a brilliant diplomatic process which Warren had engineered," [89] the Court handed down a unanimous decision in *Brown v. Board of Education* at the end of his first term. Warren was able to play a major leadership role on the Court, albeit one that was shared with and contested by some colleagues.

Warren Burger is an especially interesting case. He had considerable ambition for leadership, both within the Court and in the legal system as a whole. He achieved some success in securing administrative changes in the federal courts and procedural changes in the Court itself. But in the Court's decision making he did not establish himself as a leader comparable to Hughes or, it seems, even to Warren.

One apparent reason for Burger's limited impact on the Court's decisions was an absence of the skills needed for effective leadership. A former clerk for Justice Powell said that Burger "does not have the gift of leadership or conciliation." [90] Burger was accused of bullying the Court and of attempting to control decisions through illegitimate means, such as voting "insincerely" with the majority so he would be able to assign the Court's opinion in a case. Some colleagues reacted negatively to his efforts at leadership.

But Burger also faced obstacles that were beyond his control. Perhaps most important, any justice as conservative as Burger would have had difficulty in leading the Court of the 1970s and 1980s, because he stood near one end of an ideologically diverse group of justices. Further, the considerable time he spent on concerns outside the Court limited the energies he could devote to the Court's decision-making process. In any case, his example shows that even a chief justice who wants to be a strong leader does not always achieve that goal.

When William Rehnquist became chief justice in 1986, there was considerable speculation about his potential for Court leadership.[91] Rehnquist seemed to possess stronger interpersonal skills than Burger, but he was at the conservative end of the Court's ideological spectrum. Thus some observers suggested that he would have to moderate his positions to lead the Court effectively. In the 1986 term Rehnquist generally did not take more moderate positions, and as a result William Brennan as senior associate justice apparently gained opportunities to assign opinions and to exercise his own leadership. But even if this impression is correct, Rehnquist could well become a more powerful leader in time. Perhaps the most important factor is whether future appointments give him a strong conservative majority with which to work.

Harmony and Conflict

Disagreement is a regular feature of Supreme Court decision making and is made public in concurring and dissenting opinions. To a great extent, this disagreement reflects fundamental differences among the justices in their policy preferences.

Disagreement over decisions and policy goals need not lead to personal conflict among the justices. William Douglas and William Rehnquist, who stood at opposite ends of the Court ideologically, were personally close.[92] But the potential for such conflict always exists. Members of the Court often have intense feelings about the matters on which they differ, and they work under considerable pressure. Thus reports of personal frictions within the Court should not be surprising.

The justices have incentives to limit these frictions. A harmonious Court is, of course, a happier place in which to work. Personal relations also can affect the decisional process. A Court in which conflicts are kept under control will be able to maximize consensus in decisions, because members work easily with each other and are relatively willing to compromise. Such a Court also may function more efficiently, because good interpersonal relations speed the process of reaching decisions and resolving internal problems.

The success of the justices in limiting friction has varied. Perhaps the most conflictual Court of this century was that of the late 1940s. Hugo Black and Robert Jackson engaged in an open feud, and the papers of the Court's justices depict bitterness and distrust between other pairs of justices. In other periods personal relations have been considerably better.

But conflict within the Court is never entirely absent. The Court seemed to be relatively harmonious during the Warren era, but relations among the justices were not always smooth. Felix Frankfurter was involved in some conflicts; indeed, William Douglas in 1960 drafted (but did not send) a memorandum to his colleagues in which he complained

Table 4-3   Two Exchanges Between Opposing Opinions

Oregon v. Elstad (1985)

"In imposing its new rule ... the Court mischaracterizes our precedents, obfuscates the central issues, and altogether ignores the practical realities of custodial interrogation that have led nearly every lower court to reject its simplistic reasoning."

(Justice Brennan in dissent)

"Justice Brennan, with an apocalyptic tone, heralds this opinion as dealing 'a crippling blow to Miranda.'. . . Justice Brennan not only distorts the reasoning and holding of our decision, but, worse, invites trial courts and prosecutors to do the same."

(Justice O'Connor's majority opinion)

Bowen v. American Hospital Association (1986)

"The plurality incorrectly resolves an issue that was not fully addressed by the parties, gives no guidance to the Secretary or the other parties as to the proper construction of the governing statute, and fails adequately to explain the precise scope of the holding or how that holding is supported under the plurality's chosen rationale. From this misguided effort, I dissent."

(Justice White in dissent)

"The dissent's theory finds no support in the text of the regulation, the reasoning of the Secretary, or the briefs filed on his behalf in this Court."

(Justice Stevens's opinion for four members of the majority)

---

of Frankfurter's "continuous violent outbursts against me in Conference" and said that "in the interest of his health and long life I have reluctantly concluded to participate in no more conferences while he is on the Court." [93]

The Court of the 1980s shows some evidence of significant conflicts. Dissents appear on a variety of procedural matters, including admissions of attorneys to practice before the Court, fees paid to special masters, and the assessment of penalties for frivolous petitions. Indeed, in one 1987 case the Court split 4-3 on a litigant's request not to print portions of the appendix to a petition for certiorari. [94] Opinions often include sharp and even sarcastic language directed at the positions of other justices. Such language is exemplified by exchanges between opposing opinions in two cases, shown in Table 4-3. In speeches, several justices have attacked decisions and policy trends with which they disagree.

Such evidence aside, the Court in recent years has experienced conditions that may foster conflict. Chief Justice Burger probably was less effective than some predecessors in maintaining harmony. The more liberal members of the Court are unhappy with the Court's conservative direction, and these are the justices who have publicly attacked Court policies and written most of the strongly worded dissents. Their frustrations are summarized by the opening line of a 1985 dissent by Justice Stevens: "The Court does not appreciate the value of individual liberty." [95] Finally, the unusual stability of the Court's membership, particularly between 1971 and 1986, may have exacerbated tensions. Chief Justice Rehnquist noted in 1987 that justices had debated cases "week after week, month after month, year after year" with "the same cast of characters." "Sometimes you get the feeling: 'Jeez, I've heard all this before.'" [96]

Still, the depth of the conflicts within the Court is unclear, and the justices themselves offer differing assessments. In 1986 Justice Blackmun complained that the past term was "the most difficult" of his sixteen terms and said that it had been marked by "impatience" and "short temper." [97] Shortly afterwards, Justice Powell agreed that it had been "a difficult term" but maintained that the justices still got along well, and a year later he cautioned that "one mustn't take seriously some of the strong language that appears in dissenting opinions." [98] That caution is useful, because such signs of conflict can be found during any period, and the current Court may not be especially conflictual by historical standards.

A Final Note

This discussion of the Court as a group suggests that it is similar to other governmental institutions in its internal dynamics. Members negotiate over votes and the language of opinions as members of Congress do over legislation. Justices engage in feuds just as administrators do, and these feuds may affect the disposition of policy questions in the same way.

These characteristics of the Court's group life disturb some observers, particularly those who see the Court as standing outside "politics." Yet it is difficult to imagine how the Court could avoid them. Some people regard a process of judicial decision through negotiation as illegitimate or undesirable. But that process is necessitated by the goal of obtaining consensus on cases and encouraged by justices' interest in securing policies with which they agree. Conflict among justices may not be desirable, but it is inevitable at some times because of disagreements about policy and the pressures involved in reaching decisions. However it may differ from other institutions, the Court necessarily functions much like most other groups that make important decisions.

Conclusion

The discussions of the major factors in Supreme Court decisions suggest that the Court's policy choices cannot be explained in simple terms.

Forces as different as the state of the applicable law and the relationships among the justices help to determine what the Court decides.

Of these forces, however, one seems preeminent—the policy preferences of the justices. Because the law usually is ambiguous and environmental constraints generally are weak, the justices are largely free to choose positions in accordance with their own conceptions of good policy. The law and the environment undoubtedly limit the meaningful options for the Court at a given time on a particular issue. Within those limits, the justices can follow the lines of policy that they prefer. Thus the Court's membership and the process of selecting the justices are critical in determining the Court's policy direction.

If justices' preferences explain a great deal, of course they do not explain everything. A Court labeled as conservative can make strikingly liberal decisions in important cases. The weight of precedent can slow policy change in any direction. Effective leadership by the chief justice can help to marshal the Court behind a particular policy. One who seeks to understand why the Court does what it does must accept the complexity of the process by which the Court reaches its decisions.

Notes

1. Stephen J. Adler, "Scalia's Court," *The American Lawyer*, March 1987, 18.
2. Lyle Denniston, " 'Creation Science' Gets a Critical Reception," *The American Lawyer*, March 1987, 95.
3. William H. Rehnquist, *The Supreme Court: How It Was, How It Is* (New York: William Morrow, 1987), 277.
4. Ruth Marcus, "Alumni Brennan, Blackmun Greet Harvard Law Freshmen," *Washington Post*, September 6, 1986, 2.
5. This discussion of the conference is based in part on Rehnquist, *The Supreme Court*, 289-295.
6. Rehnquist, *The Supreme Court*, 295.
7. *Japan Whaling Association v. American Cetacean Society*, 478 U.S. 221, 250 (1986).
8. Charles Evans Hughes, *The Supreme Court of the United States* (New York: Columbia University Press, 1928), 68.
9. *Immigration and Naturalization Service v. Lopez-Mendoza* (1984).
10. *Interstate Commerce Commission v. Brotherhood of Locomotive Engineers* (1987).
11. *Board of Airport Commissioners v. Jews for Jesus, Inc.*, 96 L.Ed.2d 500, 509 (1987).
12. Evan Thomas, "Court at the Crossroads," *Time Magazine*, October 8, 1984, 31.
13. David Lauter, "The Justices Again Repudiate Rehnquist's Views," *National Law Journal*, April 1, 1985, 5.
14. "Court to Strike Deficit Law, ABC Says," *Chicago Tribune*, June 16, 1986, 1:3.
15. Robert L. Stern, Eugene Gressman, and Stephen M. Shapiro, *Supreme Court Practice*, 6th ed. (Washington, D.C.: Bureau of National Affairs, 1986), 624.
16. Black's view was expressed in his opinions in *New York Times v. Sullivan*, 376 U.S. 254, 293-297 (1964); and *New York Times v. United States*, 403 U.S. 713, 714-720 (1971). One opposing view was expressed in Leonard W. Levy, *Legacy of Suppression: Freedom of Speech and Press in Early American History*

(Cambridge: Harvard University Press, 1960).

17. *Sorenson v. Secretary of the Treasury*, 475 U.S. 851, 867 (1986).
18. Edwin Meese III, "The Attorney General's View of the Supreme Court: Toward a Jurisprudence of Original Intention," *Public Administration Review* 45 (November 1985): 701-704; John Paul Stevens, address presented at a meeting of the Federal Bar Association, Chicago, October 23, 1985; William J. Brennan, Jr., "The Constitution of the United States: Contemporary Ratification," address presented at Georgetown University, Washington, D.C., October 12, 1985. The quotation is from p. 7 of the transcript of Justice Brennan's speech.
19. *Jones v. Barnes*, 463 U.S. 745, 751 (1983).
20. *United States v. Butler*, 297 U.S. 1, 62-63 (1936).
21. Congressional Research Service, *The Constitution of the United States of America: Analysis and Interpretation* and *1986 Supplement* (Washington, D.C.: Government Printing Office, 1987).
22. *Maryland v. Wirtz* (1968); *National League of Cities v. Usery* (1976); *Garcia v. San Antonio Metropolitan Transit Authority* (1985).
23. John Brigham, *Constitutional Language: An Interpretation of Judicial Decision* (Westport, Conn.: Greenwood Press, 1978); Timothy J. O'Neill, "The Language of Equality in a Democratic Order," *American Political Science Review* 75 (September 1981): 626-635.
24. Blackmun: *Furman v. Georgia*, 308 U.S. 238, 405 (1972); Stewart: Barbara Reynolds, "It's Best to Be a Judge—Not a Philosopher," *USA Today*, January 10, 1984, 9A.
25. *Plyler v. Doe*, 457 U.S. 202, 242 (1982).
26. *Mathews v. United States*, 99 L.Ed.2d 54, 63-64 (1988).
27. C. Herman Pritchett, "The Development of Judicial Research," in *Frontiers of Judicial Research*, ed. Joel B. Grossman and Joseph Tanenhaus (New York: John Wiley & Sons, 1969), 42.
28. Mary Frances Berry, *Stability, Security, and Continuity: Mr. Justice Burton and Decision-Making in the Supreme Court 1945-1958* (Westport, Conn.: Greenwood Press, 1978), 27.
29. The discussion in this paragraph draws much from David W. Rohde and Harold J. Spaeth, *Supreme Court Decision Making* (San Francisco: W. H. Freeman & Co., 1976), 72.
30. Joseph P. Lash, ed., *From the Diaries of Felix Frankfurter* (New York: W. W. Norton & Co., 1975), 77, 155, 182, 229-230, 339-340.
31. Rehnquist, *The Supreme Court*, 94-99.
32. From an interview by Carl Stern, broadcast on "NBC Nightly News," April 21, 1986.
33. William H. Rehnquist, "Constitutional Law and Public Opinion," presented at Suffolk University School of Law, Boston, April 10, 1986, 40-41.
34. "Justice Stewart Dissents," *Wall Street Journal*, July 3, 1968, 6.
35. Anthony Lewis, "A Public Right to Know About Public Institutions: The First Amendment as Sword," in *The Supreme Court Review 1980*, ed. Philip B. Kurland and Gerhard Casper (Chicago: University of Chicago Press, 1981), 2.
36. Sheldon Goldman and Thomas P. Jahnige, *The Federal Courts as a Political System*, 3d ed. (New York: Harper & Row, 1985), 219.
37. Al Kamen, "A Shift in the Breeze at the Supreme Court—Maybe," *Washington Post National Weekly Edition*, May 20, 1985, 31.
38. Bernard Schwartz, *Super Chief: Earl Warren and His Supreme Court—A Judicial Biography* (New York: New York University Press, 1983), 311.

39. Stephen M. Shapiro, "Oral Argument in the Supreme Court: The Felt Necessities of the Time," *Supreme Court Historical Society Yearbook 1985*, 29; Anthony Lewis, *Gideon's Trumpet* (New York: Random House, 1964), 162.
40. Rebecca M. Salokar, "The Solicitor General Before the Supreme Court, 1959-1982: A Descriptive Analysis" (paper presented at the annual conference of the Law and Society Association, Washington, D.C., June 1987), 35.
41. Karen O'Connor and Lee Epstein, "Court Rules and Workload: A Case Study of Rules Governing Amicus Curiae Participation," *Justice System Journal* 8 (1983): 42.
42. Adler, "Scalia's Court," 16.
43. John P. Frank, *Marble Palace: The Supreme Court in American Life* (New York: Alfred A. Knopf, 1958), 98.
44. Schwartz, *Super Chief*, 459-460.
45. Philip Elman, "The Solicitor General's Office, Justice Frankfurter, and Civil Rights Litigation, 1946-1960: An Oral History," *Harvard Law Review* 100 (February 1987): 852.
46. Walter F. Murphy, *Congress and the Court* (Chicago: University of Chicago Press, 1962), 246.
47. Goldman and Jahnige, *Federal Courts as a Political System*, 219-220.
48. *Marsh v. Chambers*, 463 U.S. 783, 822 (1983).
49. Quoted in Alpheus Thomas Mason, *The Supreme Court from Taft to Burger* (Baton Rouge: Louisiana State University Press, 1979), 293.
50. "Remarks" by Justice Thurgood Marshall, Second Circuit Judicial Conference, September 4, 1986.
51. Examples of this work include Glendon Schubert, *The Judicial Mind Revisited* (New York: Oxford University Press, 1974); and Rohde and Spaeth, *Supreme Court Decision Making*.
52. See C. Neal Tate, "Personal Attribute Models of the Voting Behavior of U.S. Supreme Court Justices: Liberalism in Civil Liberties and Economics Decisions, 1946-1978," *American Political Science Review* 75 (June 1981): 355-367; and S. Sidney Ulmer, "Are Social Background Models Time-Bound?" *American Political Science Review* 80 (September 1986): 957-967.
53. *Craft v. Metromedia, Inc.* (1986).
54. Stuart Taylor, Jr., "Powell on His Approach: Doing Justice Case by Case," *New York Times*, July 12, 1987, 18.
55. Benjamin N. Cardozo, *The Nature of the Judicial Process* (New Haven: Yale University Press, 1921), 12.
56. Rohde and Spaeth, *Supreme Court Decision Making*, 138.
57. See Robert L. Dudley and Craig R. Ducat, "The Burger Court and Economic Liberalism," *Western Political Quarterly* 39 (June 1986): 236-249.
58. "The Supreme Court, 1985 Term," *Harvard Law Review* 100 (November 1986): 307; "The Supreme Court, 1986 Term," *Harvard Law Review* 101 (November 1987): 365.
59. Jeffrey T. Leeds, "A Life on the Court," *New York Times Magazine*, October 5, 1986, 75.
60. *Paris Adult Theatre v. Slaton*, 413 U.S. 49, 73-114 (1973).
61. Al Kamen, "Justice Sees O'Connor Becoming Independent," *Washington Post*, November 4, 1985, A13.
62. Figures on agreement between Blackmun and his colleagues are taken from the annual statistics on the Supreme Court term in the November issues of *Harvard Law Review*. See also Note, "The Changing Social Vision of Justice Blackmun," *Harvard Law Review* 96 (1983): 717-736.

63. John A. Jenkins, "A Candid Talk with Justice Blackmun," *New York Times Magazine*, February 20, 1983, 20.
64. See Lawrence Baum, "Measuring Policy Change in the U.S. Supreme Court," *Political Science Review* 82 (September 1988), 905-912.
65. Charles P. Curtis, *Law as Large as Life* (New York: Simon & Schuster, 1959), 156-157.
66. Arthur Selwyn Miller, *Toward Increased Judicial Activism: The Political Role of the Supreme Court* (Westport, Conn.: Greenwood Press, 1982), 127.
67. See, respectively, Harold J. Spaeth, "The Judicial Restraint of Mr. Justice Frankfurter—Myth or Reality?" *Midwest Journal of Political Science* 8 (February 1964): 22-38; and Wallace Mendelson, *Justices Black and Frankfurter: Conflict in the Court* (Chicago: University of Chicago Press, 1961).
68. "What the Justices are Saying . . ." *American Bar Association Journal* 62 (November 1976): 1454.
69. "Justice Revealed," *Life Magazine*, Fall 1987, 108.
70. Bob Woodward and Scott Armstrong, *The Brethren: Inside the Supreme Court* (New York: Simon & Schuster, 1979), 310-347.
71. J. Woodford Howard, Jr., "On the Fluidity of Judicial Choice," *American Political Science Review* 62 (March 1968): 43-56.
72. Richard Kluger, *Simple Justice: The History of Brown v. Board of Education and Black America's Struggle for Equality* (New York: Alfred A. Knopf, 1976), 582-699.
73. William H. Rehnquist, "Chief Justices I Never Knew," *Hastings Constitutional Law Quarterly* 3 (Summer 1976): 647.
74. Saul Brenner, "Fluidity on the Supreme Court: 1956-1967," *American Journal of Political Science* 26 (May 1982): 388-390.
75. Saul Brenner, "Reassigning the Majority Opinion on the United States Supreme Court," *Justice System Journal* 11 (Fall 1986): 189.
76. William O. Douglas, *The Court Years 1939-1975: The Autobiography of William O. Douglas* (New York: Random House, 1980), 18.
77. "The Court's Uncompromising Libertarian," *Time Magazine*, November 24, 1975, 69.
78. Merlo J. Pusey, *Charles Evans Hughes* (New York: Macmillan, 1951), 2:671.
79. H. N. Hirsch, *The Enigma of Felix Frankfurter* (New York: Basic Books, Inc., 1981), 160-161.
80. David J. Danelski, "Causes and Consequences of Conflict and Its Resolution in the Supreme Court," in *Judicial Conflict and Consensus*, ed. Sheldon Goldman and Charles M. Lamb (Lexington: University Press of Kentucky, 1986), 31.
81. Michael S. Serrill, "The Power of William Brennan," *Time Magazine*, July 22, 1985, 62.
82. James F. Simon, *In His Own Image: The Supreme Court in Richard Nixon's America* (New York: David McKay Co., 1973), 176.
83. Jeffrey B. Morris, "Can the Supreme Court Be Led? A Re-evaluation of the Role of Chief Justices" (paper presented at the annual conference of the American Political Science Association, Washington, D.C., September 1986), 31.
84. Rehnquist, "Chief Justices I Never Knew," 637.
85. The discussion of patterns in opinion assignment that follows draws heavily from the data in Elliot E. Slotnick, "Who Speaks for the Court? Majority Opinion Assignment from Taft to Burger," *American Journal of Political Science* 23 (February 1979): 60-77.

86. Saul Brenner, "The Time Taken to Write Majority Opinions as a Determinant of Majority Opinion Assignments on the Vinson Court," *Judicature* 72 (October-November 1988).
87. Marcus, "Alumni Brennan, Blackmun," 2.
88. "Retired Justice Stewart Makes Judicious Comments," *Cleveland Plain Dealer*, September 30, 1984, 3-AA.
89. Douglas, *The Court Years*, 115.
90. "Inside the High Court," *Time Magazine*, November 5, 1979, 63.
91. See Elliot E. Slotnick, "Personnel Changes on the Supreme Court and the Structure of Judicial Opportunities: The Case of Justice William J. Brennan" (paper presented at the annual conference of the Midwest Political Science Association, Chicago, April 1988).
92. John A. Jenkins, "The Partisan: A Talk with Justice Rehnquist," *New York Times Magazine*, March 3, 1985, 100-101.
93. Melvin I. Urofsky, ed., *The Douglas Letters: Selections from the Private Papers of Justice William O. Douglas* (Bethesda, Md.: Adler & Adler, 1987), 90.
94. *Clark-Cowlitz v. Federal Energy Regulatory Commission* (1987).
95. *Walters v. National Association of Radiation Survivors*, 473 U.S. 305, 308 (1985).
96. Al Kamen and Ruth Marcus, "Rehnquist Offers Candid Appraisal of Life on Court," *Washington Post*, May 30, 1987, A5.
97. David Lauter, "Recent Supreme Court Term Blackmun's 'Most Difficult,'" *Washington Post*, July 26, 1986, A2.
98. Ruth Marcus, "Powell Sees No Major Court Shift," *Washington Post*, August 13, 1986, A4; Taylor, "Powell on His Approach," 18.

5

Policy Outputs

The first four chapters have given some attention to the policies that the Supreme Court makes. This chapter will focus directly on those policies. I will examine the Court's policy outputs—the substance of what it decides—from several perspectives in order to probe the Court's role in the making of public policy.

The first section of the chapter will examine the scope of the Court's work as a policy maker in terms of the fields of policy in which the Court is most involved. The second and third sections will discuss what the Court actually decides in its fields of major activity, focusing on the extent of its activism and on the direction of its policies. The final section will consider explanations for patterns in the Court's work as a policy maker.

Areas of Activity

Chapter 3 examined the agenda-setting process in the Supreme Court, the process by which approximately one hundred fifty cases are chosen each term for full decisions on the merits. This section will adopt a different perspective on the Court's agenda, focusing on the subject matter of the cases that the Court accepts and decides fully. To help in understanding the forces that shape the Court's agenda, I will examine changes in the agenda that have occurred over time. To provide a sense of the Court's place in the larger policy-making system, I will compare its agenda with those of other courts and other branches of government.

The Court's Current Activity

The Emphases. The Court's decisions always have dealt with a broad range of subjects, and this certainly is true today. During any term the Court adjudicates a variety of issues in fields as different as antitrust, environmental protection, and freedom of speech. In this sense the Court's agenda is a highly diverse one, and the Court can help to shape public policy in a great many fields. This diversity does not mean, however, that the Court gives equal attention to a large number of policy areas. Most of its efforts are concentrated on a fairly narrow range of cases. In this sense, the Court may be viewed as a specialist.

We can gauge the Court's specialization in terms of the numbers of cases in various areas that it decides. Of course, numbers alone are an imperfect indication of the significance of the Court's work in an area. The Court decides relatively few cases concerning the balance of constitutional power between Congress and the president, but in the 1980s it had an enormous impact in that area by striking down the legislative veto of executive branch decisions and overturning the Gramm-Rudman-Hollings deficit reduction law because an official who could be removed from office by Congress was given the power to specify the level of spending reductions needed to comply with the law.[1] But the distribution of cases provides a fairly good sense of the Court's specialization, a specialization that has several aspects.

First, the overwhelming majority of cases that the Court decides involve disputes that arise out of government activity. In the 1982 through 1986 terms, 81 percent of all the Court's decisions involved at least one government agency as a party.[2] Moreover, most of the disputes between private parties were based fairly directly on government policy, such as the regulation of labor-management relations and the awarding of patent rights.

Within this broad category, the Court's primary area of activity is civil liberties. The term *civil liberties* may be given a variety of definitions. In the current era it is perhaps best defined as encompassing three general types of rights: procedural rights of criminal defendants and other people in governmental proceedings; the right of disadvantaged groups to equal treatment; and certain "substantive" rights, the most important of which are freedom of expression and freedom of religion. During the 1982 through 1986 terms, according to one calculation, 51 percent of the Court's decisions fell in those three civil liberties areas. Although civil liberties cases are a diverse lot, the fact that half of the Court's decisions involve this single kind of issue is an indication of its specialization.

Related to the Court's civil liberties emphasis is an interest in criminal law and procedure. A significant proportion of the Court's business arises out of criminal prosecutions. In the 1982-1986 period, 27 percent of the Court's decisions came in criminal appeals or other actions by prisoners to challenge their convictions. Some of the criminal cases involve statutory interpretation, but a large majority concern constitutional due process rights. These constitutional cases, and some of the other criminal cases, should be considered civil liberties cases as well.

Civil liberties constitutes the largest field of the Court's business by far, but it does not dominate the Court's agenda entirely. About half of the cases fall into other fields of policy. These other cases, like civil liberties cases, generally arise from government policy. However, they tend to involve issues of statutory interpretation rather than the constitutional issues that predominate in civil liberties cases.

A high proportion of the non-civil liberties cases involve economic issues, most commonly government regulation of economic activity. In recent years, about 30 percent of the Court's cases have dealt with some aspect of economic regulation.[3] Within this category, the largest number of cases concern labor-management relations. Other large categories include antitrust, securities regulation, and environmental protection.

Another major subject of Court activity is federalism. Issues of federal and state powers are involved in a great many cases that arise in a broad range of substantive contexts. Some cases involve disputes over federal financial aid to state governments; one important example was *South Dakota v. Dole* (1987), in which the Court ruled that the federal government could cut highway funds to states that maintain a minimum drinking age under twenty-one. Frequently the Court determines whether state economic regulations are void because they are preempted by federal laws. Still other cases concern the relationship between federal and state courts. As these examples suggest, federalism overlaps with other issues and Court concerns.

The 1987 Term. Both the diversity and the specialization of the Court's business may be understood better through a look at the agenda in a single year, the 1987 term. It will be useful to begin by describing the issues in a fairly representative sample of cases decided during that term:

— Whether a state judge has absolute immunity from a suit for monetary damages under a federal civil rights statute for demoting and dismissing a court employee. (*Forrester v. White,* 1988)
— Whether the exclusion of certain federal employees from provisions of one statute providing for review of adverse personnel actions precludes judicial review of such actions under another statute. (*United States v. Fausto,* 1988)
— Whether an Ohio statute that awards a tax credit for ethanol in gasoline only if it is produced in Ohio or in a state that grants a similar tax advantage to Ohio-produced ethanol violates the Commerce Clause of the Constitution. (*New Energy Company v. Limbach,* 1988)

—Whether the warrantless search and seizure of garbage left for collection on the curb in front of a house violates the Fourth Amendment. (*California v. Greenwood,* 1988)

—Whether the federal government may be sued for damages resulting from an assault or battery by a government employee, where other government employees allegedly were negligent in allowing the assault or battery to occur. (*Sheridan v. United States,* 1988)

—Whether a criminal defendant's constitutional rights are violated if a trial judge does not remove for cause a prospective juror in a murder case who had declared that he would vote automatically to impose the death penalty if the defendant was found guilty. (*Ross v. Oklahoma,* 1988)

—Whether a federal statute prohibiting a household from becoming eligible for food stamps while a member of the household is on strike violates the First or Fifth Amendments. (*Lyng v. United Automobile Workers,* 1988)

—Whether a federal district court decision on the merits of a case can be appealed as a final decision even though an issue concerning attorneys' fees has not been resolved. (*Budinich v. Becton Dickinson and Company,* 1988)

—Whether a state statute that imposes a financial penalty against a party who appeals unsuccessfully from a court judgment for money violates the equal protection clause of the Fourteenth Amendment. (*Bankers Life and Casualty Company v. Crenshaw,* 1988)

—Whether the federal district courts, rather than the Claims Court, have jurisdiction to review a final administrative order refusing to reimburse a state for expenditures under its Medicaid program. (*Bowen v. Massachusetts,* 1988)

As these examples indicate, the Court addressed a wide range of policy questions in the 1987 term. The examples also suggest the extent of the Court's specialization. That suggestion is confirmed by statistics on the 145 cases that the Court decided with full opinions during the term (see Table 5-1). Perhaps the most noteworthy characteristic is that a government party was present in about 75 percent of the cases. Moreover, many of the cases with only private parties arose under laws and programs of the federal government. In other words, the Court was concerned overwhelmingly with matters of government policy.

As the data in Table 5-1 indicate, constitutional cases and those with civil liberties issues each constituted more than 50 percent of the Court's decisions. Criminal cases, almost all of which concerned the constitutional rights of defendants, comprised more than 20 percent of the agenda. The other civil liberties cases were diverse, arising under a

Table 5-1 Characteristics of Cases Decided by Supreme Court with Full
Opinions, 1987 Term

Characteristic	Number	Percentage
Cases from lower federal courts	108	74
Cases from state courts	35	24
Original cases	2	1
Federal government party[a]	58	40
State or local government party[a]	51	35
No government party	36	25
Constitutional issue present[b]	73	50
No constitutional issue	72	50
Civil liberties issue present[b]	79	54
No civil liberties issue	66	46
Criminal cases[c]	32	22
Civil cases	113	78

Note: The total number of decisions is 145. The data are based on listings of cases in *Supreme Court Reports, Lawyers' Edition,* and in *United States Law Week.* Consolidated cases decided with one set of opinions were counted once.

[a] Cases with both a federal government party and another government party were listed as federal government. Government as party includes agencies and individual government officials.
[b] Cases were counted as having constitutional or civil liberties issues if the parties raised those issues, even if the Court decided them on the basis of other issues.
[c] Includes actions brought by prisoners to challenge the legality of their convictions but excludes cases involving rights of prisoners.

number of constitutional provisions as well as federal statutes protecting civil rights.

Non-civil liberties cases also were quite diverse. Many arose from federal regulation of private economic activities in areas such as labor and antitrust law. Some involved issues of federalism, such as conflicts between state regulations of economic activity and related federal laws. The primacy of civil liberties and the secondary place of economic regulation, like most other characteristics of the 1987 agenda, were typical of the Court's work in the current era.

Change in the Court's Agenda

As discussed in Chapter 3, several forces shape the Supreme Court's agenda. The most direct is the interests of the Court itself, but the agenda is also influenced by external forces, which include legislation and other government policies, patterns of litigation, and broad social trends.

As these forces change, so does the agenda. The Court's attention to specific categories of cases may rise or decline over several years. Over long periods, the agenda as a whole may undergo fundamental changes. Both types of change and their sources merit examination.

Changes in Specific Areas.   Perhaps the most common source of change in the Court's agenda is a decision by the Court or a congressional statute that in effect opens up an area of activity.[4] The legal change spurs litigation that ultimately reaches the Court, and the justices accept cases to address the issues that have arisen.

In the past few decades, the Court has issued several decisions that opened up new areas. Its decision in *Baker v. Carr* (1962) held that federal courts could deal with issues of legislative apportionment. *Roe v. Wade* (1973) limited state powers to prohibit or restrict abortion. A 1976 decision provided some constitutional protection to "commercial" speech.[5] Each of these led to a series of later decisions, as the Court refined its initial position and addressed questions that its original decision raised. Capital punishment is another, more complex example. In its major decisions in 1976 the Court took a middle position, establishing limits to the use of the death penalty but not prohibiting it altogether; since then it has had to hear several cases to clarify its position.[6]

Some pieces of legislation also have opened up new areas. Title VII of the Civil Rights Act of 1964 established a new remedy for employment discrimination, and lawsuits brought under Title VII have made this an area of considerable Court activity. The environmental protection laws of the 1960s and 1970s and the Freedom of Information Act of 1966 had similar, though less dramatic, effects. More subtly, the growth of federal programs granting money to state and local governments has led to a series of cases concerning the rules imposed on the governments that receive these grants.

By deciding several cases in an area, the Court sometimes resolves most of the legal issues involved; as a result, the Court may accept fewer cases in that area in the years that follow. This has been true of legislative apportionment since the mid-1970s. The Court may act in other ways to move away from an area. In *Miller v. California* (1973) a Court majority agreed on a definition of obscenity for the first time, at least temporarily resolving the most basic issue in this area, and in the ensuing fifteen years the number of obscenity decisions has declined considerably.

Sex discrimination cases illustrate the complex effects of social change on the Court's agenda. The Court heard virtually no cases in this area until 1971. But such cases have been common since that time. The most fundamental reasons for the change were the development of the women's movement and the associated shift in attitudes toward the roles of women. More directly, new federal statutes produced legal issues to resolve, interest groups directed more cases in this area to the Court, and the justices themselves became more concerned about sex discrimination.

Changes in the Agenda as a Whole. Beyond these changes in specific areas, the overall pattern of the Court's agenda may shift over a period of several decades.[7] Indeed, the Court's current agenda looks fundamentally different from that of fifty years ago.

The agenda of the 1937 term resembles the 1987 agenda in some respects; both were dominated by government litigants and issues arising from government policy. But the differences are far more striking. The 1937 Court was concerned primarily with economic issues; more than 80 percent of its cases fell in that category. Indeed, 20 percent of all cases dealt with one specific economic area, federal taxes. In contrast, individual civil liberties issues were barely visible, appearing in fewer than 5 percent of the cases.

The differences between the 1937 and 1987 terms highlight the changes that have occurred in the Supreme Court's agenda over the past half century. These changes are documented by findings from Richard Pacelle's study of the agenda from 1933 to 1983, shown in Table 5-2. The Court has evolved from an institution primarily concerned with economic issues to one that gives primary attention to the civil liberties of individuals. Economic questions remain on the agenda, but in a less prominent place. And, as the table shows, some specific kinds of economic cases have declined dramatically.

These changes in the agenda stem most directly from actions taken by the justices themselves. Beginning in the late 1930s, the Court showed less willingness to monitor government regulation of the economy and an increased interest in protecting individual liberties. The Court's interest in civil liberties reached an even higher level in the Warren Court of the 1950s and 1960s. The justices of that time were more willing to accept civil liberties cases than in past eras, and their receptivity and decisions creating new rights encouraged litigants to bring such cases.

Other forces also operated to bring about the growth of civil liberties as an area of concern in the Court. Congressional legislation on civil rights—especially the Civil Rights Act of 1964 and the Voting Rights Act of 1965—provided a new basis for civil rights cases. Increases in criminal prosecutions led to more procedural challenges by defendants. The activities of interest groups such as the NAACP and ACLU and people's growing consciousness of their individual rights have increased the volume of civil liberties cases before the Court, giving the justices even greater opportunity to accept cases in this area.

Table 5-2   Percentages of Supreme Court Agenda Devoted to Selected Issue Areas, Selected Five-Year Periods Between 1933 and 1983

Issue area	Terms			
	1933-1937	1948-1952	1968-1972	1978-1982
Civil liberties[a]	7.8	27.8	59.1	49.8
Racial equality[b]	0.3	2.0	6.6	5.0
Criminal procedure[b]	3.4	12.0	24.1	18.9
Federal taxation	17.8	6.5	3.6	2.5
Bankruptcy	6.0	1.6	0.5	0.6

Source: Richard Pacelle, "The Supreme Court Agenda across Time: Dynamics and Determinants of Change" (Ph.D. dissertation, Ohio State University, 1985), chap. 3. Used by permission of Richard Pacelle.

Note: Only cases decided with full opinion are included.

[a] Includes due process, equality, and substantive rights such as freedom of expression and freedom of religion.
[b] Included within civil liberties category.

As Table 5-2 suggests, there has been a slight reversal of the post-1933 trends in the last decade. Civil liberties cases have declined as a proportion of the agenda and to a lesser extent in absolute numbers. At the same time, the Court's attention to economic regulation and federalism has grown. These changes may represent the beginnings of a new set of trends; whether those trends develop further will depend in large part on the membership of the Court.

Comparison with Other Institutions

If the Court's current agenda differs from those of past Courts, it also differs from those of other policy makers. The subjects of the Court's work may be compared with the work of lower appellate courts, Congress, and the president.

Lower Courts.   The two sets of lower courts most comparable with the Supreme Court are the federal courts of appeals and the state supreme courts. The courts of appeals stand directly below the Supreme Court, and most of the cases decided by the Supreme Court come to it from the courts of appeals. The state supreme courts share with the U.S. Supreme Court a position at the top of their judicial systems, and about two-thirds share the Court's discretionary jurisdiction.

But neither level is fully comparable with the Supreme Court. The courts of appeals have a more limited control over their agendas, and the state supreme courts deal primarily with state legal issues rather than federal issues. As a result, the agendas of these lower courts differ from that of the Supreme Court in two important respects.[8]

First, cases between private parties and those in which government policy plays little direct role are more common below the Supreme Court level. This is particularly true of the state supreme courts. In these courts a large minority of cases concern essentially private disputes involving such matters as contracts, property, personal injuries, and family relations. The Supreme Court scarcely touches these areas in its decisions, chiefly because they usually do not involve federal law.

Second, civil liberties issues are relatively rare except in criminal cases. Both the courts of appeals and state supreme courts decide significant numbers of cases involving the procedural rights of criminal defendants. But cases involving rights to equal treatment under the law and freedom of expression, though they have become more common, still take up only a small proportion of their agendas.

Thus, the mix of subject matter on the Supreme Court's agenda is unique in some important respects. No court focuses as much on government and government policy, and the Court stands alone in its emphasis on civil liberties. The Supreme Court's set of concerns, as reflected in its agenda, distinguishes it from every other court in the United States.

The President.   The president's agenda is very different from that of the Supreme Court.[9] If the current Court is a specialist in civil liberties, most recent presidents have been specialists in foreign policy and management of the economy.

The president is preeminent in the making of foreign policy decisions. Moreover, foreign policy probably consumes the largest share of the time and energy that most presidents devote to policy making. This emphasis is in sharp contrast to the role of the Court, which makes few decisions that involve any questions of foreign policy.

Particularly during periods when the economy is functioning poorly, management of the economy is another central concern of the president. Presidents seek to maintain the nation's economic health by acting and proposing actions on matters such as the size of the federal budget, job creation, and regulation of energy supplies. While the Court makes a great many decisions involving government economic activity, the current Court has barely touched the function of general economic management to which presidents are so devoted.

Like the Supreme Court, presidents deal with a variety of policy issues outside their areas of specialization. Among these are education, public welfare, and health. Some of the president's agenda falls into the civil liberties field on which the Court focuses; one example is the criminal justice issues that have been important for some recent presidents. But in general the overlap between the areas of presidential interest and the fields of Supreme Court interest is relatively limited.

Congress.   Congress differs from both the president and the Supreme Court in the range of issues to which it devotes significant attention.[10] As an institution Congress is something of a generalist.

Congress plays an active role in the issue areas that concern the Supreme Court most. Certainly it makes important policy on government regulation of the economy. Civil liberties, broadly defined, are also a major focus of congressional activity.

But Congress also devotes itself to a variety of issues that the Supreme Court deals with rather little, in addition to foreign policy and management of the economy. Many of these issues involve various kinds of government benefits to sectors of society, such as agricultural programs and natural resources projects. Even where the concerns of Congress and Court overlap, relative emphases often differ. Issues of environmental quality, for instance, have been more important in Congress than in the Court. By the same token, the civil liberties issues on which the Court focuses its attention are less important in congressional policy making.

Conclusion: The Court's Position

These comparisons between the Supreme Court and other policy makers provide a useful perspective on the Court's role. Most important, they make clear the limited range of the Court's work. The Court's jurisdiction is very broad, but the bulk of its decisions are made in a few policy areas. Certainly it is appropriate to consider the Court a specialist.

The Court's concentration on a few policy areas, particularly civil liberties, has important implications for its potential role. Even in civil liberties, the Court can address only a small proportion of the policy issues that arise. But by deciding as many cases as it does in this area, the Court maximizes its opportunities to shape law and public policy on civil liberties.

In contrast, the Court's lack of activity in several major areas of policy ensures that its impact in those fields will be limited at most. The Court hardly can have much effect on development of the law in fields such as contracts and torts. The current Court has little effect on government management of the economy and even less on foreign policy, and many people would consider these the two most important areas of government policy.

This should give pause to those who believe that the Supreme Court is the most important policy maker in the United States. The Court's significance is indisputable. But how can it be regarded as preeminent when the range of its activities is so limited? The Court could not possibly be dominant as a policy maker except in federalism, civil liberties, and some limited areas of economic policy. For reasons to be discussed in the rest of this chapter and in Chapter 6, even here the Court's dominance is not at all certain.

Supreme Court Activism: Judicial Review

The preceding section has sketched out the areas in which the Court's work is concentrated. The next two sections will examine the policies that the Court makes in its major fields of activity, looking first at their activism and then at their ideological and political direction.

As noted in Chapter 1, there are many aspects to judicial activism. In this section I will concentrate on the element of activism that concerns the Court's relations with other branches of government. To what extent has the Court made decisions that conflict with the policies of Congress, the executive branch, and state and local governments? Investigation of the frequency and importance of such decisions can help in understanding the Court's position in the policy-making process.

The Court's activism in this sense often is gauged by its use of judicial review, the power to overturn acts of other policy makers on the ground that they violate the Constitution. Judicial review is not the only basis for activist policies; the Court may come into conflict with the policies of the other branches through its interpretations of statutes. But the Court intervenes in the policy-making process most directly and most clearly through its use of judicial review. For this reason I will focus on judicial review in this section, though I will give some attention to statutory interpretation as well.

Voiding Acts of Congress

The most familiar use of judicial review is over federal statutes. This form of judicial review also represents a striking assertion of power by the Court. When the Court overturns a federal law on constitutional grounds, implicitly it substitutes its judgment for that of the other branches of the federal government.

The Court first held an act of Congress unconstitutional in 1803, in *Marbury v. Madison*. Through 1987, by one count, it had overturned 120 federal laws, in whole or in part.[11] This number in itself is significant. On the one hand, it indicates that the Court has made fairly frequent use of its review power—on the average, more than once every two years. On the other hand, the laws struck down by the Court constitute a minute fraction of the more than 60,000 laws that have been adopted by Congress. But to understand the significance of the Court's decisions overturning federal laws we must take a closer look at these decisions.[12]

One question is the importance of the provisions that the Court has overturned. The Court has struck down some statutes of major significance. Among these were the Missouri Compromise of 1820, concerning slavery in the territories, which the Court declared unconstitutional in the *Dred Scott* case in 1857; the child labor laws that the Court struck down in 1918 and 1922; and the New Deal legislation that the Court overturned in 1935 and 1936.[13] But a good many of the Court's decisions declaring measures unconstitutional, perhaps a majority, were rather unimportant to the policy goals of Congress and the president. Some of the statutes involved were minor. In other instances the Court struck down relatively unimportant provisions of statutes or declared them unconstitutional only as applied to particular circumstances. In *United States v. Grace* (1983), the Court struck down a statute that prohibited picketing and distributing leaflets on Supreme Court grounds, insofar as that statute applied to public sidewalks; it is doubtful that this very narrow decision attracted much attention in the other branches.

A related question is the timing of the Court's use of judicial review. Much of the time the Court has struck down legislation well after its enactment. More than half of its decisions voiding legislation have come more than four years after enactment, and even in four years the majority in support of the statute in question may weaken or disappear.[14] More than one-quarter of the decisions overturning statutes have come at least thirteen years after enactment, some much later than that. Congress sometimes retains a strong commitment to a statute from an earlier period but often will be unconcerned by the overturning of an older law.

For these reasons, the Court's fairly frequent use of its power to review congressional acts is somewhat misleading. Any decision that strikes down a federal statute might seem to involve a major conflict between Court and Congress, but such decisions actually may attract little congressional or public notice. Generally speaking, the Court's voiding of acts of Congress is most significant when the acts themselves are important and they are overturned rather quickly. Only a minority of cases meet these criteria.

Another way to gauge the significance of judicial review is in terms of its historical patterns. As Table 5-3 shows, the Court has not overturned federal statutes at a regular pace. It voided only two statutes prior to 1865. In the following eight years the Court overturned eight laws, and for the next half century the Court attacked acts of Congress at a rate of more than one in every two years. Then the Court's use of this form of judicial review accelerated: fifteen times during the 1920s, and twelve times in the three years from 1934 to 1936. Over the next quarter century the Court employed this power sparingly. But in the twenty-five years from 1963 through 1987, it overturned forty-nine statutes, a record

Table 5-3 Provisions of Federal Law Held Unconstitutional by Supreme Court

Period	Number	Period	Number
1790-1799	0	1890-1899	5
1800-1809	1	1900-1909	9
1810-1819	0	1910-1919	5
1820-1829	0	1920-1929	15
1830-1839	0	1930-1939	13
1840-1849	0	1940-1949	2
1850-1859	1	1950-1959	4
1860-1869	4	1960-1969	16
1870-1879	8	1970-1979	19
1880-1889	4	1980-1987	14
		Total	120

Source: Congressional Research Service, *The Constitution of the United States of America: Analysis and Interpretation* and *1986 Supplement* (Washington, D.C.: Government Printing Office, 1987), updated by the author.

number for that short a period and more than one-third of the total for the Court's entire history.

On the basis of these patterns it is possible to identify periods in which the Court has been in major conflict with Congress as a legislator. The most conflictual period lasted from 1918 to 1936. During that period the Court overturned twenty-nine laws. More important, much of the legislation voided by the Court was significant. Between 1918 and 1928 the Court struck down two child labor laws and a minimum wage law, along with several less important statutes. This was a real irritant. Then, between 1933 and 1936, a majority of the Court engaged in what can only be called a frontal attack on the New Deal program, an attack that abated with the Court's retreat in 1937.

The Court overturned legislation with even greater frequency during the period from 1963 to 1987. But few of the Court's decisions overturned major laws, and much of the legislation that the Court voided was rather old. A typical overturning decision in this period struck down a minor law or an unessential provision of a major law.

There were some clear exceptions to this pattern. The Court invalidated some major provisions of the Federal Election Campaign Act concerning campaign financing in *Buckley v. Valeo* (1976) and two later decisions.[16] In *Bowsher v. Synar* (1986) the Court overturned a provision of the Gramm-Rudman-Hollings budget deficit reduction law and thereby prevented the law from operating. *Immigration and Naturalization Service v. Chadha* (1983) struck down a relatively minor provision of immigration law, but its ruling against a legislative veto provision suggested the invalidity of some much more important federal laws. (Indeed, the Court struck down two other legislative veto provisions soon afterward.) In general, however, the legislation overturned by the Court since 1963 has not been nearly as significant as the economic legislation that the Court struck down in the 1930s.

During periods other than those two, the Court made decisions that voided major pieces of legislation, decisions that sometimes had considerable impact on politics and federal policy.[16] But these decisions were sporadic; in none of these periods was there a series of decisions overturning significant congressional policies. Thus, only in the period from 1918 through 1936 was the Court's power to review federal legislation used in a sustained way to disturb a major line of federal policy.

The Court and Presidential Decisions

The Court passes on the legality of presidential orders as well as legislation. Decisions by the president may be challenged on grounds that they conflict with statutes, with the Constitution, or with both. In ruling on such challenges, the Court can overturn presidential policies just as it can overturn congressional policies.

The Court occasionally has invalidated major presidential actions. In *Ex parte Milligan* (1866), the Court held that President Lincoln had lacked the power to suspend the writ of habeas corpus for military prisoners during the Civil War. *Youngstown Sheet and Tube Co. v. Sawyer* (1952) declared that it was illegal for President Truman to order the federal government to seize major steel mills whose workers were on strike during the Korean War. Most recently, in *Train v. City of New York* (1975), the Court limited the power of the president to refuse to spend money appropriated by Congress. This practice, known as impoundment, had been used by President Nixon to reduce or eliminate programs with which he disagreed.

These examples stand out because there are few other examples of significant presidential action that the Court has overturned. Indeed, the Court seldom has invalidated even minor decisions. A review by Glendon Schubert in 1957 found only fourteen cases in which the Court had ruled that presidential actions were illegal. In about half these cases the Court's decision was based on the Constitution.[17] The Court's interventions to disturb presidential policy have been even more sporadic than its interventions in congressional policy; in general, presidents have acted without interference from the Supreme Court.

Voiding State and Local Policies

The Supreme Court has used its power of judicial review far more frequently at the state and local levels than at the federal level. One measure of the difference is the number of laws declared unconstitutional. By the end of 1987, by one count, the Court had overturned 1,151 state statutes and local ordinances, on the grounds that they directly violated the Constitution or that they were superseded by federal law under the constitutional principle of federal supremacy. In contrast, it will be recalled, the Court had struck down only 120 federal laws. The disparity is even greater than these figures suggest, because many of the Court's overturnings of state and local laws indirectly affected laws that were not involved in the cases. For instance, in 1973 *Roe v. Wade* and *Doe v. Bolton* directly struck down the abortion laws of only two states, but implicitly they invalidated similar laws in nearly all other states.

A similar disparity seems to exist in the Court's use of judicial review to strike down nonstatutory policies. A decision that declares unconstitutional the practices of an administrative body or a lower court may be as significant as the overturning of a statute. At least in the current era, the Court holds administrative and judicial policies at the state and local levels unconstitutional far more often than it does policies at the federal level. The most important area of such activity is criminal procedure, in which the Court often has ruled that police or trial court practices violate the Fourteenth Amendment rights of defendants.

As measured by the numbers of laws overturned per decade, shown in Table 5-4, the Court's voiding of state and local laws has increased tremendously over time. More than four-fifths of all the laws struck down have been overturned since 1910. The Court's use of this form of judicial review has peaked in the last three decades; between 1960 and 1987 it declared unconstitutional an average of sixteen state and local laws per year.

Prior to 1860 the Court struck down relatively few state and local laws, but its decisions during that period played an important role in limiting state powers under the Constitution. For instance, under John Marshall the Court weakened the states' role with decisions such as *McCulloch v. Maryland* (1819), which denied the states power to tax federal agencies, and *Gibbons v. Ogden* (1824), which narrowed state power to regulate commerce.

The laws overturned by the Court in more recent periods have been a mixture of the important and the minor. In the aggregate the Court's decisions have been sufficiently important to give it a significant role in shaping state policy. During the late nineteenth century and the first third of the twentieth century, the Court struck down a great deal of im-

Table 5-4   Provisions of State Laws and Local Ordinances Held Unconstitutional by Supreme Court

Period	Number	Period	Number
1790-1799	0	1890-1899	36
1800-1809	1	1900-1909	40
1810-1819	7	1910-1919	118
1820-1829	8	1920-1929	139
1830-1839	3	1930-1939	93
1840-1849	9	1940-1949	58
1850-1859	7	1950-1959	60
1860-1869	23	1960-1969	149
1870-1879	36	1970-1979	193
1880-1889	46	1980-1987	125
		Total	1,151

Source: Congressional Research Service, *The Constitution of the United States of America: Analysis and Interpretation* and *1986 Supplement* (Washington, D.C.: Government Printing Office, 1987), updated by the author.

portant state economic legislation, including numerous regulations of commercial practices and of labor-management relations. The net effect, as with the New Deal, was to turn back much of a major tide of public policy.

The Court's decisions over the last three decades also have impinged upon important elements of state policy. A series of rulings helped to break down the legal basis for racial segregation and discrimination in Southern states. The Court has limited sharply the powers of the states to prohibit and regulate abortion, declaring invalid the prevailing pattern of state laws in 1973 and striking down a number of new abortion laws since then. It imposed upon the states a new set of rules for the processing of criminal cases and the treatment of defendants. More subtly, through a series of decisions the Court has limited state powers of economic regulation in areas that Congress has preempted under its constitutional supremacy; in doing so, it has shifted power further toward the federal government and away from the states.

The Court's significance in relation to state and local governments should not be exaggerated. Its decisions have affected only a small proportion of all public policies in the states. But the contrast between its use of judicial review at the national level and at the state and local levels is striking.

Judicial Review: The General Picture

The Supreme Court's use of judicial review is difficult to characterize, in part because the record is uneven. The extent of activism has varied during the Court's history, generally increasing over time. The Court's use of judicial review has also varied among levels of government. The Court has been considerably more willing to overturn state and local policies than federal policies, and it has done more to limit the freedom of action of state and local governments on issues of central importance.

More fundamentally, the Court's record as a whole is ambiguous. On the one hand, the justices have made considerable use of the power of judicial review. By striking down a large number of government decisions, including some important ones, the Supreme Court has established itself as a major participant in the policy-making process.

From another perspective, however, the Court's use of judicial review seems limited. The Court generally has been quite selective in employing its power to strike down laws, and the great majority of public policies at all levels of government have continued in operation without interference by the Court. Indeed, some major areas of government activity, such as foreign policy, have been affected rather little by the Court's constitutional decisions. While judicial review has helped the Court to play a major role in policy making, it certainly has not made the Court the dominant national policy maker.

Statutory Interpretation

The Court's use of judicial review, of course, is not the only important element of its policy making. Although it is appropriate to focus on judicial review as a mode of activism, statutory interpretation merits some attention as well. Even today about half of the Court's decisions are statutory rather than constitutional, and these statutory decisions often have activist components.

First, the Court's interpretations of statutes sometimes overturn policies of the federal executive branch. I have noted the rare occasions on which the Court strikes down presidential actions as unauthorized by statute. The Court regularly strikes down policies of federal administrative agencies on that ground or because the agency failed to follow proper procedures in reaching its decision. The Court overruled some important policy initiatives of the Reagan administration on these bases, including the administration's extension of tax benefits to private schools that discriminate by race and its rescinding of a rule requiring passive restraints such as airbags in new cars.[18]

More broadly, the Court's statutory decisions do much to shape federal policy within the general and often vague outlines established by Congress. Individual decisions, such as the Court's 1987 rulings that ethnic minority groups could challenge discimination under two civil rights laws, may be of considerable importance.[19] The Court has handed down a series of decisions that indicate what kinds of conduct violate the federal civil rights statutes and what remedies for discrimination are appropriate under these statutes; these decisions address such major issues as affirmative action and sexual harassment. In the 1970s and 1980s the Court's statutory decisions also have had an impact on federal policy in economic fields such as labor-management relations and regulation of securities; in the area of antitrust, for instance, the Court has narrowed the range of business conduct prohibited by the law. Even when the Court's statutory decisions involve no direct conflict with other policy makers, the Court often is asserting itself as an independent policy maker through its interpretations of statutory language.

Judicial review remains the mechanism by which the Court takes an activist position most directly. The pattern of the Court's use of judicial review to strike down government policies probably is the best indicator of the Court's activism and the limits on its activism. But a general assessment of the Court's significance as a policy maker must take into account all aspects of its work.

The Direction of Policy

In the last section I considered activism as a characteristic of Supreme Court policies. Another major characteristic of the Court's policies is their ideological and political direction. The issues that come before the Court often require the justices to choose between liberal and conservative views of policy, and the Court's decisions inevitably benefit some groups in society more than others. This section will examine the substance of the Court's policies in terms of their ideological content and their beneficiaries.

The section will focus on the last century. Since the 1880s the Court's policies have taken two quite different directions in successive periods. An examination and comparison of those periods will help in understanding how and why Supreme Court policies vary.

The 1880s to the 1930s

Protecting Business from Government.   The agenda of the 1937 term reflected the Court's major emphases during the preceding half century. In that period the great majority of decisions dealt with economic issues, and the Court's primary concern was government policy that affected the activities of private businesses. At the heart of the Court's work in this area was the adjudication of challenges to government regulation of business practices toward consumers and workers. The Court also dealt with other areas of business-government relations, particularly taxation.

As earlier discussions of this period have indicated, the major theme of the Court's decisions on legislation affecting business was protection for business enterprises. The Court declared unconstitutional a great deal of legislation that limited business freedom, including some very important regulatory laws. The Court also limited the operation of some statutes by interpreting them narrowly. This was its response to two major federal laws: the Interstate Commerce Act of 1887, which was an effort to regulate the railroads, and the Sherman Antitrust Act of 1890, an effort to combat monopolies and anticompetitive practices.[20]

The strength of this theme should not be overemphasized. The Court invalidated only a minority of the laws that businesses challenged in its cases. Moreover, in some areas it interpreted government regulatory powers rather broadly.

But the theme of protecting the business community from government was fairly strong throughout this period, and it gradually grew stronger. In the first half of the period the Court's treatment of laws limiting business freedom could be characterized as mixed. By the 1920s disapproval of such laws had become dominant in the Court's decisions, and it remained dominant through 1936. The growth of the Court's opposition to government policy toward business is reflected in the number of laws involving economic issues that it overturned in successive decades: 44 from 1900 to 1909, 111 from 1910 to 1919, and 133 from 1920 to 1929.[21]

Constitutional Doctrines. In any period the Court's perspective on major issues is reflected in the doctrines that it adopts to interpret constitutional provisions. Between the 1880s and the 1930s most justices accepted a series of doctrines that limited government power over the private economy.

At the national level the powers of the federal government to regulate commerce and to tax were interpreted narrowly. In this way the Court limited the use of these powers as mechanisms to control business activities. In contrast, the Tenth Amendment's general limitation on federal power was read broadly to prohibit some federal action on the ground that it interfered with state prerogatives.

At the state level the Court interpreted the Fourteenth Amendment as a limit on the power of state and local governments to regulate business. In a decision of great importance symbolically as well as practically, the Court held in *Santa Clara County v. Southern Pacific Railroad Co.* (1886) that corporations were "persons" whose rights were protected by the Fourteenth Amendment. The Court also established the doctrine of "substantive due process." The due process clause of the

Fourteenth Amendment seems only to require that the government follow proper procedures—that it provide the "due process of law"—in making decisions. But in the late nineteenth century the Court interpreted this amendment as creating an absolute prohibition against regulation of business that interfered unduly with the liberty and property rights of corporations. In other words, certain kinds of laws would be held to violate "due process" no matter how proper the procedures under which they were adopted and carried out. Moreover, the Court interpreted the corporate rights protected by the due process clause very broadly, to include such matters as the capacity of a public utility to make what the Court deemed an adequate profit.[22]

These doctrines were important as mechanisms by which the Court could strike down legislation that affected business. They also make clear the Court's collective view of policy during this period. Given tremendous discretion in interpreting the Constitution, most justices chose interpretations that protected business from government.

The Court's Beneficiaries.   Broadly speaking, the business community in general benefited from the Court's policies during this period. But major corporations benefited the most. Much of the regulatory legislation that the Court overturned or limited was aimed primarily at the activities of the largest businesses, which were viewed by legislators as abusing their great economic power. The railroads were the most prominent example; in the decade from 1910 to 1919, the Court overturned forty-one state laws in cases brought by railroad companies. Thus major corporations such as railroads might be considered the "clientele" of the Court in that half century.

Large corporations did not simply benefit from the Court's decisions; they helped to bring about the Court's favorable policies.[23] Beginning in the late nineteenth century, the corporate community employed much of the best legal talent in the United States to challenge the validity of regulatory statutes. Doctrines such as substantive due process were formulated and urged upon the Court by attorneys representing corporations. The justices would not have accepted these doctrines had they not been basically sympathetic toward business interests. But effective advocacy by corporate attorneys certainly laid some of the groundwork for the Court's policies toward business.

The corporate interests that brought their claims to the Supreme Court focused their attention on the judiciary because of their defeats elsewhere in government. Congress and the state legislatures were not uniformly unfriendly to business interests, but there was strong legislative support for regulation of private enterprise. In accepting the business position so frequently, the Court served as a "court of last resort" for corporations in a political sense as well as the legal sense.

Civil Liberties: A Limited Concern. Civil liberties as I have defined them were only a minor concern of the Court between 1880 and the mid-1930s. When the Court did decide civil liberties issues, it was generally unsympathetic to litigants who claimed that their liberties had been violated.

One subject that the Court addressed was the civil rights of black citizens in the South. In the *Civil Rights Cases* (1883) and other decisions, the Court interpreted narrowly the power of the federal government to protect black rights. In *Plessy v. Ferguson* (1896), the Court upheld the legitimacy of racial segregation by establishing the "separate but equal" doctrine. Other decisions were more favorable to blacks, but they did not have the significance of these two lines of doctrine.

In the early twentieth century the Court began to determine how the Fourteenth Amendment affected state criminal proceedings. To what extent did the due process clause require that a state provide procedural rights specified by the Bill of Rights, such as the protection against compulsory self-incrimination? In *Twining v. New Jersey* (1908), the Court viewed the clause as "incorporating" only a select sample of these rights. This narrow interpretation of the due process clause contrasted with the Court's very broad interpretation of its protections for business enterprises.

The Court did interpret the due process clause favorably for civil liberties in the area of freedom of expression. In a series of decisions from 1925 to 1931, the Court held that the clause protected freedom of speech and freedom of the press from state violations.[24] This was an interpretation seemingly as illogical as the doctrine of substantive due process, and its adoption by the Court reflected some sympathy for freedom of expression. But in the most significant set of conflicts involving this freedom the Court gave limited support to it. In *Schenck v. United States* (1917) and later cases the Court held that the First Amendment allowed the federal government to prosecute people whose expressions allegedly endangered military recruitment and other national security interests.

Overview. In ideological terms, the Court of this period clearly was conservative. It interpreted the law so as to protect advantaged interests in society: business corporations. At the same time it did little to protect disadvantaged groups such as blacks.

This conservatism was not new; much of the Court's work in earlier periods also had a conservative slant. Particularly under John Marshall's leadership, the Court exhibited considerable support for the rights of property holders. Support for liberal values such as civil liberties was far less common.

Thus an observer of the Supreme Court in the mid-1930s had good reason to conclude that the Court was a fundamentally conservative institution. Indeed, this was the position of two distinguished observers as late as the early 1940s. According to Henry Steele Commager in 1943, the record

> discloses not a single case, in a century and a half, where the Supreme Court has protected freedom of speech, press, assembly, petition, or religion against Congressional attack. It reveals no instance [with one possible exception] where the court has intervened on behalf of the underprivileged—the Negro, the alien, women, children, workers, tenant-farmers. It reveals, on the contrary, that the Court has effectively intervened, again and again, to defeat Congressional attempts to free the slave, to guarantee civil rights to Negroes, to protect workingmen, to outlaw child labor, to assist hard-pressed farmers, and to democratize the tax system. From this analysis the Congress, and not the courts, emerges as the instrument for the realization of the guarantees of the Bill of Rights.[25]

Attorney General Robert Jackson, soon to join the Court, put the matter more simply in 1941: "Never in its entire history can the Supreme Court be said to have for a single hour been representative of anything except the relatively conservative forces of its day." [26]

The 1930s to the Present

As of the late 1930s, the Court's conservatism seemed to be deeply rooted. Yet, within a few years after its confrontation with the New Deal, the Court changed its ideological position drastically. That change was reflected both in its treatment of economic issues and in its positions on civil liberties questions.

Acceptance of Government Economic Policy.   Beginning in 1937, it will be recalled, the Court shifted its position on government economic powers. In a series of decisions, majorities accepted the constitutional power of government—particularly the federal government—to regulate and to manage the economy. The Court abandoned altogether the antiregulatory spirit that had developed over the previous half century.

The Court's collective change of heart proved to be long-standing. Since the late 1930s the Court has been fairly consistent in viewing government economic power broadly. This position is reflected in its treatment of federal legislation. Between 1937 and 1987 the Court struck down only seven federal laws dealing with regulation of the economy and of business enterprises.[27] Two of these laws involved civil liberties issues concerning inspections of businesses, three concerned the separation of powers within the federal government, and none affected basic powers over the economy. Upholding federal supremacy in economic matters, the Court has struck down many state laws on the grounds that they impinged on the constitutional powers of the federal government or that they were preempted by federal statutes. But in other respects state governments have been given more freedom to make economic policy.

The current Court also addresses nonconstitutional economic issues that arise from decisions of federal regulatory agencies such as the Interstate Commerce Commission and the National Labor Relations Board. The Court has deferred to decisions of federal agencies in some instances, while in others it has intervened to hold that agency policies are contrary to statute. Some of the Court's interventions have been significant. But the Court has not challenged the basic economic programs of the federal government.

Support for Civil Liberties.   When the Court renounced its opposition to government economic policies, it began to adopt a new activist position in support of civil liberties. That position was signaled in Justice Harlan Stone's opinion for the Court in *United States v. Carolene Products Co.* (1938). This case was simply one of many in which the Court upheld federal economic policies. But in what has become a famous footnote, Stone argued that the Court was justified in taking a tolerant view of government economic policies, while it gave "more exacting judicial scrutiny" to policies that infringed on civil liberties.

The Court gradually adopted the position that Stone laid out. As we have seen, civil liberties issues came to occupy the largest share of the agenda. Moreover, the Court generally has been quite favorable to civil liberties in judging conflicts between those liberties and other values.

The Court's commitment to civil liberties has been uneven. In the 1940s the Court gave fairly strong support to civil liberties but dealt with only a limited range of issues in this area. After a more conservative period in the early 1950s, the early Warren Court in the rest of that decade took positions more supportive of civil liberties. *Brown v. Board of Education* (1954) was perhaps the Court's most important decision favorable to individual liberties up to that time.

The Court's liberalism in this area peaked in the 1960s. Decisions of the Court expanded liberties in many fields, from the civil rights of blacks to the rights of criminal defendants to freedom of expression. In comparison with that extraordinary decade the record of the Court in the 1970s and 1980s is considerably more conservative on civil liberties issues. In comparison with the pre-1937 period, however, the recent Court has been highly favorable to civil liberties.

The development of the Court's policies is illustrated by the pattern of decisions that declared laws unconstitutional. Figure 5-1 depicts the numbers of economic statutes and statutes limiting civil liberties that were overturned by the Court in successive decades. As the figure

Figure 5-1   Number of Economic and Civil Liberties Laws (Federal, State, and Local) Overturned by Supreme Court, by Decade

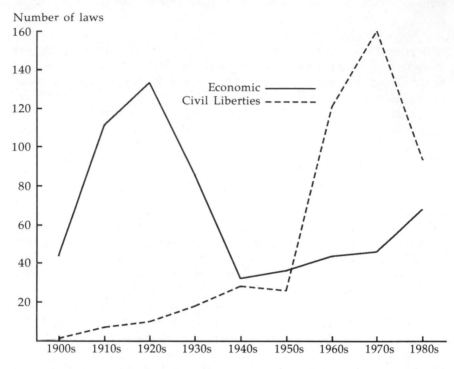

Number of laws

Economic ————
Civil Liberties — — — — —

1900s   1910s   1920s   1930s   1940s   1950s   1960s   1970s   1980s

Source: Congressional Research Service, *The Constitution of the United States of America: Analysis and Interpretation* and *1986 Supplement* (Washington, D.C.: Government Printing Office, 1987), updated by the author.

Note: Civil liberties category does not include laws supportive of civil liberties. The figures for the 1980s are based on the actual numbers for 1980-1987, multiplied by 1.25 to create a ten-year "rate" for that decade.

shows, the number of laws involving the economic system that the Court struck down declined precipitously between the 1920s and 1940s and has remained relatively low since that time. Meanwhile, the numbers of statutes struck down on civil liberties grounds became significant in the 1940s and 1950s and then grew tremendously in the two decades that followed. That growth reflects the Court's increasing liberalism. The reversal of this trend in the 1980s is also noteworthy; its implications will be considered later in this section.

Constitutional Doctrines.   The Court's liberalism on civil liberties has been reflected in a set of constitutional doctrines. Perhaps the most important of these is the Court's broad interpretation of the due process clause of the Fourteenth Amendment to encompass a wide range of procedural rights. Nearly all the rights of criminal defendants that are protected against federal violation by the Bill of Rights have been applied to the states through the due process clause. These include, among others, the right to a public trial (*In re Oliver*, 1948), the right to a trial by jury (*Duncan v. Louisiana*, 1968), and the protection against compulsory self-incrimination (*Malloy v. Hogan*, 1964). The clause also has been interpreted as establishing procedural rights for groups other than criminal defendants, such as recipients of public welfare benefits.[28]

Two other doctrines are notable because they underline the Court's willingness to depart from conventional interpretations of the Constitution to support civil liberties. The Constitution contains no protection against discrimination by the federal government, but in *Bolling v. Sharpe* (1954) the Court interpreted the due process clause of the Fifth Amendment to prohibit federal denials of equal protection of the laws. Like some interpretations of the Fourteenth Amendment due process clause in an earlier era, this interpretation seems to have little basis in the words of the Constitution itself. *Griswold v. Connecticut* (1965) created a new constitutional right to privacy. The opinions in the case based this right on several provisions of the Constitution, including the rather vague and previously dormant Ninth Amendment.[29]

In interpreting the equal protection clause of the Fourteenth Amendment, the Court gave greater emphasis to a doctrine that already existed in implicit form. Under this doctrine, some government policies would be given "strict scrutiny" when challenged as violations of equal protection, because of the identity of the groups who were treated differently or the significance of the rights that the policies affected. Increasingly government has been given a burden of proof to establish the legitimacy of its policies under the equal protection clause.

The Court's Beneficiaries. The groups that have benefited most from the Court's policies in the current era, of course, are those that bring civil liberties claims before the Court. These include socially and economically disadvantaged groups, criminal defendants, and people who take unpopular political stands. In 1967, during the Warren Court's most active period, an unsympathetic editorial cartoonist depicted the Court as a Santa Claus whose list of gift recipients included Communists, pornographers, extremists, drug pushers, criminals, and perverts.[30] Whatever one may think of this characterization, it underlines the change in the Court. A historian summarizes the change: "Whereas the beneficiaries of the Court before 1937 had been businessmen and other propertied interests, after 1937 they became the less advantaged groups in America." [31]

The sector of the population that the Court has aided most is black citizens. Since the 1940s the Court has given extraordinary support to black civil rights, particularly in the fields of education and voting rights. The Court also took great efforts to protect the civil rights movement when it was under attack in the late 1950s and 1960s. Southern statutes designed to cripple the NAACP were struck down. In addition, the Court overturned criminal convictions of civil rights activists in more than 50 cases arising from "sit-ins" and other demonstrations against segregation.

The Court's support for black civil rights was never absolute, however, and that support declined somewhat in the 1970s. But the Court usually has been more favorable to civil rights than have the other branches of government. Congress did not adopt a major civil rights statute until 1964, and from the late 1960s until the early 1980s it did relatively little to advance black rights. Some presidents, such as Lyndon Johnson, gave strong support to black civil rights; others, such as Dwight Eisenhower and Richard Nixon, seemed indifferent. In a real sense, black citizens have been a special clientele of the Supreme Court during much of the current era.

The Court's support for some other groups has diverged even more from the positions of the other branches of government. Convicts have had few advocates in the executive branch and the legislature. Leftist political groups such as the Communist party have been subject to a good deal of congressional attack. As it did when it supported business interests, the Court has provided relief for groups that fare badly elsewhere in government.

The Burger and Rehnquist Courts. The Supreme Court of the 1970s was distinctly more conservative than the Warren Court that preceded it, and the Court of the 1980s has been even more so. As yet, however, the Court has not departed clearly from the policy positions that characterize the period since 1937. Both the Court's policy change and the limited extent of that change should be noted.

In civil liberties, there are several signs of growing conservatism. As shown in Table 4-2 (page 146), parties with civil liberties claims have won a declining proportion of cases—though the first two terms of the Rehnquist Court brought a moderate upsurge in that proportion. While the number of laws overturned on civil liberties grounds increased in the 1970s, this number has declined substantially in the 1980s. Major expansions of particular liberties have been relatively rare over the last decade. And the Court has cut back some rights that were established by the Warren Court, especially in criminal procedure—the area in which its conservatism has been strongest.

But the changes in the Court's policies have fallen far short of a complete policy reversal. In the late 1930s and 1940s, the Court abandoned its economic conservatism through a general rejection of the legal rules that supported intervention in the field of government regulation. Nothing like such a rejection has yet occurred in civil liberties. Few civil libertarian rulings of the Warren Court have been overturned, and the Court's protections for liberties remain far broader than they were in 1937. Indeed, even the Court of the late 1980s sometimes expands rights significantly. One example is *Batson v. Kentucky* (1986), in which the Court ruled that prosecutors could not exclude blacks from juries through peremptory challenges on racial grounds; the Court had to overrule a Warren Court decision to reach this ruling.

The Court of the 1970s and 1980s also has been more conservative than its predecessor on economic issues, but it has not departed from the general position of upholding government regulatory power over the economy. In 1987 the Court showed signs of such a departure in two rulings that limited state powers to regulate land use, but these rulings were balanced by others that reaffirmed broad government powers in the economic arena.[32] While the Court of the 1980s has struck down an increased number of economic statutes, the great majority were state laws that conflicted with federal powers. Here, too, a fundamental change from the post-1937 pattern of Supreme Court policy has not yet occurred.

At least in civil liberties, such a change certainly could occur in the relatively near future. Indeed, the battle over the nomination of Robert Bork to the Court in 1987 reflected a widespread perception that the Court was close to making a big step in a conservative direction. For two decades observers of the Supreme Court "have been waiting for the other shoe to drop"—for the appointments of conservative justices to produce a Court that fully rejects a commitment to the protection of civil liberties.[33] It is still quite possible that the other shoe will drop and that the Court will once again become highly conservative.

This point should be emphasized. Because the current era has lasted for several decades, some observers of the Court see its role as a liberal institution and a strong supporter of civil liberties as both permanent and inevitable. Our examination of the Court's policies over an entire century makes it clear that this is not the case. Rather, the Court's support for civil liberties developed late in its history. For most of its history, the Court was devoted far more to the interests of business than to what we think of as civil liberties. In ideological terms the Court was generally a conservative institution until the era that began in the late 1930s. Certainly it might become a conservative institution once again.

This discussion raises questions of explanation for the Court's policy positions over time. What accounts for the patterns that I have described, and how can we understand changes in those patterns? The next section will examine the forces that have shaped the Court's policies.

Explaining the Court's Policies

The preceding sections of this chapter have examined several facets of the Supreme Court's policy outputs. A number of patterns have emerged. Some of these are particularly important:

—During a particular historical period the Court may devote a large portion of its output to a particular policy goal, such as the protection of civil liberties.

—This goal may be quite different from the positions of other public policy makers on the set of issues in question.

—The Court's collective policy goal underwent a fundamental change rather rapidly in at least one instance, beginning in the late 1930s.

—The Court has actively scrutinized policies of the national government and often struck them down, but only during one limited time period did the Court use judicial review to overturn a major line of congressional and presidential policy.

—The Court has been considerably more active in striking down significant policies of state and local governments.

In this section I will seek to provide a brief and partial explanation for these patterns. To do so, I will draw upon the discussion in Chapter 4 of the major factors that shape Supreme Court decisions. Two of these factors are particularly useful in understanding broad patterns of policy: the Court's environment and its members' policy preferences.

The Court's Environment

Freedom from External Pressures.   Perhaps the most important characteristic of the Supreme Court's environment is its limited impact on the Court's decisions. Compared to policy makers such as legislators or trial judges, Supreme Court justices have unusual freedom to adopt the policies that they prefer.

This freedom explains a great deal about the Court's policies, because it allows justices to take positions that diverge from the local and national consensus of opinion. The Court's decisions on black civil rights in the 1950s and early 1960s illustrate the potential for divergence. During that period the strong opposition of constituents prevented southern policy makers in other institutions from supporting civil rights. Members of Congress from the Deep South were likely to be defeated for reelection if they voted for any civil rights legislation. For this reason, even the liberals among them generally felt compelled to oppose this legislation. The federal district judges of the South held lifetime terms, but they faced possible ostracism by their friends and violence from their neighbors if they favored the interests of blacks. In contrast, southern members of the Supreme Court had both lifetime tenure and physical separation from the South. As a result, they were relatively free to support civil rights, and they frequently did so. The unanimous Court in *Brown v. Board of Education,* for instance, included members from Kentucky, Texas, and Alabama.

In the same way, justices' freedom from popular control allows them to take other relatively unpopular positions. The Court could resist the national tide of opinion that favored regulation of business in the early twentieth century. In the current era it can take policy positions that lack anything like majority support, such as protection of the rights of criminal defendants and prohibition of organized prayer in public schools.

Influence of the Societal Environment. Yet the Court is not entirely free from the influence of its environment; the society in which it operates affects its policies in subtle but important ways. Most fundamentally, despite their independence, it would be difficult for the justices to take a position on an important set of issues if that position enjoyed no approval at all outside the Court. Such a position might make the Court vulnerable to attack, and major decisions that were universally unpopular would be vulnerable to widespread noncompliance. More broadly, as discussed in Chapter 4, the justices undoubtedly are influenced by the state of opinion in the general public and in the sectors of society to which they are closest.

The environment has a more direct impact as well. The Court acts on the litigation that is brought to it, and concerted litigation on a set of issues usually requires considerable group activity. The more support a policy position enjoys, the more likely it is that the Court will receive the cases that would allow it to develop that position.

In most respects, both the distinctive policy positions that the Court has taken during this century had only minority support in society, but the level of support was sufficient to make it possible for the Court to adopt them. The Court's resistance to government economic policy before 1937 was supported actively by most of the business community and much of the legal profession. The Court received considerable praise for its economic decisions from respected individuals and groups. Moreover, through the efforts of corporations and their representatives the Court received a steady flow of litigation on this subject and strong legal arguments against government economic policies.

Similarly, the Court's expansions of civil liberties in the past few decades have had considerable support. A great many legal commentators view such expansions favorably, as does a significant minority of political and social leaders. The NAACP, the ACLU, and a variety of other groups bring civil liberties cases to the Court and argue for broad interpretations of legal protections for civil liberties. On some issues, a majority of the public approves of such interpretations.

At the beginning of the twentieth century, little of this support for civil liberties existed. At that time it would have been difficult for the Court to take strong positions in favor of black civil rights or the rights of criminal defendants. For the same reason, the Court today would find it difficult to limit government management of the economy significantly even if most of its members wished to do so; there simply is too little support for that position. Societal opinion does create subtle boundaries on the range of policies that the Court can adopt.

Congressional Sanctions.   A more concrete constraint on the Court is the array of potential sanctions that Congress possesses, such as the power to limit the Court's jurisdiction. Congress seldom employs these sanctions but frequently threatens to do so. The existence of this authority gives justices an incentive to minimize direct conflicts with Congress.

Occasionally congressional sanctions have a very clear impact on Supreme Court policy. This was the case with the Court's "retreats" on economic policy in 1937 and on civil liberties policy in the late 1950s. Even when there is no direct threat, however, the Court may be cautious about opposing the direction of national policy in order to avoid incurring congressional wrath.

This caution probably is reflected in the Court's limited use of judicial review at the national level. As we have seen, only in the 1920s and 1930s has the Court overturned a set of major congressional policies. In contrast, the Court has been far more active in striking down state and local laws. This difference stems from several factors. One important factor is the power of Congress to injure the Court in significant ways and the more limited ability of state and local policy makers to do so.

Policy Preferences and the Appointment Power

The Importance of Preferences.   Though these constraints are significant, the Court does possess considerable autonomy. As a result, the single most important influence on the Court's direction is the values held by its members—specifically, their preferences on the policy issues that the Court addresses.

From this perspective, a great deal about the Court's direction can be explained quite simply. During any given period in its history, the Court's policies have reflected the collective preferences of its membership. The justices who served during the half century from the 1880s to the 1930s were primarily political conservatives. As such, they supported government restrictions on civil liberties but were highly skeptical of economic policies that infringed upon the freedom of business enterprises. Most of the justices who have served since that time are liberals by historical standards—people who are favorable to civil liberties and to government management of the economy. The shift from the first of these eras to the second was fairly abrupt, reflecting a rapid change in the Court's membership.

This explanation is not entirely satisfying, because it does not tell why certain preferences predominated on the Court during particular eras. Several factors may help to explain the patterns of preferences over time. One is the dominant national values during the periods in which justices developed their attitudes. Another is the social class backgrounds of the justices, particularly the predominance of higher-status backgrounds for most of the Court's history. Also, the dominant ideology in elite segments of the legal profession can shape the views of its members, including future Supreme Court justices.

But the most direct explanation for the collective preferences of the Court is the decisions that presidents make in appointing justices. Chapter 2 examined these decisions in some detail. In this section I will look at the broad impact of these appointment decisions on Supreme Court policy.

The Impact of Appointments. We have seen that the Court's policy direction is largely a function of the appointments that presidents make. If a series of appointees are political conservatives, the Court is likely to become a conservative body. Moreover, because vacancies occur on the Court with some frequency—on the average, once every two years—most presidents can have a significant impact on the Court's direction.

Thus, Robert Dahl has argued that "the policy views dominant on the Court are never for long out of line with the policy views dominant among the lawmaking majorities of the United States." [34] In Dahl's judgment, the president's power to make appointments has limited the number of major statutes overturned by the Court. For the most part, justices view policy in the same ways as do Congress and the president, so they seldom upset the policies of these branches.

I think that there is much to Dahl's argument. The Court's general willingness to accept national public policy can be traced in part to the selection process. Certainly this process helps to explain the Court's greater propensity to overturn state policies. State governors and legislators, unlike their federal counterparts, cannot shape the Court's collective views. Yet the process of control through appointments is imperfect, because of several complicating factors.

One of these is time lag. The average justice serves for several years after the departure of the appointing president, so that the Court nearly always reflects the views of past presidents and "lawmaking majorities" at least as much as those of the present time. Fred Rodell has suggested that the aphorism, "the Supreme Court follows the election returns" be amended to refer to the returns "of ten or twelve years before." [35]

The extent of the lag may vary, chiefly because presidents have differing opportunities to make appointments. President Nixon was able to select four justices during his first term in office, while Franklin Roosevelt and Jimmy Carter made none in that period. Roosevelt's bad luck in this respect helped to produce his conflict with the Court over its handling of the New Deal legislation. Had he been able to replace two conservative justices early in his tenure, the Court would not have served as a major roadblock to his program. Carter's luck was even worse; the absence of vacancies during his term, combined with his defeat for reelection in 1980, made him the first president in more than a century who made no appointments to the Court. As a result, he had no opportunity to strengthen the Court's liberalism. Of course, as the example of Roosevelt illustrates, a president's influence over the Court's direction depends only in part on the number of appointments to be made. It also depends on the ideological configuration of the Court and on the identity of the members who leave it.

Another factor is deviation of justices from presidential expectations. Presidents usually get most of what they want from their appointees, but this is not an absolute rule. Wilson's selection of the conservative McReynolds affected the Court's balance for two decades. The unprecedented liberalism of the Court in the 1960s resulted in part from Eisenhower's miscalculations in his nominations of Warren and Brennan.

Finally, appointments reflect not the views of a "lawmaking majority" so much as the views of the president. A conservative Republican who perseveres in selecting like-minded nominees to the Court, such as Richard Nixon, will obtain a more conservative Court even when Congress is Democratic and liberal. Nor do all appointments reflect a national consensus about policy. John Kennedy in 1960 and Richard Nixon in 1968 won the presidency by very small margins; their elections hardly represented general endorsements of their views. But the narrowness of their victories did not prevent either from reshaping the Court.

For these reasons, Dahl's argument is valid only as a statement of a general tendency. The process of appointment does limit the Court's disagreement with the policies of Congress and the president. But the lag that is inherent in the selection process weakens the relationship between the Court and current lawmaking majorities. Moreover, the element of chance in the timing of vacancies in the Court and in the performance of appointees makes the Court's reflection of even past majorities somewhat uneven. The two policy orientations that have prevailed on the Supreme Court over the last century reflected in part the existence of strong lawmaking majorities during particular time periods: the conservative Republican governments that dominated much of the period from the Civil War to the Great Depression, and the unprecedented twelve-year tenure of Franklin D. Roosevelt. However, they also reflected patterns of resignations and deaths, unexpected behavior on the part of justices, and other factors that were a good deal less systematic. The forces that shape the Court's role as a policy maker, like so much about the Court, are highly complex.

Conclusions

This chapter has examined a wide range of subjects concerning the Supreme Court's policy outputs. Among all the patterns that have been discussed, a few merit emphasis.

First, during particular periods the Court's policy-making activity often has fairly strong themes. In the past half century, for instance, the dominant theme has been a concern for civil liberties. The Court devotes a large proportion of its agenda to civil liberties issues. Although its support for civil liberties has varied over time and among issues, in general the Court has expanded legal protections for liberties. Similarly, the dominant theme in an earlier Court was scrutiny of government economic policies.

Second, these themes and the Court's work as a whole reflect both the justices' preferences and the influence of the Court's environment. In large part the Court's policies are what its members would like them to be. But the Court is subject to environmental constraints, which limit the divergence between Supreme Court decisions and the policies of the rest of government. In particular, the president's appointment power establishes a direct link between the justices' preferences and their environment.

Finally, the Court's role as a policy maker—though clearly significant—is a limited one. The Court specializes in some fields of policy, while it scarcely touches several major policy areas. As a result, critical matters such as foreign policy are left almost entirely to the other branches. Even in the areas to which the Court gives the greatest attention, it does not often disturb the basic features of national policy.

The significance of the Supreme Court as a policy maker ultimately depends on the impact of its decisions. This impact will be the subject of the final chapter. After examining the effect of the Court's decisions, we can make a firmer assessment of the Supreme Court's role in the policy-making process.

Notes

1. The cases were, respectively, *Immigration and Naturalization Service v. Chadha* (1983) and *Bowsher v. Synar* (1986).
2. This figure and the figure on criminal cases below were calculated from data in the summaries of Supreme Court business in November issues of the *Harvard Law Review,* volumes 97-101.
3. This figure is based in part on data in Richard L. Pacelle, Jr., "The Supreme Court and the Growth of Civil Liberties: The Process and Dynamics of Agenda Change" (paper delivered at the annual conference of the American Political Science Association, Chicago, September 1987), 32.
4. This discussion of changes in specific areas draws much from Arthur D. Hellman, "Case Selection in the Burger Court: A Preliminary Inquiry," *Notre Dame Law Review* 60 (1985): 947-1055.
5. *Virginia State Board of Pharmacy v. Virginia Citizens Consumer Council* (1976).
6. The most important of these decisions was *Gregg v. Georgia* (1976).
7. This discussion of changes in the agenda as a whole draws much from the work of Richard Pacelle, including "Supreme Court and Growth of Civil Liberties" and "The Supreme Court Agenda across Time: Toward a Theory of Agenda-Building" (paper delivered at the annual conference of the Midwest Political Science Association, Chicago, April 1986).
8. The primary source for this discussion of the agendas of the courts of appeals was Administrative Office of the United States Courts, *1986 Annual Report of the Director* (Washington, D.C.: Government Printing Office, 1987), 142-145. The sources for the state supreme courts were Robert A. Kagan, Bliss Cartwright, Lawrence M. Friedman, and Stanton Wheeler, "The Business of State Supreme Courts, 1870-1970," *Stanford Law Review* 30 (November 1977): 121-156; Burton M. Atkins and Henry R. Glick, "Environmental and Structural Variables as Determinants of Issues in State Courts of Last Resort," *American Journal of Political Science* 20 (February 1976): 97-115; and selected official reports of state supreme court decisions for 1985.
9. This discussion is based in part on data provided by John Kessel and on Paul C. Light, *The President's Agenda: Domestic Policy Choice from Kennedy to Carter* (Baltimore: Johns Hopkins University Press, 1982).
10. This discussion is based in part on material in Aage R. Clausen, *How Congressmen Decide: A Policy Focus* (New York: St. Martin's Press, 1973); and Barbara Sinclair, *Congressional Realignment, 1925-1978* (Austin: University of Texas Press, 1982).
11. Because of ambiguities, different observers reach different totals of laws overturned. This and later figures on numbers of federal and state laws struck down by the Court are based on data in Congressional Research Service, *The Constitution of the United States of America: Analysis and Interpretation* and *1986 Supplement* (Washington, D.C.: Government Printing Office, 1987), updated by the author. There appear to be some inconsistencies in the criteria used in the Congressional Research Service source to identify state laws that were overturned.
12. The distinctions made in the paragraphs that follow are drawn chiefly from Robert A. Dahl, "Decision-Making in a Democracy: The Supreme Court as a National Policy-Maker," *Journal of Public Law* 6 (Fall 1957): 279-295.
13. *Scott v. Sandford* (1857); *Hammer v. Dagenhart* (1918); *Bailey v. Drexel Furniture Co.* (1922). Among the 1935-1936 decisions were *United States v. Butler* (1936) and *Schechter Poultry Corp. v. United States* (1935).

14. Based on data in Congressional Quarterly, *The Supreme Court: Justice and the Law,* 3d ed. (Washington, D.C.: Congressional Quarterly Inc., 1983), 159-164, updated by the author.
15. *Federal Election Commission v. National Conservative Political Action Committee* (1985); *Federal Election Commission v. Massachusetts Citizens for Life* (1986).
16. See William Lasser, "The Supreme Court in Periods of Critical Realignment," *Journal of Politics* 47 (1985): 1174-1187.
17. Glendon A. Schubert, Jr., *The Presidency in the Courts* (Minneapolis: University of Minnesota Press, 1957), 354-365.
18. The decisions were, respectively, *Bob Jones University v. United States* (1983) and *Motor Vehicle Manufacturers Assn. v. State Farm Mutual* (1983).
19. *Saint Francis College v. Al-Khazraji* (1987); *Shaare Tefila Congregation v. Cobb* (1987).
20. The decisions were, respectively, *Cincinnati, New Orleans, and Texas Pacific Railway Co. v. Interstate Commerce Commission* (1896) and *United States v. E. C. Knight Co.* (1895).
21. To provide these figures and some others to be presented later, I have categorized decisions that struck down laws as involving economics, civil liberties, or other subjects. The criteria that I used necessarily were arbitrary; other criteria would have resulted in slightly different totals.
22. *Newton v. Consolidated Gas Co.* (1922); *Ottinger v. Brooklyn Union Co.* (1926).
23. Benjamin Twiss, *Lawyers and the Constitution* (Princeton: Princeton University Press, 1942).
24. *Gitlow v. New York* (1925); *Fiske v. Kansas* (1927); *Stromberg v. California* (1931); *Near v. Minnesota* (1931).
25. Henry Steele Commager, "Judicial Review and Democracy," *Virginia Quarterly Review* 19 (Summer 1943): 428.
26. Robert H. Jackson, *The Struggle for Judicial Supremacy* (New York: Alfred A. Knopf, 1941), 187.
27. *United States v. Cardiff* (1952); *National League of Cities v. Usery* (1976); *Marshall v. Barlow's, Inc.* (1978); *Railway Labor Executives' Association v. Gibbons* (1982); *Northern Pipeline Construction Co. v. Marathon Pipe Line Co.* (1982); *Process Gas Consumers Group v. Consumer Energy Council* (1983); *United States Senate v. Federal Trade Commission* (1983).
28. *Goldberg v. Kelly* (1970).
29. The Ninth Amendment reads as follows: "The enumeration in the Constitution, of certain rights, shall not be construed to deny or disparage others retained by the people."
30. *San Francisco Examiner,* December 14, 1967, 42.
31. William E. Leuchtenburg, "Franklin D. Roosevelt's Supreme Court 'Packing' Plan," in *Essays on the New Deal,* ed. Harold M. Hollingsworth and William F. Holmes (Austin: University of Texas Press, 1969), 108.
32. The two 1987 rulings were *Nollan v. California Coastal Commission* and *First Lutheran Church v. Los Angeles County.* The decisions on the other side were *Fisher v. City of Berkeley* (1986) and *Pennell v. City of San Jose* (1988).
33. Lawrence Baum, "Explaining the Burger Court's Support for Civil Liberties," *P.S.* 20 (Winter 1987): 21.
34. Dahl, "Decision-Making in a Democracy," 285.
35. Fred Rodell, *Nine Men* (New York: Random House, 1955), 9. The original aphorism was coined by Finley Peter Dunne and put in the mouth of his character Mr. Dooley in 1901. See Finley Peter Dunne, *Mr. Dooley on Ivrything and Ivrybody,* selected by Robert Hutchinson (New York: Dover Publications, 1963), 160.

6

The Court's Impact

Supreme Court decisions receive attention chiefly because of their potential effects. A tax decision may affect business practices. A decision on campaign finance laws may shape future election campaigns. But the actual effects of the Court's decisions are not always easy to predict. First of all, their direct effects depend in part on the actions of other government institutions. When the Court prohibits a government practice, some policy makers nonetheless may continue the practice. An interpretation of a federal statute may be negated by the adoption of a new statute. Second, the long-term effects of the Court on matters such as labor-management relations and the status of women are inherently uncertain, because the Supreme Court's decisions are only one of many forces that affect such matters.

This chapter will examine what we know about the impact of Supreme Court policies. Among all the types of impact that the Court may have, the chapter will focus on three that are particularly important. The first section will discuss the implementation of Supreme Court decisions by lower courts and administrative agencies. The second section will examine the responses of legislatures and chief executives to the Court's policies. The final section will deal with the societal impact of the Court's decisions.

Implementation of Decisions

After the Supreme Court makes a decision, that decision must be carried out by other public policy makers. Most commonly, the Court's decisions are to be put into effect by lower court judges and by administrators. The tasks of these policy makers take two different forms: the implementation of a decision as it concerns the litigants in the case, and the implementation of the legal rules and general policy established in the decision by applying them to other cases and other situations. I will examine the application of decisions to the litigants briefly and then consider in more detail the broader implementation of decisions by judges and administrators.

Treatment of the Litigants

When the Supreme Court affirms a lower court decision, that decision becomes final. If the Court vacates (makes void), reverses, or modifies a decision, the case may be handled in two ways. First, the Court may simply return the case to the lower court to reach a new decision dictated by the Court's ruling. For instance, in *Lyng v. United Automobile Workers* (1988), the Court ruled that Congress could deny eligibility for food stamps to striking workers; its decision required that the lower court rule against the parties that had challenged this statutory provision. Second, more often the Court remands (sends back) the case to the lower court for reexamination. In doing so it directs that the case be given "further proceedings consistent with this opinion," or the like. Remands occur not only in full decisions but also in brief orders directing that a lower court reconsider a case in light of a recent Supreme Court decision on the same issue.

When it issues a remand, the Court often leaves considerable leeway to the lower court in its reconsideration of the case. As a result, that court may rule in favor of the same party as in its original decision, the one overturned by the Supreme Court. Such a result is not necessarily illegitimate; the judges may have taken the Court's decision into account but concluded that the same outcome still was justified.

Yet lower court judges occasionally seem to behave in an evasive manner, using the leeway that the Supreme Court provided to reach a result that conflicts with the Court's intent. In rare instances the lower court's disobedience is clear. In *Sullivan v. Little Hunting Park, Inc.* (1968), the Court directed the state Supreme Court of Virginia to reexamine the case in light of a Supreme Court decision in another case. On remand, the Virginia court simply refused on jurisdictional grounds to consider the case further, thereby failing to follow the Court's instructions.

More often, the picture is ambiguous. In *Sumner v. Mata* (1981, 1982), the Supreme Court twice vacated decisions of the Ninth Circuit Court of Appeals after that court had overturned a murder conviction, but the court of appeals reinstated its earlier decision even after the second Supreme Court remand. The majority on the court of appeals sought to show that its reinstating decisions were consistent with the Supreme Court's decisions, but a dissenter was dubious: in one of the decisions he declared, "I cannot join in this disregard of the Supreme Court's authority." [1] Even the Supreme Court may be unsure how to interpret a lower court's action; in *City of Riverside v. Rivera* (1986), the

Court divided 5-4 on the question as to whether a district court and court of appeals had followed its remand properly.

As these two cases illustrate, a litigant who feels that a lower court has failed to follow the Supreme Court's lead after a remand often brings a case back to the Court for a second decision. The Court may then issue a decision with more specific instructions to the lower court, perhaps accompanied by criticism of that court's behavior. The Court took this course in the *Sullivan* case. In a less dramatic and more typical example, the Court in 1986 ruled that the Seventh Circuit Court of Appeals had misinterpreted its earlier ruling on federal regulation of commodities brokers.[2]

To secure compliance with its rulings, the Court can go even further. It might direct that a case be assigned on remand to a different judge, as it did in a 1967 antitrust case.[3] If a lower court demonstrated disobedience, the Court could exercise its power to render a final judgment in the case rather than returning it to the lower court. Alternatively, it could issue a writ of mandamus to the lower court, requiring it to take specified action. If the writ was disobeyed, the judges could be cited for contempt of the Supreme Court.

Despite this considerable arsenal, lower court judges who are determined to subvert a decision on remand may be successful. Perhaps the major reason is the Court's extreme reluctance to do more than reverse and criticize the judges involved. For instance, the Court never has held a judge in contempt, although it nearly did so in *In re Herndon* (1969). It refrained from issuing a writ of mandamus to a district court in 1979, despite the district court's long-standing resistance to the Court's rulings on reapportionment of the Mississippi legislature.[4] Judges who strongly oppose the Court's position in a case can refuse to comply with the terms of the remand, knowing that they will have ample warning if the Court contemplates the use of strong measures to attack the lower court's resistance. In the face of continued resistance, either the Supreme Court or the litigant it seeks to benefit may give up, leaving the lower court triumphant.

An extreme but illustrative case of successful lower court resistance was the futile effort of Virgil Hawkins to enter the University of Florida. Hawkins, a black man, sued in 1949 for admission to the law school of the all-white university. In 1952 the Florida Supreme Court dismissed his suit. Two years later the U.S. Supreme Court remanded the case back to the Florida Supreme Court for reconsideration in light of *Brown v. Board of Education*. On rehearing, the Florida court said that Hawkins was entitled to admission, but it allowed that admission to be delayed indefinitely. Hawkins returned to the Supreme Court, which held in 1956 that he was "entitled to prompt admission." Nonetheless, the Florida court ruled in the following year that the Supreme Court could not have meant to limit the prerogatives of a state supreme court in such a way, and it refused to order Hawkins's admission. The Supreme Court then refused to hear the case a third time, suggesting in a brief note that Hawkins might try his luck in federal district court—which he did without success, as the district court in 1958 also prevented his admission. Thus, after nine years of litigation and two favorable Supreme Court decisions, Virgil Hawkins was unable to enter the University of Florida law school.[5]

After a Supreme Court remand, a state supreme court or federal court of appeals often returns the case to trial court. If the Court overturns a criminal conviction on procedural grounds, the prosecutor usually is free to initiate a new trial that follows the Court's procedural guidelines. Thus Ernesto Miranda, in whose case the Court made its famous 1966 decision on police interrogation of criminal suspects, was retried without the evidence based on his interrogation. He was convicted once again and sentenced to prison—a common result in such cases, since there is nothing inappropriate about it if the Court's ruling is followed at retrial. Considerable time may be required for a case to reach its final resolution; after Anthony Herbert won an important Supreme Court decision in 1979 on the use of evidence in his libel suit against CBS News, the litigation continued for seven more years before Herbert ultimately lost the case.[6]

Like other court cases, those in which the Supreme Court has ruled may end in a variety of ways. Sometimes a case is resolved out of court after the Court's ruling, with the ruling serving as leverage for the party that won in the Court. This was the outcome of *Silkwood v. Kerr-McGee Corp.* (1984), a case that became famous when a movie was made about the atomic energy worker whose death brought about the case. Cases decided by the Supreme Court ultimately may be resolved in settings that are considerably less lofty. After a 1977 defeat in the Court, the state of New Hampshire owed court costs to a married couple; they sought to collect by dispatching a federal marshal to a state liquor store to seize some of its inventory. The marshal refrained from seizing state assets after the couple's attorney received a pledge from the governor that the costs would be paid in a more conventional manner.[7]

Implementation of General Policies: An Overview

Ordinarily, the outcome of a Supreme Court decision for the litigants in the case is far less important than the application of the rules laid down in the decision to other cases and other litigants. It is generally accepted that lower courts are obliged to apply Supreme Court rules of law to cases in which those rules are relevant. When the Court adopts an interpretation of an antitrust statute, federal district judges who hear other cases under the statute must follow that interpretation.

With some disagreement, it is also widely accepted that other government officials are under a similar obligation; if a Supreme Court ruling impinges upon the practices of a government body, its members must ensure that their practices are consistent with the ruling. Thus, when the Court forbids a police search procedure, any department that uses this procedure must eliminate it. The officials whose practices are affected most often by the Court's decisions are administrators, and I will focus on them. (I will use the term *administrators* broadly, to refer to officials such as teachers and police officers as well as members of administrative agencies.)

As the discussion so far suggests, the responses of judges and administrators to the Court's rules of law can be examined in terms of their compliance and noncompliance with these rules. But the Court's decisions can evoke responses that range from complete rejection to enthusiastic acceptance and extension, and the concept of compliance does not capture all the possible variations.

The application of Supreme Court rulings to other cases and situations is similar to other implementation processes in government. Like the Court, Congress, the president, and other appellate courts all require action by administrators and judges to put their decisions into effect. Implementation is a basic process of government in each of the branches and at both the federal and state levels.

Wherever it is found, implementation is an imperfect process. Observers of politics sometimes assume that when Congress adopts a statute or the Supreme Court makes a decision, other policy makers automatically do what the statute or decision requires to make it effective. This assumption is faulty; effective implementation is far from automatic. Indeed, policies frequently fail to achieve their objectives because they are carried out poorly, as a result of intentional resistance or problems that implementors cannot overcome.

This does not mean that implementation always works badly. Rather, any policy maker is likely to have a mixed record in getting its policies put into effect. This certainly is true of the Supreme Court. Some of the Court's decisions have been implemented more successfully than others, and the effectiveness of implementation for a specific decision often varies considerably among geographical areas or types of policy makers.

Three Case Studies

These generalizations about the implementation process can be illustrated with a look at three areas of policy in which the Court has suffered from serious implementation problems but achieved some successes as well. After these illustrations, I will discuss the Court's record more broadly.

School Desegregation.   Prior to the Supreme Court's 1954 decision in *Brown v. Board of Education,* separate sets of schools for black and white students existed throughout the Deep South and in most border state districts. The Court's decision required that these dual systems be eliminated. In the border states considerable compliance with the Court's ruling came within a few years. In contrast, policies in the Deep South changed extremely slowly. As late as 1964-1965, there was no Deep South state in which as many as 10 percent of the black students went to school with any white students—a rather minimal definition of desegregation.[8] This resistance demands a closer look.

Judges and school officials responded to the *Brown* decision in an atmosphere hostile to desegregation. Visible white opinion was strongly opposed to desegregation, and black opinion was largely irrelevant because a high proportion of black citizens were prevented from voting. Southern public officials encouraged resistance to the Supreme Court. In 1956, ninety-six southern members of Congress signed a "Southern Manifesto" that attacked the *Brown* decision. Governors and legislatures throughout the South expressed a distaste for desegregation and took official action to prevent it. Governor Orval Faubus of Arkansas, for instance, interceded to prevent desegregation in Little Rock in 1957.

In this atmosphere school officials generally sought to maintain the status quo. Most administrators personally favored segregation and did everything possible to preserve it. Administrators who were willing to adopt the Court's policy were deterred from doing so by pressure from state officials and local citizens.

In the absence of voluntary compliance by school administrators, black citizens could bring suits to the federal district courts to challenge the continuation of segregated systems. In many districts no suits ever were brought. One reason was black parents' fear of retaliation if they actively supported integration in their communities.

Even where suits were brought, they were not always successful. In its second decision in the *Brown* case in 1955, the Supreme Court gave great freedom to district judges to determine the appropriate timing for desegregation in their areas. Many judges themselves disagreed with the *Brown* decision, and all felt some local pressure to proceed slowly if at all. As a result, few demanded speedy desegregation of the schools, and many abetted school officials in resisting change. Judges William Atwell and T. Whitfield Davidson of Dallas, for instance, struggled mightily to maintain segregation.

Some judges did support the Court wholeheartedly. But they had some difficulty in overcoming dilatory tactics by school administrators and elected officials. In New Orleans Judge J. Skelly Wright worked hard to bring about desegregation, but his efforts were fought by the governor and legislature with considerable success.

Table 6-1 Percentages of Black Elementary and Secondary Students Going to School with Any Whites, in Eleven Southern States

School year	Percentage
1954-1955	0.001
1956-1957	0.14
1958-1959	0.13
1960-1961	0.16
1962-1963	0.45
1964-1965	2.25
1966-1967	15.9
1968-1969	32.0
1970-1971	85.6
1972-1973	91.3

Sources: Southern Education Reporting Service, *A Statistical Summary, State by State, of School Segregation-Desegregation in the Southern and Border Area from 1954 to the Present* (Nashville: Southern Education Reporting Service, 1967) (for 1954-1967); U.S. Bureau of the Census, *Statistical Abstract of the United States* (Washington, D.C.: Government Printing Office, 1971 and 1975) (for 1968-1973).

Note: The states are Alabama, Arkansas, Florida, Georgia, Louisiana, Mississippi, North Carolina, South Carolina, Tennessee, Texas, and Virginia.

This multileveled opposition to the Court's decision helps to explain the absence of desegregation in the Deep South until the mid-1960s. After that time, the southern states began to comply. In the second decade after *Brown* the dual school systems of the South finally were dismantled. Although school segregation was not eliminated altogether, the proportion of black students attending school with whites rose tremendously. That growth is illustrated in Table 6-1.

This change occurred in part because the Court made a series of decisions between 1968 and 1971 that demanded effective desegregation without further delay. However, earlier congressional action was more important. The Civil Rights Act of 1964 allowed federal funds to be withheld from institutions that practiced racial discrimination. In carrying out that provision, the Department of Health, Education, and Welfare (HEW) required a "good-faith start" toward desegregation if schools were to receive federal aid. Faced with a threat to important financial interests, school officials felt some compulsion to go along. The 1964 act also allowed the Justice Department to bring desegregation suits where local residents were unable to do so, and this provision greatly enhanced the potential for litigation against school districts that refused to change their policies. In an indirect way the Voting Rights Act of 1965 also played a significant role, because it increased the numbers of black voters in the South and thus made it more risky for officials to attack civil rights as vehemently as they had in the past.

In the 1970s the Court turned its attention to the North. In many northern cities a combination of housing patterns and school board policies had created a situation in which white and nonwhite students tended to go to different schools. In a Denver case, *Keyes v. School District No. 1* (1973), the Court held that government-induced segregation in such cities violated the Fourteenth Amendment and required a remedy. In a series of decisions over the next decade, the Court spelled out rules with which to identify constitutional problems and to fashion remedies for northern-style segregation.

On the whole, federal district judges in the North have been more supportive of the Court than their southern counterparts were. Indeed, some judges had acted against segregated districts even before the *Keyes* decision. Others adopted remedies for segregation that the Court found too sweeping, as in Detroit and Pasadena,[9] or that it accepted with some reluctance. While some foot dragging occurred in the lower courts, it has been much less extensive than in the South.

Keyes and later Supreme Court decisions left a great deal of ambiguity in the law, especially as to appropriate remedies for northern segregation. The Court's rulings, however, indicated that the existing arrangements in many school districts were unconstitutional. In response, some districts changed their practices voluntarily. But strong public opposition to remedies for segregation, especially busing, meant that local governments generally have not taken strong action until faced with a court order or pressure from federal administrators. As a result, change in northern districts has come slowly and unevenly. For the most part, however, school districts faced with desegregation orders have complied grudgingly rather than resisting. Compliance has been increased by the willingness of district judges such as W. Arthur Garrity in Boston to supervise school action directly.

When the courts began to attack northern school segregation, Congress became less supportive of their efforts. Over the past two decades Congress has enacted into law some antibusing provisions, largely symbolic, and has considered many others. More important has been the unwillingness of some presidents to support desegregation through litigation and financial pressure, thereby slowing the process.

Overall, the record of implementation in school desegregation is a mixed one. In the Deep South the Court's decisions ultimately were implemented, but only with major help from the other branches. In the border states the Court secured substantial change even before receiving outside aid. In the North the Court has helped to bring about major changes in school practices, and the degree of change is striking in light of the Court's mixed and ambiguous position on the scope of remedies.

Police Investigation. The Warren Court imposed heavy procedural requirements on the police in two areas of criminal investigation, with a landmark decision in each area. In search and seizure cases, *Mapp v. Ohio* (1961) applied to the states the "exclusionary rule," under which evidence illegally seized by the police could not be used against a defendant in court. The *Mapp* decision thereby provided a possible incentive for police to follow rules for legal searches that were established in other decisions. In the area of interrogation *Miranda v. Arizona* (1966) required that suspects be given a series of warnings prior to police questioning if their statements were to be used as evidence.

The Burger Court subsequently weakened the *Mapp* and *Miranda* decisions in some respects, and some commentators viewed its 1984 decisions on the exclusionary rule as negating much of the rule's force. But the basic rules of both decisions remained standing at least until 1984. How have judges and police officers responded to those rules?

Lower court responses to *Mapp* and *Miranda* have been mixed. Some state supreme courts criticized the decisions and interpreted them narrowly. Others were more supportive. Indeed, supreme courts in several states have evaded the Court's narrowing of *Mapp* and *Miranda* over the last two decades by holding that their state constitutions provide broader protection of defendants' rights.[10] At the trial level, where judges frequently deal with challenges to searches and confessions, the record also varies. Clearly many judges who are sympathetic toward the police have been reluctant to order the exclusion of evidence from trials.

The evidence on police response to the Court's requirements is not as extensive as we might like, but we know a good deal about that response. Most police officers seek maximum freedom for their investigative activities and resent the Court's efforts to impose constraints on those activities. At the same time, they want their evidence to stand up in court. The result has been a complex pattern of police behavior.

In the case of *Miranda*, studies in New Haven and Washington, D.C., shortly after the decision found that police officers usually failed to give suspects all the warnings required by the Court.[11] In 1970, former justice Tom Clark complained that "the police just will not give the warnings required."[12] Since that time the level of literal compliance with the *Miranda* rules apparently has become rather high. But officers often make it difficult for suspects to make effective use of the rights contained in the warnings. For instance, as a study in Denver found, officers sometimes put great pressure on suspects to waive their rights and to answer questions.[13] Even without such pressure, most suspects disregard the *Miranda* warnings and talk to the police. As a result, officers have found that they can live with the decision; as a public defender has noted, they even gain an advantage from it.

> Police *love* the *Miranda* decision. They speed-read the suspect his rights and tell him to fill in and sign a printed waiver form. He's frightened; he doesn't understand what was read to him; he's afraid he'll look guilty if he doesn't sign; he signs, and school's out. The signed waiver is almost impossible for the defense to overcome.[14]

In search and seizure, there is disagreement about the extent of police compliance with rules established by the Court. This disagreement reflects a mixed and ambiguous picture.[15] There is some evidence that *Mapp* produced changes in police behavior, including a major increase in the use of search warrants in some departments.[16] But it appears that the Court has faced more noncompliance in this area than in interrogations, because the Court's search requirements are more difficult to reconcile with police needs: compliance with rules for searches sometimes makes it impractical to obtain needed evidence. After *Mapp*, observers of police activities in cities such as Oakland and New York City reported that illegal searches were common.[17] Studies indicate that in a relatively small but significant number of cases, prosecutors drop charges because of illegally seized evidence or judges grant motions to suppress illegal evidence; such actions occur most often for "search-intensive" crimes such as drug offenses.[18]

The imperfect adherence of police to court-mandated rules for searches may be puzzling, because noncompliance jeopardizes the use of evidence in court. One reason for rule violations is that officers do not always concern themselves with obtaining convictions, particularly in minor cases. In addition, illegal searches may not prevent convictions. A great many defendants plead guilty, thereby waiving their right to challenge the legality of evidence against them. Sympathetic trial judges may give the benefit of the doubt to police officers on borderline evidentiary questions. All these factors reduce the risks in departing from judicial rules.

School Religion. In *Engel v. Vitale* (1962) and *Abington School District v. Schempp* (1963), the Supreme Court ruled that public schools could not hold prayer and Bible-reading exercises for their students. Information on the responses of schools to these decisions is incomplete and somewhat contradictory, but it seems clear that within a few years a high proportion of schools had eliminated religious exercises prohibited by the Court. By 1964-1965, according to one survey, the proportion of classrooms with prayers declined from 60 percent to 28 percent; for Bible reading, the decline was from 48 percent to 22 percent.[19]

The decline, of course, still left a large number of schools in noncompliance with the Court's rulings. Such noncompliance is not difficult to explain. Prayer and Bible reading were deeply rooted in many schools, with a good deal of strong support from school personnel and people in the community. In many school districts there was no open opposition to the religious observances, in part because few people disagreed with them and in part because potential opponents were afraid to come forward. Under these conditions it was easiest for school officials simply to maintain the observances. Some reconciled that policy with the Supreme Court's decisions through reinterpretation of the decisions—as allowing prayers where participation was voluntary, for instance.

In the late 1970s and 1980s there seemed to be a mild resurgence in school religious observances; according to one expert in 1980, "Prayer is creeping back into public schools rather sporadically." [20] School officials in some districts established new observances or proclaimed existing ones more openly. Legislatures in several states, including Louisiana, Massachusetts, and West Virginia, adopted laws providing for school prayers in some form. A more conservative political climate probably helped to bring about this activity.

When legal challenges are brought against school religion, judges generally have supported the Supreme Court. Lower courts have acted quickly to strike down state laws mandating prayer and religious observances in local schools. One exception was an Alabama federal judge who upheld both a state prayer law and local observances in 1983, declaring that "the United States Supreme Court has erred" in its interpretation of the Constitution.[21] In that case, the Supreme Court ultimately struck down the Alabama law and chastised the judge who upheld it. A study of one Alabama county after the Court's decision, however, indicated that many teachers continued practices that the state law had mandated.[22]

The Case Studies and the Broader Picture. School desegregation, police investigation, and school religion all illustrate the imperfections of the implementation process for Supreme Court decisions. These examples of implementation problems are not unique in recent history. Several of the Warren and Burger Court decisions concerning criminal trials, such as the ruling that juvenile defendants are entitled to basic procedural rights, have been widely violated by trial judges. Some law enforcement agencies and movie censorship boards have failed to follow the Court's definitions of obscenity and rules for its control. The federal Patent Office essentially ignored the Court's long effort to establish a higher standard for the assessment of patent applications.

Yet we should not conclude from this record that the implementation of Supreme Court policies invariably is poor. First of all, even in the areas that I have discussed, the Court has had significant successes as well as failures. Desegregation of schools in the border states, widespread modification of police practices, and elimination of prayers in thousands of classrooms are all substantial policy changes that the Court secured. Under difficult circumstances the Court has had a considerable impact on judicial and administrative behavior.

Further, the rulings that have suffered from serious implementation problems do not represent the whole picture. The Court has been more successful with major policy initiatives in other areas. One particularly clear example is legislative apportionment, where the Court secured general compliance with its requirement for massive restructuring of state legislatures under the "one person, one vote" principle. And the implementation of relatively minor, uncontroversial decisions probably is more successful on the whole than that of the major decisions that arouse strong opposition. Given the traditional expectation that Supreme Court decisions are carried out faithfully, it is understandable that the negative side of the record has received more attention, but the negative side is only part of the picture.

We have seen considerable variation in the success of implementation. Some decisions seem to fare better than others. Major decisions have elicited quite different responses from different officials, and the case studies suggest that judges—especially appellate judges—tend to implement the Court's rulings more fully than do administrators. This variation requires explanation.

Explaining the Implementation Process

The effectiveness with which public policies are implemented depends upon a variety of factors. My discussions of three policy areas may have suggested the complexity of these factors for Supreme Court decisions. Five general factors seem to be particularly important in explaining the responses of judges and administrators to the Court's decisions. Each may be viewed as a potential source of difficulties and as a basis for differences in the ways that decisions are carried out.

Clarity and Ambiguity. The opinions that proclaim Supreme Court policies frequently are unclear as to what they require of judges and administrators. To a great extent, this ambiguity is unavoidable. The Court's opinions proclaim general principles in the context of specific cases. These opinions cannot cover all contingencies that arise in other cases or situations. This is especially true in areas where the application of the Court's rulings depends on specific facts, such as the content of an allegedly obscene book or the circumstances under which two companies merged.

The likelihood of ambiguity is increased by some characteristics of the Court as a policy maker. The Court's group decision process works against clarity, because the justice who writes a majority opinion often needs to compromise on language to obtain agreement from other justices. The result may be an opinion that fails to address important questions clearly or one that makes inconsistent statements on an issue.

The existence of multiple opinions in a case also can create confusion, particularly where concurring or dissenting opinions "interpret" the majority opinion. In *Hodel v. Irving* (1987), one concurring opinion stated that "I find nothing in today's opinion that would limit Andrus v Allard . . . to its facts," while another said that "our decision effectively limits Allard to its facts." Of course, confusion is almost guaranteed when the Court fails to produce a majority opinion at all.

Ideally, a series of decisions on an issue increases clarity by spelling out the Court's position more fully. In legislative apportionment the Court established a somewhat vague principle of equality in district population, but it then decided a large number of additional cases to clarify the application of that principle. Similarly, the Court gradually clarified its position on state regulation of abortion after its initial decision in *Roe v. Wade* (1973). But if the Court is inconsistent, multiple decisions can increase confusion rather than alleviating it. Inconsistency is especially likely when the Court's collective views change over time. On issues related to police searches and questioning of suspects, for example, the current body of law includes decisions from the 1960s that were generally favorable to the rights of defendants as well as decisions from the 1970s and 1980s that are less favorable.

The most obvious result of ambiguity is that judges and administrators are uncertain as to what the Court wants: officials may not carry out the Court's intent properly because they misunderstand it. A more subtle but equally important problem for the Court is that ambiguity provides judges and administrators who seek to avoid implementing the Court's policies with some leeway to do so. Judges routinely "distinguish" the cases before them from those decided by the Supreme Court in order to take a different direction. In this way, for example, the state supreme court of Oregon in 1986 allowed garnishment of the wages of an out-of-state worker despite a 1980 Supreme Court decision that had limited the power of state courts to do so.[23]

A more striking example is the implementation of *Brown v. Board of Education*. It will be recalled that the Court gave district judges a free hand to determine the timing for desegregation rather than setting a firm timetable itself. As a result, those judges were under great pressure to allow delay by school districts. Had the Court taken the responsibility for timing on itself, this pressure might have been removed. "If the Supreme Court had issued unequivocal mandates insisting that the district judge promptly order recalcitrant boards to act, the board could blame the district judge and he could blame the Supreme Court." [24] As a result, desegregation might have come about more quickly.

More generally, clarity in the Court's position increases the chances of effective implementation. The Court's success in securing reapportionment of state legislatures was partly a function of its efforts to establish unambiguous rules in this field. But, for the reasons that I have discussed, the Court often fails to achieve the clarity that would aid its cause.

Communication of Decisions.   We tend to assume that officials who are affected by Supreme Court decisions automatically become aware of those decisions. But communication of decisions is not automatic. Few officials monitor the Supreme Court's output systematically to identify relevant decisions; even federal judges generally are too busy to do so. Instead, decisions must come to people's attention in other ways. Decisions are transmitted to judges and administrators through several channels, which may be only partially effective in informing them of Supreme Court policies.

One of these channels is the mass media. A few Supreme Court decisions are sufficiently important or interesting that they receive heavy publicity in newspapers and on television. Because of this publicity, many policy makers quickly become aware of decisions such as the Court's 1987 decision on racial discrimination and the death penalty and its 1988 decision on censorship of student newspapers.[25] But not everyone is aware of even these well-publicized decisions, and most decisions receive much less attention from the mass media.

Moreover, what the mass media report about a decision may be misleading or simply incorrect. In 1956 most newspapers reported that the Supreme Court had banned racial segregation on intrastate bus lines when the Court actually had refused to hear a case on that question. Before the mistake was discovered, eleven southern cities had desegregated their bus lines in what they thought was compliance with the Court's ruling.[26] While media coverage of the Court has improved in accuracy since that time, errors are still possible.

Attorneys serve an important communication function for some officials. Through their arguments in court proceedings and administrative hearings they bring favorable precedents to the attention of judges and administrators. Lawyers on the staffs of administrative agencies often inform agency personnel of relevant decisions. In these ways attorneys help to ensure that Supreme Court policies are communicated to some policy makers, especially appellate judges.

But where attorneys do not come into direct contact with policy makers or where their role is somewhat informal, their impact necessarily will be more limited. Even when a school system employs an attorney, for instance, that attorney is likely to provide little information on court decisions to teachers. The atmosphere of some trial courts is sufficiently "nonlegal" to limit the role of lawyers as communicators there as well. A study of juvenile justice in rural Kentucky found that many judges simply were unaware of the Supreme Court's landmark ruling on procedures in juvenile cases. In part this was because juveniles seldom were represented by counsel in some areas.[27]

For judges and administrators at low levels in their professional hierarchies, officials at higher levels often play an important role in providing information about Supreme Court decisions. State trial judges become aware of those decisions largely as they are cited by state appellate courts. Police officers often learn of decisions from departmental superiors. There is an inevitable loss of information in this process; those who communicate a Supreme Court policy generally will give a partial and distorted picture of that policy. The distortion will be particularly great where the communicator disapproves of a decision. Many state supreme courts and most police officials offered negative views of liberal criminal justice decisions by the Warren Court as they informed their subordinates of those decisions.

Effective communication of decisions depends on the receivers as well as the channels of transmission. Legally trained officials are best able to understand decisions and their implications. Nonlawyers who work regularly with the law, such as police officers, have the same advantage to a lesser degree. Teachers and other people who work outside the legal system are likely to have the greatest difficulties in interpreting what they learn of Supreme Court rulings.

Because the communication of decisions is imperfect, they frequently are misunderstood by the policy makers who must respond to them. In the mid-1970s, for instance, only 17 percent of a sample of Florida school teachers knew that the Court had prohibited the recitation of the Lord's Prayer in public schools. The same survey found higher levels of knowledge for judges and law enforcement officers. But even the judges showed limitations in their understanding of some of these policies.[28]

Thus, the justices cannot assume that their messages are being heard, and heard accurately, by all the policy makers who must carry them out. And, where communication problems exist, they have an obvious and significant impact. Policy makers who do not know of a decision, such as the rural Kentucky judges, cannot implement it. Teachers who believe that the Supreme Court has allowed the recitation of voluntary prayers will continue their recitation. Police officers whose superiors portrayed *Mapp* and *Miranda* in a negative light as they communicated these decisions thereby developed a bias against compliance. Certainly weaknesses in the communication process help to explain inadequate implementation of the Court's decisions.

Motivations for Resistance. Once policy makers become aware of a relevant Supreme Court policy, they must choose a response to it. In large part, their responses are determined by their agreement or disagreement with the policy and by their assessment of its effect on their self-interest. Where these factors are favorable, as they often are, officials are likely to carry out a policy faithfully. It will be useful, however, to focus on situations in which the policy preferences or interests of officials provide incentives to resist Supreme Court policies.

In appellate courts, disagreement with Supreme Court policies is probably the most common reason for refusals to implement them faithfully. Particularly when the Court adopts a controversial new policy, many lower court judges may conclude that the Court has made a serious mistake. Occasionally, this belief is expressed clearly in an opinion. In the late 1970s, the chief justice of the Utah Supreme Court wrote of the U.S. Supreme Court's position on obscenity that "it would appear that such an argument ought only to be advanced by depraved, mentally deficient, mind-warped queers." [29] More often, judges who disagree with the Court's positions quietly work to limit their impact. In the 1980s, some liberal appellate judges have resisted the Court's conservative rulings on civil liberties issues through narrow interpretations of those rulings or, in the case of state supreme courts, by finding broad protections of liberties in their own state constitutions.

Of course, trial judges and administrators also disagree with some Supreme Court decisions. A great many teachers, for instance, disapproved of the Court's decisions limiting school religious observances. Similarly, most police officers regard decisions that limit their investigative powers as bad policy. In three of four Wisconsin cities surveyed, more than 80 percent of the officers who were questioned disagreed with *Miranda*.[30] This level of disagreement ensured that implementation would be imperfect in both areas.

Supreme Court policies can conflict with officials' self-interest when those policies threaten existing practices that serve important purposes. Law enforcement officers feel that decisions which constrain their investigations of crime will make their jobs more difficult. Detectives, for instance, could expect to have more difficulty in achieving a satisfactory "clearance rate" of crimes solved by arrests. Members of some administrative agencies may feel that compliance with Supreme Court rulings would damage important relationships with private interest groups. State trial judges who need to dispose of criminal cases rapidly may resist implementing due process decisions that would slow the rate of dispositions. This factor helps to account for noncompliance with such decisions as *Argersinger v. Hamlin* (1970), which extended the right to counsel for indigent defendants to some misdemeanor cases, and *Tate v. Short* (1972), which held that defendants cannot be jailed because of their inability to pay fines. In administrative agencies and even in trial courts, organizational inertia gives officials an incentive to maintain existing practices, and decisions that require massive changes may be resisted for that reason alone.

Another interest that can conflict with the Court's decisions is the desire to maintain public standing. Elected officials often shy away from supporting unpopular Supreme Court decisions. Conservative groups recently have enjoyed some success in campaigning against judges who strongly support the rights of criminal defendants, so some judges may avoid vigorous implementation of decisions that expand those rights.

Federal judges, who are appointed for life, might seem to be immune from these political concerns. But they too may wish to avoid incurring public wrath. Full adherence to *Brown v. Board of Education* would have made district judges' lives less pleasant because of the reactions of their friends and neighbors. J. Skelly Wright of Louisiana, who did adhere to *Brown*, found that his life was affected a great deal. "You never know whether people really want to talk with you and I don't see a lot of people any more." [31] Wright also had to endure public attacks, which included a demonstration in which parents and children from integrated New Orleans schools brought an effigy of him in a coffin into the state capitol to the applause of legislators.[32] Robert Taylor of Tennessee reported, "Some of my best friends turned against me on account of the way I ruled in segregation cases. They never forgave me and never will. It was terrible and very emotional." [33]

These judges were willing to accept the costs of supporting the Supreme Court, and northern federal judges such as W. Arthur Garrity in Boston have ordered school desegregation despite the prospect of severe public criticism. But these are exceptions to the general pattern. Where the perceived impact of carrying out a decision is highly negative, most people will offer less than total support to the Court. Few southern officials supported desegregation in the face of strong public disapproval. Most police officers grudgingly implement decisions that limit their investigative activities.

As is true of any government policies, the varying implementation of Supreme Court policies results primarily from differences in the policy preferences and self-interest of implementers. Police departments tend to resist decisions that limit their powers but follow with alacrity those that expand police powers; they have followed *Miranda* more faithfully than limitations on searches because *Miranda* causes them fewer difficulties in practice. The difference between the responses of the Deep South and the border states to the *Brown* decision was primarily a function of different attitudes toward race and segregation in the two regions.

Acceptance of the Court's Authority.   Policy makers may implement the Supreme Court's decisions even when they have incentives not to do so. One important reason is the Court's authority as interpreter of the law. Most people believe that the Court's decisions are authoritative judgments about the law and that there is an obligation to comply with those decisions. Because of this belief, even officials who are disposed to disobey the Court's decisions may choose not to do so. Certainly a policy maker who is indifferent toward a policy issued by the Supreme Court will be inclined to go along because of the Court's authority.

The Court's authority is strongest for judges, primarily because they have been socialized to accept the leadership of higher courts. The attitude of most judges is reflected in the statement of one member of a federal court of appeals: "Our job is to follow the Supreme Court whether we like the decisions or not." [34] Judges occasionally use their opinions to express strong disagreement with the Court's policies but to indicate that they feel duty-bound to go along. One federal court of appeals judge responding to a remanded case in 1980 noted his belief "that the decision of the Supreme Court in this case is profoundly wrong," but he added that lower court judges "must either obey the orders of higher authority or yield up their posts to those who will. I obey. . . ." [35]

Yet few judges hold an absolute loyalty to the Court. Their acceptance of the duty to obey its decisions often is leavened with a resentment of the Court that resembles the feelings of subordinates in other organizations toward their superiors. Further, state judges may divide their loyalties between the Court and their own state supreme court.[36] Thus judges enjoy a degree of psychic independence from the Supreme Court. Because of this independence, judges who dislike a particular Supreme Court policy may not feel compelled to implement it fully. Rather, they can take a middle course, following the Court where the language of its opinions leaves no choice but using the ambiguity that often exists in the Court's decisions to limit their impact. One member of a somewhat rebellious lower court put the matter flatly: "We follow Supreme Court decisions when we can't get around them." [37]

A few judges have gone even further and refused to follow the Court when its position was quite clear. In 1958 a federal district judge in Texas disregarded a long-standing and fundamental Supreme Court decision by ruling that federal power to regulate agriculture was limited.[38] Brevard Hand, the district judge in Alabama who held in 1983 that the Court had "erred" on school prayer, provides another example.

The Court holds authority for administrators as well as judges. Studies of the school prayer decisions found that some school officials were willing to eliminate religious observances that they would have preferred to maintain, because they accepted a duty to follow Supreme Court rulings.[39] But the Court's authority for administrators as a group is weaker than it is for judges. Administrative agencies are somewhat removed from the judicial system and its norm of obedience to higher courts. Moreover, administrators such as police officers and school personnel usually have not received law school socialization in this norm. As a result, administrative officials find it somewhat easier to justify deviation from Supreme Court policies than do judges. Certainly the most blatant noncompliance with the Court's decisions comes primarily from the administrative sector.

The weight of the Court's authority tends to decline as organizational distance from the Court increases. Officials at the grassroots level, far removed from direct contact with the Court, may feel little need to adjust their policies to the Court's decisions. This feeling is typified by the experience of a legal scholar who was caught in a speed trap in Pennsylvania and was brought before the local justice of the peace. The scholar pointed out that the J.P.'s practice of taking part of each fine as a personal fee was unconstitutional. " 'Who said that?' he was asked. Upon learning that it was the United States Supreme Court, the J.P. shrugged and said, 'Oh well, I didn't think it was any Pennsylvania court.' " [40]

The Court's authority, then, is an important force for acceptance of its policies, but not an overwhelming one. Particularly for judges, the authority attached to Supreme Court decisions reduces noncompliance with those decisions. But the Court's authority is not so strong as to prevent all subversion of the Court's policies where other motivations incline judges and administrators toward subversion.

Sanctions for Disobedience.　More tangible than the Court's authority as a force for compliance is the potential application of sanctions for noncompliance. Judges and administrators might follow the Court's lead despite negative inclinations because they wish to avoid those sanctions.

For judges, the primary sanction is reversal. If a judge fails to follow an applicable Supreme Court policy, the losing litigant may appeal the case and secure a reversal of the decision. This sanction is significant, in part because the ability to avoid reversals is one major criterion by which the performance of judges is measured. When the Ninth Circuit Court of Appeals suffered an unusually large number and proportion of Supreme Court reversals in the mid-1980s, that record led to questions about the quality of the Ninth Circuit's work and put its chief judge in the uncomfortable position of trying to defend his court publicly.[41]

Judges express a variety of attitudes toward reversal, but because of professional pride few are indifferent toward it. One judge on a federal court of appeals said of reversals, "Everybody minds it. Don't believe that business about 'I don't mind a bit'—at least from any judge who is any good."[42]

The possibility of reversal not only discourages noncompliance with the Court's decisions but, more broadly, encourages lower courts to follow the Supreme Court's general line of policy. If the Court begins to adopt more conservative policies on civil liberties issues, the proportion of conservative rulings in the lower courts is likely to increase, as judges shift their positions to reduce the chances of reversal. Indeed, studies have found that decisional trends in some policy areas in the lower federal courts move in the same direction as Supreme Court policy.[43]

But reversal is not an overwhelming sanction. A judge who feels strongly about an issue such as abortion may be willing to accept a few reversals on that issue as the price of following personal convictions. Nor does reversal follow inevitably from a failure to accept the Supreme Court's policies, particularly where that failure is somewhat ambiguous. The losing litigant may not appeal. Moreover, the great majority of judges are reviewed by a court other than the Supreme Court, and the reviewing court may share their opposition to the Court's policies. After several state supreme courts in the 1970s and 1980s expressed their lack of sympathy for the Court's conservative positions on criminal procedure, lower court judges in those states could feel fairly safe in deviating from the Court's positions.

For administrators, the most common sanction is a court order that directs compliance with a decision. If a public welfare agency fails to follow an applicable Supreme Court policy, a person who is injured by its failure may bring a lawsuit to compel compliance with the Court. Such a suit in itself is undesirable, because of the trouble and expense that it entails. A successful suit is even worse, because an order to comply with a Supreme Court rule may be an embarrassment and puts an agency under judicial scrutiny that officials would prefer to avoid.

But this sanction suffers from the weaknesses of reversal in even stronger form. First, it depends on people's willingness to bring litigation challenging agency behavior. Frequently noncompliant policies will continue unchallenged. This was the case with school religious and racial policies in many communities. Where a lawsuit appears to be unlikely, officials may see no reason to change their practices. Moreover, a potential court order is not a tremendously powerful sanction. Officials can live with the possibility of such an order if they have reason to oppose a Supreme Court policy. In the unusual event that an order actually is issued, they can then comply and avoid possible penalties.

Administrators who are directly dependent upon the courts have a stronger incentive to follow Supreme Court decisions. Police officers who wish to secure convictions of defendants may jeopardize those convictions with illegal searches. A federal regulatory agency whose decisions are enforced by the courts is in a similar position. As the discussion of the police indicated, however, even these administrators may feel some freedom to depart from the Court's rules.

But the impact of potential sanctions on administrators is hardly trivial. To follow a policy that is inconsistent with a Supreme Court ruling carries some risks, often substantial ones, and officials would like to avoid these risks. This attitude helps to account for the frequency with which administrative organizations eliminate practices prohibited by the Court on their own initiative.

This discussion suggests two conditions that affect the enforcement process. First, enforcement of a Supreme Court decision is enhanced when groups act to challenge noncompliance. The NAACP Legal Defense Fund and the American Civil Liberties Union are important not only because they bring cases to the Supreme Court but also because they bring legal actions against policy makers who disobey the Court. Schools probably are more likely to follow Supreme Court decisions on such issues as religious observances and procedures for suspension of students in cities where the ACLU plays an active role.

Second, the Court's decisions are easiest to enforce when the affected policy makers are small in number and highly visible. It was relatively simple for the Court to oversee the fifty state legislatures that ultimately were responsible for carrying out the first wave of reapportionment decisions. Interested groups easily could bring actions against any legislature that refused to reapportion, and the Court itself could hear all the necessary cases. It is a far more difficult matter to oversee the day-to-day activities of thousands of police officers involved in the investigation of crime.

In general, the sanctions available to the Court are fairly weak. Faced with resistance to its policies, the Court can do relatively little to overcome that resistance. Thus the willingness of Congress and the president to offer their help can make a great deal of difference when the Court faces widespread noncompliance. Ultimately it was federal legislation and its enforcement by the executive branch that brought about the beginning of real school desegregation in the Deep South.

Conclusions.   The factors that I have examined can explain a great deal about the success and failure of implementation for Supreme Court policies, just as similar factors help to explain implementation results for other government policies. Perhaps most important are the motivations that judges and administrators may have to resist carrying out the

Court's policies. When these policy makers like a decision, they can be expected to carry it out enthusiastically. But when a high proportion of officials oppose a Court ruling, successful implementation is much less likely. Other factors, such as the degree of clarity in the Court's policies and the effectiveness of their communication, also affect the implementation process and its outcomes.

The workings of these factors suggest some patterns in the implementation of Supreme Court decisions. First, we can expect judges generally to carry out the Court's policies more effectively than do administrators. Communication of decisions to judges is relatively good, most judges accord the Court a high level of authority, and their self-interest seems less likely to conflict with the implementation of decisions. For some of the same reasons, federal judges and administrators probably are better implementers of decisions than their state counterparts. They are "closer" to the Supreme Court, so the Court's decisions are communicated to them relatively well, and its authority and sanctions impinge on them more directly.

We do not yet have sufficient evidence to assess the overall effectiveness with which Supreme Court decisions are carried out. That effectiveness probably is greater than the existing evidence indicates, because scholars and other observers have paid attention primarily to implementation difficulties and failures. Still, it is clear that the Court's decisions are implemented with only partial success; the gap between the rules that the Court hands down and the actions that judges and administrators take is often considerable.

In this respect, as I have noted, the Court is not unique. Congress and the president also suffer from significant problems in securing implementation for their policies. The Court does have special problems, because it can exert little control over the implementation process. Most notably, the sanctions that it can apply to disobedient officials are weaker than those available to policy makers such as the president. But more striking than this difference is the similarity in the basic positions of Court, Congress, and president: each proclaims policies that face uncertain and often unsuccessful results in the implementation process.

Responses by Legislatures and Chief Executives

After Supreme Court decisions are handed down, Congress, the president, and their state counterparts may play a variety of roles in responding to those decisions. They may help or hinder the implementation of decisions, they may act to change the Court's interpretations of the law, and they can attack the Court or its members. In addition, they may themselves be required to comply with the Court's decisions. In this section I will examine these various roles, both for their own significance and for what they tell about the Court's relationships with the other branches of government.

Congress

Responding to Decisions: Statutory Interpretation.   In the interpretation of federal statutes, the Supreme Court's legal position is inferior to that of Congress. If an effective majority in Congress disagrees with the Court's interpretation of a provision, that provision simply can be changed in new legislation to overcome the Court's interpretation.

Members of Congress undertake efforts to overturn only a minority of the Court's statutory decisions, and most of these efforts are unsuccessful. Beth Henschen found that Congress seriously considered bills to modify or reverse 26 of the 222 decisions in labor and antitrust law that the Court issued between 1950 and 1972. Only nine such bills were enacted.[44] These figures are not surprising. Many statutory decisions are uncontroversial or deal with minor matters, so that they attract little congressional attention. When attempts are made to overturn decisions, they face the same roadblocks that lead to failure for most significant legislation of any sort.

Even though most of the Court's statutory decisions are unchallenged in Congress, enough face serious challenges to make this a significant congressional activity. Table 6-2 lists some acts adopted by Congress since 1984 to overturn or limit statutory decisions. As the table shows, a wide range of policy issues—from civil rights to patent law— were involved. In the same period there were numerous other efforts to overturn statutory decisions. The subjects of these efforts included the right of military personnel to sue the government for injuries, the application of mail fraud statutes to government corruption, and state sales taxes on out-of-state mail order business.

In most respects, the politics of congressional response to the Court's statutory decisions resembles congressional politics generally.[45] Some bills to overturn decisions receive serious consideration because of spontaneous action by members of Congress, but interest groups that are hurt by specific Court decisions play the primary role in getting such bills on the agenda. Just as groups that fail to achieve their goals in Congress often turn to the courts for relief, so groups whose interests suffer in the Supreme Court may turn to Congress. Labor unions, for instance, attacked the Court's *Bildisco* decision allowing companies to abrogate union contracts unilaterally when they filed for bankruptcy. In recent years business groups and local governments also have sought congressional action to overturn unfavorable Supreme Court decisions.

Similarly, the success or failure of efforts to overturn statutory decisions depends on the same factors that influence other congressional

Table 6-2   Selected Legislation Adopted by Congress to Overturn or Limit Supreme Court Statutory Decisions, 1984-1988

Bankruptcy Amendments and Federal Judiciary Act of 1984.   Overturned in part *National Labor Relations Board v. Bildisco and Bildisco* (1984) by prohibiting companies from altering the terms of their labor contracts unilaterally after filing bankruptcy claims.

Patent Law Amendments of 1984.   Overturned *Deepsouth Packing Co. v. Laitram Corp.* (1972) by prohibiting manufacturers in the U.S. from supplying components of patented products for assembly and use in other nations.

Local Government Antitrust Act of 1984.   Overturned *Community Communications Co. v. City of Boulder* (1982) by protecting local governments from damage suits under certain provisions of the antitrust laws if the governments act within their authority.

Fair Labor Standards Amendments of 1985.   Modified *Garcia v. San Antonio Metropolitan Transit Authority* (1985) by allowing state and local governments to make compensatory time available to their employees in lieu of overtime pay.

Handicapped Children's Protection Act of 1986.   Overturned *Smith v. Robinson* (1984) by allowing parents of handicapped children to bring lawsuits under one statute and to be awarded attorneys' fees for successful suits under another statute.

Civil Rights Restoration Act of 1987 (adopted in 1988).   Overturned *Grove City College v. Bell* (1984) by establishing institution-wide coverage for four federal laws that prohibit discrimination by recipients of federal funds.

---

outcomes. Some efforts achieve success in part because they are attached to broader bills with popular features; this was true, for instance, of the 1984 expansion of the definition of patent infringement. More generally, as for other legislation, the balance of party and ideological positions in Congress and the relative strength of interest groups on the two sides help to determine whether a bill will be successful.

One overturning of a statutory decision in recent years, the bill to negate *Grove City College v. Bell* (1984), became a matter of widespread interest and controversy. The decision limited the reach of the statutes that prohibit discrimination by recipients of federal funds. After it was handed down, a wide range of civil rights groups immediately began to pressure Congress to overturn it. The House passed such a bill later in the year, but the Senate did not act. Later efforts to overturn the decision were stalled by disputes over the implications of proposed bills for the abortion issue. Legislation to overturn *Grove City* finally was adopted in 1988 when an amendment satisfied the concerns of antiabortion groups, though some conservative groups and the Reagan administration remained strongly opposed. The president vetoed the bill; a week later, after heavy public and private lobbying from groups on both sides of the issue, the veto was overridden.

Some element of institutional conflict usually is present when Congress overturns a statutory decision. Members of Congress often criticize the Court for what they see as a misguided reading of the law. But this element of conflict should not be exaggerated. Friction between branches of government in policy making is common and generally does not indicate deep hostility.

Indeed, the Court sometimes encourages Congress to overturn a decision. We would expect dissenters to do so when a decision distresses them; dissenting in a 1986 civil rights case, for instance, Justice Brennan said that "it is to be hoped that Congress will repair this Court's mistake." [46] But even the Court majority may invite reversal. In *McCarty v. McCarty* (1981), the Court ruled that under federal law state courts could not order military retirement pay to be shared with a spouse as part of a divorce settlement. Justice Blackmun's opinion for the Court alluded to the negative effects of the decision: "We recognize that the plight of an ex-spouse of a retired service member is often a serious one." Then he reminded Congress of its ultimate responsibility: "Congress may well decide ... that more protection should be afforded a former spouse of a retired service member. This decision, however, is for Congress alone." [47] Blackmun probably was not unhappy when Congress acted the next year to negate the Court's interpretation of the law.

Responding to Decisions: Constitutional Interpretation. When the Court makes a decision on the basis of the Constitution, Congress cannot overturn the decision directly through statute. But Congress sometimes can negate a constitutional decision, or at least reduce its effects, through statutory action.

If the Court has nullified a statute on constitutional grounds, Congress can write a second statute to try to meet the Court's objections. It has engaged in at least two such efforts in the 1980s. In 1982 the Court ruled that the existing form of the bankruptcy system was unconstitutional because bankruptcy judges were given too little independence in relation to their powers. Congress had no choice but to adopt a new system, one that its members hoped the Court would find acceptable. [48]

In 1983 the Court struck down the legislative veto device by which Congress or a subunit of Congress can overrule administrative decisions made under certain laws. Despite the Court's ruling, Congress has continued to include similar legislative veto provisions in some statutes; almost surely, these provisions would be struck down if they were contested in court. But in other instances Congress has amended statutes to require the president's approval of legislative vetoes, thus eliminating the feature that the Court had found to be unconstitutional. [49]

Statutes also may be used to limit the impact of a constitutional decision. Since 1976, three years after the Supreme Court struck down government prohibitions of abortion, Congress each year has adopted provisions that greatly restrict the use of federal Medicaid funds to pay for abortions. In *Maher v. Roe* (1977) and *Harris v. McRae* (1980) the Court indicated that these provisions were constitutionally acceptable.

When the Supreme Court rules that a right is not protected by the Constitution, Congress ordinarily is free to establish such a protection through statute. Congress seldom takes such action. It did so, however, after *Zurcher v. Stanford Daily* (1978), in which the Court held that newsrooms could be searched on the basis of warrants even if no news personnel were suspected of crimes. In 1980 Congress negated *Zurcher* by requiring that most such searches operate through subpoenas, a procedure providing greater protection for news organizations in that a subpoena can be challenged in court before a search takes place.

Constitutional decisions, of course, may be overturned directly by constitutional amendment. Congress formally has proposed and sent to the states amendments to reverse Supreme Court decisions at least five times. The Eleventh Amendment, which broadened state immunity from lawsuits, overturned *Chisholm v. Georgia* (1793). The Fourteenth Amendment's provision upholding the right of citizenship for black persons nullified part of the *Dred Scott* decision of 1857. The Sixteenth Amendment, allowing a federal income tax, reversed *Pollock v. Farmers' Loan and Trust Co.* (1895). Congress proposed the Child Labor Amendment in 1924 to overcome the Court's rulings that Congress lacked the power to regulate child labor. This amendment, however, was not ratified by the states. The Twenty-sixth Amendment nullified the Court's limitation on congressional power to reduce the legal voting age in *Oregon v. Mitchell* (1970). A few other amendments also can be interpreted in part as attacks on the Court's positions.

The constitutional decisions that Congress has acted to overturn are only a small proportion of those that aroused congressional displeasure. This small proportion reflects the difficulty of the amendment process. Members of Congress are hesitant to tamper with the Constitution, especially to limit the protections of civil liberties in the Bill of Rights, and the requirement of a two-thirds majority in each house presents a formidable obstacle to action.

It is especially striking that Supreme Court decisions expanding civil liberties in the past quarter century have not led to formal amendment proposals. Conservative members of Congress frequently have been distressed by decisions supporting civil liberties during this period. In several instances they have urged the adoption of constitutional amendments to overturn these decisions. This was the case with the school prayer decisions of 1962 and 1963, the reapportionment decisions of 1962 and 1964, the abortion decision of 1973, and the decisions that allowed busing of public school students for purposes of racial integration.

Because most of these decisions were highly unpopular in Congress, favorable congressional action on amendment efforts would seem likely. But in no instance has either house provided the necessary two-thirds majority for an amendment resolution. In 1979 an antibusing amendment failed even to obtain a majority in the House, despite overwhelming congressional opposition to busing. The election of President Reagan and of a more conservative Congress in 1980 seemed to ease the way for amendments on abortion and school prayer. But in 1983 the Senate defeated an amendment to allow Congress and the states to prohibit abortion, and in 1984 it defeated an amendment to allow school prayer exercises. In 1988 it was Senate liberals who supported an amendment to overturn a decision, the Court's 1976 ruling prohibiting mandatory limits on campaign spending; this amendment was killed by a filibuster.

Attacks on the Court and Individual Justices.   When members of Congress are dissatisfied with the Supreme Court's behavior, they may attack the Court as an institution or individual justices as well as the Court's policies. The simplest and easiest form of such attacks is verbal, and members of Congress frequently express their disapproval of the Court by denouncing it. Unhappy with a 1956 decision on state regulation of subversive activities, for instance, one member of the House announced that the Court was "a greater threat to this Union than the entire confines of Soviet Russia. If some way is not found to stop them, God help us." [50]

This kind of verbal attack may injure the Court by reducing public esteem for it, but its impact is uncertain. Congress can have a more direct impact by taking legislative action against the Court or its members. This action may take several forms.

One very important but disputed power of Congress over the Court as an institution is its capacity to limit the Court's appellate jurisdiction. The Constitution gives Congress control over the appellate jurisdiction through simple legislation, though there is some question as to whether Congress could limit the Court's jurisdiction to prevent it from protecting constitutional rights. Congress has used its power over the Court's jurisdiction to control the Court only once, in a rather unusual situation; in 1869 it withdrew the Court's right to hear appeals in habeas corpus actions in order to prevent it from deciding a pending challenge to the post-Civil War Reconstruction legislation. In the case, *Ex parte McCardle* (1869), the Court ruled that the congressional action was proper.

In recent years Congress has considered several bills that would have limited the Court's jurisdiction in areas of civil liberties activism. In 1964 the House actually passed a bill to remove the jurisdiction of all federal courts over state reapportionment, and in 1979 the Senate adopted a provision that would eliminate the federal courts' jurisdiction over cases involving school prayer. Both the 1964 and 1979 bills died in the other house. In the 1980s a variety of bills have been introduced to limit the Court's jurisdiction in the areas of abortion, school busing, and prayer, but none have passed either house—even in the Republican-controlled Senate of 1981-1986. Indeed, in 1985 the Senate defeated a bill to prohibit all federal courts from hearing school prayer cases by a decisive 62-36 vote, with many conservatives joining the opposition.

Another kind of proposal that was popular in the past would have required extraordinary majorities of justices to declare acts of Congress unconstitutional. A 1923 proposal set the required number at seven, a 1936 proposal at six. No bill of this kind has been adopted.

The device of adding members to the Court in order to change its policies was made famous by President Roosevelt's Court-packing plan in 1937, which would have increased the Supreme Court at least temporarily to fifteen members. The size of the Court was altered several times in the nineteenth century, and a desire to affect its policies played a part in some of the changes. However, the Court's size has not changed since 1869, and by now it seems rather firmly set at nine.

Along with these means to affect the Court as an institution, Congress also may attack its members. The most extreme method of individual attack is impeachment. As noted in Chapter 2, one justice was impeached by the House—though not convicted by the Senate—in the early nineteenth century, and impeachment has been threatened in several other instances.

Congress holds power over the Court and its justices through its control over the Court budget, limited only by the constitutional prohibition against reducing the justices' salaries. With a few exceptions, Congress has refrained from attacking the Court openly through its budget.[51] But in 1964 Congress singled out the justices when it increased their salaries by $4,500, $3,000 less than the raises given to other federal judges. That action was motivated by displeasure with the Court's civil liberties policies. A year later Representative Robert Dole of Kansas expressed that displeasure in speaking against a bill to eliminate the $3,000 gap:

> . . . whenever thinking about the Supreme Court, I think of last June 15, 1964, and the reapportionment decisions handed down in *Reynolds against Simms* and the related cases. It has been suggested that perhaps Section 2 of this bill might be amended whereby the effective date of the pay increase, if adopted by this House, would be the date the Supreme Court reverses the decision in *Reynolds against Simms.*[52]

For whatever reasons, the bill to restore the gap was defeated by twenty-six votes.

That attack on the justices' salaries was perhaps the most serious concrete action that Congress has taken against the Court in this century; Congress has made rather little use of its enormous powers over the Court. Why has it been so hesitant to employ these powers even during those times when most members were unhappy about the Court's direction?

The answer seems to have several parts. To begin with, there always are a good many members of Congress who agree with the Court's policies and lead its defense. Further, serious forms of attack against the Court such as impeachment and reduction of jurisdiction seem illegitimate in many people's minds. In part this is because most members of Congress believe that the Court should have some independence from the other branches of government. This widespread perception of illegitimacy is a powerful weapon with which to defend the Court. Finally, when threatened with serious measures the Court sometimes has retreated to reduce the impetus for action.

All of these factors can be seen at work in the failures of the most serious attacks on the Court in this century. Both the Court's economic conservatism during the 1930s and its support of civil liberties since the 1950s accorded with the views of many members of Congress, who worked hard to defeat anti-Court legislation. Even some legislators who disagreed with the Court were troubled by the extreme character of bills to "pack" the Court or to limit its jurisdiction. In both the 1930s and the late 1950s, the Court abandoned some of the policies that were under attack, though in more recent years it has maintained highly unpopular policies and still avoided the imposition of limits on its jurisdiction.

Affecting the Implementation of Decisions. Through legislation Congress can influence the implementation of Supreme Court decisions. Its most important tool is budgetary. Congress can provide or fail to provide funds to carry out a decision. Furthermore, Congress can help the Court by withholding federal funds from state and local governments that refuse to comply with the Court's decisions.

This latter power has played an important role in the process of school desegregation. As noted earlier, the 1964 Civil Rights Act gave to the Department of Health, Education, and Welfare (HEW) the power to withhold funds from school districts that refused to desegregate and gave to the Justice Department the power to sue such districts. The Johnson administration's fairly enthusiastic implementation of these provisions was crucial in bringing about the first meaningful compliance with *Brown v. Board of Education* in the Deep South. Later, after the federal courts began to require desegregation of northern school systems, Congress reversed its role. Beginning in 1975 appropriations bills for HEW were adopted with provisions that forbade the department to use its financial powers in support of school busing. In 1980 the appropriations bill for the Justice Department prohibited government lawsuits that might bring about busing; President Carter vetoed the bill because of that provision.

Occasionally a Supreme Court decision requires implementation by Congress itself. *Powell v. McCormack* (1969), for instance, required the House of Representatives to admit Representative Adam Clayton Powell, who earlier had been excluded from membership for misconduct and misuse of public funds. In these situations Congress generally has accepted its obligation with little resistance. However, after the Court held in *United States v. Lovett* (1946) that Congress could not withhold salaries from three federal employees who were accused of subversive affiliations, the House agreed to appropriate the required money by only a single vote.

An Overview.   Two themes in congressional response to the Court should be emphasized. The first is that this response is "political," in that members of Congress react to Court decisions largely in partisan and ideological terms. During any controversy the major defenders of the Court are those who agree with its policies, while the major opponents are those who find its policies unpalatable. As the Court's policies change, former supporters may become opponents and vice versa. Conservatives who supported the Court when Roosevelt offered his Court-packing plan later denounced the liberal Court that developed from Roosevelt's appointments.

Second, despite frequent disagreement between Congress and the Court, congressional attacks on the Supreme Court generally are limited in severity and scope. While Congress acts to limit or overturn some decisions, it makes surprisingly little use of its powers to propose constitutional amendments and to attack the Court as an institution. On the whole, the congressional bark at the Supreme Court has been a good deal worse than its bite.

The President

Influencing Congressional Response.   The president may influence congressional action concerning the Supreme Court by taking a position on proposals for action. However, presidents often remain aloof from debates over the Court. For example, in 1957 President Eisenhower refused to express a clear position on legislation to attack the Warren Court. One reason for this lack of involvement is a reluctance to take sides in a conflict that may have little relevance to the president's own goals.

Sometimes, however, the president actually proposes anti-Court action by Congress. Thomas Jefferson attempted to curb the Federalist judiciary through Congress. Acting largely behind the scenes, he helped to engineer the removal of a lower court judge as well as the impeachment of Justice Chase. Jefferson sought ultimately to remove other justices, including Chief Justice Marshall. This effort was unsuccessful, in part because of Marshall's deft maneuvering. Jefferson also considered other anti-Court measures, such as a constitutional amendment to allow the removal of judges by the president, but none of these were adopted.

Franklin Roosevelt's Court-packing plan is by far the most dramatic presidential intervention in this century. It is striking that the plan received considerable support in Congress despite the radical impact that it would have had on the Court. This support reflected the power of a very strong president in Congress.

Shaping the Implementation Process. The president also can seek to influence the responses of judges and administrators to Supreme Court decisions. Most directly, the president must choose whether to support the Court with the power of the federal government when its decisions meet with open resistance. The president's legal duty in cases of resistance is somewhat uncertain. Practically speaking, the president has pretty much a free hand.

The most coercive form of federal power is the military. In the famous aftermath of *Worcester v. Georgia* (1832), where the Court ruled that a state lacked power to pass laws affecting Indians living on Indian territory within that state, President Jackson refused to provide military force to overcome Georgia's noncompliance with the Supreme Court mandate. Legally and practically, the situation was highly ambiguous. It became famous because Jackson is purported to have said, "John Marshall has made his decision; now let him enforce it." Real or apocryphal, that statement expresses the Court's dependence on other institutions for help in enforcing its decisions.

When southern defiance of *Brown v. Board of Education* began, President Eisenhower indicated that he would not use troops to enforce the decision. By doing so he may have encouraged efforts to prevent desegregation. In 1957 a combination of state interference and mob action prevented court-ordered desegregation of the schools in Little Rock, Arkansas. At that point Eisenhower abandoned his earlier position and brought in troops. In 1962 President Kennedy used federal troops to enforce desegregation at the University of Mississippi.

Federal funds and litigation have become important instruments of national power, as demonstrated by their use in the desegregation controversy. The vigorous use of these mechanisms in the Johnson administration was most directly responsible for breaking down dual school systems in the Deep South. More recent administrations have varied in their use of money and litigation as means to support desegregation in the North and South.

The president may seek to influence implementation indirectly by shaping public opinion. President Eisenhower seemed to be personally unsympathetic to the *Brown* decision, and he refused to encourage compliance with it. Rather, he made ambiguous statements that indicated some support for white southerners who opposed the decision. This position undoubtedly hurt the Court; given Eisenhower's enormous popularity, wholehearted support of the Court might have quieted some opposition to desegregation. "If Mr. Eisenhower had come through," Justice Tom Clark later said, "it would have changed things a lot." [53] Several other justices expressed resentment at Eisenhower's failure to support the *Brown* decision.[54]

President Kennedy played a very different role in the controversy over *Engel v. Vitale* (1962), the first of the decisions that declared school prayer exercises to be unconstitutional. Asked about the decision, Kennedy responded:

> The Supreme Court has made its judgment. Some will disagree and others will agree. In the efforts we're making to maintain our Constitutional principles, we will have to abide by what the Supreme Court says. We have a very easy remedy here, and that is to pray ourselves.[55]

While Kennedy's statement certainly did not produce perfect compliance with the Court's decision, it may have increased the level of compliance marginally.

Presidential Compliance.   Occasionally a Supreme Court decision requires compliance by the president, either as a party in the case or—more often—as the person who controls action by a federal agency involved in litigation. Some presidents and commentators have argued that the president need not accede to an order of the Supreme Court, which is only a coequal body rather than a legal superior. Indeed, in a few instances presidents have indicated that they would not obey an adverse decision in a pending case. Franklin Roosevelt did so twice, in a 1935 challenge to New Deal legislation that limited gold backing for the dollar and in a 1942 challenge to his establishment of a military tribunal to try eight alleged German saboteurs.[56] In both of these cases a confrontation was avoided when the Court ruled in favor of the president.

In terms of power, the president would seem to be in a position to disobey the Court with impunity. In reality, the president's position is not quite that strong. The political power of the president is rather amorphous, based largely on the capacity to obtain support from other policy makers. This capacity in turn is dependent in part on perceptions of the president's legitimacy. Disobedience of the Court would threaten this legitimacy. For this reason, Samuel Krislov has argued that presidents "cannot afford to defy the Court." [57]

That statement is supported by the presidential response to the two most visible Court orders in this century. In *Youngstown Sheet and Tube Co. v. Sawyer* (1952) the Court ruled that President Truman had acted illegally in seizing steel mills to keep them operating during a wartime strike and ordered that they be released. The president immediately complied.

The case of President Nixon's tape recordings, *United States v. Nixon*, is even more striking. During investigation of the Watergate episode, Nixon withheld recordings of certain conversations in his offices that special prosecutor Leon Jaworski sought. A federal district judge ruled that Nixon must yield the tapes, and the case went to the Supreme Court on an expedited appeal in July 1974. Shortly afterward, the Court ruled against Nixon by a unanimous vote.

In oral argument before the Court, the president's lawyer had indicated that Nixon might not comply with an adverse decision. After the decision was handed down, Nixon apparently considered noncompliance; by the end of the day, however, it was announced that he would comply. The administration sent the recordings to the district court as required, and in early August it released transcripts of the tapes to the public.

Information in the transcripts provided strong evidence of presidential misdeeds, especially an effort by Nixon to halt the investigation of the Watergate break-in primarily for political reasons. Support for Nixon against impeachment evaporated, and three days after the transcripts became public he announced his resignation.

Why did President Nixon comply with the Court when the result was to assure his removal from office? He apparently did not realize how damning the evidence in the tapes actually was. Just as important, however, noncompliance would have damaged his remaining legitimacy fatally. For many members of Congress noncompliance in itself would have constituted an impeachable offense, one on which there would be no dispute about the evidence. Under the circumstances compliance may have been the better of two unattractive choices.

This episode suggests that even an official as powerful as the president cannot disobey a direct order from the Court with impunity. Indeed, the president probably is in a particularly weak position to do so because of the need for public legitimacy. In any case, the compliance by President Nixon creates a powerful precedent for similar compliance by future presidents.

The Reagan Administration.   When they came into office, President Reagan and many members of his administration were unhappy with the Supreme Court's liberal policies on civil liberties. Their desire to move the Court in a conservative direction was reflected in Reagan's nominations to the Court and in the work of the solicitor general's office in cases before the Court.

Reagan also encouraged efforts in Congress to limit or overturn some of the Court's decisions. Congress did continue to limit federal funding of abortion, but initiatives to attack the prayer and abortion decisions more directly were unsuccessful. Frustrated by these failures, some critics complained that Reagan had not given these issues a high priority on his agenda. These complaints reflect the reality that only decisions that impinge on foreign policy, economic management, and presidential power are likely to be of central importance to presidents in the current era.

Especially during Reagan's second term, members of his administration criticized the Court with unusual frequency and severity. Secretary of Education William Bennett expressed opposition to some Court decisions in his field, and in one speech he said that his department "will do our best to nullify the damage" caused by a decision concerning government financial aid to parochial schools.[58] Particularly strong in their criticisms were Attorney General Edwin Meese and Assistant Attorney General William Bradford Reynolds. Meese attacked the Court's liberal activism on several occasions, once referring to the *Miranda* decision as "infamous." [59] In a 1986 speech, Meese offered a limited view of the Court's authority, arguing that its decisions—unlike the Constitution—are not the "supreme law of the land." Some people read Meese as saying that officials are not always bound to follow the Court's interpretations of law, though he disavowed this interpretation after his speech drew criticism.[60] Excerpts from other statements by Meese and Reynolds are shown in Table 6-3.

The goals behind these attacks are not clear. If they were intended to pressure the Court to change its positions, they apparently failed; indeed, the attacks may have reduced the administration's influence over Court decisions. One motivation may have been a desire to shape opinion in the legal community and thus to encourage judicial conservatism in the long term. To some degree, the anti-Court statements simply may have reflected frustration that the Court was maintaining a set of policy positions with which administration officials disagreed fundamentally.

State Legislatures and Governors

State governments have no direct powers over the Supreme Court as an institution. They interact with the Court primarily through their

Table 6-3 Statements About the Supreme Court by Justice Department Officials in the Reagan Administration

"To put it succinctly, the jurisprudential theories approved by the federal courts generally and the Supreme Court in particular have, through the years, been largely at odds with the basic principles of our Constitution."
> *Assistant Attorney General William Bradford Reynolds, in an address at the University of Texas, Austin, February 19, 1987.*

"*Garcia* [a 1985 decision] deserves a place among what University of Chicago Professor Philip Kurland calls the 'derelicts of Constitutional law,' cases such as *Dred Scott* and *Plessy v. Ferguson* that cried out for reversal."
> *Attorney General Edwin Meese, in an address to the Judicial Conference of the Tenth Circuit, San Diego, July 31, 1987.*

"What is bothersome is Justice Brennan's abiding belief in what he regards as the sanctity of a judicial power that ranges, largely unchecked, across an ever expanding moral landscape described loosely as 'judicial interpretation'. . . . This brand of jurisprudence and its policy particulars derive primarily from a liberal social agenda in which Justice Brennan shares. And that agenda has little or no connection with the Constitution, the Bill of Rights, or any subsequent amendment."
> *Reynolds, in a lecture at the University of Missouri School of Law, Columbia, September 12, 1986.*

responses to decisions that strike down statutes or other government policies at the state level. These responses help to determine how decisions are implemented and their ultimate impact on state policy.

State governments sometimes aid in the implementation of a decision. Legislatures allocated a good deal of money to help fund legal services for indigent criminal defendants after *Gideon v. Wainwright* (1963) required that such services be available. A number of states changed their laws concerning juvenile criminal proceedings to incorporate the rights established in *In re Gault* (1967).[61] In 1984 the Ohio legislature adopted a statute to enforce *Tate v. Short* (1971), which prohibited the jailing of indigent defendants who were unable to pay a fine. But efforts to overcome decisions have been more prominent.

Like Congress, state legislatures can rewrite statutes to try to meet the Court's constitutional objections. The Supreme Court struck down the existing death penalty statutes in *Furman v. Georgia* (1972), with some members of the five-justice majority emphasizing the arbitrary element in the use of the penalty. Afterwards, thirty-five states adopted new capital punishment laws that were designed to avoid arbitrary sentencing. In a series of cases from 1976 on, the Court upheld some of the new statutes and overturned others. States whose laws were rejected by the Court then adopted the forms that the Court had found acceptable. As a result, the impact of *Furman* has been nearly nullified.

The states also have been successful in attacking hostile takeovers of in-state companies despite an adverse Supreme Court decision. In *Edgar v. MITE Corporation* (1982), the Court ruled that a type of antitakeover law that existed in thirty-seven states was unconstitutional because it conflicted with the federal government's power to regulate interstate commerce. In response, a number of states adopted new types of laws to prevent takeovers. Lower federal courts consistently struck down these laws, but in *CTS Corporation v. Dynamics Corporation of America* (1987), the Court ruled that one of the new laws was acceptable. Within eight months of the decision, twelve legislatures passed similar laws.[62]

In other instances state legislatures have adopted statutes that seem clearly to violate the Court's decisions, in order to limit the Court's impact and express opposition to its rulings. A striking example is the body of southern statutes designed to prevent school desegregation in the decade after *Brown v. Board of Education.* During one period of several weeks at the end of 1960, the Louisiana legislature passed more than forty laws to maintain segregation in New Orleans, all of which were overturned by the federal courts. Another example is state statutes that simply reinstated school religious observances that the Supreme Court had declared unconstitutional. In 1981 the Colorado and Montana legislatures passed bills to limit procedural rights for defendants that the Court had established; the Montana bill was vetoed by the governor.[63]

On abortion, state legislative action has been quite diverse. After the Court struck down state prohibitions of abortion in 1973, most states adopted laws to regulate abortion. Many of these laws were neutral regulations of a sort clearly acceptable to the Court, such as a requirement that abortions be performed by licensed physicians. But other laws were motivated by disagreement with the Court's ruling and a desire to limit its impact by making abortions more difficult to obtain. Rhode Island sought to nullify the Court's decision altogether with a new statute. Ultimately, lower federal courts and the Court itself overturned much of this restrictive legislation. However, the Court did allow states as well as Congress to limit government funding of abortions.

Governors, like presidents, help to determine legislative responses to the Court and the general atmosphere in which decisions are carried out. Southern governors such as Orval Faubus of Arkansas and George Wallace of Alabama helped to block school desegregation in the 1950s and 1960s through their efforts to stir up resistance. Governors also have been prominent in state controversies over the school prayer and abortion decisions, most often in opposition to the Court.

It is difficult to compare the responses of state legislatures and governors to Supreme Court decisions with congressional and presidential responses. Perhaps the clearest difference is that state governments engage in more direct defiance of Court decisions. This difference may result from the sheer number of states rather than from differences between state and federal officials in their attitudes toward the Court. Even so, it suggests that the Court may face special difficulties when it seeks to bring about fundamental changes in state policies.

Impact on Society

A General View

The Importance of Societal Impact. Supreme Court decisions are directed at other public policy makers, establishing legal rules to govern policy decisions within government. But the ultimate importance of the Court's decisions rests primarily on their impact outside government, on American society as a whole. For example, the Court's rulings in labor law are important chiefly because of their potential effects on the relationship between employees and employers; its decisions on sex discrimination, because of their impact on the status of women. The responses of other policy makers to Supreme Court decisions can be considered a kind of intermediate step, albeit a crucial one.

One way to assess the impact of the Court on society is in terms of the goals that seem to underlie the Court's policies. The Supreme Court generally does not proclaim long-term goals in its opinions. However, the intent of the justices often is fairly clear from what the Court does. *Brown v. Board of Education* certainly was intended to improve the quality of education for black children and eventually to improve the status of blacks in American life. Some of the Court's antitrust decisions have been efforts to increase competition in particular sectors of the economy. Beginning with these implicit goals, we may examine the Court's success in advancing them.

Yet the Court's effects are not limited to those intended by its members. Critics of decisions often charge that the Court's efforts to serve one goal damage the achievement of another. Some people view decisions that support the rights of criminal defendants, for instance, as a cause of increases in crime rates. On another level, a Supreme Court policy can influence the course of action by political and social groups. The Court's decision in *Roe v. Wade,* for instance, helped to bring about a mass antiabortion movement in the United States. As these examples suggest, it is important to look widely in order to gauge the Court's full effects on American society.

Assessing the Court's Impact. Observers of the Supreme Court often ascribe tremendous impact to its decisions. This is especially true of people who disagree with the Court's policies. Commentaries on decisions concerning the schools provide some examples. In 1985 a high school principal argued that the *Tinker* decision giving protection to students' freedom of speech had produced an "insidious and subtle mutation of pupil-teacher relationships" and helped to weaken the quality of education.[64] Commentator William F. Buckley concluded a year later that the Court's decisions limiting religious observances in the schools had helped to cause a rise in teen-age pregnancies.[65] In 1972 George Wallace said that the school prayer decisions had been followed by an increase in crime, "an epidemic" of drug abuse in schools, and the appearance of "hard-core pornographic filth . . . on our newsstands and in our theaters." "This may be coincidence," Wallace concluded, "but I don't think so." [66]

Such statements deserve a degree of skepticism, for they seem to ignore limits on the Court's impact. In reality, the effects of Supreme Court decisions on society are constrained a great deal by the context in which those policies operate.

Part of that context is governmental. As we have seen, the impact of decisions is often narrowed by other policy makers who fail to implement them fully or who take other action to limit them. For example, George Wallace based his complaints about the school prayer decisions on the assumption that "public school prayer has been nearly nonexistent for the past eight years," [67] but in fact prayers remained widespread after the Supreme Court's decisions prohibiting them. The Court's voiding of existing death penalty laws was superseded by legislative action to restore capital punishment.

More generally, the Court seldom is the only government agency that deals with a particular set of issues. Rather, in most areas the Court is one policy maker among many that make decisions and undertake initiatives. In the regulation of labor-management relations, for instance, Congress sets the basic rules, administrative agencies elaborate on these rules and apply them to specific cases, and lower courts resolve most disagreements over agency decisions. The Court's participation is limited to the resolution of a few of the legal questions that arise in the lower courts. Under these circumstances, the Court still can have considerable impact. But it hardly could determine the character of labor relations by itself.

The Court's policies also operate within a context of nongovernment action. Even the direct impact of most decisions depends largely on the responses of people outside government.[68] Perhaps most important are the actions of a decision's beneficiaries, such as hospitals that become free to provide abortions or welfare recipients who gain new procedural rights. These beneficiaries may not take full advantage of the opportunities that the Court provides them. One reason is that communication of decisions to the general public is even less effective than communication to policy makers. Many people give little attention to the Court; in 1986, when William Rehnquist had been a justice for fifteen years and his nomination as chief justice was a subject of great controversy, a survey found that only one quarter of the public could identify him as a member of the Court.[69] Thus, individuals may not know of decisions that could help them. But even those who are aware of favorable decisions do not always act on them. For example, welfare recipients may not insist on their procedural rights because they fear alienating officials who hold power over them.

Nongovernment forces also are important in determining the broad impact of Supreme Court decisions on society. Phenomena such as crime and sex discrimination are affected by family socialization, the mass media, and the economy. These kinds of forces are likely to exert a more fundamental impact on the propensity to commit crimes or to discriminate than does a Supreme Court policy. The effects that the Court does have will occur within the context of more basic and more powerful influences.

This limitation is one common to all public policies, whatever their sources. The effects of government, good or bad, are constrained by other social forces. We have learned in recent years that government policies have only a limited capacity to reduce crime or to strengthen the economy. But the Supreme Court is in an especially weak position to shape American society, because it has little direct control over behavior in the private sector and because it seldom makes comprehensive policy in a particular area.

All this does not mean that Supreme Court decisions cannot have a significant impact on society. Frequently their direct impact is considerable, and they may play a part in shaping important social phenomena. The Court's decisions striking down barriers to advertising and price competition among lawyers led to major changes in the legal profession.[70] By striking down major provisions of the Federal Election Campaign Act, the Court has influenced the course of national politics over the last decade. But we should not expect the Court generally to exert a dominant influence on society. Nor should we declare that the Court's policies have failed because their impact is limited.

Problems in Determining Impact. The Court's impact is often quite difficult to ascertain, in part because of the forces that limit and channel it. Most fundamentally, as legal scholar Jesse Choper has written, "the repercussions of all government actions . . . interrelate with other phenomena, both public and private, many of which simply cannot be quantified and indeed often cannot even be identified." [71] Thus, the effects of the Court's policies must be investigated rather than assumed. Even careful investigation, however, cannot produce a precise measure of the impact exerted by a Court policy. The broader the policy, the greater will be the difficulty of measurement.

A good example is the tremendous growth in the number of legal abortions since 1970. The Supreme Court struck down state prohibitions on abortion in 1973, so we might assume that the Court was responsible for the change in the abortion rate. But the picture is not that simple.[72] Changing social attitudes led a large minority of states to ease restrictions on abortion prior to 1973, and the sharpest increase in legal abortions occurred in the pre-1973 period. If the Supreme Court had not acted, the process of legal change would have continued. Indeed, the Court's decision helped to mobilize opposition to abortion that in turn led to new limits on access to abortion in some states. Although the Court has affected the abortion rate, then, its effect has been more limited than we might have predicted in 1973 and less extensive than the increase in legal abortions suggests.

Thus the task of determining the Court's impact is not easy. But it is possible to reach some tentative conclusions about the effects of Supreme Court policies in particular areas. Two important areas that illustrate some aspects of the Court's impact are black civil rights and freedom of expression.

Black Civil Rights

Chapter 5 discussed the high level of support that the Supreme Court has given to the civil rights of blacks since the 1940s. This support has not been total, and it has declined markedly from its peak in the 1960s. But the general thrust of the Court's policies has been quite favorable by most measures. The Court has supported civil rights in substantive areas such as education and voting. It also did much to protect the civil rights movement when the movement came under attack in the South in the 1950s and 1960s. In recent years it has upheld the use of affirmative action programs in a broad range of situations.

The implicit goal that underlies the Court's work in this area has been improvement of the status of blacks in American society. To what extent have the Court's policies actually furthered that goal? Although that question cannot be answered with certainty, we can get some sense of the Court's contribution.

Change in the Status of Blacks.   The process of change in the situation of black Americans has been complex and ambiguous. Understandably, commentators disagree as to how much blacks have gained since the 1940s. Perhaps the best generalization is that progress has varied among the major areas of black disadvantage.

The clearest change has been political. Black political power has grown tremendously in the past three decades. One important reason is the increased ability of southern blacks to vote. In eleven southern states, 29 percent of the nonwhite adults were registered to vote in 1960;

by 1986, 61 percent of the black adults were registered.[73] Another is the development of a vastly strengthened civil rights movement. The growth in political power is reflected in the increase in black elected officials from about 100 in 1964 to 6,600 in 1987 [74] and in Jesse Jackson's strong campaigns for the Democratic presidential nomination in 1984 and 1988. Another reflection is a growing willingness of white officials to respond to black concerns. Some former advocates of white supremacy, such as Senator Strom Thurmond of South Carolina, now feel compelled to seek black votes.

Socially, the segregation of American life has broken down to some degree. Dual school systems no longer exist in the Deep South and border states. Black access to accommodations in hotels and restaurants has improved tremendously throughout the country. But education in practice remains largely segregated in much of the United States, including many large northern cities. Nationally, 18 percent of all nonwhite public school students attended schools whose enrollments were less than 1 percent white in 1980.[75] This segregation in turn results in part from continuing segregation of housing. It is in the area of housing that discrimination has been most unyielding.

Economic status may be the most important issue of all, because of its own significance and its implications for social and political gains. Here the picture is confused and a matter of heated debate. By some measures, there has been an improvement in economic equality. But the average income of blacks remains a good deal lower than that of whites; in 1986 the median income for black families was about $17,600, compared with $30,800 for white families.[76] As these figures suggest, a disproportionate number of blacks live in poverty. On the basis of this continuing disparity and other measures, some observers argue that the change in black economic status has been minimal.

The Court's Role. To some degree, at least, the position of blacks has improved. How much of this improvement can be ascribed to the Supreme Court? Certainly the Court has worked alongside other important sources of change. Particularly during the 1960s, Congress and the federal executive branch made some significant contributions to equal rights. So did state and local governments in much of the country. Nongovernment forces for change include the mass media and, more important, the civil rights movement itself.

The limits of the Court's impact are clear in the two substantive areas in which it has been most active, education and voting. Despite *Brown v. Board of Education,* school segregation in the Deep South did not break down until the Civil Rights Act of 1964 provided financial inducements for desegregation. The Court's decisions eliminated some barriers to black voting, but those decisions did not bring about full access to the ballot box in the South. That access came after the Voting Rights Act of 1965 created administrative mechanisms for effective enforcement of the right to vote.

The Court has played a more limited role in some other areas, including employment and housing. In both of these areas the major government initiatives in support of black rights came from the legislative and executive branches. Because constitutional protections do not apply directly to private discrimination, the Court's activity has been limited chiefly to interpretations of federal legislation. If government has contributed to an improvement in black economic status, it is primarily Congress that is responsible.

It is more difficult to determine whether the Court played an indirect role by spurring federal legislation on civil rights and strengthening the civil rights movement itself. One careful commentary concluded that the Court's impact in both areas was minimal.[77] But a case can be made that the Court contributed significantly to these changes.

The development of the mass civil rights movement in the South probably was inevitable, and the Supreme Court was hardly the major force leading to that movement. But the Court may have speeded its growth. Its decisions in education and other areas created hope for change and established rights to be vindicated by political action. This is particularly true of the *Brown* decision, which had considerable symbolic importance for some people.[78] Its protection for the movement itself did not eliminate harassment of civil rights groups in the South or violence against their members, but the Court did help to ensure that the movement was able to withstand the pressures against it.

The series of civil rights laws that were adopted from 1957 on also seems to owe much to the Court. In the areas of education and voting the Court initiated government action against discrimination and helped to create expectations that Congress and the executive branch were pressed to fulfill. It is true that congressional action was most directly responsible for bringing about school desegregation in the Deep South. But if the Court had not made the *Brown* decision, Congress might have had no impetus to act against segregation at all. After civil rights legislation was adopted, the Court affirmed the validity of laws that were challenged and increased their effectiveness through a general pattern of broad interpretations for a number of years. And the Court's support for affirmative action programs in education and employment has allowed existing programs to continue and has encouraged the establishment of new ones.

General Assessment.   The example of black civil rights illustrates both the strengths and limitations of government in society. Public policy has helped to bring about significant reductions in the disadvantages of blacks. Yet these disadvantages hardly have been wiped out, and even a stronger government commitment to equality could not have eliminated them altogether.

For the Supreme Court specifically, the assessment also is mixed. The Court has had little direct impact on discrimination in the private sector. Even in the public sector it has been weak in the enforcement of rights. But it has played a role in initiating and supporting processes of change, and its members probably can take some credit for improvements in the status of black Americans. If the Court's effects have been far more limited than many observers had hoped, still the Court has demonstrated a capacity to contribute to significant social change.

Freedom of Expression

The Supreme Court's policies on freedom of expression issues have been less consistent than its policies on black civil rights. But since the 1940s the Court has done much to expand legal protection for speech and writing. Certainly the Court has been far more supportive of First Amendment rights than the other branches of government, whose policies frequently have been antagonistic to these rights. How much impact has this line of policy had on the effective state of freedom in the United States? [79]

The Court's Policies. To answer this question, it is necessary first of all to examine briefly the Court's work in this field. There are several areas in which the Court has been active in providing legal protection for expression. One is the area of conflict between freedom of expression and national security. During the Cold War era, the Court gave mixed support to the constitutional rights of people who were accused of subversive activities and associations. Later, during the war in Vietnam, the Court was more consistent in protecting freedom of expression for opponents of the war.

A second area might be called "public speech." It involves efforts by local authorities to restrict picketing, demonstrations, speeches, and other forms of expression in public places. The Court has acted against arbitrary prohibitions of these activities that authorities justify by the need to maintain public order.

A third area is that of "commercial speech." In 1976 the Court overturned a long-standing doctrine and held that expression that is commercial in nature enjoys broad constitutional protection.[80] Since that time the Court has loosened government restraints on such commercial expression as advertising by attorneys.

Two other areas affect primarily the print media. Beginning with its decision in *New York Times Co. v. Sullivan* (1964), the Court established rules that limited the ability of public officials and public figures to bring libel suits. In doing so it broadened the freedom of newspapers and magazines to comment on public issues.

In the area of obscenity, the Court has taken a series of complicated and contradictory positions, but since the late 1950s it has been consistent in giving government only limited power to censor materials or to prosecute on grounds of obscenity. The Burger Court was more favorable to regulation of obscenity than was the Warren Court. But its guidelines for the definition of obscenity, though less protective of expression than those of the Warren Court, indicated that only the most offensive and least serious material may be held obscene.[81]

The Court's Effects.   It is not possible to speak precisely about the impact of these policies, but it is possible to reach some general conclusions. To begin with, it appears that the Court has expanded freedom in practice as well as legal rights in each of the five areas that I discussed.

For instance, the Court's protection of people who opposed the war in Vietnam probably encouraged the open expression of dissent. This was particularly true of its decisions that disallowed retaliation by the Selective Service System against antiwar protesters.[82] By increasing the safety of opposition to American policy, the Court may have contributed subtly to the growth of the antiwar movement.

In obscenity cases the Court has contributed to a general trend toward freer publication and distribution of materials containing sexual matter.[83] The Court's decisions have been only one element in a general process of social change. But by reducing the risk of successful prosecution for obscenity the Court has had an impact on the practices of groups such as booksellers.

Yet the Court's policies on freedom of expression have not eliminated all constraints on speech and writing. The press frequently reports actions such as the following:[84]

—The Federal Aviation Administration fired a supervisor who spoke in support of the air traffic controllers who walked out on strike in 1981.

—The FBI undertook an investigation of an eleven-year-old boy in New Jersey, apparently because he had written a letter to the Soviet government asking for information about the country.

—After a Colorado resident spoke against an effort to remove certain books and areas of instruction from the local schools, callers threatened her and her children, and bricks were thrown through her windows.

Such attacks on expression remind us that the Supreme Court has not brought about a state of total freedom for speech and writing.

Explaining the Court's Limited Impact. Why has the Supreme Court not had a greater effect in this area? There appear to be several reasons. First, the Court's support for freedom of expression has been limited both in degree and in scope. By no means has the Court invalidated all governmental restrictions on expression. For instance, it has limited prosecutions for obscenity and libel suits by public officials but has not prohibited them altogether. And the Court has done very little to curb some important government policies that limit freedom of expression, such as surveillance of political dissenters by law enforcement agencies.

Second, other policy makers do not always implement the Court's decisions effectively or follow them faithfully. On issues such as censorship of school library books, the Court has not been clear in its position; on issues such as libel of public figures, the Court has been inconsistent as well as unclear. This ambiguity limits the Court's impact. But even where the Court is clear, strong-minded officials sometimes choose to ignore its rulings. Some movie censorship boards have operated in violation of the Court's guidelines. And local officials occasionally restrict demonstrations in ways that the Court has prohibited.

For these reasons people cannot feel entirely safe from punishment for what they speak or write. Despite the Court's decisions, a person who protested against the war in Vietnam still might suffer government harassment or even prosecution. A book publisher may fear that a local prosecutor or a jury will depart from the Court's guidelines on obscenity or libel, with devastating results.

But the most important limitation on the Court's impact concerns restrictions on freedom of expression from nongovernment sources. Arguably, the most powerful deterrents to free expression come primarily from the private sector rather than from government. People may refrain from saying what they think because they fear their friends and neighbors will ostracize them, community groups will attack them, customers will withdraw their business, or employers will fire them. While economic pressures have the most obvious impact, these prospects are all unattractive.

The Supreme Court and other courts have little control over these private actions, because constitutional protections for freedom of expression apply only to government action. With a few exceptions, primarily in the area of labor-management relations, there are no legal protections for expression against private action. Certainly, the courts can do nothing directly to prevent unpopular statements from making people unpopular. Thus, even if the Court had taken a stronger stand against government restrictions on expression, it could not have guaranteed anything like full freedom for speech and writing.

General Assessment.   The Supreme Court has had a real impact on freedom of expression. At least some groups in society—booksellers, critics of public officials, dissenters against American foreign policy— have had more freedom because of the Court's decisions. But Supreme Court support for First Amendment rights has not brought about total protection for speaking and writing. Indeed, the constraints that remain seem much more important than those that the Court has eliminated.

In some respects this picture parallels what has happened in the field of black civil rights. There is at least one important difference, however. In civil rights the Court's policies have been reinforced by other institutions working in the same direction, including Congress and a major social movement to achieve racial equality. Indeed, in recent years Congress has supported equality more strongly than the Court on some issues. In freedom of expression the Court has lacked that kind of reinforcement. The private forces that support free expression, such as the ACLU, are hardly comparable in strength with the civil rights movement. The other branches of government tend to restrict freedom of expression rather than working for it. In this situation, the Court's impact necessarily has been a modest one.

The Court, Public Policy, and Society

It is now possible to reach some general conclusions about the role of the Supreme Court as a public policy maker. As the material in these last two chapters suggests, that role is fundamentally limited in some respects but nonetheless quite important.

The most obvious limitation on the Court's role lies in the small number of issues that it addresses. In a great many policy areas, including some of the most important, the Court rarely makes decisions. The Court is at most a minor participant in the making of foreign policy, to use the most notable example. Moreover, it takes only a small part in a good many areas of "legal" policy, such as contract law and family relations.

Even in the areas in which the Court specializes, its intervention in the policy-making process is limited. It addresses only a small sample of the issues that arise concerning the rights of criminal defendants or freedom of expression. Its intervention also is limited in the sense that it has been cautious about substituting its judgment for that of Congress and the president.

Where the Court does intervene, its impact may be minimized by the actions of other institutions and individuals. A ruling that schools must eliminate prayer exercises does not guarantee that those exercises will disappear. Efforts to broaden freedom of expression may be stymied by conditions in government and society that the Court cannot reach.

These limitations must be balanced against the Court's considerable strengths. Certainly a great many Supreme Court decisions have significant direct effects. Antitrust decisions determine whether companies can merge. School desegregation decisions determine which schools students attend. Interpretations of the Voting Rights Act shape the course of local politics. The effects of capital punishment decisions literally are matters of life and death for the defendants.

The Court also plays a major part in processes of political and social change. The Court's opposition to government regulation of private business ultimately was overcome, but it delayed a fundamental change in the role of government in the United States. If *Roe v. Wade* (1973) was not as critical as often thought, nonetheless this decision has been the centerpiece of a major national debate and struggle for more than fifteen years. The Court's decisions have not brought about racial equality, even in conjunction with other forces, but they have done much to shape the process of change in the status of blacks.

As the examples of abortion and civil rights suggest, the Court is perhaps most important in creating the conditions for action by others. Its decisions put issues on the national agenda so that other policy makers and the general public consider them. The Court generally does not do well in enforcing rights, but it often legitimates efforts to achieve them and thus provides the impetus for legal and political action. The Court's decisions affect the positions of interest groups and social movements, strengthening some and weakening others.

The Supreme Court, then, is neither all-powerful nor insignificant. It is one of many public and private institutions that shape American society in significant ways. That is a smaller role than some have claimed for the Court. But the role that the Court does play is an extraordinary one for a single small body that holds little concrete power. In this sense, perhaps more than any other, the Supreme Court is a remarkable institution.

Notes

1. *Mata v. Sumner*, 649 F.2d 713, 718 (9th Cir. 1981).
2. *Commodity Futures Trading Commission v. Schor* (1986).
3. *Cascade Natural Gas Corp. v. El Paso Natural Gas Co.* (1967).
4. *Connor v. Coleman* (1979).
5. The history of the *Hawkins* case is described in Darryl Paulson and Paul Hawkes, "Desegregating the University of Florida Law School: Virgil Hawkins v. The Florida Board of Control," *Florida State University Law Review* 12 (Spring 1984): 59-71.
6. The case was *Herbert v. Lando* (1979).
7. The case was *Wooley v. Maynard* (1977). The outcome is described in "Marshals Seek Costs for Motto Lawsuit," *Valley News*, December 3, 1977, 1, 24.

8. Harrell R. Rodgers, Jr., and Charles S. Bullock III, *Law and Social Change: Civil Rights Laws and Their Consequences* (New York: McGraw-Hill Book Co., 1972), 75.
9. *Milliken v. Bradley* (1974); *Pasadena Board of Education v. Spangler* (1976).
10. "Developments in the Law: The Interpretation of State Constitutional Rights," *Harvard Law Review* 95 (1982): 1367-1398; "State Constitutional Law," *National Law Journal*, September 29, 1986, S-9, S-12.
11. Michael Wald et al., "Interrogations in New Haven: The Impact of *Miranda*," *Yale Law Journal* 76 (July 1967): 1519-1648; Richard J. Medalie, Leonard Zeitz, and Paul Alexander, "Custodial Police Interrogation in Our Nation's Capital: The Attempt to Implement *Miranda*," *Michigan Law Review* 66 (May 1968): 1347-1422.
12. *United States v. Jackson*, 429 F.2d 1368, 1372 (7th Cir. 1970).
13. Lawrence S. Leiken, "Police Interrogation in Colorado: The Implementation of *Miranda*," *Denver Law Journal* 47 (1970): 1-53.
14. James S. Kunen, *"How Can You Defend Those People?": The Making of a Criminal Lawyer* (New York: Random House, 1983), 132.
15. See Richard Van Duizend, L. Paul Sutton, and Charlotte A. Carter, *The Search Warrant Process: Preconceptions, Perceptions, and Practices* (Williamsburg, Va.: National Center for State Courts, 1984).
16. Bradley C. Canon, "Is the Exclusionary Rule in Failing Health? Some New Data and a Plea Against a Precipitous Conclusion," *Kentucky Law Journal* 62 (1974): 702-725.
17. Jerome H. Skolnick, *Justice Without Trial: Law Enforcement in Democratic Society* (New York: John Wiley & Sons, 1966), 164-181; Comment, "Effect of *Mapp v. Ohio* on Police Search-and-Seizure Practices in Narcotics Cases," *Columbia Journal of Law and Social Problems* 4 (1968): 87-104.
18. Thomas Y. Davies, "A Hard Look at What We Know (and Still Need to Learn) About the 'Costs' of the Exclusionary Rule: The NIJ Study and Other Studies of 'Lost' Arrests," *American Bar Foundation Research Journal* (Summer 1983): 611-690.
19. H. Frank Way, Jr., "Survey Research on Judicial Decisions: The Prayer and Bible Reading Cases," *Western Political Quarterly* 21 (June 1968): 191. See also Donald R. Reich, "The Impact of Judicial Decision Making: The School Prayer Cases," in *The Supreme Court as Policy-Maker: Three Studies on the Impact of Judicial Decisions*, ed. David H. Everson (Carbondale: Southern Illinois University, 1968), 45-52.
20. Diane Henry, "Prayer: An Issue Without an Amen," *New York Times*, April 20, 1980 (Education), 3.
21. *Jaffree v. Board of School Commissioners*, 554 F. Supp. 1104, 1128 (S.D. Alab. 1983).
22. The Supreme Court's decision was *Wallace v. Jaffree* (1985); Jaffree's role as a litigant was discussed in Chapter 3. The study was Kenneth Paul Nuger, "Teacher Compliance With *Wallace v. Jaffree* in Mobile County Schools" (paper presented at the annual conference of the Midwest Political Science Association, Chicago, April 1987).
23. Conrad E. Yunker, "Oregon Court OK's Garnishment of Minn. Worker's Pay," *National Law Journal*, February 10, 1986, 14. The case was *State ex rel. Department of Revenue v. Control Data Corp.* (Oregon Sup. Ct. 1986).
24. J. W. Peltason, *Fifty-Eight Lonely Men: Southern Federal Judges and School Desegregation*, 2d ed. (Urbana: University of Illinois Press, 1971), 246.
25. The decisions were *McCleskey v. Kemp* (1987) and *Hazelwood School District v. Kuhlmeier* (1988).

26. Stephen L. Wasby, *The Impact of the United States Supreme Court: Some Perspectives* (Homewood, Ill.: Dorsey Press, 1970), 94-95.
27. Bradley C. Canon and Kenneth Kolson, "Rural Compliance with Gault: Kentucky, a Case Study," *Journal of Family Law* 10 (1971): 300-326.
28. Larry C. Berkson, *The Supreme Court and Its Publics* (Lexington, Mass: Lexington Books, 1978), 79-86.
29. *Salt Lake City v. Piepenburg*, 571 P.2d 1299 (Utah Sup. Ct. 1977).
30. Neal Milner, "Comparative Analysis of Patterns of Compliance with Supreme Court Decisions: *Miranda* and the Police in Four Communities," *Law & Society Review* 5 (August 1970): 126.
31. Peltason, *Fifty-Eight Lonely Men*, 9.
32. "Parents Stage Demonstration," *New Orleans Times Picayune*, November 24, 1960, quoted in Robert Coles, *Children of Crisis: A Study of Courage and Fear* (Boston: Little, Brown, 1967), 385, n. 2.
33. "Judge Robert L. Taylor Recalls School Integration Cases, Efforts to Reduce Huge Docket Backlog," *The Third Branch* 17 (August 1985): 6.
34. Sheldon Goldman, "Conflict and Consensus in the United States Courts of Appeals," *Wisconsin Law Review* (1968): 477.
35. *Weber v. Kaiser Aluminum & Chemical Corp.*, 611 F.2d 132, 133 (5th Cir. 1980).
36. See Robert S. Gerstein, "Serving Two Masters: The California Courts of Appeal and Criminal Procedure" (paper presented at the annual conference of the American Political Science Association, Denver, September 1982).
37. Interview by the author with a federal appellate judge.
38. *United States v. Haley* (N.D. Texas 1958).
39. William K. Muir, Jr., *Prayer in the Public Schools: Law and Attitude Change* (Chicago: University of Chicago Press, 1967); Richard Johnson, *The Dynamics of Compliance* (Evanston, Ill.: Northwestern University Press, 1967).
40. George D. Braden, "Legal Research: A Variation on an Old Lament," *Journal of Legal Education* 5 (1952): 41, n. 1.
41. Charles Maher, "Engine, Engine Number 9 . . ." *California Lawyer*, February 1985, 38-43, 66-67; James B. Stewart, "Judicial Mavericks," *Wall Street Journal*, December 19, 1984, 1, 18; Robert Bartlett, "A Rare Victory for Court in S.F.," *San Francisco Chronicle*, June 27, 1984, 12.
42. J. Woodford Howard, Jr., *Courts of Appeals in the Federal Judicial System: A Study of the Second, Fifth, and District of Columbia Circuits* (Princeton: Princeton University Press, 1981), 140, n. j.
43. See Donald R. Songer, "The Impact of the Supreme Court on Trends in Economic Policy Making in the United States Courts of Appeals," *Journal of Politics* 49 (August 1987): 830-841; and Ronald Stidham and Robert A. Carp, "Trial Court Responses to Supreme Court Policy Changes: Three Case Studies," *Law & Policy Quarterly* 4 (April 1982): 215-234.
44. Beth Henschen, "Statutory Interpretations of the Supreme Court: Congressional Response," *American Politics Quarterly* 11 (October 1983): 444-446; Note, "Congressional Reversal of Supreme Court Decisions: 1945-1957," *Harvard Law Review* 71 (May 1958): 1324-1337.
45. See Beth M. Henschen and Edward I. Sidlow, "The Supreme Court and the Congressional Agenda-Setting Process" (paper presented at the annual conference of the Midwest Political Science Association, Chicago, April 1988).
46. *Evans v. Jeff D.*, 89 L.Ed.2d 747, 781 (1986).
47. *McCarty v. McCarty*, 453 U.S. 210, 235-236 (1981).
48. The Court's decision was *Northern Pipeline Construction Co. v. Marathon Pipe Line Co.* (1982).

49. The Court's decision was *Immigration and Naturalization Service v. Chadha* (1983). On congressional action after the decision, see Elder Witt, "High Court to Clarify Sweep of Its Legislative Veto Ruling," *Congressional Quarterly Weekly Report* 44 (December 6, 1986): 3025-3030; and Louis Fisher, "Judicial Misjudgments about the Lawmaking Process: The Legislative Veto Case," *Public Administration Review* 45 (November 1985): 705-711.

50. U.S. Congress, House, *Congressional Record*, 84th Cong., 2d sess., 1956, 102, pt. 5:6385.

51. Dean L. Yarwood and Bradley C. Canon, "On the Supreme Court's Annual Trek to the Capitol," *Judicature* 63 (February 1980): 324.

52. U.S. Congress, House, *Congressional Record*, 89th Cong., 1st sess., 1965, 111, pt. 4:5275. The misspelling of "Sims" was in the *Record.*

53. Richard Kluger, *Simple Justice: The History of Brown v. Board of Education and Black America's Struggle for Equality* (New York: Alfred A. Knopf, 1976), 753.

54. Bernard Schwartz, *Super Chief: Earl Warren and His Supreme Court—A Judicial Biography* (New York: New York University Press, 1983), 175.

55. "Transcript of President's News Conference on Foreign and Domestic Affairs," *New York Times*, June 28, 1962, 12.

56. *Norman v. Baltimore and Ohio Railroad Co.* (1935); *Ex parte Quirin* (1942).

57. Samuel Krislov, *The Supreme Court in the Political Process* (New York: Macmillan, 1965), 140.

58. Keith B. Richburg, "Bennett Links Religion, Democracy," *Washington Post*, August 8, 1985, A11.

59. Mary Thornton, "Meese Attacks Miranda Decision," *Washington Post*, August 26, 1985, A6. Meese made the statement on an ABC television news program.

60. Stuart Taylor, Jr., "Meese Says Court Doesn't Make Law," *New York Times*, October 23, 1986, A1, A20; Edwin Meese III, "The Tulane Speech: What I Meant," *Washington Post*, November 13, 1986, A21.

61. Jesse H. Choper, "Consequences of Supreme Court Decisions Upholding Individual Constitutional Rights," *Michigan Law Review* 83 (October 1984): 49 n. 298.

62. Daniel B. Moskowitz, "Takeover Ruling Opens the Floodgates in State Legislatures," *Washington Post*, Washington Business, December 21, 1987, 28.

63. William J. Mertens and Silas Wasserstrom, "The Good Faith Exception to the Exclusionary Rule: Deregulating the Police and Derailing the Law," *Georgetown Law Journal* 70 (1981): 369 n. 29.

64. H. Wesley Smith, "Holding Court in the Schools," *Newsweek*, February 4, 1984, 13. The decision was *Tinker v. Des Moines School District* (1969).

65. William F. Buckley, Jr., ". . . And Religion," *Washington Post*, April 6, 1986, A23.

66. Jack Bass and Walter De Vries, *The Transformation of Southern Politics* (New York: Basic Books, 1976), 67.

67. Bass and De Vries, *Transformation of Southern Politics*, 67.

68. Charles A. Johnson and Bradley C. Canon, *Judicial Policies: Implementation and Impact* (Washington, D.C.: CQ Press, 1984), ch. 4.

69. "What America Really Thinks about Lawyers," *National Law Journal*, August 18, 1986, S-6.

70. The decisions were *Bates v. State Bar* (1977) and *Goldfarb v. State Bar* (1975).

71. Choper, "Consequences of Supreme Court Decisions," 7.

72. Susan B. Hansen, "State Implementation of Supreme Court Decisions: Abortion Rates Since *Roe v. Wade*," *Journal of Politics* 42 (May 1980): 372-395; Michael Barone, "The Court's Politics Backfired," *Washington Post*, September 1, 1983, A23.

73. U.S. Bureau of the Census, *Statistical Abstract of the United States, 1984* (Washington, D.C.: Government Printing Office, 1983), 261; U.S. Bureau of the Census, *Statistical Abstract of the United States, 1988* (Washington, D.C.: Government Printing Office, 1987), 250.
74. Charles S. Bullock III and Harrell R. Rodgers, Jr., *Racial Equality in America* (Pacific Palisades, Calif.: Goodyear Publishing Co., 1975), 172; U.S. Bureau of the Census, *Statistical Abstract of the United States, 1988*, 247.
75. U.S. Bureau of the Census, *Statistical Abstract of the United States, 1984*, 149.
76. U.S. Bureau of the Census, Current Population Reports, Series P-60, No. 157, *Money Income and Poverty Status of Families and Persons in the United States: 1986* (Washington, D.C.: Government Printing Office, 1987), 9.
77. Gerald N. Rosenberg, "The Courts, Congress and Civil Rights: Comparing Institutional Capabilities" (paper presented at the annual conference of the American Political Science Association, Chicago, September 1983).
78. See Jesse H. Choper, *Judicial Review and the National Political Process* (Chicago: University of Chicago Press, 1980), 93-94.
79. The discussion that follows draws in part from Samuel Krislov, *The Supreme Court and Political Freedom* (New York: Free Press, 1968), 165-200.
80. *Virginia State Board of Pharmacy v. Virginia Citizens Consumer Council* (1976).
81. *Miller v. California* (1973).
82. *Oestereich v. Selective Service System* (1968); *Gutknecht v. United States* (1970).
83. See Choper, "Consequences of Supreme Court Decisions," 68-74.
84. These incidents were reported in the following sources, respectively; Pete Earley, "FAA Supervisor, Strike Victim, Gets Job Back," *Washington Post*, May 23, 1984, A19; Nat Hentoff, "Hold It There, Kid, This Is the FBI," *Washington Post*, June 4, 1988, A27; and "Vandals Lay Siege to Pair Fighting Censors," *Columbus Citizen Journal*, June 28, 1982, 1.

Glossary

Legal Terms Related to the Supreme Court

Affirm.   In an appellate court, to reach a decision that agrees with the result reached in the case by the lower court.

Amicus curiae.   "Friend of the court." A person, private group or institution, or government agency, not a party to a case, that participates in the case (usually through submission of a brief) at the invitation of the court or at its own initiative.

Appeal.   In general, a case brought to a higher court for review. In the Supreme Court, certain cases are designated as appeals under federal law; formally, these must be heard by the Court.

Appellant.   The party that appeals a lower court decision to a higher court.

Appellee.   A party to an appeal who wishes to have the lower court decision upheld and who responds when the case is appealed.

Brief.   A document submitted by counsel to a court, setting out the facts of the case and the legal arguments in support of the party represented by the counsel.

Certiorari, Writ of.   A writ issued by the Supreme Court, at its discretion, to order a lower court to prepare the record of a case and send it to the Supreme Court for review. Most cases come to the Court as petitions for writs of certiorari.

Civil cases.   All legal cases other than criminal cases.

Class action.   A lawsuit brought by one person or group on behalf of all persons in similar situations.

Concurring opinion.   An opinion by a member of a court that agrees with the result reached by the court in the case but disagrees with or departs from the court's rationale for the decision.

Dicta.   See Obiter dictum.

253

Discretionary jurisdiction. Jurisdiction that a court may accept or reject in particular cases. The Supreme Court has discretionary jurisdiction over most cases that come to it.

Dissenting opinion. An opinion by a member of a court that disagrees with the result reached by the court in the case.

Habeas corpus. "You have the body." A writ issued by a court to inquire whether a person is lawfully imprisoned or detained. The writ demands that the persons holding the prisoner justify the detention or release the prisoner.

Holding. In a majority opinion, the rule of law necessary to decide the case. That rule is binding in future cases.

In forma pauperis. "In the manner of a pauper." In the Supreme Court, cases brought in forma pauperis by indigent persons are exempt from the Court's usual fees and from some formal requirements.

Judicial review. Review of legislation or other governmental action to determine its consistency with the federal or state constitution, with the power to strike down policies that are inconsistent with the Constitution. The Supreme Court reviews governmental action only under the federal constitution.

Jurisdiction. The power of a court to hear a case in question.

Litigants. The parties to a court case.

Majority opinion. An opinion in a case that is subscribed to by a majority of the judges who participated in the decision. Also known as the opinion of the court.

Mandamus. "We command." An order issued by a court that directs a lower court or other authority to perform a particular act.

Mandatory jurisdiction. Jurisdiction that a court must accept. Cases falling under a court's mandatory jurisdiction must be decided officially on their merits, though a court may avoid giving them full consideration.

Modify. In an appellate court, to reach a decision that disagrees in part with the result reached in the case by the lower court.

Moot. A moot case is one which has become hypothetical, so that a court need not decide it.

Obiter dictum. (Also called dictum or dicta.) A statement in a court opinion that is not necessary to resolve the case before the court. Dicta are not binding in future cases.

Original jurisdiction. Jurisdiction as a trial court.

Per curiam. "By the court." An unsigned opinion of the court, often quite brief.

Petitioner. One who files a petition with a court seeking action or relief, such as a writ of certiorari.

Remand. To send back. When a case is remanded, it is sent back by a higher court to the court from which it came for further action.

Respondent.   The party in opposition to a petitioner or appellant, who answers the claims of that party.

Reverse.   In an appellate court, to reach a decision that disagrees with the result reached in the case by the lower court.

Standing.   A requirement that the party who files a lawsuit have a legal stake in the outcome.

Stare decisis.   "Let the decision stand." The doctrine that principles of law established in earlier judicial decisions should be accepted as authoritative in similar subsequent cases.

Statute.   A written law enacted by a legislature.

Stay.   To halt or suspend further judicial proceedings. The Supreme Court sometimes issues a stay to suspend action in a lower court while the Supreme Court considers the case.

Vacate.   To make void or annul. The Supreme Court sometimes vacates a lower court decision, requiring the lower court to reconsider the case.

Writ.   A written court order commanding the designated recipient to perform or not perform acts specified in the order.

Supreme Court Nominations, 1789-1988

Name	Nominated by	Service
John Jay	Washington	1789-1795
John Rutledge	Washington	1789-1791
William Cushing	Washington	1789-1810
Robert H. Harrison	Washington	(D, 1790)
James Wilson	Washington	1789-1798
John Blair	Washington	1789-1796
James Iredell	Washington	1790-1799
Thomas Johnson	Washington	1791-1793
William Paterson	Washington	(W, 1793)
William Paterson[a]	Washington	1793-1806
John Rutledge[b]	Washington	(R, 1795)
William Cushing[b]	Washington	(D, 1796)
Samuel Chase	Washington	1796-1811
Oliver Ellsworth	Washington	1796-1800
Bushrod Washington	J. Adams	1798-1829
Alfred Moore	J. Adams	1799-1804
John Jay[b]	J. Adams	(D, 1801)
John Marshall	J. Adams	1801-1835
William Johnson	Jefferson	1804-1834
H. Brockholst Livingston	Jefferson	1806-1823
Thomas Todd	Jefferson	1807-1826
Levi Lincoln	Madison	(D, 1811)
Alexander Wolcott	Madison	(R, 1811)
John Quincy Adams	Madison	(D, 1811)
Joseph Story	Madison	1811-1845
Gabriel Duval	Madison	1811-1835
Smith Thompson	Monroe	1823-1843
Robert Trimble	J. Q. Adams	1826-1828
John J. Crittenden	J. Q. Adams	(P, 1829)

Name	Nominated by	Service
John McLean	Jackson	1829-1861
Henry Baldwin	Jackson	1830-1844
James M. Wayne	Jackson	1835-1867
Roger B. Taney	Jackson	(P, 1835)
Roger B. Taney[a]	Jackson	1836-1864
Philip P. Barbour	Jackson	1836-1841
William Smith	Jackson	(D, 1837)
John Catron	Jackson	1837-1865
John McKinley	Van Buren	1837-1852
Peter V. Daniel	Van Buren	1841-1860
John C. Spencer	Tyler	(R, 1844)
Reuben H. Walworth	Tyler	(W, 1844)
Edward King	Tyler	(P, 1844)
Edward King[a]	Tyler	(W, 1845)
Samuel Nelson	Tyler	1845-1872
John M. Read	Tyler	No action
George W. Woodward	Polk	(R, 1846)
Levi Woodbury	Polk	1846-1851
Robert C. Grier	Polk	1846-1870
Benjamin R. Curtis	Fillmore	1851-1857
Edward A. Bradford	Fillmore	No action
George E. Badger	Fillmore	(P, 1853)
William C. Micou	Fillmore	No action
John A. Campbell	Pierce	1853-1861
Nathan Clifford	Buchanan	1858-1881
Jeremiah S. Black	Buchanan	(R, 1861)
Noah H. Swayne	Lincoln	1862-1881
Samuel F. Miller	Lincoln	1862-1890
David Davis	Lincoln	1862-1877
Stephen J. Field	Lincoln	1863-1897
Salmon P. Chase	Lincoln	1864-1873
Henry Stanbery	Johnson	No action
Ebenezer R. Hoar	Grant	(R, 1870)
Edwin M. Stanton[c]	Grant	1869
William Strong	Grant	1870-1880
Joseph P. Bradley	Grant	1870-1892
Ward Hunt	Grant	1872-1882
George H. Williams	Grant	(W, 1874)
Caleb Cushing	Grant	(W, 1874)
Morrison R. Waite	Grant	1874-1888
John M. Harlan	Hayes	1877-1911
William B. Woods	Hayes	1880-1887
Stanley Matthews	Hayes	No action

Name	Nominated by	Service
Stanley Matthews[a]	Garfield	1881-1889
Horace Gray	Arthur	1881-1902
Roscoe Conkling	Arthur	(D, 1882)
Samuel Blatchford	Arthur	1882-1893
Lucius Q. C. Lamar	Cleveland	1888-1893
Melville W. Fuller	Cleveland	1888-1910
David J. Brewer	Harrison	1889-1910
Henry B. Brown	Harrison	1890-1906
George Shiras Jr.	Harrison	1892-1903
Howell E. Jackson	Harrison	1893-1895
William B. Hornblower	Cleveland	(R, 1894)
Wheeler H. Peckham	Cleveland	(R, 1894)
Edward D. White	Cleveland	1894-1921
Rufus W. Peckham	Cleveland	1895-1909
Joseph McKenna	McKinley	1898-1925
Oliver W. Holmes	T. Roosevelt	1902-1932
William R. Day	T. Roosevelt	1903-1922
William H. Moody	T. Roosevelt	1906-1910
Horace H. Lurton	Taft	1909-1914
Edward D. White[b]	Taft	1910-1921
Charles E. Hughes	Taft	1910-1916
Willis Van Devanter	Taft	1910-1937
Joseph R. Lamar	Taft	1910-1916
Mahlon Pitney	Taft	1912-1922
James C. McReynolds	Wilson	1914-1941
Louis D. Brandeis	Wilson	1916-1939
John H. Clarke	Wilson	1916-1922
William H. Taft	Harding	1921-1930
George Sutherland	Harding	1922-1938
Pierce Butler	Harding	1922-1939
Edward T. Sanford	Harding	1923-1930
Harlan F. Stone	Coolidge	1925-1946
Charles E. Hughes[b]	Hoover	1930-1941
John J. Parker	Hoover	(R, 1930)
Owen J. Roberts	Hoover	1930-1945
Benjamin N. Cardozo	Hoover	1932-1938
Hugo L. Black	F. Roosevelt	1937-1971
Stanley F. Reed	F. Roosevelt	1938-1957
Felix Frankfurter	F. Roosevelt	1939-1962
William O. Douglas	F. Roosevelt	1939-1975
Frank Murphy	F. Roosevelt	1940-1949
Harlan F. Stone[b]	F. Roosevelt	1941-1946

Name	Nominated by	Service
James F. Byrnes	F. Roosevelt	1941-1942
Robert H. Jackson	F. Roosevelt	1941-1954
Wiley B. Rutledge	F. Roosevelt	1943-1949
Harold H. Burton	Truman	1945-1958
Fred M. Vinson	Truman	1946-1953
Tom C. Clark	Truman	1949-1967
Sherman Minton	Truman	1949-1956
Earl Warren	Eisenhower	1953-1969
John M. Harlan	Eisenhower	1955-1971
William J. Brennan Jr.	Eisenhower	1956-
Charles E. Whittaker	Eisenhower	1957-1962
Potter Stewart	Eisenhower	1958-1981
Byron R. White	Kennedy	1962-
Arthur J. Goldberg	Kennedy	1962-1965
Abe Fortas	Johnson	1965-1969
Thurgood Marshall	Johnson	1967-
Abe Fortas[b]	Johnson	(W, 1968)
Homer Thornberry	Johnson	No action
Warren E. Burger	Nixon	1969-1986
Clement Haynsworth Jr.	Nixon	(R, 1969)
G. Harrold Carswell	Nixon	(R, 1970)
Harry Λ. Blackmun	Nixon	1970-
Lewis F. Powell Jr.	Nixon	1971-1987
William H. Rehnquist	Nixon	1971-
John Paul Stevens	Ford	1975-
Sandra Day O'Connor	Reagan	1981-
William H. Rehnquist[b]	Reagan	1986-
Antonin Scalia	Reagan	1986-
Robert H. Bork	Reagan	(R, 1987)
Douglas H. Ginsburg[d]	Reagan	(W, 1987)
Anthony M. Kennedy	Reagan	1988-

[a] Earlier nomination not confirmed.
[b] Earlier Court service.
[c] Died four days after confirmation.
[d] Withdrew before formal nomination.
Boldface type indicates nomination as chief justice.
(D) Declined
(P) Postponed
(R) Rejected
(W) Withdrawn

Sources: Leon Friedman and Fred L. Israel, eds., *The Justices of the United States Supreme Court, 1789-1969* (New York: R. R. Bowker Co., 1969); Executive Journal of the U.S. Senate, 1789-1975; *Guide to the U.S. Supreme Court* (Washington, D.C.: Congressional Quarterly Inc., 1979); updated by author.

Selected
Bibliography

The books listed below may be useful to readers who would like to explore further the subjects discussed in this book. Books that are general in their subject matter are listed first, followed by books that are especially relevant to specific chapters.

General

Congressional Quarterly. *Guide to the U.S. Supreme Court.* Washington, D.C.: Congressional Quarterly Inc., 1979.

Douglas, William O. *The Court Years 1939-1975: The Autobiography of William O. Douglas.* New York: Random House, 1980.

Goldman, Sheldon, and Jahnige, Thomas P. *The Federal Courts as a Political System,* 3d ed. New York: Harper & Row, 1985.

Goldman, Sheldon, and Sarat, Austin, eds. *American Court Systems: Readings in Judicial Process and Behavior,* 2d ed. New York: Longman, 1989.

Krislov, Samuel. *The Supreme Court and Political Freedom.* New York: Free Press, 1968.

Lewis, Anthony. *Gideon's Trumpet.* New York: Random House, 1964.

Murphy, Bruce Allen. *Fortas: The Rise and Ruin of a Supreme Court Justice.* New York: William Morrow, 1988.

Schmidhauser, John R., and Berg, Larry L. *The Supreme Court and Congress: Conflict and Interaction, 1945-1968.* New York: Free Press, 1972.

Scigliano, Robert. *The Supreme Court and the Presidency.* New York: Free Press, 1971.

Shapiro, Martin. *The Supreme Court and Administrative Agencies.* New York: Free Press, 1968.

Simon, James F. *Independent Journey: The Life of William O. Douglas.* New York: Harper & Row, 1980.

Ulmer, S. Sidney, ed. *Courts, Law, and Judicial Processes*. New York: Free Press, 1981.

Wilkinson, J. Harvie III. *Serving Justice: A Supreme Court Clerk's View*. New York: Charterhouse, 1974.

Chapter 2: The Justices

Abraham, Henry J. *Justices and Presidents: A Political History of Appointments to the Supreme Court*, 2d ed. New York: Oxford University Press, 1985.

Danelski, David J. *A Supreme Court Justice Is Appointed*. New York: Random House, 1964.

Friedman, Leon, and Israel, Fred L., eds. *The Justices of the United States Supreme Court 1789-1969: Their Lives and Major Opinions*. New York: R. R. Bowker Co., 1969. (Updated with an additional volume in 1978.)

Schmidhauser, John R. *Judges and Justices: The Federal Appellate Judiciary*. Boston: Little, Brown & Co., 1979.

Shogan, Robert. *A Question of Judgment: The Fortas Case and the Struggle for the Supreme Court*. Indianapolis: Bobbs-Merrill Co., 1972.

Simon, James F. *In His Own Image: The Supreme Court in Richard Nixon's America*. New York: David McKay Co., 1973.

Chapter 3: The Cases

Caplan, Lincoln. *The Tenth Justice: The Solicitor General and the Rule of Law*. New York: Alfred A. Knopf, 1987.

Casper, Gerhard, and Posner, Richard A. *The Workload of the Supreme Court*. Chicago: American Bar Foundation, 1976.

Casper, Jonathan D. *Lawyers Before the Warren Court: Civil Liberties and Civil Rights, 1957-66*. Urbana: University of Illinois Press, 1972.

Craig, Barbara Hickson. *Chadha: The Story of an Epic Constitutional Struggle*. New York: Oxford University Press, 1988.

Epstein, Lee. *Conservatives in Court*. Knoxville: University of Tennessee Press, 1985.

Estreicher, Samuel, and Sexton, John. *Redefining the Supreme Court's Role: A Theory of Managing the Federal Judicial Process*. New Haven: Yale University Press, 1986.

Kluger, Richard. *Simple Justice: The History of Brown v. Board of Education and Black America's Struggle for Equality*. New York: Alfred A. Knopf, 1976.

O'Connor, Karen. *Women's Organizations' Use of the Courts*. Lexington, Mass.: Lexington Books, 1980.

Provine, Doris Marie. *Case Selection in the United States Supreme Court*. Chicago: University of Chicago Press, 1980.

Sorauf, Frank J. *The Wall of Separation: The Constitutional Politics of Church and State.* Princeton: Princeton University Press, 1976.

Tushnet, Mark V. *The NAACP's Legal Strategy Against Segregated Education, 1925-1950.* Chapel Hill: University of North Carolina Press, 1987.

Vose, Clement E. *Constitutional Change.* Lexington, Mass.: D. C. Heath & Co., 1972.

Chapter 4: Decision Making

Hirsch, H. N. *The Enigma of Felix Frankfurter.* New York: Basic Books, 1981.

Howard, J. Woodford, Jr. *Mr. Justice Murphy: A Political Biography.* Princeton: Princeton University Press, 1968.

Murphy, Walter F. *Elements of Judicial Strategy.* Chicago: University of Chicago Press, 1964.

Rohde, David W., and Spaeth, Harold J. *Supreme Court Decision Making.* San Francisco: W. H. Freeman & Co., 1976.

Schwartz, Bernard. *Super Chief: Earl Warren and His Supreme Court—A Judicial Biography.* New York: New York University Press, 1983.

Schwartz, Bernard. *Swann's Way: The School Busing Case and the Supreme Court.* New York: Oxford University Press, 1986.

Steamer, Robert J. *Chief Justice: Leadership and the Supreme Court.* Columbia: University of South Carolina Press, 1986.

Woodward, Bob, and Armstrong, Scott. *The Brethren: Inside the Supreme Court.* New York: Simon & Schuster, 1979.

Chapter 5: Policy Outputs

Blasi, Vincent, ed. *The Burger Court: The Counter-Revolution That Wasn't.* New Haven: Yale University Press, 1982.

Casper, Jonathan D. *The Politics of Civil Liberties.* New York: Harper & Row, 1972.

Halpern, Stephen C., and Lamb, Charles M., eds. *Supreme Court Activism and Restraint.* Lexington, Mass.: Lexington Books, 1982.

Horowitz, Donald L. *The Courts and Social Policy.* Washington, D.C.: Brookings Institution, 1977.

Mason, Alpheus Thomas. *The Supreme Court from Taft to Burger,* 3d ed. Baton Rouge: Louisiana State University Press, 1979.

McCloskey, Robert G. *The American Supreme Court.* Chicago: University of Chicago Press, 1960.

Miller, Arthur Selwyn. *The Supreme Court and American Capitalism.* New York: Free Press, 1968.

Schubert, Glendon. *The Constitutional Polity.* Boston: Boston University Press, 1970.

Shapiro, Martin. *Law and Politics in the Supreme Court.* New York: Free Press, 1964.

Chapter 6: The Court's Impact

Becker, Theodore L., and Feeley, Malcolm M., eds. *The Impact of Supreme Court Decisions*, 2d ed. New York: Oxford University Press, 1973.

Bullock, Charles S. III, and Lamb, Charles M., eds. *Implementation of Civil Rights Policy*. Monterey, Calif.: Brooks/Cole Publishing Co., 1984.

Dolbeare, Kenneth M., and Hammond, Phillip E. *The School Prayer Decisions: From Court Policy to Local Practice*. Chicago: University of Chicago Press, 1971.

Jenson, Carol E. *The Network of Control: State Supreme Courts and State Security Statutes, 1920-1970*. Westport, Conn.: Greenwood Press, 1982.

Johnson, Charles A., and Canon, Bradley C. *Judicial Policies: Implementation and Impact*. Washington, D.C.: CQ Press, 1984.

Milner, Neal A. *The Court and Local Law Enforcement: The Impact of Miranda*. Beverly Hills: Sage Publications, 1971.

Muir, William K., Jr. *Prayer in the Public Schools: Law and Attitude Change*. Chicago: University of Chicago Press, 1967.

Murphy, Walter F. *Congress and the Court*. Chicago: University of Chicago Press, 1962.

Peltason, J. W. *Fifty-Eight Lonely Men: Southern Federal Judges and School Desegregation*, 2d ed. Urbana: University of Illinois Press, 1971.

Tarr, George Alan. *Judicial Impact and State Supreme Courts*. Lexington, Mass.: Lexington Books, 1977.

Wasby, Stephen L. *The Impact of the United States Supreme Court: Some Perspectives*. Homewood, Ill.: Dorsey Press, 1970.

Case Index

In this index the titles of cases are followed by citations to the legal reports in which they are contained. The abbreviation for the title of the set of reports is preceded by the volume number and followed by the page on which the case begins. The citations for nearly all Supreme Court decisions are to *U.S. Reports* (U.S.), the official report of Court decisions. Until 1875, a citation to a volume of official reports was to the name of the Court's reporter at the time. Citations for cases from the 1986 and 1987 terms that are not yet published in *U.S. Reports* are to the "Lawyer's Edition" (L. Ed. 2d), another set of reports of Supreme Court decisions. Lower court decisions have citations to the most commonly available set of reports for the courts involved.

Abington School District v. Schempp, 374 U.S. 203 (1963), 210
Argersinger v. Hamlin, 407 U.S. 25 (1972), 217
Ashwander v. Tennessee Valley Authority, 297 U.S. 288 (1936), 7

Bailey v. Drexel Furniture Co., 259 U.S. 20 (1922), 198
Baker v. Carr, 369 U.S. 186 (1962), 23, 170
Baldwin v. Alabama, 472 U.S. 372 (1985), 111
Bankers Life and Casualty Company v. Crenshaw, 100 L. Ed. 2d 62 (1988), 168
Bates v. State Bar, 433 U.S. 350 (1977), 250
Batson v. Kentucky, 476 U.S. 79 (1986), 191
Betts v. Brady, 316 U.S. 455 (1942), 120
Board of Airport Commissioners v. Jews for Jesus, Inc., 96 L. Ed. 2d 500 (1987), 159
Board of Education v. Dowell, 93 L. Ed. 2d 370 (1986), 112
Bob Jones University v. United States, 461 U.S. 574 (1983), 199
Bolling v. Sharpe, 347 U.S. 497 (1954), 189
Bowen v. American Hospital Association, 476 U.S. 610 (1986), 157
Bowen v. Massachusetts, 101 L. Ed. 2d 749 (1988), 168
Bowsher v. Synar, 478 U.S. 714 (1986), 5, 177-178, 198

Brown v. Board of Education, 347 U.S. 483 (1954), 349 U.S. 294 (1955), 23, 85, 129, 132, 150, 155, 187, 193, 203, 206-207, 213, 217-218, 229, 231-232, 236-237, 241-242
Brown v. Herald Co., Inc., 464 U.S. 928 (1983), 111
Buckley v. Valeo, 424 U.S. 1 (1976), 86, 177
Budinich v. Becton Dickinson and Company, 100 L. Ed. 2d 178 (1988), 168
Burke v. Barnes, 93 L. Ed. 2d 732 (1987), 112

California v. Carney, 471 U.S. 386 (1985), 112
California v. Greenwood, 100 L. Ed. 2d 30 (1988), 168
Carter v. Carter Coal Co., 298 U.S. 238 (1936), 26, 198
Cascade Natural Gas Corp. v. El Paso Natural Gas Co., 386 U.S. 129 (1967), 247
Chisholm v. Georgia, 2 Dallas 419 (1793), 19, 226
Cincinnati, New Orleans and Texas Pacific Railway Co. v. Interstate Commerce Commission, 162 U.S. 184 (1896), 199
City of Riverside v. Rivera, 477 U.S. 561 (1986), 202
Civil Rights Cases, 109 U.S. 3 (1883), 185
Clark-Cowlitz v. Federal Energy Regulatory Commission, 98 L. Ed. 2d 239 (1987), 163
Colorado v. Connelly, 474 U.S. 1050 (1986), 111
Commodity Futures Trading Commission v. Schor, 478 U.S. 833 (1986), 247
Community Communications Co. v. City of Boulder, 455 U.S. 40 (1982), 224
Connecticut v. Barrett, 93 L. Ed. 2d 920 (1987), 112
Connor v. Coleman, 440 U.S. 612, 441 U.S. 792 (1979), 247
Craft v. Metromedia, Inc., 475 U.S. 1058 (1986), 161
CTS Corporation v. Dynamics Corporation of America, 95 L. Ed. 2d 67 (1987), 236

Darden v. Wainwright, 477 U.S. 168 (1986), 120
Deepsouth Packing Co. v. Laitram Corp., 406 U.S. 518 (1972), 224
Doe v. Bolton, 410 U.S. 179 (1973), 179
Duncan v. Louisiana, 391 U.S. 145 (1968), 189

Edgar v. MITE Corporation, 457 U.S. 624 (1982), 236
Engel v. Vitale, 370 U.S. 421 (1962), 86, 210, 232
Evans v. Jeff D., 475 U.S. 717 (1986), 249
Ex parte McCardle, 7 Wallace 506 (1869), 227
Ex parte Milligan, 4 Wallace 2 (1866), 21, 178
Ex parte Quirin, 317 U.S. 1 (1942), 250

Federal Election Commission v. Massachusetts Citizens for Life, 93 L. Ed. 2d 539 (1986), 199
Federal Election Commission v. National Conservative Political Action Committee, 470 U.S. 480 (1985), 199
First Lutheran Church v. Los Angeles County, 96 L. Ed. 2d 250 (1987), 110, 199
Fisher v. City of Berkeley, 475 U.S. 260 (1986), 199
Fiske v. Kansas, 274 U.S. 380 (1927), 199
Forrester v. White, 98 L. Ed. 2d 555 (1988), 167
Furman v. Georgia, 408 U.S. 238 (1972), 118, 160, 235

Gannett v. DePasquale, 443 U.S. 368 (1979), 130
Garcia v. San Antonio Metropolitan Transit Authority, 469 U.S. 528 (1985), 160, 224, 233
Gault, In re, 387 U.S. 1 (1967), 235
Gibbons v. Ogden, 9 Wheaton 1 (1824), 20, 179

Gideon v. Wainwright, 372 U.S. 335 (1963), 23, 79, 120, 132, 235
Gitlow v. New York, 268 U.S. 652 (1925), 199
Goldberg v. Kelly, 397 U.S. 254 (1970), 199
Goldfarb v. State Bar, 421 U.S. 773 (1975), 250
Green v. Zant, 469 U.S. 1143 (1985), 25
Gregg v. Georgia, 428 U.S. 153 (1976), 198
Griswold v. Connecticut, 381 U.S. 479 (1965), 126, 189
Grove City College v. Bell, 465 U.S. 555 (1984), 224
Gutknecht v. United States, 396 U.S. 295 (1970), 251

Hammer v. Dagenhart, 247 U.S. 251 (1918), 82, 198
Harris v. McRae, 448 U.S. 297 (1980), 25, 226
Hazelwood School District v. Kuhlmeier, 98 L. Ed. 2d 592 (1988), 248
Hepburn v. Griswold, 8 Wallace 603 (1870), 26
Herbert v. Lando, 441 U.S. 153 (1979), 247
Herndon, In re, 394 U.S. 399 (1969), 203
Hodel v. Irving, 95 L. Ed. 2d 668 (1987), 213
Home Building & Loan Assn. v. Blaisdell, 290 U.S. 398 (1934), 126
Honig v. Doe, 98 L. Ed. 2d 686 (1988), 112

Immigration and Naturalization Service v. Cardoza-Fonseca, 94 L. Ed. 2d 434
  (1987), 111
Immigration and Naturalization Service v. Chadha, 462 U.S. 919 (1983), 25, 114-
  115, 178, 198, 250
Immigration and Naturalization Service v. Lopez-Mendoza, 468 U.S. 1032 (1984),
  159
In re Gault, 387 U.S. 1 (1967), 235
In re Herndon, 394 U.S. 399 (1969), 203
In re Oliver, 333 U.S. 257 (1948), 189
Interstate Commerce Commission v. Brotherhood of Locomotive Engineers, 96 L.
  Ed. 2d 222 (1987), 159

Jaffree v. Board of School Commissioners, 554 F. Supp. 1104 (S.D. Alab. 1983),
  248
Japan Whaling Association v. American Cetacean Society, 478 U.S. 221 (1986),
  159
Johnson v. Transportation Agency, 94 L. Ed. 2d 615 (1987), 25
Jones v. Barnes, 463 U.S. 745 (1983), 124, 160

Karcher v. May, 98 L. Ed. 2d 327 (1987), 112
Keyes v. School District No. 1, 413 U.S. 189 (1973), 208
Kolender v. Lawson, 461 U.S. 352 (1983), 110

Legal Tender Cases, 12 Wallace 457 (1871), 26
Lowe v. Virginia, 475 U.S. 1084 (1986), 112
Lynch v. Donnelly, 465 U.S. 668 (1984), 110, 134
Lyng v. United Automobile Workers, 99 L. Ed. 2d 380 (1988), 168, 202

Maher v. Roe, 432 U.S. 464 (1977), 226
Malloy v. Hogan, 378 U.S. 1 (1964), 189
Mapp v. Ohio, 367 U.S. 643 (1961), 23, 73, 209-210, 215
Marbury v. Madison, 1 Cranch 137 (1803), 19, 20, 175
Marsh v. Chambers, 463 U.S. 783 (1983), 161

Marshall v. Barlow's, Inc., 436 U.S. 307 (1978), 199
Maryland v. Wirtz, 392 U.S. 183 (1968), 160
Massachusetts v. Laird, 400 U.S. 886 (1970), 25
Mata v. Sumner, 649 F. 2d 713 (9th Cir. 1981), 247
Mathews v. United States, 99 L. Ed. 2d 54 (1988), 160
McCardle, Ex parte, 7 Wallace 506 (1869), 227
McCarty v. McCarty, 453 U.S. 210 (1981), 225, 249
McCleskey v. Kemp, 95 L. Ed. 2d 262 (1987), 248
McCulloch v. Maryland, 4 Wheaton 316 (1819), 20, 179
Miller v. California, 413 U.S. 15 (1973), 24, 170, 251
Milligan, Ex parte, 4 Wallace 2 (1866), 21, 178
Milliken v. Bradley, 418 U.S. 717 (1974), 248
Miranda v. Arizona, 384 U.S. 436 (1966), 23, 209-210, 215-217, 234
Mora v. McNamara, 389 U.S. 934 (1967), 25
Motor Vehicle Manufacturers Assn. v. State Farm Mutual, 463 U.S. 29 (1983), 198
Muller v. Oregon, 208 U.S. 412 (1908), 115

National Labor Relations Board v. Bildisco and Bildisco, 465 U.S. 513 (1984), 223-224
National Labor Relations Board v. Jones & Laughlin Steel Corp., 301 U.S. 1 (1937), 26
National League of Cities v. Usery, 426 U.S. 833 (1976), 160, 199
Near v. Minnesota, 283 U.S. 697 (1931), 199
New Energy Company v. Limbach, 100 L. Ed. 2d 302 (1988), 167
New Jersey v. T.L.O., 468 U.S. 1214 (1984), 111
New York Times Co. v. Sullivan, 376 U.S. 254 (1964), 159, 243
New York Times Co. v. United States, 403 U.S. 713 (1971), 159
Newton v. Consolidated Gas Co., 258 U.S. 165 (1922), 199
Nollan v. California Coastal Commission, 97 L. Ed. 2d 677 (1987), 110, 199
Norman v. Baltimore and Ohio Railroad Co., 294 U.S. 240 (1935), 250
Northern Pipeline Construction Co. v. Marathon Pipe Line Company, 458 U.S. 50 (1982), 199, 249-250

Oestereich v. Selective Service System, 393 U.S. 233 (1968), 251
Oliver, In re, 333 U.S. 257 (1948), 189
Oregon v. Elstad, 470 U.S. 298 (1985), 157
Oregon v. Mitchell, 400 U.S. 112 (1970), 226
Ottinger v. Brooklyn Union Co., 272 U.S. 579 (1926), 199

Paris Adult Theatre I v. Slaton, 413 U.S. 49 (1973), 161
Pasadena Board of Education v. Spangler, 427 U.S. 424 (1976), 248
Pennell v. City of San Jose, 99 L. Ed. 2d 1 (1988), 199
Pennzoil Co. v. Texaco, Inc., 95 L. Ed. 2d 1 (1987), 110
Petty v. United States, 95 L. Ed. 2d 810 (1987), 111
Plessy v. Ferguson, 163 U.S. 537 (1896), 185, 235
Plyler v. Doe, 457 U.S. 202 (1982), 24, 160
Pollock v. Farmers' Loan & Trust Co., 158 U.S. 601 (1895), 226
Powell v. McCormack, 395 U.S. 486 (1969), 230
Process Gas Consumers Group v. Consumer Energy Council, 463 U.S. 1216 (1983), 199

Quirin, Ex parte, 317 U.S. 1 (1942), 250

Railway Labor Executives' Association v. Gibbons, 455 U.S. 457 (1982), 199
Regents of the University of California v. Bakke, 438 U.S. 265 (1978), 89, 118
Reynolds v. Sims, 377 U.S. 533 (1964), 228
Richmond Newspapers, Inc. v. Virginia, 448 U.S. 555 (1980), 130
Riddick v. School Board, 93 L. Ed. 2d 370 (1986), 112
Roe v. Wade, 410 U.S. 113 (1973), 4, 24, 81, 170, 179, 213, 237, 247
Rook v. Rice, 478 U.S. 1040 (1986), 25
Ross v. Oklahoma, 101 L. Ed. 2d 80 (1988), 168

Saint Francis College v. Al-Khazraji, 95 L. Ed. 2d 582 (1987), 199
Shaare Tefila Congregation v. Cobb, 95 L. Ed. 2d 594 (1987), 199
Salt Lake City v. Piepenburg, 471 P. 2d 1299 (Utah Sup. Ct. 1977), 249
Santa Clara County v. Southern Pacific Railroad Co., 118 U.S. 394 (1886), 183
Sarnoff v. Shultz, 409 U.S. 929 (1972), 25
Schechter Poultry Corp. v. United States, 295 U.S. 495 (1935), 26, 198
Schenck v. United States, 249 U.S. 47 (1919), 185
Scott v. Sandford (Dred Scott case), 19 Howard 393 (1857), 20, 176, 198, 226, 235
Sheet Metal Workers' International Assn. v. Equal Employment Opportunity
  Commission, 478 U.S. 421 (1986), 25
Sheridan v. United States, 101 L. Ed. 2d 352 (1988), 168
Silkwood v. Kerr-McGee Corporation, 464 U.S. 238 (1984), 204
Smith v. Robinson, 468 U.S. 992 (1984), 224
Sorenson v. Secretary of the Treasury, 475 U.S. 851 (1986), 160
South Dakota v. Dole, 97 L. Ed. 2d 171 (1987), 167
State ex rel. Department of Revenue v. Control Data Corp., 713 P. 2d 30 (Ore.
  Sup. Ct. 1986), 248
Steward Machine Co. v. Davis, 301 U.S. 548 (1937), 26
Stromberg v. California, 283 U.S. 359 (1931), 199
Sullivan v. Little Hunting Park, Inc., 392 U.S. 657 (1968), 396 U.S. 229 (1969),
  202-203
Sumner v. Mata, 449 U.S. 539 (1981), 455 U.S. 591 (1982), 202

Tate v. Short, 401 U.S. 395 (1971), 217, 235
Thompson v. City of Louisville, 362 U.S. 199 (1960), 11
Thornburgh v. American College of Obstetricians and Gynecologists, 476 U.S.
  747 (1986), 25
Tinker v. Des Moines School District, 393 U.S. 503 (1969), 237-238, 250
Train v. City of New York, 420 U.S. 35 (1975), 178
Twining v. New Jersey, 211 U.S. 78 (1908), 185

United States v. Butler, 297 U.S. 1 (1936), 26, 160, 198
  v. Carolene Products Co., 304 U.S. 144 (1938), 187
  v. E. C. Knight Co., 156 U.S. 1 (1895), 199
  v. Fausto, 98 L. Ed. 2d 830 (1988), 167
  v. Grace, 461 U.S. 171 (1983), 176
  v. Haley, 166 F. Supp. 336 (N.D. Texas 1958), 249
  v. Jackson, 429 F.2d 1368 (7th Cir. 1970), 248
  v. Leon, 468 U.S. 897 (1984), 24
  v. Lovett, 328 U.S. 303 (1946), 230
  v. Nixon, 418 U.S. 683 (1974), 5, 17, 24, 42, 114, 149, 233
  v. Will, 449 U.S. 200 (1980), 129
United States Senate v. Federal Trade Commission, 463 U.S. 1216 (1983), 199

Virginia State Board of Pharmacy v. Virginia Citizens Consumer Council, 425
  U.S. 748 (1976), 198, 251

Wainwright v. Booker, 473 U.S. 935 (1985), 25
Wallace v. Jaffree, 472 U.S. 38 (1985), 110, 248
Weber v. Kaiser Aluminum & Chemical Corp., 611 F.2d 132 (5th Cir. 1980), 249
Weinberger v. Wiesenfeld, 420 U.S. 636 (1975), 111
West Coast Hotel Co. v. Parrish, 300 U.S. 379 (1937), 26
Wolston v. Reader's Digest Association, 443 U.S. 157 (1979), 24
Wooley v. Maynard, 430 U.S. 705 (1977), 247
Worcester v. Georgia, 6 Peters 515 (1832), 231

Young v. Town of Atlantic Beach, 462 U.S. 1101 (1983), 110
Youngstown Sheet and Tube Co. v. Sawyer, 343 U.S. 579 (1952), 178, 233

Zurcher v. Stanford Daily, 436 U.S. 547 (1978), 226

Index

Abortion
   as Court concern, 170
   Court policies, 4, 24, 179-180, 213
   impact of decisions, 134, 226-228,
      236-238, 240, 247
   in selection of judges, 40-41, 50
Abraham, Henry J., 25, 69
Adams, John
   campaigning by Chase, 66
   selection of justices, 19
Adler, Stephen J., 159, 161
Administrative agencies
   comparison with Court, 2, 6, 127,
      136
   Court review of actions, 181
   role in implementing decisions, 7,
      201-222
   as sources of justices, 56-57, 61
Affirmative action
   as Court concern, 182
   Court policies, 4, 119, 136-137
   litigation, 103
Agricultural Adjustment Act, 21
Alexander, Paul, 248
American Anti-Boycott Association,
   82
American Bar Association (ABA)
   Powell's background, 56
   on proposal for a new court, 109
   in selection of judges, 31-33, 58
American Civil Liberties Union
   (ACLU)
   in litigation, 77, 82, 84, 86-87, 171,

193, 221, 246
   in selection of justices, 34
American Conservative Union, 34
American Federation of Labor-Con-
   gress of Industrial Organizations
   (AFL-CIO)
   in selection of justices, 34
   in litigation, 78
American University, 51
Americans for Effective Law Enforce-
   ment, 83
Amicus curiae briefs, 80-81, 83, 86-88,
   90, 99, 102, 131
Antitrust
   as Court concern, 33, 165, 167
   Court policies, 182-183
   impact of decisions, 223-224, 247
Armstrong, Scott, 162
Atkins, Burton M., 198
Attorneys. See Lawyers
Atwell, William, 206

Baker, Howard, 37-38
Bankruptcy
   as Court concern, 172
   Court policies, 225
   impact of decisions, 224-225
Barbash, Fred, 70
Barnes, Fred, 69
Barone, Michael, 251
Bartlett, Robert, 249
Bass, Jack, 250
Bennett, William, 234

Berkson, Larry C., 249
Berry, Mary Frances, 160
Bill of Rights, 185, 189. *See also* Civil
  liberties; specific constitutional provisions and specific categories of
  civil liberties
Black, Hugo
  appointment to Court, 28, 53
  background, 54, 56-57
  as commentator, 53, 147
  as justice, 23, 120, 151, 155-156, 159
  retirement, 64-65, 146
Black civil rights. *See also* Black civil
  rights issues; School desegregation;
  National Association for the Advancement of Colored People
  as Court concern, 22, 170, 172
  Court policies, 23, 145, 185-187,
    189-194
  impact of decisions, 223-224, 240-
    243, 246-247
  litigation, 84-86, 105-106
  in selection of justices, 33-34, 49,
    51
Black civil rights issues
  citizenship, 226
  education. *See* School desegrega-
    tion
  employment, 85, 170, 241-242
  housing, 242
  transportation, 214
  voting, 85, 190, 240-242, 247
Blackmun, Harry
  appointment to Court, 29, 35, 41-
    42, 48-50, 146
  background, 55, 131
  as commentator, 15, 127, 144, 154,
    158
  extra-Court activity, 15
  as justice, 41-42, 92, 116, 123, 127,
    131, 139-142, 144, 146, 160, 225
  nonretirement, 64-65
Blasi, Vincent, 26
Bodine, Laurence, 70
Bork, Robert
  as commentator, 6, 25
  nomination and Senate defeat, 1,
    24, 27, 29, 32, 34-35, 38, 44-46, 48,
    52
Braden, William, 249

Brandeis, Louis
  appointment to Court, 28, 33, 39,
    45
  as attorney, 115
  as justice, 7
Brennan, William
  appointment to Court, 29, 37, 40-
    41, 43, 48, 196
  background, 54, 56
  as commentator, 108, 111, 124, 129,
    131, 160
  extra-Court activity, 15, 67
  as justice, 23, 40-41, 91-92, 94-95,
    127, 134, 136-137, 139-144, 151-
    152
  nonretirement, 64
Brenner, Saul, 150, 162-163
Brigham, John, 160
Buckley, William F., 238, 250
Budgetary policy. *See* Gramm-Rudman-Hollings deficit reduction law;
  Impoundment of funds
Bullock, Charles S., III, 248, 251
Burger, Warren
  appointment to Court, 23, 29, 37,
    48-50, 62, 146
  background, 55-57, 60-61
  as chief justice, 15, 92, 108-109, 112,
    133, 154-155, 157
  as commentator, 93
  as justice, 90, 120, 124, 127, 129,
    142-144, 149
  retirement, 23, 38, 50, 63-65, 146
  in selection of justices, 35
Burger Court
  comparison with Warren Court,
    23-24, 100, 145-147, 190-191
  intracourt relations, 151
  policies, 23-24, 100, 190-191, 209
Burton, Harold
  appointment to Court, 29, 43
  background, 54, 56
  as commentator, 128
  as justice, 95
Business corporations
  as litigants, 77, 184
  as subjects of decisions, 21, 182-
    185, 193. *See also* Economic policy
Butler, Pierce, appointment to Court,
  28, 35

Byrnes, James
  appointment to Court, 28, 42-43
  background, 53-54, 56
  resignation, 63, 66

Caldeira, Gregory, 98-100, 112
Canon, Bradley C., 25, 248-250
Capital punishment
  as Court concern, 170
  Court policies, 119, 127
  impact of decisions, 119, 214, 235,
    247
  litigation, 85
  stays of execution, 15
Caplan, Lincoln, 111
Cardozo, Benjamin
  appointment to Court, 28, 32-33,
    35, 39
  background, 39
  as commentator, 137, 161
Carp, Robert A., 249
Carswell, G. Harrold, nomination
  and Senate defeat, 29, 32-35, 46, 48,
  51-52
Carter, Charlotte A., 248
Carter, Jimmy
  in litigation, 89
  response to decisions, 230
  selection of judges, 30, 37, 40, 196
Cartwright, Bliss, 198
Caseload of Court, 105-109
Casper, Gerhard, 112, 160
Certiorari, 12, 90
Chadha, Jagdish Rai, 114-115
Chambers, Marcia, 25
Chase, Harold W., 55
Chase, Samuel, impeachment, 66
Chief justice. *See also* individual
  names
  conference leadership, 116, 153
  duties and powers, 15, 153-154
  influence over Court, 153-155
  opinion assignment, 117, 153-154
  selection, 30
  in selection of justices, 35
Choper, Jesse, 239, 250-251
Circuit justices, 14-15
Circuit-riding, 14, 43-44
Civil liberties. *See also* specific issues
  as Court concern, 6, 22-24, 82-83,
    88, 166-169, 171-175, 185-188, 197

Court policies, 22-24, 106, 134-135,
    148-149, 185-195, 197
  impact of decisions, 134, 202-247
  litigation, 82-83, 105
  in selection of justices, 52
Civil rights. *See* Black civil rights; Sex
  discrimination
Civil Rights Act of 1964, 72, 85, 170-
  171, 107-208, 241
Civil War and Reconstruction, 20-21,
  133-134, 227
Claims Court, 9
Clarity, James F., 25
Clark, Ramsey, 66
Clark, Tom
  appointment to Court, 29, 37, 48
  background, 54
  as commentator, 209, 232
  as justice, 131
  retirement, 65-66, 146
Clarke, John
  appointment to Court, 28
  resignation, 63
Clausen, Aage R., 198
Coles, Robert, 249
Commager, Henry Steele, 186, 199
Committee on Federal Judiciary
  (ABA), 31-33
Communist party, 189-190. *See also*
  Internal security and free expression
Concurring opinions, 119-120
Conference (of Court)
  process and impact, 93-94, 116-117,
    149-153
  schedule, 17-18
Congress. *See also* Senate
  attacks on Court, 23, 133-135, 222,
    227-229
  comparison with Court, 2, 14, 60,
    73-74, 127-128, 136, 174, 192, 205
  effect on Court's agenda, caseload,
    and jurisdiction, 19, 72-73, 106-
    108, 133-134, 170-171
  impeachment of justices, 20, 66-67,
    228, 231
  influence on Court decisions, 132-
    136
  interpretation of legislation by
    Court, 4, 123, 166-167, 181-182
  lobbying by justices, 107-109, 133

policy response to decisions, 7,
207-208, 222-227, 229-230
provisions for judicial retirement,
63-64
review of legislation by Court,
175-178
as source of justices, 56-57
as subject of decisions. *See* specific
issues
Constitution, U.S. *See also* Judicial
review
as basis for litigation, 5, 9, 11, 105
provisions concerning Court, 9, 11,
13
as source of law, 4, 123-124
Constitutional provisions. *See also*
specific issues
commerce clause, 183
contract clause, 126
Article III, 18
1st Amendment, 23, 123, 130, 243,
246
4th Amendment, 4, 123
5th Amendment, 189
9th Amendment, 189, 199
10th Amendment, 183
11th Amendment, 19, 226
14th Amendment
due process, 123, 179, 183-185,
188-189
equal protection, 139, 189, 208
general, 21, 183, 226
16th Amendment, 226
22nd Amendment, 122
26th Amendment, 226
Coolidge, Calvin, selection of justices, 41, 43
Court of Appeals for the Federal Circuit, 9, 109
Court of International Trade, 9
Court of Military Appeals, 9
"Court-packing" plan. *See* Franklin
Roosevelt
Courts of appeals (federal), 9-10, 72,
172, 173. *See also* Lower courts
Courts of Appeals Act of 1891, 107
Covington, Hayden, 79
Cowan, Ruth B., 110
Criminal law and procedure. *See also*
Capital punishment; Police
as Court concern, 12, 22, 73, 166-

169, 171
Court decision making, 132
Court policies, 23-24, 100-101, 106,
128, 139, 185, 187-189, 194
impact of decisions, 204, 209-211,
215-217, 221, 235, 239
litigation, 100, 105-106
in selection of justices, 40
Curtis, Charles P., 162

Dahl, Robert A., 195-196, 198-199
Danelski, David J., 162
Davidson, T. Whitfield, 206
Davies, Thomas Y., 248
Davis, John W., 37
Day, William, appointment to Court,
28
Death penalty. *See* Capital punish-
ment
Denniston, Lyle, 159
Desegregation. *See* School desegrega-
tion
De Tocqueville, Alexis, 5, 25
De Vries, Walter, 250
Discuss list, 93, 153
Dissents and dissenting opinions, 94,
119-120
District courts (federal), 9-10, 192. *See
also* Lower courts
Dole, Robert, 228
Douglas, William
appointment to Court, 28, 37
background, 54, 56, 58
as commentator, 36, 69, 78, 89, 108,
110, 151, 155, 162-163
extra-Court activity, 67
as justice, 129, 151, 155-157
retirement, 64-65, 146
threat of impeachment, 64, 67
Ducat, Craig R., 55, 161
Dudley, Robert L, 161
Dunne, Finley Peter, 199

Earley, Pete, 251
Economic policy. *See also* specific issues
as Court concern, 20-22, 33, 167,
169, 171-175, 177-178, 182-183
Court policies, 20-22, 82, 148, 179-
180, 183-188, 191, 193-194, 197
impact of decisions, 218

litigation, 82
in selection of justices, 40
Ehrlichman, John, 37, 69-70
Eisenhower, Dwight D.
policy positions, 190
response to decisions, 230-232
selection of justices, 30-31, 37, 40-
43, 196
Elections, Court as issue in, 2
Elman, Philip, 89, 161
Environmental protection
as Court concern, 1, 72, 166-167,
170
Court policies, 97
litigation, 82, 97
Epstein, Lee, 83, 101, 110-112, 161
Everson, David H., 248
Executive Committee of Southern
Cotton Manufacturers, 82

Faubus, Orval, 206, 236
Federal Aviation Administration, 244
Federal Bureau of Investigation, 244
Federal courts, structure and jurisdic-
tion, 7-9. *See also* Courts of appeals;
District courts; Lower courts
Federal Election Campaign Act, 86,
239
Federal government as litigant, 88-
90, 101-102, 131, 135, 169, 207-208,
229-230
Federalism
as Court concern, 20, 99, 167, 169-
170, 172, 175
Court policies, 126, 180
Fish, Peter G., 25
Fisher, Louis, 250
Ford, Gerald
effort to impeach Douglas, 23, 64,
67
selection of justices, 31, 42, 64
Foreign policy
as Court concern, 173, 181, 246
Court policies, 115
Fortas, Abe
appointment as associate justice,
29, 37, 41, 48, 146
as attorney, 79, 132
background, 55-57
extra-Court activity, 15-16, 67, 135
nomination as chief justice, 29, 39,

45-46, 48, 51
resignation, 51, 65, 67, 146
threat of impeachment, 67
Forte, David F., 25
Frank, Jerome, 12, 25
Frank, John, 132, 161
Frankfurter, Felix
appointment to Court, 28
background, 54, 56-57
as commentator, 61
as justice, 148-149, 151-152, 155-157
retirement, 145
in selection of justices
Fraternal Order of Police, 34
Freedom of expression. *See also* specific issues, 36
as Court concern, 22, 166, 170
Court policies, 23, 130, 134, 176,
185-187, 189-190, 226
impact of decisions, 134, 214, 226,
238, 243-246
litigation, 86
Freedom of Information Act, 170
Fried, Charles, 90
Friedman, Lawrence M., 198
Friedman, Leon, 55
Fuller, Melville, 66
Fund for a Conservative Majority,
121

Galanter, Marc, 102, 112
Garrity, W. Arthur, 208, 217
Gerstein, Robert S., 249
Getty Oil, 77
Gideon, Clarence Earl, 79, 103
Ginsburg, Douglas, announced
nomination to Court, 29, 38-39, 44,
46, 48, 68
Glick, Henry R., 198
Gold, Laurence, 78
Goldberg, Arthur
appointment to Court, 29, 44, 48,
145
background, 55-57
resignation, 63, 65-66, 146
Goldman, Sheldon, 70, 160-161, 249
Goodman, James, 68
Governors, response to Court deci-
sions, 234-237
Gramm-Rudman-Hollings deficit re-
duction law, 5, 82, 121, 166, 177-178

Greenberg, Jack, 79
Greenhouse, Linda, 111
Greenya, John, 110
Gressman, Eugene, 25, 111-112, 159
Griswold, Erwin, 78, 89, 111
Grossman, Joel B., 36, 69, 160

Habeas corpus, 178
Halpern, Stephen C., 25
Hand, Brevard, 218
Hand, Learned, 36
Hansen, Susan, 250
Harbaugh, William H., 69
Harding, Warren, selection of justices, 35-36
Harlan, John
  appointment to Court, 29, 48-49
  background, 54
  as commentator, 131
  as justice, 151
  retirement, 64-65, 146
Harlan, John Marshall, 66
Hawkes, Paul, 247
Hawkins, Virgil, 203-204
Haynsworth, Clement, nomination
  and Senate defeat, 33, 39, 45-46, 48,
  51-52
Health, Education, and Welfare, De
  partment of, 207, 229-230
Hellman, Arthur D., 110-111, 198
Henry, Diane, 248
Henschen, Beth M., 223, 249
Hentoff, Nat, 251
Herbert, Anthony, 204
Hirsch, Harry N., 162
Hollingsworth, Harold M., 199
Holmes, Oliver Wendell
  appointment to Court, 28, 39
  background, 39
  as commentator, 147
  retirement, 35
Holmes, William F., 199
Hoover, Herbert, selection of justices, 32-33, 39, 46
Hoover, J. Edgar, 131
Howard, J. Woodford, Jr., 110, 149,
  162, 249
Hughes, Charles Evans
  appointment as associate justice, 28
  appointment as chief justice, 28, 68
  as chief justice, 154-155

as commentator, 21, 26, 120, 159
as justice, 22
resignation as associate justice, 63,
  68
Hutchinson, Dennis J., 112

Immigration and Naturalization
  Service, 5
Impeachment
  of justices, 20, 66-67, 228, 231
  of presidents, 5, 67-68, 114, 223
Impoundment of funds, 178
Interest groups
  influence over Court decisions, 87-
    88
  in litigation, 2, 79-88, 171, 221
  in selection of justices, 33-34, 49-
    52, 80
Interstate Commerce Act of 1887, 183
Interstate Commerce Commission,
  120, 187
Internal Revenue Service, 4
Internal security and freedom of ex-
  pression
  Court policies, 185, 190, 243
  impact of decisions, 244
Israel, Fred L., 55

Jackson, Andrew, response to deci-
  sions, 231
Jackson, Robert
  appointment to Court, 29
  background, 54
  as commentator, 186, 199
  as justice, 156
Jaffree, Ishmael, 77, 248
Jahnige, Thomas, 70, 160-161
Jay, John, resignation, 19, 63
Jefferson, Thomas, relations with
  Court, 20, 66-67, 231
Jehovah's Witnesses, in litigation, 79,
  82
Jenkins, John A., 69, 162-163
John Birch Society, 67
Johnson, Andrew, impeachment, 67
Johnson, Charles A., 250
Johnson, Lyndon
  policy positions, 190
  relations with Court, 15-16, 39
  response to Court decisions, 231-
    232

role in resignations and retirements, 66
selection of justices, 41-42, 46, 51
Johnson, Richard, 249
Judicial activism and restraint, 5-7,
175-182
Judicial Conference, 15
Judicial review
development of power, 19-20
exercise of power, 19-22, 175-182,
194
Judiciary Act of 1789, 19
Judiciary Act of 1925, 107, 133
Jurisdiction
of courts generally, 7-9, 97
of Supreme Court, 9-12, 19, 96-97,
227-228
Justice Department
in litigation, 88-90, 101-102, 131,
135, 169, 207-208, 229-230
response to Court decisions, 135-
136, 234-235
in selection of judges, 37-38, 41
as source of justices, 42, 56-57, 62
Justices. *See also* individual names
ages, 58, 63-66
backgrounds, 2, 53-62, 68, 137
duties, 14-16
impeachment, 20, 66-67, 228, 231
nominations, 1789-1988, 257-260
nominations, 20th century, 28-29
number, 13-14, 21-22, 228
resignation and retirement, 63-68
salaries, 14, 228-229
selection, 27-52
in selection of colleagues, 34-36

Kagan, Robert A., 198
Kamen, Al, 112, 160-161, 163
Kennedy, Anthony
appointment to Court, 14, 29, 32,
38, 46, 48-49, 52-53, 146
background, 55
as justice, 109
Kennedy, John
response to decisions, 231-232
selection of justices, 42, 44, 62, 145,
196
Kessel, John, 198
Kluger, Richard, 162, 250
Kolson, Kenneth, 249

Krislov, Samuel, 233, 250-251
Kunen, James S., 248
Kurland, Philip B., 112, 160

Labor, organized, in selection of justices, 33-34, 49, 51
Labor-management relations
as Court concern, 166-167
Court policies, 180, 182, 202
impact of decisions, 223-224, 226,
238
in selection of justices, 33, 34, 49,
51
Lamar, Joseph, 28
Lamb, Charles M., 25
Lash, Joseph P., 160
Lasser, William, 199
Lauter, David, 110, 159, 163
Law clerks
backgrounds, 16
role on Court, 16-17, 94-95, 107,
116
Law reviews, influence on Court,
130-131
Lawyers
admission to practice before Court,
18
communication of Court decisions,
214-215
role in Court, 78-79, 115-116, 184
in selection of judges, 31-33
as subject of Court decisions, 239
Leadership Conference on Civil
Rights, in selection of justices, 34, 50
Lee, Rex, 78, 90
Leeds, Jeffrey T., 161
Legal Defense Fund. *See* NAACP
Legislative apportionment
as Court concern, 103, 170
Court policies, 23, 203, 213
impact of decisions, 134, 212, 221,
226-229
Legislative veto
Court policies, 114-115, 178, 225
impact of decisions, 225
Leiken, Lawrence S., 248
Leuchtenburg, William E., 199
Lewis, Anthony, 130, 160-161
Libel
Court policies, 23-24, 243-244
impact of decisions, 245

Light, Paul C., 198
Lincoln, Abraham, Court's review of
  actions, 178
Litigants in the Court, 74-77
Litigation volume in the Court, 104-
  109
Lower courts
  comparison with Supreme Court,
    37-40, 43, 45-46, 73-74, 172-173,
    192-193, 205
  role in implementing decisions, 7,
    201-222
  selection of judges, 37-40, 45
  as sources of justices, 40-41, 56-57,
    60-61
Lukas, J. Anthony, 69
Lurton, Horace, appointment to
  Court, 28

Maher, Charles, 249
Malone, Patrick, 110
Mandamus, 203
Mann, Jim, 110
Marcus, Ruth, 70, 159, 163
Marshall, John
  background, 61
  as chief justice, 19-20, 133, 153, 185
  threat of impeachment, 231
Marshall, Thurgood
  appointment to Court, 29, 34, 45,
    48-49, 146
  as attorney, 79, 132
  background, 55, 59
  as commentator, 161
  as justice, 92, 94, 101, 119, 136, 139-
    143
  nonretirement, 64, 66
Mason, Alpheus Thomas, 161
Mass media
  communication of decisions, 214
  influence on Court, 130
Mayo Clinic, 131
McCloskey, Robert G., 25
McReynolds, James
  appointment to Court, 28, 41, 43,
    196
  as justice, 41, 43, 151
Medalie, Richard J., 248
Meese, Edwin
  as commentator, 6, 25, 124, 160,
    234-235, 250
  in selection of justices, 38, 40
Mendelson, Wallace, 162
Mertens, William J., 250
Mexican-American Legal Defense
  and Education Fund, 82
Miller, Arthur Selwyn, 162
Milner, Neal, 249
Minton, Sherman
  appointment to Court, 29, 36, 48
  background, 54
Miranda, Ernesto, 204
Missouri Compromise of 1820, 20,
  176
Mock, Carol, 11, 14
Moody, William, 28
Mootness, 96-97
Morris, Jeffrey B., 111, 153, 162
Morris, Thomas R., 111
Morrison, Alan, 83
Moskowitz, Daniel B., 250
Muir, William K., Jr., 249
Murphy, Frank
  appointment to Court, 28
  background, 54
Murphy, Walter F., 69, 161

Nader, Ralph, 83
National Association for the Ad-
  vancement of Colored People
  (NAACP) and NAACP Legal De-
  fense and Education Fund
  in litigation, 79, 81-86, 97, 101, 171,
    193, 221
  Marshall's background, 60
  in selection of justices, 33-34, 51
  as subject of decisions, 190
National Conservative Political Action Committee, 34
National Consumers' League, 82
National Industrial Recovery Act, 21
National Labor Relations Board, 187
National Organization for Women
  in litigation, 82
  in selection of justices, 34
National Right to Work Legal Defense Fund, 83
New Deal, Court policies toward, 21-
  22, 134, 176, 180, 196. *See also* Franklin Roosevelt

Nixon, Richard
  policy positions, 190
  pressure on justices, 66-67
  response to decisions, 42, 233
  selection of justices, 23, 30-33, 37,
    40-43, 46, 50-51, 62, 146, 196
  as subject of decisions, 5, 24, 99,
    114, 178, 233
  threat of impeachment, 5, 67-68,
    114, 233
  and Warren appointment, 43
Nuger, Kenneth Paul, 248

Obscenity
  as Court concern, 73, 170
  Court policies, 23-24, 144, 244
  impact of decisions, 211, 216, 244-
    245
O'Connor, Karen, 83, 101, 110-112,
    161
O'Connor, Sandra Day
  appointment to Court, 29, 35, 41,
    44, 48-50, 62, 146
  background, 55-56, 59-60, 137
  as commentator, 62
  as justice, 129, 137, 140-142, 144,
    157
Olson, Elizabeth, 69
O'Neill, Timothy J., 160
Opinions
  announcement, 121
  assignment, 117, 153-154
  concurring and dissenting, 94, 119-
    120
  per curiam, 91, 94
  use and purposes, 114-115, 119-120
  writing and reaching agreement,
    117-119
Oral argument
  impact, 131-132
  interest group participation, 80
  schedule and procedure, 17-18,
    115-116
  use, 94

Pacelle, Richard, 171-172, 198
Parker, John, nomination and Senate
  defeat, 28, 33, 46
Patent Office, 211
Paulson, Darryl, 247

Paupers' petitions, 92, 96
Peltason, J.W., 248-249
Pennzoil Company, 77, 79
Perry, H.W., Jr., 98, 100, 111-112
Petzinger, Thomas, Jr., 110
Pitney, Mahlon, appointment to
  Court, 28
Police. *See also* Criminal law and pro-
  cedure
  Court policies toward, 23, 179, 209,
    213
  response to decisions, 209-211, 215-
    217, 219, 221
Political parties and partisanship
  in justices' backgrounds, 43, 57, 61-
    62
  in selection of justices, 43, 47, 49,
    51-52, 61-62
Pollak, Louis, 33
Posner, Richard A.. 112
Powell, Adam Clayton, 230
Powell, Lewis
  appointment to Court, 29, 37, 42-
    43, 48-49, 146
  background, 55-57, 137
  as commentator, 149, 158
  as justice, 14, 42, 137, 140-143, 151
  retirement, 14, 34, 38, 52, 64-65,
    146
Precedents, 124-127
President. *See also* individual names
  comparison with Court, 173-174,
    205
  Court's review of actions, 129, 178,
    181, 232-233
  influence on Court, 132-133, 135-
    136
  pressures on justices to resign, 66-
    67
  response to decisions, 7, 135, 230-
    235
  selection of justices, 27-52, 68, 135
Prettyman, E. Barrett, 78
Pringle, Henry F., 69
Pritchett, C. Herman, 127, 160
Privacy, Court policies on, 126, 189.
  See also Abortion
Provine, Doris Marie, 111-112
Public Citizen Litigation Group, 83
Public interest law firms, 82-83

Public opinion, influence on Court, 128-131, 144
Pusey, Merlo J., 162

Race, in selection of justices, 44, 59-60
Racial discrimination. *See* Black civil rights
Railroads, as litigants and subjects of decisions, 183-184
Reagan, Ronald
  Court review of policies, 181
  and Justice White, 66
  in litigation, 89-90, 102
  response to decisions, 135-136, 234
  selection of judges, 1, 23, 32, 37-38, 40-42, 44, 46, 52
Reapportionment. *See* Legislative apportionment
Recess appointments to Court, 30
Reed, Stanley
  appointment to Court, 28
  background, 54
Rehnquist, William
  appointment as associate justice, 29, 42, 48, 50-51, 136, 146
  appointment as chief justice, 23, 29, 34, 38, 48, 50-51, 68
  background, 16, 55
  as chief justice, 109, 155-156
  as commentator, 16-17, 94, 99, 112, 117, 129, 150, 153, 158-160, 162
  extra-Court activity, 14, 128
  as justice, 16, 116, 139-144, 151, 156, 238-239
  in selection of justices, 35, 41
Rehnquist Court
  comparison with predecessors, 146-147, 190-191
  policies, 100-101, 147, 190-191
Religion, in selection of justices, 43-44
Religious freedom and church-state issues. *See also* School religious observances
    as Court concern, 22
    Court policies, 77, 134
    litigation, 77, 79, 82
Remands
  lower court responses, 202-204
  procedure, 202

Revesz, Richard, 111
Reynolds, William Bradford, 234-235
Richburg, Keith B., 250
Roberts, Owen
  appointment to Court, 28
  as justice, 22, 125
Robertson, Pat, 64
Rodell, Fred, 196, 199
Rodgers, Harrell R., Jr., 248, 251
Rohde, David W., 69, 138-139, 160-161
Roosevelt, Franklin
  Byrnes resignation, 66
  "Court-packing" plan, 13-14, 21-22, 133-135, 228-230
  response to decisions, 21-22, 232
  selection of justices, 22, 27, 40-42, 196-197
Roosevelt, Theodore, and pressure on justices to resign, 66
Rosenberg, Gerald N., 251
Rowan, Carl, 70
Rule 17 (of the Court), 96-99
Rutledge, John, resignation, 19
Rutledge, Wiley
  appointment to Court, 29, 36, 43
  background, 54, 56

Safire, William, 69
Salokar, Rebecca M., 112, 161
Sanford, Edward, appointment to Court, 28
Scalia, Antonin
  appointment to Court, 29, 37-38, 44, 48-50, 146
  background, 55-56
  as justice, 109, 120, 139-142
Schmidhauser, John, 59, 69-70
School desegregation
  Court decision making, 129, 132, 155
  Court policies, 23, 128-129, 190
  impact of decisions, 129, 134, 203-204, 206-209, 213-214, 217, 227-230, 232, 236-237, 240-242, 247
  legislative policies, 207-208, 241-242
  litigation, 85, 103
School religious observances
  Court policies, 73, 128-129
  impact of decisions, 134, 210-211,

215, 218-219, 226-228, 232, 236, 238

litigation, 77

Schubert, Glendon, 161, 178, 199

Schwartz, Bernard, 132, 160-161, 250

Scigliano, Robert, 39, 41, 69

Selective Service System, 244

Semonche, John E., 70

Senate, in selection of justices, 30-35, 45-52, 68. *See also* Congress

Senatorial courtesy, 45

Serrill, Michael S., 162

Sex, in selection of justices, 44, 59-60

Sex discrimination

as Court concern, 103, 170-171, 182

Court policies, 24, 60, 137, 145

impact of decisions, 239

litigation, 84, 87

Shapiro, Stephen M., 25, 111, 159, 161

Sherman Antitrust Act of 1890, 183

Sidlow, Edward I., 249

Sierra Club

in litigation, 82

in selection of justices, 34

Simon, James F., 162

Sinclair, Barbara, 198

Skolnick, Jerome H., 248

Slotnick, Elliot E., 162-163

Smith, H. Wesley, 250

Social class, backgrounds of justices, 59-60

Social Security Act of 1935, 106

Solicitor general, 88-90, 101-102, 131, 135

Songer, Donald R., 249

Spaeth, Harold J., 69, 138-139, 160-162

Standing to sue, 96-97

State courts. *See also* Lower courts

comparison of state supreme courts with Court, 172-173

structure and jurisdiction, 8-9

State legislatures

Court's review of legislation, 179-180

response to decisions, 221

Statutes

as source of law, 4

congressional response to interpretations, 223-225

Stays, 14-15

Stern, Robert L., 25, 111, 159

Stevens, John Paul

appointment to Court, 29, 48-49, 146

background, 16, 55

as commentator, 94, 111-112, 124, 155, 160

extra-Court activity, 15

as justice, 16, 90, 92, 94-95, 98, 100, 120-121, 123, 139-142, 157-158

nonretirement, 64

in selection of justices, 35

Stewart, James B., 249

Stewart, Potter

appointment to Court, 29, 48-49

background, 55, 58

as commentator, 127

as justice, 127, 130, 144, 152, 160

retirement, 64-65, 146

Stidham, Ronald, 249

Stone, Harlan Fiske

appointment as associate justice, 28, 41, 43

appointment as chief justice, 28, 68

as chief justice, 154

as justice, 41, 43, 151, 187

in selection of justices, 35

Study Group on the Caseload of the Supreme Court, 108

Sutherland, George, appointment to Court, 28

Sutton, L. Paul, 248

Taft, William Howard

appointment to Court, 28, 36

as chief justice, 13

influence on legislation, 133

as president, 36, 40

in selection of justices, 35

Tanenhaus, Joseph, 160

Taney, Roger

as chief justice, 20

as justice, 20

Tate, C. Neal, 161

Tax Court, 9

Taxation policy

as concern of Court, 172, 183

Court policies, 183

impact of decisions, 226

Taylor, Robert, 217

Taylor, Stuart, Jr., 161, 163, 250
Texaco, Inc., 77, 79
Thomas, Evan, 69, 159
Thornberry, Homer, nomination to
  Court, 29, 48
Thornton, Mary, 250
Thurmond, Strom, 241
Tocqueville, Alexis de, 5, 25
Totenberg, Nina, 112
Truman, Harry
  compliance with decisions, 233
  Court's review of actions, 129, 178,
    233
  selection of justices, 36-37, 40, 42-
    43
Tushnet, Mark V., 110
Twiss, Benjamin, 199

Ulmer, S. Sidney, 112, 161
United States government, as litigant, 88-90, 101-102, 131, 135, 207-
  208, 229-230
Urofsky, Melvin I., 163

Van Devanter, Willis, appointment
  to Court, 28
Van Duizend, Richard, 248
Vietnam War
  Court avoidance of challenges, 7,
    103
  Court policies, 129, 244-245
Vinson, Fred
  appointment to Court, 29
  background, 54, 56
Voting Rights Act of 1965, 88, 171,
  208, 242, 247

Wald, Michael, 248
Wall Street Journal, 130
Wallace, George, 236, 238
Warren, Earl
  appointment to Court, 29, 40-43,
    48, 196
  background, 54, 56-57, 60-61
  campaign for impeachment, 67
  as chief justice, 23, 154-155
  as justice, 40-41, 143
  retirement, 23, 65, 146

Warren Court
  comparison with Burger and
    Rehnquist Courts, 23-24, 100, 145-
    147, 190-191
  intracourt relations, 151
  policies, 22-23, 51, 100, 130, 171,
    189-190, 209, 230
Wasby, Stephen L., 69, 85, 110, 249
Wasserstrom, Silas, 250
Way, H. Frank, Jr., 248
Weaver, Warren, Jr., 25
Wheeler, Stanton, 198
White, Byron
  appointment to Court, 29, 48, 62,
    145
  background, 16, 55, 57-58, 62
  as commentator, 111
  as justice, 98, 120, 139-142, 144, 157
White, Edward
  appointment as chief justice, 28,
    36, 68
  death, 36
Whittaker, Charles
  appointment to Court, 29, 48
  background, 54
  resignation, 145
Wiesenfeld, Stephen, 87
Williams, Richard L., 25
Wilson, Woodrow, selection of jus-
  tices, 36, 39, 41, 43, 196
Wolfson Foundation, 67
Witt, Elder, 250
Women's groups
  influence on Court, 145, 170-171
  in litigation, 82
  in selection of justices, 34
Women's rights. *See* Sex discrimina-
  tion
Woodward, Bob, 162
Wright, J. Skelly, 6, 25, 206, 217
Wright, John, 98-100, 112

Yarwood, Dean L., 250
Young, Cecelia, 76
Yunker, Conrad E., 248

Zeitz, Leonard, 248